HOSHUN

PERRY P. STEADMAN

Order this book online at www.trafford.com
or email orders@trafford.com

Most Trafford titles are also available at major online book retailers.

Printed in the United States of America.

ISBN: 978-1-4669-7375-6 (sc)
ISBN: 978-1-4669-7376-3 (hc)
ISBN: 978-1-4669-7377-0 (e)

Library of Congress Control Number: 2012924021

Trafford rev. 01/15/2013

 www.trafford.com

North America & international
toll-free: 1 888 232 4444 (USA & Canada)
phone: 250 383 6864 ♦ fax: 812 355 4082

Dedication

This story is dedicated to
the perpetual regeneration
of the ties that bind;
to our family, and to all families.

Preface

In the year of 1167 A.D., beside the river Onon, a son was born to the Mongol tribal chief Yesugei. Yesugei named his son Temujin, taken from a rival Tatar chief he had slain a short time previous, in the belief that all of the better qualities of his enemy would magically be inherited by his son. Whether any of the desired traits were actually transferred is not a matter of history, but his arrival and subsequent achievements were to affect a vast portion of the known world for the next three hundred years.

At the age of nine, Temujin was betrothed to a girl of the Konkirat tribe. His bride to be, Burte, was one year his senior and destined to play the lead role in his life by presenting him a son that would sire the man responsible for the fulfillment of Temujin's ambitions.

While making the long journey home from the betrothal, Yesugei was poisoned by Tatars. He died shortly after Temujin's return from the camp of his bride, whereas custom bade, he had taken up residence. The property of his family and leadership of the clan was taken over by jealous kinsmen; fearing later reprisals they enslaved Temujin and would doubtlessly have put him to death if he had not escaped.

By the age of fifteen, Temujin was a warrior with a sizable following and he returned to claim his bride. With the aid of Burte's dowry, he allied his forces with the powerful Ong Khan, ruler of the Kereit, a large tribe of central Mongolia.

With shrewd diplomacy and an unaccountable foresight, he made and broke many pacts with other tribal chieftains, as it suited his purpose. Warfare among the numerous tribes provided the stepping stones to ultimate power and before he was thirty he was acclaimed Genghis Khan (Universal Monarch) by the chiefs supporting him. By the year 1206 he had subjugated the Kereits, Tatars, Merkits, Oirots and the Tumats plus numerous smaller tribes to unify Mongolia under a single ruler. The Mongol Princes proclaimed him Supreme Khan and his conquest of China proper began.

Genghis Khan did not live long enough to see the capitulation of Linan (Hangchow), capital city of the Sung Dynasty. He died in 1227. However, the Empire he had established reached from Korea in the east to cover most of northern China, Mongolia, and Manchuria, Afghanistan and on to the Caspian Sea. The Khanate passed to the hands of Ogadai, Genghis' third oldest son and from him to Guyuk, Ogadai's son. Guyuk's reign was short and upon his death Mangu was made Khan. Mangu was the eldest son of Genghis' youngest son, Tolui. It was Mangu, with the aid of his brother Kublai, who launched the final assault on the Sung Dynasty and total conquest of China.

Mangu died during the campaign in Szechwan province in 1259. Under Kublai Khan, the war was pressed for another seventeen years and the dream of Genghis was realized with the surrender of the Emperor at Linan in 1276. Mopping-up operations were not completed in southern China and the Imperial Navy there, until three years later. In 1279, Kublai Khan proclaimed himself Emperor of all China and thereby established the Yuan Dynasty. Within a hundred years, the Dynasty Kublai fought so long to establish was overthrown by the peasant classes and the Mongols were either destroyed or driven out. Through violent measures, lasting nearly three hundred years, the Ming Dynasty reestablished Chinese rule over their country.

In the sixty years following Genghis' death, his sons and grandsons extended his Empire to incorporate all lands east of the Danube in central Europe including Kiev, the Russian capital, south to the deserts of Arabia, Iran and the Persian Gulf. Western Siberia and the south Russian steppes were ruled by other offspring of Genghis not mentioned before; additional armies in the southeast captured and sacked the capital cities of Hanoi in Vietnam and Pagan of Burma.

The concomitant factors resulting in the ever escalating successes of Genghis Khan, his sons and grandsons, has been argued by historians for the past four hundred years; a few of them have written Temujin off as nothing more than a lucky barbarian bandit chieftain, even to the time of his death.

Little imagination is required to question this belief if consideration is given to the fact that the population of China alone was then 60,000,000 people and the maximum strength of Genghis' army less than half of one percent of that, a meager 250,000 fighting men. To further complicate this assumption, a large portion of his soldiers were not Mongolian, but instead volunteers from other lands he had conquered.

Temujin's early intellect was demonstrated by his successful escape from enslavement to become a mature, highly capable warrior. His magnetic character and personality were displayed by his return six years later as the leader of a fighting unit of his own and his tenacity is shown at the same time by his demand for his bride.

Genius exceeds the mere ability to think more accurately than the average, it is also being able to perceive and utilize all of the prevailing conditions, no matter how small, to their best advantage. Such was the case of Temujin. The religion of the Mongol tribes was Tengri, worship of the spirit of the blue sky, and it contained no provisions for mercy or charity to one's enemies. Temujin therefore used the faith to unite the individual units of his armies as well as fan their ardor. Many shamans accompanied the troops to the very threshold of battle.

The military code, Yasa (or Yassa), was strict and rigidly enforced. Though it contained many superfluous and superstitious rules, such as forbidding a blade being thrust into a fire, it also offered a positive system of reward and advancement for those of intelligence and valor. It spelled out the prescribed disposition for traitors and cowards, which resulted in the iron discipline of the Mongol Cavalry. The Great Book of Yasa was compiled by Genghis and his advisors.

In addition to the Yasa, the oath of Anda and the declaration of Nukur were encouraged by Temujin. By taking the "oath", a relative, no matter how far removed, could become a blood brother, and greatly reinforce their tie. The "declaration" freed any man of all other responsibilities and loyalties, including kinship to another and proclaimed himself solely "the man" of a freely chosen war leader. A large percentage of Genghis Khan's generals, captains, and advisors were either one or both.

The love and pride each Mongolian had for his horses may not seem connotative and yet through these affections he had inadvertently bred the finest cavalry mount in the world, comparable to the cow ponies of the American West. In addition, each man owned several horses, as many as six or eight, enabling him to ride for days and still have a fresh mount to take him into battle. A good portion of his own nourishment came from these herds in the form of mare's milk and its fermented form, koumiss.

Being an Arat (nomad), the Mongol did not need to adapt to life in the field. His natural way of existence molded him into an expert equestrian; he was able to perform dexterous feats from the back of his galloping pony that his adversaries had difficulty duplicating on the ground.

The Mongol warrior's laminated re-curved bow was the most powerful in the world and he used it to rout and demoralize his enemies. He followed this up with lightening charges of lance and sword to finish the carnage. His light armor of woven lacquered leather and small circular shield allowed him both speed and maneuverability and enabled him to strike lethal blows and retreat before his foe could regroup.

Genghis Khan implemented the amazing mobility of his cavalry by forming them into graduations of ten. Ten men to the troop, ten troops to the squadron, ten squadrons to the regiment and ten regiments to the touman, or division. The touman was the largest of the independent units and normally three of them comprised an army. This arrangement simplified many of the operational problems including supply, replacement and table of organization. In battle, all orders were transferred by the use of black and white flags, eliminating the confusion of oral or written directives. His staff officers directed the engagements from vantage points encompassing the entire action, free from distraction and harm. Communication was greatly speeded by Genghis' establishment of Urton, a mounted relay service with bases nineteen miles apart, manned with fresh riders and horses twenty four hours a day. The same system was adopted by the Pony Express five hundred years later in the American West. For the tremendous distances of the western campaigns he instituted the use of homing pigeons in relay.

From the mind of Genghis Khan came the spearhead maneuver, penetrating a hundred miles or more behind enemy fortifications, or flanking and isolating one particular force. Spies, propaganda, psychological warfare, fifth columnists, and bypassing bastion-like cities were a few more of his innovations that were not remembered until a man named Hitler began his invasion of some of the same territory, Poland, six hundred years later, and called it blitzkrieg. He also perfected collapsible boats for transporting his armies across rivers and lakes.

The macabre brutality administered to cities that resisted spread before his armies like wildfire. In one instance, he ordered all living creatures within a city put to the sword, including the dogs and cats. On the other hand, if they accepted his terms of surrender, they were not harmed and many of them were taken into his service, especially those of outstanding quality in trades, engineering and crafts.

It is possible that one of Genghis Khan's greatest assets were his advisors that came from almost every faction of importance. Many of these men performed a dual role, as they were also officers in his armies. One in particular was a visionary with extreme accuracy; he was a general of the touman, brother of Temujin by the oath of Anda, and Nukur to him through declaration.

These are the facts, relevant to, and concerning the only total conquest of China from outside. There is one more that should be brought to light, for in essence it is the beginning of a series of events that take place much later, perhaps part of it in your time. When Kublai became Emperor, many of his followers could not abide in a life of peace among the strange subjects and environments they had conquered. They left in groups, large and small, to return to their native lands; to find the excitement and riches of new battlefields, or to make new homes in a land they had seen in their travels.

From this point on there can be no corroboration from the annals of history; for the withdrawal of General Kirghiz, the visionary, and a tenth part of his touman along with their families and livestock, was not important. All of the predictions he had made for Genghis Khan, his sons, and their sons had come true. All of the battles he had fought in had been victories and all of the advice he had given had been sound. The fighting was done, he was old, his advice no longer needed and the ultimate goal had been achieved. Kublai Khan kept the promise made by his grandfather and ordered the arrangements with Phags-Pa, the King Priest of Tibet (predecessor of the Dali Lamas). The land Kirghiz wanted for his Hoshun there was his and those that would go with him. The debt of three generations was paid, but the payment was over-shadowed by the magnitude of the victory celebrations and the crowning of a new Emperor. Kublai and his staff listened to the warnings Kirghiz gave them of the future, but they paid him little attention. They had done the impossible and nothing could harm them now; the fighting and the dying were in the past and so was the usefulness of the old man called Kirghiz.

Author's Note

The only precise date in the life of Genghis Khan is his death August 25, 1227. All other times and periods concerning him are arbitrary to a maximum difference of six years at his birth (1161). Variations of calendar, lack of documents and translation of widely scattered accounts are responsible.

With the exception of actual historical personages identified as such, the characters, organizations and events herein are entirely the product of the author's imagination and have no relation to any person or persons in real life. The emergence of the Mongol from the mating of the blue wolf (Borte Chinua) and the gray doe (Gooa Maral) is a Mongol tribal totem, pre-Buddhist influence.

To the memory of Temujin, my cousin, my brother and my Lord:

Banner of the Blue Wolf

The predominant truths of antiquity grow weary with the passage of time. Yesterday they are a dull memory, today forgotten and tomorrow buried in the dust of the ages. In the never ending cycle of man's evolution, a searching warrior shall stumble in the blackness; groping in the unknown, he will find the lance of the silver point. He will raise it high for all to see and the masses shall gasp in astonishment that such as this could ever be. Once again the banner of the Blue Wolf shall be riffled by the chilly morning wind that announces the coming of Tengri, the blue sky and a new day.

.... Kirghiz 1227 A. D.

BOOK ONE

Kula Kangri, 1890, Year of the Tiger

CHAPTER 1

I f a king had lived to mark his hundredth year, his subjects
would have rejoiced throughout the land and claimed it to
be a remarkable reign; to their Gods it would have been as
the winking of an eye. The rule of the ancient Vedic Deity was to be
forever, from the beginning until only the mist remained. They gave
no thought to the feeble attempts of man to lengthen his life span,
nor the measuring of his years. They did not fear usurpation, for
there were none to touch their supremacy. Mankind was the flock to
be led and tolerated, to be soothed and pitied, to be comforted and
scorned but he never feared, for sheep do not revolt. Their visions
did not tell them of the Triad of Vishnu, Shiva and Brahma, or of
the one that would give up his riches to walk barefoot and ragged
so that he might preach his concepts living in the Middle Way and
attaining Enlightenment, the one later called Buddha. Nor did they
see the coming of the Carpenter and the Seller of Tents. The voices
of Christ and of Mohammed were dull whisperings in their ears
until the time they went to sleep. When they awoke, there were none
left to bow before them. They were alone and unwanted in their
home above the sea.

Each time they woke they were discontent and their raging
could be heard and seen quite plainly. The blackness of their wrath

boiled over the length and breadth of the Bay of Bengal and was punctuated by streaks of jagged fire and earsplitting roars. As their indignation of being deposed reached unbearable dimensions, they began to weep. Their tears drowned all that lay in the path of the land-bound hurricane. The screaming monkeys of the tree tops became mute in their dismay, for the time of the monsoon rains was two months distant. The tiny creatures of the mangroves were torn from their perches and flung to the churning crocodile infested waters of the Sunder bans. The reptiles paid them scant attention for their concern was trying to keep the water from their lungs and stave off a ridiculous death for an amphibian. The end came despite their attention and effort for the swamp was a boiling mass of vines, leaves, limbs, bodies, and the poisonous mixture of water and air.

There was little here to hold the interest of a God for it was man that defied, and abandoned him, and to man the greatest torment would be delivered. The unabated fury swept inland smiting the ungrateful of both East and West Bengal, then onward and upward across the broad Ganges Plain. Death, destruction and misery were meted out to men of all rank, for they must all learn not to trifle with the Divinities.

The borders of Bhutan, Sikkim and Nepal were the barriers of man and offered no resistance to the onslaught of the Holies. However, the Gods in their madness had forgotten the barriers of nature that had been in existence even longer than they. As the wind plowed into the majesty of the mighty Himalayas, it recoiled in surprise. The current, rushing in reverse, countered its own strength, and the lofty peaks became traps for high velocity air streams that have lost direction. The coldness of the heights transformed the harshness of the deluge to soft floating bits of snow that dropped harmlessly to the ever waiting ledges.

The unplanned wrath of the vanquished came to an orderly end. Only a slight breeze managed to escape through the mountain pass high above Darjeeling and was lost on the vastness of the Tibetan Plateau, the Top of the World.

All of the lofty peaks were not behind and the small breeze lost even more of its strength as it pushed up the lower reaches of the mountain Kula Kangri. One third of the way to the top the wind entered the broad and sheltered valley of the Kirghiz, people of the Blue Wolf and Arat, remnant of the Khans. The dark shapes of the yurts were there below, but the people were asleep within, for it was an hour before dawn. The wind could go no further for it was snared in the vertical cliffs at the head of the valley; it could only circle weakly, waiting for the sun that would put an end to it and the anger would be fully spent.

A soft caress of the dying air touched the broad bronze face of Mango as he sat perched on a high outcrop of rock waiting for sunrise and the time of his morning ritual with Tengri. He breathed deeply and as his nostrils flared wide, he could smell and taste the dampness the air still carried. He stared southwest into the darkness and smiled inwardly as he recalled the many pleasures of the past at the southern end of the caravan trail. Darjeeling was a wonderful place to end a long trek and then spend a week or two resting up for the trip back. As captain of the caravan guard, he was a man of rank and most doors of the Indian city were open to him. His inward pleasure remained as he recalled the times he considered youth's folly. His thoughts meandered and time slipped by unnoticed. The faint skyline of the mountain became visible, and he was startled back into the present.

From somewhere below he could hear the periodic scrape of leather against rock, and he knew someone was climbing up to him. He peered down and could dimly make out the yurts far below, but it was not yet light enough to see who approached. With noiseless caution he raised the near-new breach loader rifle from its resting place across his thighs, and centered the muzzle on the break in the rocks directly beneath him. The only approach to his lofty bastion was protected from surprise attack so he waited in silence.

"Mango, Mango Noyan are you there?" The deep whispering voice of Gariu shattered the morning stillness.

"Yes, noble kinsman, I am here," Mango answered softly, as a broad smile creased the squarish features of Mango's face, and his teeth glistened with the predawn light in fond recognition of his cousin's presence. "Come join me, Gariu Taiji, for it will soon be time to welcome the new day, and pray to the blue sky for its blessing."

Gariu's head and shoulders appeared in the cleft between the rocks. His short-cropped black hair was covered by a square fur cap with a long flap reaching to the center line of his shoulders. The mate to Mango's rifle was slung over his back so that he might use both hands in the steep ascent. His searching brown eyes grew wide as his gaze came to rest on his Prince, and his entire face radiated the pleasure he felt within. With a final heave he raised himself to stand beside Mango who had done him this courtesy in greeting.

"I had hoped you would come," said Mango with sincerity as each man took a pressing grip on the others forearms in salutation. "I could not sleep in the late hours of the night. I thought perhaps this solitude would smooth the waters of my thoughts, and give reason to the actions we must take as the leaders of our people. I would have called you, but I knew you were extremely tired from the long journey on the Tsangpo to our summer home. As the only Taiji left us, yours is a difficult task. I do not envy you. It is much easier for me to say that which is to be done, than it is for you to see that it is accomplished."

"No, Mango, I do not think this is so," replied Gariu. "I have the full cooperation from all of the clan, and even though our lot is trying, it is shared by all, and therefore minimized. We work hard at the chores that must be done to exist, but we live well and there is little complaining. If only it could continue as it has I would be more than gratified. Without you, as the living spirit of the Khan, there would be no point in our struggle, and the Clan of the Blue Wolf would dissipate as does the morning dew." Gariu paused and then went on, "To decide which is right, and which is wrong, for our people is beyond my capabilities. This is not so with you, my Prince. It has been proven during the past ten years of your leadership!"

"The test of any ruler is not conclusive until his reign has finished, Gariu," Mango replied. "That which is upon us now may well prove to be the end of the people of Kirghiz as well as my rule of them. Enough for now, my brother, Tengri approaches and it is time to commune."

While they had spoken, the clear morning sky had turned from gray to blue; the faintness of the stars had paled and melted into nothing; the wind that blew almost continually died. As the two men peered south and west, the snow crested peaks of the giant Himalayas clutched at the first rays of the morning sun. Their whiteness transformed to pink, then red and finally brilliant gold framed in the vast blueness of the sky to which the pair directed their thoughts of worship. The features of the two men were visible now, the wide expanse of Mango's face compared to the smooth lines of Gariu. Gariu stood nearly half-a-head taller than Mango, and even though he was the tallest man of the clan, he was an even two inches short of six feet. His body was well proportioned to his height, broad shoulders and strong limbs. Mango, on the other hand, compensated for his shortness in the breadth of his chest, the thickness of his neck, arms and legs. The light hickory color of Mango's skin was constant, even to the expanse of exposed torso left by his open tunic. The temperature was barely above the freezing mark, but Mango paid it little heed.

The minutes ticked by silently as each man exposed his soul to the spirit of Tengri. The air began to warm as the sun lifted itself free from the chains of darkness and drove the shadows from the ledge on which they stood.

At last Mango's meditations were complete. He turned to stare directly above him, more than a mile up into the dazzling heights of Kula Kangri. The sun caressed the wind swept rock glistening in shades of gray and brown. In the ravines and low spots the snow and ice reflected so bright it hurt his eyes. His brown orbs stared long and hard at each projection, each depression, as though appraising an enemy. There was no malice in his scanning, only wonder and desire.

Gariu watched for some time in silence, for he knew what was on Mango's mind. At last he spoke, "Perhaps, my Prince, this will be the year you will find out what is up there that has drawn you for so long."

"Yes, this may well be the time," Mango replied abstractly. His gaze finally settled on a broad shelf of rock a few hundred feet below the mountain summit. "It has been an exceedingly long time since I first stood here with my father, and he related the story the ancients told Kirghiz when he passed this place on his mission of conquest. To the natives of the plateau, this entire mountain was sacred; for it was from up there that life began anew after the great waters had covered the earth. Only those that were on that high bench survived to start the world again. How long ago this was supposed to have happened they did not know; for the ancients were taught when they were children by those that were aged beyond counting. It was the same many times over before their time. The legend said that only the tops of the mightiest of peaks were exposed when they finally did start down, accompanied by a giant three legged turtle. It was the turtle that formed the rivers, streams, and gorges to drain the land, and make it livable once more. It was also he that showed them how to plant and water the rice, and how to live when there was very little dry land. He stayed with them for a great long time, but when his work was finished he left the same way he had come. He swam out into the big waters that remained and was never seen again." Mango lowered his gaze to Gariu's face, and he smiled at the intentness he saw there. "I think I bore you with this tale you have heard as many times as I."

"No, Mango," Gariu responded, "I never tire, for I believe there must be some truth to it or it could not have endured for such a great length of time. Kirghiz, our ancestral grandfather, believed it, and he was the wisest of all our people. It is widely known that Kirghiz could see into the future, even unto this time. Why then could he not know the past as well?"

"Yes, Gariu," Mango conceded, "these have been my thoughts also, and that is one more reason that I must know if there is anything left up there to support this belief. But, there is more to it than that with me. I am drawn to those heights as your knife is drawn to the lodestone. It has been so since I was a child, and it becomes stronger with each passing year." The tone of Mango's voice now held an imploring edge, as though he craved release from this desire.

"Then why not do it this time?" inquired Gariu. "We will have the council meeting when the sun is high. You have said you would give them twelve days to deliberate, and render their opinions on what you must do to preserve our way of life. I cannot leave with the horse herd for Maleek of Chamdo until you have reached a decision. This would give you more than enough time to climb four such mountains. Knowing your persistence and endurance, I have little doubt that you could make the entire trip in three days if you were of a mind to!"

"I believe you torment me, Gariu," Mango laughed. "It is possible I could make it in four or five days, but never in three. I have plotted the route I must take many times and even with a large amount of good fortune it will take two or three days going up."

"Perhaps I do overrate your abilities somewhat, but I have seen you in action of insurmountable odds before. Think on it! When in the past have you ever had twelve days to wait before you could act? When in the future will it come again? Besides, if you rid your mind of this obsession there will be more room for our problems of survival." Gariu smiled at the truth of his last remark.

"Leave it to the Taiji to resolve two dilemmas with one piece of action," responded Mango with like levity. "As you say, brother, let us think on it. In the meantime we had best return to the Bag, for I see many of our people are up and about."

Gariu nodded his approval as Mango slung his rifle over his back in anticipation of their descent.

*   *   *   *   *

As wife of Noyan, it was Baikali's habit to rise before the first light of dawn so that his nourishment would be ready when he opened his eyes. This morning, however, she had heard him rise in the still black hours and she knew he would not return until the sun was up. She cherished each extra moment among the warm fur robes. The chill began to leave the air inside the yurt and the light increased so that she could make out the soft dark curls of their girl child asleep on the far side of the tent. Silently she rolled back the covers and stood, stretched both arms wide and high, then rubbed her eyes with clenched fists to rid them of sleep completely. Her form was slight and well-rounded with smooth skin the color of burnt gold. She found the stiff bristle brush for her hair and stood in the center of the room brushing out the tangles of her hair after the night's sleep. The slight crispness of the air nipped at her bare flesh speeding her mind to full awareness. Two long braids hung below her waist when she finished, their shiny blackness contrasting with her bareness. Next she donned the trousers and tunic, inner and outer, both fitting snugly. She placed a wide leather belt with a diamond shaped silver buckle about her waist, pulled on the loose knee high boots and was ready to start the day.

The strong aroma of thick buttered tea met Mango at the entrance to his home. As he stepped inside, Baikali rose from beside the brazier to greet him. "Welcome home, my Khan. Has my companionship grown so dull that you seek the embrace of the night?" she teased.

"The warmth of your arms is the only embrace I shall ever seek my heart, until all the ice has melted from the mountains of the south," Mango breathed as he held her to him. "How many times must I tell my Princess that she must not refer to me as the Khan? I am the Noyan, the Wang or Prince of the Kirghiz; a blood descendent of Temujin, but I am no Khan!"

"To me, my Lord, you are the Khan, a King of Kings outshining Genghis or Kublai in all their magnificence. Where you walk goes the light that I see by and the only air that I can breathe." She pulled herself closer to him as she spoke seeking the inner warmth that came to her with his touch.

"How can there be a Khan or King for little more than one hundred souls and most of them the very old or the very young? Kirghiz himself was cousin and Nukur to Temujin, general of more than ten thousand, first Prince of our people and touched by the clear vision of Tengri. Yet, he claimed to be no more than a Prince! Do you place me above even him?" Mango's voice was low, and a pleased smile curved his lips.

"I hold you greater than any man that has ever lived or ever will be," Baikali whispered, looking up to him searchingly.

Mango drew her as tight as he could without breaking any of her small ribs, nuzzled her cheek, but did not answer. He did not because he had seen the two wide brown eyes watching them from the small couch near the lattice work of the yurt wall. He grinned and the pair of eyes smiled back.

"It would seem that once again I am trapped in the paradox of my existence," Mango said. "I am wanted in two different places at the same time. We have a small audience we were not aware of my love."

"That child!" Baikali exclaimed with mock severity, "She pretends she cannot speak, but I am positive she understands every word, even though it may be a whisper, and the opening of a flower bud can wake her from a sound sleep." Baikali pulled free of Mango's embrace, went to the tiny bed, and lifted Menilan to her breast. The tender adoration of a mother replaced the passion of Baikali's small face and the child snuggled close to the sweet warmth of her personal goddess. Baikali took her to her own couch and commenced to brush and braid the child's fine tresses, unaware of the infant's nakedness as she had been of her own. As she started to dress the smiling Menilan, she spoke once again to Mango as though she had momentarily forgotten him, "Why do you stand there grinning like an over fed yak, my lover Prince? Your morning meal is still warm at the side of the brazier, but if you do not partake of it soon, it will be dry and unsavory. Have you never seen your Princess daughter before? Do you believe you are the only man to ever sire a beautiful girl child?" Her inquiries were meant to be terse, but her own pride and love punctured the illusion before it could form.

"I marvel only that the magnificent pair of you could have been given to me. In the many years I spent with the caravan guard I wondered a few times if I would live to see the day I would be the ruler of our people. But, almost every day of that time I dreamed of what it would be like to have you for my own and what our life would be. I recalled you most often as the skinny little daughter of Blate, the one that refused to wear the long skirts and headdress of the sex, the one with the blue black hair and diamond bright eyes. If my memory does not fail me, you were eight summers and I fourteen when our fathers made the arrangements." As Mango spoke, he seated himself beside the brazier, poured a steaming mug of the pungent tea, and began munching on a thick slice of mutton and a brown barley cake.

Baikali's head snapped erect to stare directly at him, "How could you dream of a lean stick of a girl that thought only of horses and had the disposition of a mountain bear? My father said this was the only impression I could have given you that day, and it was the only time we were together before you left to go to the service of Maleek of Chamdo."

"It may have been the only time we were together," Mango replied with a smile, "but it was not the only time I saw you. In the years that followed I remember observing you standing by the rope stops as I worked with the ponies; or when I stood guard, you would be tending a flock near my post. Somehow, nearly every time my father would send me to the caves to fetch the barley beer, you would be on a similar mission for cheese or milk. I am sure that these many occasions were purely coincidence, but they did occur frequently and regularly until the day of my departure." The smile deepened on Mango's features and as he jerked his head forward to hide his mirth, a lock of his black hair fell between his dancing eyes.

"Now you taunt me, my prince," responded Baikali with pleasure at his past attention. "It would not be the truth for me to say that all of these encounters were accidental. If I must speak the truth, I would say that all of my attention from then on was not directed at the horse herds."

Baikali finished dressing Menilan without speaking. The many fond memories of her girlhood passed leisurely through her mind and a lingering smile transfixed her small red mouth. She dressed the child with unconscious effort and twice the small round eyes looked up at her questioningly, but were unnoticed. When fully clothed, she slipped from her mother's arms and returned to her couch. From beneath the warm robes, she removed her doll with tender hands. With great diligence she prepared the stuffed sheepskin toy for the new day just as she had been prepared, but her fingers were not nimble enough to braid the horse tail that served as hair. Because of this, the doll received a double dose of brushing. During the entire process Menilan did her best to softly croon a melody she had not yet learned herself. She gazed fondly into dried berries that were sewn into place for eyes and innocently patted the bulging cheeks of her cherished and only possession.

As Mango ate his meal, his eyes would shift from one to the other, the mother then the child, and a warm glow began to light the darkness that had been within him in the early hours of the morning.

The chill he had not felt during his predawn vigil, the full meal he had consumed, and the heat from the brazier began to take effect. Drowsiness clouded his eyes. He watched the thin blue curl of smoke that rose from the white heat of the burning argil as it lazily made its way to the wooden ring surrounding the smoke hole in the top of the yurt. His gaze traveled down, then up the two gaily painted posts that supported the ring and the dozens of thin round roof poles that protruded from their sockets like the many spokes of a wheel. The poles were dull orange color with bright blue points doweling into the ring, and bright green resting on the lattice work of the yurt side. Unwittingly, he was playing an old game with Baikali, seeing if any of the poles had been placed wrong end to. Some of them would go either way, but not fit snugly; this could spell disaster in a bad storm. This morning he could find none that were wrong, but he said nothing; he was tired and sleepy; he could have missed one.

Baikali busied herself with her morning chores of shaking and airing the sleeping robes, then rolling each up tight so that it would not be under foot during the day. Her eyes darted occasionally to Mango still seated where he had finished his breakfast. Without asking if he were going to sleep, she remade his couch then turned to him. "Your sleep was not good, I felt you toss and turn during most of the night before you finally arose; your climb of this morning must have wearied you. I would be grateful if you were rested and fresh when it is time for the council meeting. Would it be too much if I ask my Lord to take a slight nap?" she inquired with an impish grin.

For a brief moment Mango's chin did not rise from his chest where it had come to rest, but then he roused his head and spoke.

"You mock me, woman, when I am unable to properly defend myself. It is the heat of this confinement that makes me sleepy. But you are right, I am tired for I have not slept well for some time, and I think a nap might refresh me."

"I do not order, my Lord," chided Baikali, "I only implore."

"Whichever way it might be, I will comply," laughed Mango as he stretched-out on the new laid robes.

"I must go to the cave this morning for butter, milk and cheese. Also, I have promised to help some of the young girls with their sewing lessons; this will be an ideal time for you to have some peace and quiet. I shall wake you in plenty of time for the meeting," Baikali informed him.

She turned and spoke to Menilan, who was playing hide and seek with her doll. "Come precious, we will take a nice long walk to the cave; you can play with some of the other children."

As she took the child by the hand and stepped through the double flaps of the yurt door, Mango grunted his approval and dropped instantly into a deep sleep.

Outside the yurt, Baikali stopped for a moment. She and Menilan stood motionless between two long lances impaled solidly, butt-first, into the turf. At the point of each was attached a tightly woven pennant of gold color with a wolf's head adorning the center, fangs exposed and eyes ablaze. The morning breeze came down the valley from the icy top of the mountain at a brisk pace. The pennants stood out almost vertically from the shafts and the rippling motion caused by the wind gave life to the two blue heads. The eyes never stopped roving, and the fangs constantly tore at an unseen foe. With her free hand Baikali, gently patted the bright purple felt of the yurt as though saying goodbye to a friend, then started walking down the valley toward the horse corrals where she had glimpsed Gariu before he disappeared into the herd.

*   *   *   *   *

Gariu had no inkling of how long his audience had been in attendance. He had been working with the horses since the time he had departed from Mango, save for the few moments he had allowed himself to swallow his morning meal. To each animal he gave a thorough inspection, first with his eyes and then with his hands: each muscle and joint, eyes and mouth, teeth, each ear cavity for burrs or sticks that may have lodged there during a strong wind, and lastly the currying of the mane and tail. It took a great deal of his day for there were fifty choice animals in this herd. Gariu was down on his haunches looking at a dark spot on the cannon of a chestnut mare. The spot was the stain of a green berry she had rubbed against. He was about to stand when he saw a curious thing; two round brown shining eyes were watching him through the countless legs of the other horses. At first glance he was startled and then he recognized the cherubic face framed in the bright yellow hood and tunic. With quick care he made his way through the herd to the corral ropes and his unexpected company.

"Greetings, my princess, and little princess," Gariu beamed as he stepped through the ropes of the enclosure. He bowed his head and shoulders low to each of them before he finished. "It is indeed a pleasure to have a visit of two such beautiful ladies on a morning as fine as this." Menilan bubbled with unrestrained glee as he swept her from the ground up into his arms. "How is my most favored and only niece this day?" He laughed as she nuzzled his cheek and ran her fingers through the stubble of his uncovered hair.

"Oh, we are fine or even better," Baikali replied with pleasure. "As you undoubtedly know, we were afforded the opportunity to sleep in today and we both took advantage of it. Menilan is learning the expedience of her royal blood quite early, I think." She watched fondly as Gariu played affectionately with her child and the thought came to her once again that if Mango had decided not to return as the ruler of her people, this man would be the ruler and her husband as well. She flushed inwardly and tried to push the notion from her mind, but being honest with herself admitted that she was indeed fortunate to have had such an alternative.

"I hardly think that such an infrequent indulgence will spoil either of you for your duties," Gariu laughed. "How often does this occur? Once or twice each year?" As he spoke, he turned toward the stream about a hundred yards distant. "I need to quench my thirst and rinse my face. It is warm work being pressed between the bodies of those ponies."

Baikali followed Gariu as he carried Menilan to the water. The blue-green grass of the valley floor was ankle high to her boots, spangled with myriads of edelweiss, iris and rhododendron and small clumps of wild rose bushes invaded the water's edge. She smiled as she recalled the fantasies of her early youth, believing the flowers to be sacred and trying not to trample the ground plants. The smooth, round, gray and brown rocks of the floor were not enough, nor close enough to each other to form a path and the blossoms too numerous. She finally yielded to logic and the inevitable. She giggled aloud as she caught herself changing course to avoid a particularly large cluster of the brilliant petals.

Gariu turned and smiled as he sat Menilan on a large round stone beside the stream. Here in the upper valley the water's flow was smooth and slow. A thin skin of ice covered the stream near the bank. Gariu broke the crust with his heel before lowering his head and a good portion of his neck into the tingling waters. When he had finished wiping most of the moisture from his face and neck, he cupped both hands, dipped them into the creek again and carried a refreshing drink to his little princess waiting on the rock.

Menilan drank deeply, laughing happily each time she came up for air; she paid scant attention to the coldness that filled her eyes and nose and dribbled down the soft warm skin of her chest.

Baikali followed Gariu's example of drinking while lying on her belly. After rising and brushing the bits of sand from her tunic and trousers, she wondered idly if the clan elders would have approved of her prostrating herself before the Taiji, even though it was in the act of drinking. She dismissed the thought irritably; the elders and some of their notions of what she should and shouldn't do made her angry. "Do you think Maleek of Chamdo will be pleased with the horses you take him, Gariu?"

"He very well should be!" replied Gariu with conviction. "These are the finest of the fine. Nowhere in the world could he find horses like these in this day and age. In the time of the great Khans, there were many more animals than there were warriors. But when the glory of the Khanate disintegrated, so did the vast herds of their fabled ponies. Perhaps there is a moral here: The most ambitious have, and deserve, the best of everything; but when they lose sight of their objective, and lose interest in the betterment of their belongings, then they will lose everything that is worth-while. At any rate, the people of Kirghiz were the only ones to protect the purity of their herds. As a consequence, we are the only ones to have this pure strain of animals today. There are things I could tell you about." Gariu had gotten carried away and would have gone on for an hour or more if he hadn't seen the corners of Baikali's mouth quiver in her attempt to stifle a grin. "Alright, alright, you she-devil that my prince has chosen for a wife; once more you have tricked me with your sly queries, knowing you will lead me into making lengthy and ridiculous statements that you know as well as I do. Why do this to me? Am I not like your brother?"

"Perhaps," answered Baikali seriously, "that is why I do it. I have great fondness for you, my Taiji, as you well know and it pleases me to see you slightly confused, a little bit entrapped and ever so joyous when you work your way out of it. I would not injure your pride, your honor, or your intelligence with small bits of humor, and I am sure you know I treasure your friendship dearly, or I would not jest with you."

The serious tone of her voice, the tenderness of her eyes, and the warmth of a half-formed smile melted his slight resentment. "Yes,"

Gariu responded, "I know you would not injure me intentionally, but there are fleeting instants that my short temper sweeps past my control and I am sorry."

"Come," said Baikali, "let us sit over there on that little knoll for a moment and enjoy the beauty of this summer day."

When they reached the top of the little mound, Baikali stood on tiptoe to survey the entire valley. From her vantage point, the valley was nearly a mile wide in each direction, sloping gently upward from the stream toward the bases of the sheer walls on each side. The last hundred feet beneath the cliffs tilted very sharply and were completely covered with a dozen varieties of brush and berry bushes, all of them an emerald green. She looked northward to the head of the valley where the caves were, and the rock rose vertically from the smooth floor as a mammoth wall towering five hundred foot high. She turned southward to peer down stream, her eyes following the winding silver ribbon to where it entered the narrows nearly five miles below. She could not see from this distance, but knew there would be at least two men on guard at the other end of the deep ravine. There would be one on a high pinnacle above them able to see an enemy far out on the plain that stretched out beneath for twenty miles in all three directions. It was a spectacle of beauty this time of year and a comforting thought to know that an alert sentry could spot an intruder at least a day before he would reach the guards at their outposts. She knew that ten good men, or less, could hold off an army there at the narrow entrance to her sanctuary. "Gariu," she said dreamily, "I wish we could stay here the entire year. It's so pretty and so comforting. When we leave here each fall and start the circuit of the Hoshun, I feel as though I am naked until we return next year. The waters of the Pomo Tsho, Yamdrok Tsho, nor the canyons along the river Tsangpo do not exhilarate me as they do the other people of our clan. I have a sense of dread whenever I am away from here. Do you feel it too?" She asked hopefully.

"Yes," he replied earnestly, "I do have a deep love for this place, but for many more reasons than my personal safety. Here the horses and the rest of the stock grow sleek and glossy on the abundant grass and browse. The bears cannot reach the colts or the snow leopards the young of the yak and sheep. In this valley, and up there on the mountain, I feel much closer to the spirit of Tengri. You will recall that I was born in this haven and both my mother and father died here. If it is possible for our people to call any one place home, I believe it would be here for me. But we both know when winter comes to this land, the creek turns to near solid ice and the snow is more than five feet deep. The temperature drops to the point where nothing could live, even if there were something for it to eat."

"Yes," responded Baikali, "I know this too. I guess I was merely dreaming the foolishness of a woman. There are times when I find it hard to live up to the mandate of being a princess. None the less, it is still my most cherished place on earth. To get back to the horses, I know how hard you have worked this past year preparing this lot for Maleek and you can be very proud, for you have done a remarkable job. He will probably want you to stay with them for a while, I imagine."

"If he does," replied Gariu, "he will just have to want, for I have too much to attend to here. I cannot play nursemaid to his stock when I have ours to take care of and we do not have enough men to properly form the guard compliment as it is. Which reminds me, I was supposed to inspect the timber shoring of the cave mouth first thing this morning and I have forgotten. I must go there at once, Princess!"

"We will go with you," beamed Baikali. "That is where we were going when I spied you among the horses. This way we will keep your company longer than I had hoped!"

"Come along then," ordered Gariu good naturedly, "and I will get us some mounts. Perhaps you enjoyed the walk down from the Bag, but I do not like walking anywhere if I can possibly ride."

"The sons of the Blue Wolf are all alike," laughed Baikali with unfeigned pleasure, "you may be born of woman in a yurt, but you will all die on the back of a hapless pony."

"That is true," replied Gariu with a wide smile, "or at least the way we would like it to be."

Gariu held Menilan in his lap with one hand and the reins in the other, as they moved toward the Bag. Unwittingly, he scanned the half circle of the thirty odd yurts. The brilliance of their colors did not impress him, nor did the banners flying before the larger one in the center. Directly behind the living quarters of the Prince and a long bow shot closer to the caves stood the council chambers, the largest and most impressive tent of all with its dazzling yellow top and blue sides. Here too the entrance was flanked by the standards of the clan. As they rode past the deserted council house, Gariu recalled that in the days of his childhood two guards had stood beside the lances from daybreak unto dark. "Times have changed," he mused.

*   *   *   *   *

The air seeping from the entrance of the cave felt warm as the trio entered, but only because the sun was not yet at its zenith. By afternoon, when the temperature outside neared the mid-sixties, it would be cold as the icy winds from above. The morning sun still lit the passage clear into the first large room-like cavern, and they could see it was empty of people. The sides of the entrance for the first three hundred feet were close together, allowing no more than two people to enter at the same time. The stone walls and roof were badly shattered fragments of an ancient upheaval, held in place for the past six centuries by the implementations and ingenuity of man. Large timbers, that had been hauled on the backs of yak more than fifty miles, supported and retained the thousands of tons of rock and debris that should have fallen long ago.

Each year when the Arats returned, Gariu would inspect the entire structure, and replace every piece that showed signs of dry rot or splintering. At the base of each upright stall was driven a wide wooden wedge which could, if necessary, be removed without difficulty. This feature made for simple and expeditious changing of the uprights and the caps, but its design served a far more serious purpose. Long, long ago Kirghiz had known that someday they might be trapped in this valley by their enemy, the Uli Prang. After installing the timber supports, he had ordered all of the facing rocks outside loosened from their natural sockets. This disruption of weight distribution placed the stabilization directly on the internal timbers. If several sets of these timbers were removed from near the entrance, a violent landslide would occur within seconds, sealing off the cave forever.

Kirghiz had been a man of great wisdom, one whose eyes saw beyond the shadows of tomorrow. He knew that once in the dim past, this cavern served as the underground channel for the stream that gave life and beauty to the valley above. He was sure that it had to emerge somewhere further down the mountain side. After two summers of relentless exploration of miles upon miles of subterranean chasms, one of his most trusted captains discovered the exit far down upon the mountain, in a remote and narrow canyon to the west. The place where it emerged he had ordered sealed by large boulders from within, keyed to where they could not be removed from the outside. The existence of this egress was kept secret from all save the noble Taiji and the captains. So it had been for six hundred years and more. If this were to be a last ditch defense, logic decried that only the trusted and proven leaders of the clan should know of its whereabouts.

As Gariu went about his business of inspection, he was somewhat amused that the secret had been kept so long and with so little effort. Almost every person of the Bag came to the cave for some purpose at least once each day, and sometimes more often. The first large chamber served as a communal storage vault of all foodstuffs, and the women and children had worn the passage floor smooth with their countless trips to fetch their table needs. This first chamber was the most expansive, its walls and domed roof as solid as the mountain itself. The floor and sides were damp and cold, but dozens of large rock slabs lying on the floor had dry tops, and these were the storage spots of the milk, cheeses by the hundreds, both fresh and dried meats, berries and grains, the koumiss, barley beer, and the distilled arch. The second and third rooms were much drier, and therefore the cache for furs, hides, clothing and the extra felts for the yurts, which would require many more layers as the temperature began to drop in the fall. From each of these rooms many small cavities extended out into the rock in diverse directions, but the majority of them dead ended within a short distance. The main passageway leading to the fourth, fifth and last room was easy to follow, for it was wide and clear of rubble. Beyond the first room, however, the gloom thickened with each step, and at least one butter lamp was needed to light the way, two made even a strong minded man feel more comfortable. A large supply of these devices lay on the first large stone to one's right upon entering the first room. The lamps were filled daily by the children, and none would venture beyond this point without one and at least two companions equally equipped. Proceeding to the last room gave a person the strange feeling of compression. As one progressed along the path each room became smaller and the linking caverns more confining. Contrary to the other rooms, the last one had five other exits. Each one of them continued on into the mountain in opposite directions and angles, later joining other channels coming from directly overhead at times, or dropping straight down into yawning crevasses, seemingly without bottom. No child had ever been known to explore beyond the third room, and very few men even yards beyond the sixth. Only those select few that had been informed of what lay beyond had the courage to make the long and perilous trip to view the sealed exit of Kirghiz.

Gariu trembled slightly as he recalled his one and only trip with his adopted father when he was twelve. Mango had made the trip the summer before with his father, the same man. For a youngster Gariu's age, it had been an awesome and terrifying time, but more startling was the knowledge that Mango had made the journey, and had revealed nothing in the following months. For a long time he felt hurt at Mango's lack of trust, but in due course he realized that this was one of the tests of being a true Prince, or a true Noble, and he had followed Mango's example. The last of the timbers were past, and he made mental note of those to be replaced; there weren't many this year. He removed flint, steel and tinder from one of the voluminous pockets of his trousers and lit two of the lamps.

"What would my lady wish in the way of edibles?" Gariu inquired lightly to break the strain of his thoughts.

"Only a few things," Baikali replied. "One of the older cheeses, a skin of fresh milk, a small bucket of butter and some barley flour."

Gariu held both the lamps and Menilan, as Baikali went from one stone table to the next selecting the items she had mentioned. As the three of them moved about the grotto their greatly magnified shadows followed them grotesquely along the high stone walls. The eyes of the child were fascinated by the weird images.

When the trio emerged in the full sunlight, they experienced a momentary blindness. After a few moments, Baikali raised her head to position the sun. "It will soon be time for the council meeting," she said, "and I must wake Mango." Gariu nodded in reply as they mounted the waiting horses.

*   *   *   *   *

The sun was directly overhead, and its light flooded the interior of the council house through the double smoke holes of the roof. Near thirty men, mostly old, were seated upon the fur robes that completely covered the chamber floor. A heavy yellow silk screen divided the rear third of the yurt; a long mortared stone dais, nearly chest high, stood directly in front. The lattice work of the walls was not visible, for the silk screening of the partition had been extended to cover it. At each end of the stone altar a stripped birch pole, of two arm's length, had been inserted into a socket, and a long gold banner with the Blue Wolf's head stretched tautly between them. On the pole to the assembly's right hung a four-foot unstrung composite bow, once black in color, but faded now to a dull gray. Beside the bow hung a leather quiver containing twelve long arrows, ebony black in hue, with fine gold lacquered symbols and inscriptions of a language no one present understood. On the pole to the left a small brass shield hung, scarcely more than a foot in diameter, its only decoration being a raised center with enclosing circles, each one larger than the last, radiating to the perimeter. The leather straps that bound it to the wearer's forearm had long since deteriorated into dust. A spear with a long brightly polished head and a shattered shaft stood upright wedged between the shield and the pole. At the table's center, an object about ten inches high and twice as long was covered with a light silk drape, pure white with interspaced threads of gold and silver.

Of all the men seated on the floor, there were only two that could be considered young, and they were by themselves close in front of the dais. The slender one of the two betrayed his nervousness with the occasional darting movements of his hands. His companion sat stoically gazing at the stone base in front of him; neither his eyes nor his chubby limbs displayed his inner feelings. The silence in the chamber was absolute. When the slender young man thought he could contain himself no longer, the curtains separated and Gariu strode out to stand before the dais. His head was covered with an iron helmet that came down nearly to his ears with an attached flap of mail extending down his neck to the area around his shoulder blades. The head piece was smooth in contour, with an arched dome; a heavy projection resembling a swan's head extended upward from between his eyes. A short shirt of chainmail covered his shoulders and upper chest ending well above his navel; a two-foot curved sword was sheathed in a plain silver scabbard hanging at his right side. His tunic, pants and boots were close fitting of heavy leather designed purposely for combat. The sword hanging at his side was the only weapon carried within the walls of the council house.

Gariu let his gaze rest briefly on each man's eyes before he spoke; except for the two nearest his feet, his gaze was met with intense sincerity. His voice rang loud and clear, "Arise you men of Kirghiz. Arise and raise your lance arm in tribute to Mango Noyan, direct descendant of Kirghiz, the gifted one: blood relative of Temujin, Genghis Khan, the chosen one of Tengri and the warrior father of the Blue Wolf." There was no sound as the assemblage rose to their feet, and thrust high either right or left arm in greeting to their Prince. Fierce pride reflected from the face of each man as Mango stepped up behind the altar.

Mango's attire was nearly identical to Gariu's with the exception of his helmet, which displayed a ten-inch tuft of horse tail sprouting from the top center. There was no array of riches or finery, or jewels or gold to enchant the elders of the clan. The elegance lay within the men themselves, and it was there for all to see.

Mango looked out upon his audience, then down at the white drapery before him as though deliberating what he would say. When he spoke his voice was low, but audible. "When I was very young," he began, "I remember that at the beginning of each council in this valley the legend of our people was recounted, from its origin unto the present, so that the greatness of our past, and the purpose of our being would be with our people at all times. Those that attended these meetings were charged with the recital to all of their ancestors, so that the young and the old, the women and the infirm, would all know our history. There have been many changes in the past two decades, most of them necessary, and this practice has fallen with many of our customs. I believe now, regarding matters at hand, that the story should be told again so that you might all reflect upon it in your deliberations of the coming days."

CHAPTER 2

———◆·◆·◆———

"When the earth was young, before the time of our people, it was inhabited only by the animals roaming in the mountains, and the forests of the lower country. Each of these animals stayed with its own kind and time went on without count. Then, at a point unknown, a male wolf was born that grew to be huge in size, fearless in courage, and as he got older his coat turned blue in color. This one was called Borte Chinua. He knew that he was different from others of his species for none of the females of his own kind appealed to him. He searched for a long time, not knowing even what he was looking for. In his seeking, his reputation spread far and wide as being of great strength, and possessing both wit and cunning. Finally he came upon a gray doe, with gentle eyes and a graceful form; he knew it was she he had been seeking. He called her Gooa Maral, and it was from the mating of these two, so different in all aspects, that the Clan of the Blue Wolf was born." At this juncture Mango stopped speaking, looked down, and removed the drape from the object at the center of the dais. Beneath was a magnificent scene in many different hues of jade. The base of the carving was made of silver, inlaid with branches and leaves of gold. Above the base, a long slab of green jade formed the background of a hill. Near the top, the figure of a gray doe lay sleeping at the foot of a cream colored rock. Atop the boulder stood the lifelike miniature of a blue wolf, his eyes scanning for any intruder, and his fangs bared to protect his mate. The workmanship of the carving was smooth and immaculate, perfect in every detail. With only a slight amount of imagination, Mango thought he could almost hear the deep throated growl of the Blue Wolf.

He waited a few minutes while all present looked at the symbol of their birth as a people; he knew that most of them saw it only once each year.

At length he continued, "It is said that this was a gift direct from Tengri, and no one knows how long it has been with us. It was placed in the care of Kirghiz by the shaman, after he had taken the oath of Anda with Temujin. Let us go back for a moment, so you might truly understand. By the time Temujin was born, a great many tribes had resulted from this union," Mango stated, resting his left hand upon the back of the standing wolf. "These tribes, even though they were brothers, had been warring against one another for centuries. When Temujin was still a boy, his father died of poison and his family was stripped of their possessions by their kin. Temujin, himself, was placed in the yoke of slavery, a cangue about his neck. Even the stout cangue could not hold one destined to be a Khan and he escaped. The true blood of the Blue Wolf boiled within his veins, and within a short while, his courage, wit and daring gained him many followers. While still a very young man, he was made Khan of many tribes. It was then that Kirghiz, a distant cousin and a mere boy of thirteen, came forward to offer his services. Temujin was not impressed with the skinny lad and his visions of the future. He was not enthused, that is, until several pertinent forecasts proved to be true. Temujin then eagerly appointed him as an advisor to his staff. This was the period that Kirghiz took the oath of Anda, and honored it until the spirit had left Temujin many years later. Within four years, Temujin made Kirghiz captain of his personal guard. When Temujin had united all of the tribes, he was proclaimed universal monarch of all Mongolia,

Genghis Khan, and his eyes turned east and south to the vast kingdom of China. He appointed Kirghiz general of the touman, ten thousand of his finest cavalry, and was never to regret his choice."

Mango stopped only long enough to catch his breath and observe that the listening men were engrossed in his story. Then he resumed, "It was with the aid of Kirghiz that Temujin enacted the code of Yassa, the laws his warriors lived by. Together they devised his system of relay messengers, many of his war tactics, and methods of supply. Kirghiz became a formidable warrior, a rarity in that he was a revered general as well as a talented one. His greatest asset to Temujin was his ability to see into the future. Details of coming events were not always clear to him, but the generalities rarely escaped. The only secret Kirghiz ever kept from Temujin was that he, the Khan, would never live to see the surrender of Lin'an and the Song dynasty."

"Before Temujin died, he asked Kirghiz what his reward would be for all those years of faithful service. Kirghiz answered that when all the fighting was finished, and he had found the land he fancied, that he be allowed to take all of his touman that would follow, and retire there to live in peace. Temujin ordered that this should be, even after his death. And that is the way it was, for it was the grandson of Genghis Khan, the one called Kublai, that rode into Lin'an as the Emperor and granted Kirghiz his reward."

"The clear vision of Tengri did not tell Kirghiz that only one in ten of the touman would want to follow him to this land he had chosen many years before. He explained to them that the rule of the Mongols in China would be of short duration, and that when it was finished they would be massacred by the thousands, or driven from the country like dogs from a lambing fold. He told them that the Khanate would vanish from the earth as the leaves from the trees, and that the revenge of the Ming Dynasty to come would last one hundred years. Still they would not follow him, only one in ten."

"Kirghiz came here with his thousand men, their wives, and offspring with the blessing of Kublai and the King Priest of Tibet, for he swore to protect the pilgrims of all faiths that should wander within the limits of his Hoshun."

"Before Kirghiz died, at the age of ninety-six, he learned there were other things his visions had not told him. Even some of those that had followed him could not adjust to a life of peace. It was because of this that he arranged to provide the caravan guards for the Merchants of Chamdo. At first it was only through this country of the Lama's, but in time the warriors of the Blue Wolf ranged to Kabul in the west through the Khyber Pass, north through the Gobi to the homeland of our ancestors and south to the plain of the Ganges."

"The Yassa of Temujin proved to be too harsh for men of peace to live by, and there were no provisions for the women or children. Kirghiz rewrote his own Yassa, and it is the one we live by to this day. He established the rights of inheritance from father to sons, the equal distribution of communal wealth in accordance with individual productivity, and the rights of women to accept or deny their fathers choice of a husband. Through the Merchants of Chamdo, he established the trade we needed for the items we could not produce ourselves. He wrote the advice and guidelines that our people have lived by these past six hundred years and more, to become the most prosperous people of this land."

"The only enemies we have had all this time were there at the beginning, the Uli Prang. They have lived for centuries by raiding defenseless caravans, and the small villages of the lowlands. They range from the salt marshes south of the Gobi to the northwest steppes, from the edges of the jungles of the peninsula to the highest mountains of the west. And yet, they are the only ones that dispute our claim to this land, saying it has always been theirs. They do not raise flocks or herds of any kind, nor do they plant as the farmers of the deep valleys; still they say we trespass in a land they were afraid to camp on before our people came. The ancient taboo of this mountain kept them away as it did all others!"

Mango's throat was dry from his lengthy discourse, and he stopped momentarily. After quenching his thirst from a skin bag Gariu had set near his feet, he continued, "When Kirghiz first came here, the Uli Prang tried to force our people out, but they soon found they were no match for the fighting men of the Blue Wolf. Since that time their only assaults have been from ambush, or on highly outnumbered parties. Our people soon learned that we must always have superior weapons, a highly effective guard system, and never travel in small groups."

"Until the past few years, these safeguards have worked extremely well. However, the Yassa of Kirghiz allowed any man or woman, or group of them to leave the Hoshun for another land and life, if they so desired. Over the centuries a great many have done so; it has decimated our ranks until only we few remain. We do not have enough young men to properly man the guard posts here in this natural fortress. On the trail, or by the lakes, we have been forced to use deception by changing the sentries more often, and dressing them differently. At a distance they appear as other men, making out that we have twice the fighting force we have. But, this sham cannot continue much longer. The chief of the Uli Prang, Tal Rashi, has sworn that he will rid this land of us. His father died twelve years after being wounded by one of us. For this, he has also pledged that he will drink farewell to us from a cup fashioned from the top portion of my skull. I have no fear of this boast he made, but I am informed he is the most capable leader they have ever had, and is not a man to make idle threats. I believe that in the near future he plans some definite action, and whatever this may be, we must be prepared for it. For the moment I would like all of you to consider the possibilities. We have another matter before this council, and at this time I will interrupt and defer to it."

*   *   *   *   *

Mango looked down steadily at the two young men seated before him. "Plauyat and Jebtsun, sons of Hankar, stand before the council." The two young men rose to their feet instantly and stood at attention. "The two of you have recently returned from the service of Maleek, the Merchant of Chamdo. It was at your request before this council one year ago that you were assigned to that service. The reasons you were allowed that request were not that you were outstanding as warriors or guards, but instead that you both were of little use to the clan in any of your duties other than guard. You have returned empty handed and without explanation. This is not the custom of Maleek; he is generous with those who serve him well. All others that have gone before you were reluctant to return so soon. In addition to this, you demand your share of all the wealth of the clan, and a wife that each of you has chosen. I am told that the maids you have selected have refused you both, and that their fathers have denied intervention on your behalf. Why then, do you petition this council?"

At first neither of the men spoke, one only looked at the other. Finally the slender one, Jebtsun, older brother, answered, "We claim our share of the horse herd and the flocks by right of inheritance. Our mother died with a still born, and our father was killed by a fall from a horse."

"Your father would not have died if he had not consistently over indulged in the drinking of koumiss," Mango interrupted.

"This may be true," Jebtsun answered his narrow chin jutting forward as he gained confidence, "but then again the horse may have shied or stumbled. The point of the matter is that he was a member of this clan, and had a share in all things of value."

"It is true," countered Mango, "that he was one of us those many years ago; he was concerned only with the spirits he could drink, and his contribution to the rest of us scarcely warranted that." Mango shifted his gaze to Plauyat's round face with its vacant eyes. "How do you claim the two girls you would have to wife?"

The vacant look vanished from Plauyat's eyes, and was replaced by a piercing stare. His voice was deep and resonant as he spoke, "Under the Yassa of Temujin, any warrior returning from a campaign lasting more than six months may choose and be given any unwed woman or girl of the tribe. We have been gone a year and it was under the order of this council that we left!"

"You would have me re-enact laws that have been abolished for more than six hundred years?" Mango asked incredulously.

"For the warriors that do the fighting, these laws are irrevocable. The Yassa of Kirghiz was made for the herders of yaks and goats, and the breeders of horses." Plauyat's voice never changed. There was no malice, nor venom, only a matter of fact attitude that showed he believed what he said. Jebtsun looked at his brother and nodded his approval.

"If it were possible," Mango began evenly, "for me to use these extinct laws, applying as you say to returning warriors, then you must understand that I would be forced to use all of the rules that so applied."

The two brothers nodded in agreement.

"Did you know also," Mango inquired, "that any warrior that returned without honor, or failing in his mission, could at the discretion of his captain, be put to death immediately?" Mango watched as the heads of the two men jerked in unison. "Furthermore," he added, "there was even a prescribed manner of death. The offender would have an arm or leg fastened to a line of four unbroken horses, and then the animals would be spooked. Or, he could be given a running chance against two or more mounted lancers. If the troops needed some entertainment he might be buried up to his neck, and his head used for archery practice." With each word he spoke, Mango could see some of the color drain from their faces.

"The mission that you claim to have been on is in question. The manner of your return suggests that either you deserted your posts, or were dismissed for reasons unknown to us at this time."

The tone of Mango's voice now became icy, "In twelve days Gariu Taiji will deliver a horse herd, to the camp of Maleek of Chamdo at Shigatse. He will inquire as to why you are no longer in the service of the merchant, and when he returns, we will decide what is to be done about your demands. For now, you are dismissed; return to your posts immediately. I need not warn you about leaving the area of this valley; it would be construed as an admission of guilt, and you would be hunted down. That is all!"

For a stunned moment the two men stared at the Prince in disbelief; then recovering they left the council in extreme haste.

*   *   *   *   *

"Now," said Mango, his voice returning to normal, "We will return to the purpose of this meeting. I chose to impart the knowledge of our past to those two men in the event of their innocence, but I'm sorry to say that I fear it was a waste. I believe that they have neglected their duties to the Merchant, or even worse, may have allowed some of his property to fall into the hands of Tal Rashi. In this event, I did not want either of them to know what we will speak of from this point on."

Mango's voice picked up timbre as he began anew, "We cannot continue to exist as we have in the past! The defects of our defenses will surely come to light. It is only a matter of time until Tal Rashi discovers how under manned we are. I have given the matter considerable thought; we have several choices, one or more of which we must make immediately. The first choice is that we change our way of life completely. We could dispose of most of our stock, and with the earnings buy land in the valleys or the city. We could learn trades, or till the soil. The second alternative is that we who are able could take service with the Dali Lama in the city of Lhasa; those that earn could provide for the young and the old. It would be necessary that we adopt the faith of Buddha, in the Lamaist version, to take this step. The final possibility, and the one I prefer, is that we could rewrite the Yassa forbidding anyone to leave the clan for any reason. In perhaps two generations we could then take care of ourselves. In the meantime, it would be mandatory that we hire skilled and trusted fighting men to protect us and our property. What say you?"

The reaction was instantaneous! The quiet of the last hour was shattered by the hum of voices as each man addressed his neighbor. A slight man of near fifty, with wispy gray hair, rose to his feet. "Mango Noyan, May I?" he inquired.

"By all means," Mango encouraged, "that is the purpose of the council."

"To bring armed strangers into our camp to stand guard over us while we sleep would be much the same as appointing the snow leopards the guardians of the colts. Is this not so?" he queried.

"Not so!" replied Mango, "for the past ten years we have not been able to supply Maleek of Chamdo with his full need of guards, and lately we have furnished him none. He has found that the Singhs of India are valiant and even though they are not familiar with these mountains and our ways, we could train them. If we decide upon this choice, I would ask Maleek to loan us at least ten of these men until such time as we could establish our own compliment. Gariu Taiji leaves for Shigatse in twelve days, and we must decide by then!"

One man over sixty, and unique by his bushy gray hair, took one step toward the dais, and then raised his right arm for silence. "I, Belan Deem, have served the clan of the Blue Wolf in every capacity from a dung bearer to the captain of the guard. I am proud to say I served as caravan captain under two of the Merchants of Chamdo, Maleek and his father before him. I am the father of eight children. Only two of them remain with us, so I feel that I am qualified to speak. I too have had many fears for our safety, and I know of these Singhs. In their own land they are known as the Keshdhari, the Hairy Ones; they dress strangely, adorning themselves with a top knot, combs, and bracelets as women do. They claim to worship the god of Akal, The Timeless, but they also revere the old gods of Sat Nam, Granth and Nanak. How can we trust our lives to men so fickle in their appearance and with the inability to make up their minds as to which gods to worship?"

"What you say Belan Deem is true to a degree," Mango replied with a warm smile, "but being a traveler as you are you must admit that the dress and habit of other lands are different than ours, and by no means demean the people. As for their god, they set Akal above all, and the others you mention are the remains of ancient times, just as the Lamaists we share this land with were once of the religion of Bon. They are, none-the-less, a very loyal and dependable people, and have earned a great deal of respect with the armies of the British in the land of India."

"The seeds of truth may be in what you say," replied Belan Deem. "I speak only that our people may know as much of them as I do; my contacts with the Singhs have been limited I must admit."

"That is the primary purpose of this meeting," Mango stated. "All known facts and beliefs should be brought to light before we make our decision; we will only have the one choice, and it must be made wisely."

A slight man in his middle forties spoke next, "I, Lacomata, know nothing of these Singhs, their habits or their gods, but I am confident that I would rather die by a musket ball of the Uli Prang or even the hand of the Singhs, than the slow death of city life in the service of the Dali Lama, or that of a farmer of the stifling deep valleys."

A loud grunt of approval issued from the assembly. Close by the entrance to the council chamber an old man sat on a high pile of robes. It was evident that his bones were stiff with age. If he were to sit on the floor as the others, he would suffer pain, and would have great difficulty in rising. His skin was pale, bleached, and wrinkled lacking the smoothing effect of flesh to cover the sharpness of his skull bones. A tall rectangular cap covered his snow white hair, and his tunic was black and long, ending well below his knees. The bottoms of his trousers were frayed and worn, and his soft skin boots exhibited many cracks and holes. In his hand he carried a six-foot staff of birch wood, worn smooth by generations of handling. The girth of the staff was more than two inches thick, and nine deep notches were carved one above the other beginning at the mid-point. Dilow Kampi, the shaman of the Blue Wolf, had neither moved nor spoken since the council started, but now he leveled his gaze upon Mango with a stare that could not be misinterpreted nor ignored.

"Dilow Kampi will speak," Mango announced, "Open your ears and hearts, and hear the thoughts of Tengri!"

The old man did not attempt to rise, but his sharp encompassing gaze held the attention of all. "By my count this is the one hundred and twenty sixth time I have camped in the valley of Kirghiz. I have watched many of your grandfathers at play when they were small boys. I have healed their battle wounds, and cured their sicknesses, and accompanied them to the nether land after death. I have preserved and interpreted the Yassa of Kirghiz, and that of Temujin. I have kept the records of your past, and that of your ancestors, and have enlightened all that came to me as to the nature of Tengri. These abilities, and my many years of useful life are my gift from Tengri, just as Kirghiz was able to see beyond tomorrow. I have never seen a vision, nor could I even guess what lies beyond each hill, and until today, I have never felt the need to do so. In the past, I have given advice upon logic and experience that I myself have known, and I must now do as I have always done."

Dilow Kampi closed his eyes as he stopped speaking. For a long moment he looked as though he had gone to sleep. At length he opened his eyes to look upon the Jade carving on the dais, his head never turned from it until he finished speaking, and his voice gained deep resonance for one with a frame so frail. "Kirghiz alone knew the future of his people and of us. He knew that many of the young would leave and that eventually we would come to this; yet he did not change his laws. His desires were that we live in peace wherever possible, but that we keep our lance and sword arm strong to protect ourselves and other men of peace against the Uli Prang and others like them. He did not say that we should not hire out to others; however, he did say that we should live in such a manner as to make all of us happy and harmonious, and to hold our honor close to our hearts at all times. He further knew that time changes all things from kings to rivers, and from mountains to people, that there is nothing upon this earth that will endure forever."

The Shaman paused once more, but this time his eyes did not close. "From the final chapter of the Yassa of Kirghiz, written by his hand, I shall quote his words; perhaps his wisdom will aid in our decision. The last paragraph states, 'Moreover, the Princes of the Blue Wolf shall abide in this valley forever, looking out upon the world from both on high and from within.' These were his thoughts; he put them in the Yassa only a few days before he died. The meaning of this is clear to me only to the extent that this valley and the Hoshun is our home, and that we will not leave it now or in the future. Whatever decision we come to must be in accord with the final words of Kirghiz." The old man closed his eyes again and spoke no more.

The stillness within the chamber was expectant. From without came the shouts of the children at play, and the bleating of some distant goats. All eyes remained fastened upon the shaman, but he had nothing further to impart.

Finally, Gariu cleared his throat, and looked expectantly at Mango.

"Our people have lived by the words of Kirghiz for the past six centuries and we have prospered," Mango picked up. "We shall not deviate from his words now, but within the scope of his laws he has given us broad latitude to preserve ourselves. This is what we should all think upon in the course of the next twelve days. At that time, Gariu Taiji and a few guards will take the horse herd of fifty to

Maleek who will be in Shigatse for a few weeks. If we are to seek the service of the Singhs, he must do it then. Does anyone else care to speak, or will we adjourn until the next meeting?" A few of the men nodded, some grunted, and others made a downward gesture with the flat of their hand indicating that the talk was done for now.

When the chamber had cleared, and only the leaders remained, Mango covered the carving of the Blue Wolf and Gray Doe with the silk cloth. Gariu busied himself with dismantling the birch poles, the lance, bow, shield and the arrows. While he was so occupied, Mango had dropped to his haunches and was manipulating four small stones on the rear side of the dais. He nodded to Gariu, and he in turn grasped the long flat rock just above the ground level. There wasn't much to get a hold of, and at first it did not move. Then slowly under Gariu's steady pressure it slid outward revealing a large interior vault going three feet or more below the ground, completely lined with stone. Several layers of twigs covered the rock bottom; this in turn was overlaid with hides to keep out the moisture. The jade icon and the personal armament of Kirghiz were gently laid within. The large rock slab was replaced and the small stones returned to their original positions locking the ancient safe so that only those that knew its secret would be able to open it. Kirghiz himself had built and mortared the dais; it had yielded to neither man nor the elements since his time.

Their ritual chores completed, the two men left the council house and stepped outside to watch the children. Five young boys between eight and thirteen were lined up at a toe mark shooting at targets set up fifty yards distant, with bows resembling the one within the dais. To their immediate right four more boys, even younger, were stripped to the waist and engaged in a wrestling match. Two older ones, of maybe fifteen, were racing their ponies well out beyond the line of yurts. Small groups of women, girls and tiny children moved from one scene to the next displaying fancy headdresses sparkling with coins and other elaborate adornments. Their long ankle-length dresses were multicolored with rich embroidery, and a great deal of piping. The older men walked back and forth nodding their approval of both the boys and the females. The young men were conspicuous by their absence.

"The homecoming Naadam Festival of this valley has come to a sorry pass, hasn't it?" asked Gariu with visible sadness.

"So it has," Mango replied with gravity. "When we were boys there were enough of us to provide twenty archers, a like amount of wrestlers, and twice that number of riders. As I recall, there were many injuries incurred during the tournament. We did not have to worry that a man or a boy would be laid up for one day, or several. There were enough, and some to spare, to tend the herds and flocks, enough to stand the watches without weariness, and each of them had time for the pleasures of living. All that has truly changed, perhaps it will soon be that way again, let us hope so!"

"Yes," Gariu responded positively, "and let us hope that there will be more smiles upon the faces of the young girls that seldom see what few young, available men we have. Are you still considering the trip up the mountain?"

"Not merely considering," replied Mango, "my mind is made up; I will do it in two more days. In the meantime, I will rest and gather what few things I will need. I could start sooner, although there is little point in hurrying after all these years. Oh, Gariu, I almost forgot, I would prefer that only yourself and Baikali know what I am about. I doubt that the rest of our people would understand my reasons, and if they did, they might think me unbalanced." Mango smiled briefly at this notion.

"There is little doubt in my mind that that is exactly what they would think," Gariu chuckled. "To them it is only another mountain made of stone, ice and snow. It is the site of their valley and beyond that it holds no importance. Why should anyone be foolish enough to want to climb to its barren top? But then, they do not feel the link with the past that you and I do, nor do they have the curiosity; that is why they are content to live as they do, otherwise they would be gone with those that left before to seek out new land and lives. I will say nothing!"

"It is settled then; I will start in two days," Mango stated flatly, and felt relieved with his decision.

*   *   *   *   *

When Jebtsun and Plauyat left the council chamber, their haste was obvious; but when they were out of sight from the Bag, they slowed their mounts to a leisurely walk. For many minutes neither of them spoke. Intermittently Jebtsun would look questioningly at his younger brother then lower his glance to the wide worn trail that led directly to the valley entrance. The vacant stare returned to Plauyat's eyes even before he was in the saddle, and his expression gave the impression of a blank mind to match.

Finally, Jebtsun could continue the silence no longer, "Well, what do you think we ought to do now?" he ask softly.

The empty look vanished from Plauyat's face immediately. "Why ask me what I think we ought to do now?" he snapped crisply. "You're the one that has done all the thinking to get us into this mess. Right from the very start, remember, it was you that decided we should go to the service of Maleek. It was you that said we were being used and abused here. It was also you that decided we should talk to the man that turned out to be a scout for Tal Rashi. You decided we could turn our back at the right time, and be well paid for our lack of attention. And, remember also, that it has always been you that constantly told me I was not too bright, and that you should do the thinking for both of us. Well, I admit that I am slow minded, but never dumb enough to lead us into a mess like this. You should have known people would die if Tal Rashi were involved. You should have known that if we were paid well, the Uli Prang would receive a thousand times more; and that we could be held responsible for all of it. As ignorant and dumb as I am, I can see it now, and you should have seen it from the beginning. As for what to do, I don't have any idea of how we're going to get out of this! It's too complicated for me to understand all that has happened. I do not know. It is beyond me!"

As Plauyat began speaking, Jebtsun sat bolt upright in his saddle. The words he heard, the tone and the attitude were not that of his brother; he looked again to see if he was riding with another. A slight panic began to rise within him as he listened, and at first he could believe neither his ears nor his eyes. Soon the crispness left Plauyat's voice, the lifted chin lowered to his chest, and before he finished his speech began to falter. The panic left Jebtsun as he realized his brother had been thinking of some of these things for weeks; that most of what he said, he had probably rehearsed many times, and that he would have little to say for some time. He would be submissive as he had always been.

There was a great deal of truth in what his brother said, and Jebtsun knew it. The business with the Uli Prang had not gone as he thought it should. He knew there would be blood spilled and goods stolen, but he had been sure the pair of them would appear blameless. The guard captain had been suspicious of them immediately. Jebtsun knew they had to leave the caravan, and soon. Everything had gone wrong when they returned home too. He was sure they could come back, claim their inheritance and a wife each, then leave as so many of the others had done in the past; but inquisitive doubt waited for them even in the clan of the Blue Wolf. Jebtsun soon began to wonder if the odor of treachery might not be carried on the wind, or if it clung to a man's body as does the fragrance of musk.

"There isn't much of a choice for us, my brother," Jebtsun replied easily. "We can either stay here until the Taiji returns from Shigatse and be executed by the words of Maleek, or we can leave before he returns. We do have a choice as to how and when we leave!"

Plauyat turned to face him, the vacant look remained. "The Noyan said that if we left, we would be hunted down as guilty," he quoted flatly.

"They have barely enough men to man the sentry and send guards with the Taiji; with us gone they will have two less," countered Jebtsun. "They could ill afford to send a party looking for us even for a few days. But, if we manage it right, we might not even have to worry about pursuit. We might be able to leave with our stock, the girls we want, and possibly even more!"

"How could this be?" queried Plauyat without turning.

"Did not Tal Rashi say that in the future there might be a place for us with his people? Did he not say that if we were ever in need of help that he considered himself in our debt? And, did he not say there would always be a scout within signaling distance?" Jebtsun eyed his brother avidly.

"Yes, those were his words, I remember," Plauyat answered with new interest. "Well then, why not contact the scout; tell him of our dilemma, and ask for sanctuary with his people. He might even offer to help us take our share of the herds and the girls we want. After all, he is partially responsible for the way things happened and the position we are in. In truth, he owes this much, for he has under-paid us up till now," Jebtsun finished with a note of indignation.

"What about the Noyan, the Taiji and the rest of our people?" Plauyat wondered, sounding concerned.

"What of them?" Jebtsun spat. "They are the ones that could condemn us to die. They have truly never been our people, or the people of our father. You heard how the Noyan spoke of him at the council. Besides, they all think in the old way, and they do not understand our younger generation. That is why most men our age have gone. We live in a new world, and they are living in the past. The ways of Temujin were far superior to the boredom of existence here. There are not enough of us young people to change them, so we must do the next best thing; we will leave as the others did, and make a new life for ourselves."

"What makes you so certain Tal Rashi will be willing to help us?" ask Plauyat, now thoroughly interested.

"Because of what he said, and the light in his eyes when he spoke," answered Jebtsun. "I am sure he's honestly sincere. He is a great leader in the history of the Uli Prang, and you saw for yourself there were many more of them than of the Blue Wolf."

Plauyat nodded in agreement, but did not reply.

"When we reach the guard post," Jebtsun proposed, "we must make certain there is no one out on the plateau. After the others have gone, you must climb to the lookout point. Use the polished silver plate the scout gave you, and make the signal in all directions. When he replies, make certain you note exactly where he is hidden; then I will ride out to make contact with him. Do you understand?" Jebtsun ask softly.

"Yes, I understand," Plauyat returned placidly, "but what if someone comes down from the Bag while you are out there with him? What will I say? I can't think too good if taken by surprise or frightened, and I might be both."

"Tell them I was in the lookout and thought I saw a pair of snow leopards, and went out to investigate. Any of the rest of them would do the same thing, liking to hunt as they do."

"That's good thinking, brother!" Plauyat exclaimed. "How soon do you think we will be able to leave? I have a feeling I will be more content when we are gone from here. I did not like the look of Mango Noyan when he told us his intentions and our rights. It made my belly heavy, and it still is."

"Nor did I like it," agreed Jebtsun, "but do not be frightened. Remember that we have Tal Rashi on our side, and once we are with his people, we will be safe from all of them. It will take a day or two and we will have to work out the details very carefully. Our first watch of the day is four hours before dawn, and that will be an ideal time for our departure. We will have to have help to drive our share of the animals, and maybe take the girls by force. But there is nothing to worry about really; Tal Rashi will surely know how to handle it. This will probably be the beginning of our real good fortune!"

"I hope you're right, brother; I am in need of that," Plauyat breathed almost prayerfully.

The gray stone walls of the valley drew together sharply ahead of them and the descent steepened considerably. The stream beside the trail made a singing noise as it plunged headlong between the vertical walls, leaving only enough room on the westward side for the trail. Five hundred feet directly above the horsemen a great brown hawk shrieked out his warning as he abandoned his lofty perch. Jebtsun looked up and smiled inwardly; soon he would be as free as that bird of prey and that was the life he had dreamed of.

The narrow ravine meandered slightly first this way and then the other. The trail remained on the same side and the torrential stream ripped at the cliff base on the opposite. At some time in the long distant past, the water had cut into the stone at each curve of the trail side, forming several undercut caves of varying depths. Then eons later, as the water cut deeper into the rock floor, the caves were left high and dry forming natural bastions that had only to be walled up a few feet on the open side. These small forts were in readiness, but not in use, being intended only to fall back upon in the event of a prolonged assault from outside. A quarter mile from the upper end the sheer rock walls spread wide, folding back on the mountain itself, leaving only a low boulder-studded ridge on each side of the valley as it descended to the plateau another two miles below. At the entrance, on either side, the water had eroded large overhangs and these were the main outposts. Well back within the protection of the gorge, a series of natural projections, improved by many men, formed a stairway to the lookout niche high upon the outward face of the cliff. It was from this position Plauyat was to signal the spy of the Uli Prang.

As they approached the guard station, Jebtsun whistled sharply several times alerting the sentries of their coming. "Remember," he admonished, "act natural, and do as I have told you. In two or three days we will be on our way to riches and a good life!"

"This time I hope you're right brother," replied Plauyat, and he smiled for the first time.

CHAPTER 3

———————◆◆◆———————

"Woman!" Mango addressed Baikali with mock sternness. "If I were to take along all of these things you think necessary for my trip, I would need six porters to carry them."

"How will you sleep warm if you don't take extra robes?" Baikali asked. "And you know you will need more to eat in the extreme bitterness up there. You have said yourself that all men need more food when the weather turns cold, why not now?" Baikali inquired plaintively.

"I will also need both hands free to climb with; the larger the load I carry, the more it will slow me down. The air is very thin up there and a man cannot do what he could do normally down here. I must get up and down in the shortest possible time; in order to accomplish this there are some things I will have to do without, and there is some discomfort I will have to bear. Don't you see dear heart?" Mango pleaded.

"I think I'm beginning to wish you had never decided to make this trip. No one has ever dreamed of doing this before, and I can't imagine what you expect to find up there now. Even if the legends were true, which I doubt, after all this time there would surely be nothing left, would there?" Baikali's shoulders slumped; her soft dark eyes were pleading.

Menilan sat beside one of the roof poles, her doll pulled closely to her breast. She listened attentively as each of her parents spoke, for she had never seen them in disagreement before, and she did not comprehend what they were talking about. Occasionally she would glance down at her toy as if anticipating an explanation. When none came forth, she would return her scrutiny to the grown-ups.

"My Prince," Baikali began hesitantly, "why not think on this a few days more? I am frightened, and it is not a girlish whim. I don't like the notion of you being by yourself in the event anything should happen. No, don't stop me," she interjected as Mango raised his hand. "What would you do if a bad storm came up? It has happened this late in the year. You would be trapped up there and we could not help you. Or you could fall, a rock could fall on you; there have been landslides before, and you know it. Any number of things could happen, and I don't like it one bit. Please," she implored, "don't go now; wait at least until it gets a little warmer and the chance of a storm is lessened!"

"Heart of my heart," Mango replied in deep seriousness, "there is a certain amount of risk in our lives every day that we live. Many things could happen either here or any place else in the Hoshun, but they normally don't. This is a thing I have wanted to do for more years than you have lived; now is probably the only opportunity I will have to see it through. Don't ask me why I must do it, for I don't really know myself, except to say that it is a compulsion that has been with me all my life. Perhaps I will find nothing, and my time and energy will be wasted; but at least I will have it out of my system, and no longer haunted by the burning questions that have tormented me for so long." Mango ran his hand through his hair in a gesture of his concern; a dark forelock fell across his wide brow to dangle between his eyes. He brushed it back with indifference, then went on, "It's really not going to be as difficult as you imagine. I have already been part way up, one quarter of the distance I would judge. The part I have traveled several times is as steep and treacherous as any of the rest of it. Also, I have plotted the entire journey and it looks as though there is actually a trail of sorts from where I stopped on up to the top. There will be some hardship of course, but I shall not freeze to death nor starve. I am certainly more familiar with this mountain than any other man on earth. "Please," he begged, "have a little more faith in me, and don't worry so much!"

"Alright, alright, I do have faith in you. A great deal more than you know, but I still worry and I am afraid. Maybe it is only silly female intuitive nonsense as I know you believe it to be, so now I will be silent. What else can I do to help with your packing?" Baikali asked with resignation.

"Nothing," replied Mango, "I have everything I will need to last me six days, and I shall not be gone that long. Gariu Taiji will accompany me until the sun is high tomorrow, and then he will return to the Bag. He will carry the food and water we will need for the morning and I will take my evening meal from him when we part."

"Now," said Mango with a wide smile, "let us follow the example set by our daughter and get some rest." He gestured toward the sleeping form of Menilan slumped against the yurt pole, the doll still cradled in her arms.

"It has been a long and tiring day for her. I hope she doesn't wake while I undress her," Baikali breathed tenderly. Mango was already in the folds of the sleeping robes as Baikali extinguished the last butter lamp. As his eyes adjusted to the gloom, he found he could see quiet plainly by the blue-white glow still emanating from the brazier. He watched with fascination as Baikali shed her clothing, folded it neatly in a pile, then stretched her bare form before the dying warmth of the fire; the pale light gave a strange radiating effect to the golden brownness of her skin.

Beneath the robes he pulled her closely to him, and he imagined he could feel the radiance he had seen only a few moments before. She nuzzled her nose playfully into the hollow of his neck.

"Tomorrow I will go to Dilow Kampi, and ask him to summon the spirit of Tengri to assist you in your safe return," Baikali whispered.

"If it pleases you to do so, then do it," laughed Mango softly. "But as the winds return each afternoon, then so shall I, and to this very spot with as much anticipation as I have at this very moment." He pulled her even closer to him, and her fears of the day dissolved in an instant.

*   *   *   *   *

The limpid light of a quarter-moon made the going easier for the first hour of the climb. Mango and Gariu were nearly a thousand foot above the outcrop of rock they often used to commune with Tengri. The wind was light and timid, and each rest stop was welcomed for its cooling effect to their overheated bodies. Neither of them had spoken since leaving the Bag; they needed all their strength and concentration for the ascent. The gray-brown limestone wall they climbed was slightly less than vertical, highly fractured, and provided easy footing and hand holds.

They stopped to rest and do homage to Tengri as the sun burst forth. An hour later they had breasted the wall, and began working their way up the eastern side of a long spiny ridge that steeply angled its way toward the summit of the mountain. Their footing remained good and the patches of ice and snow were still easily avoided.

Midmorning came and the pair of them found a wide fissure in the rock facing directly into the sun, focusing its warmth, and shutting out the wind that had risen. Mango loosened his pack, then shed his mittens and sat down. Gariu stood looking back down the ridge from where they came, his small pack and rifle still on his back.

"We have made good progress, Mango," he announced as he turned and lowered himself to sit.

"Excellent, excellent!" agreed Mango. "I thought we would find more snow and ice on this side of the ridge and that it would make the going slower. I would like a drink of water and some koumiss to warm my bones. How about you brother Taiji?"

"Sounds good," Gariu answered with a grin as he stripped the rifle and pack from his shoulders. "By the way, where did you leave your weapon?"

"At the yurt with Baikali," responded Mango. "It would only be in the way and I'm sure I'll find nothing up there to shoot at," he laughed.

"No, I don't think you will," Gariu agreed, "but I would find it hard to do after all these years. I feel completely naked without mine."

"That is how I feel at the moment, but with my pack, the rope, hook and my knife, I have all I wish to carry." Mango drank deeply from the water skin and then more sparingly from the smaller one Gariu had tendered him. "That makes my blood tingle, Gariu," Mango stated with relish.

"Yes, it really does," Gariu accorded as he lowered the small skin. "This climbing is hard work, you know?"

"Indeed I do," chirped Mango, "and it's going to get more difficult the higher we go. A man has to breathe many more times up here to get the air he needs and he tires much more rapidly."

"You must go at a slower pace when you start on alone Mango," Gariu suggested. "Travel too fast and you might collapse in the wrong place!" He glanced significantly at the sheer drop below them.

"I know what you mean," said Mango, "and I will pace myself accordingly. Come, I feel rested now. Let us continue." They again shouldered their gear and began inching their way upward.

By the time the sun had reached its zenith, the two mountaineers had scaled the uppermost reaches of the ridge, and stood looking westward over a broad expanse of ice curving inward for nearly half a mile to the next exposed ledges of rock. Mango eyed the terrain carefully, selecting the route he would follow.

"Let us eat now, my brother," he addressed Gariu, "for my hunger is great."

"Mine also," replied Gariu, "and I am tired. There looks to be a spot up ahead," he pointed.

"Yes, this is fine," Mango said as they slipped into the warmth of the crevice. Though the sun shone brightly, the wind was cold, and carried particles of ice picked up from the face of the glacier.

"How much farther do you believe you will be able to go before dark?" asked Gariu with serious concern.

"On the far side of the ledges, beyond the ice, the rock curves inward to form a wide funnel where a deep canyon ends. From below, I could see the impression of a jutting shelf or trail that inclines upward across the face of it. The shelf traverses clear around and up the side of another ridge resembling the one we just came up. I should make it around the point at least."

"What lies beyond there?" Gariu inquired.

"As I recall," Mango answered, "it curves inward again, but the area above is a series of short ledges, one directly above the other. It might be that I can take this route, and if not, I will continue westward to the next spur that leads to the summit. It would take longer that way, but the going would be easier."

"How long?" Gariu ask bluntly.

"Tomorrow night, or the next day," said Mango, "depending on which way I am able to take."

"What are your plans when you return from Shigatse?" Mango asked, changing the subject deliberately.

"It's hard to say precisely," Gariu returned a trifle wistfully. "If we decide to bring in additional men, I believe I will look for myself a bride."

"That's wonderful news!" beamed Mango. "Both Baikali and I believe you should have done so before now."

"Oh," Gariu answered, "I have given it a great deal of thought, but there were many things to be considered. Until now I have had no time to give to a wife. All of my efforts have been required elsewhere. Then too, there are none to my liking here in the clan of the Blue Wolf. Not that they are not good enough, nor handsome enough, but instead they are all so young. There is not a woman available among us near my age, nor my temperament. I thought I might enlist the aid of Maleek; being a Muslim he is inclined to be a romantic, and has broad connections. He, if anyone, could find me a bride of good blood. One that would be fair to look upon and at the same time suited for our way of life. Don't you agree?"

"I do wholeheartedly," laughed Mango.

"What do you find so amusing, Mango Noyan?" Gariu asked, taken aback.

"Only that this is a strange time and place for the two of us to be discussing your future mate," Mango assured him.

"Yes, it is, isn't it?" Gariu's smile returned. "I had best be going now, brother, for I am stealing valuable moments from you. Good fortune to you, my Prince," he intoned as he took Mango by the forearms in farewell greeting.

"And to you, my Taiji," responded Mango with deep emotion.

The two men shouldered their burdens, looked each other in the face, then turned and went their separate ways without further words.

Crossing the glacier proved to be an easy accomplishment for Mango. The surface of the ice was extremely roughened by the constant erosion of the wind and the frozen particles it carried. The same wind bit at his face and neck where the flesh was exposed, and he drew the fur hood closer about him with his free hand. The slant of the floe was minimal where he crossed, but a few hundred yards below, it pitched sharply downward ending in a vertical drop of more than a thousand feet. His surroundings did not bother him as much as the knife-like edge of the wind. Out here on the ice there was nothing to break the force of it, and he was thankful when he reached the protection of the ledges once more.

The ridge he skirted at a steep upward course was very similar to the one Gariu was descending. He crowded close to the rock as he moved up, keeping his eyes constantly ahead, and never once looked back. His lungs started to ache just as he emerged at the top of the ridge and the ground leveled a bit. It was becoming more and more difficult to continue any appreciable distance before he must stop and rest.

He seated himself with his back braced against the base of a high rising tor, his mouth and nostrils gasping for air, producing a wheezing sound he tried to stop, but could not. Gariu's advice to slow down came to his mind and he decided now was the time to pace his advance and conserve his strength.

When he was well rested, he rose and continued around the base of the rock spire. Upon emerging at the opposite side, he was amazed to find himself at the foot of the wide rock shelf he had spoken of. It apparently extended further down than he had been able to see from below and was much broader than he thought.

His way was much easier now; the shelf was smooth and the incline gradual, but he had made up his mind to take it slowly. Fifty steps, stop and rest, then go on again for another fifty. He was headed in toward the heart of the mountain; the wall at his right rose straight up, and he could not see the top. To his left, it dropped at first in a smooth roll changing gradually to another wall with an outward thrust; it's height increased as he progressed upward and the canyon bottom fell way below.

By the time he reached the midpoint of the traverse, the shelf had narrowed to less than three feet in width. The near vertical drop was close to half a mile, interrupted by occasional knobby projections of stone. He paid no attention to the void beneath him, but kept his eyes

on the trail that curved and headed nearly opposite to the direction
he had been going. As he proceeded, the shelf once more broadened,
but the pitch became steeper. In a few minutes he was forced to cut
his traveling distance to twenty five steps. Mango wanted to hurry
now, for the top of the ridge was near at hand, and so was the setting
of the sun. Below, the upper end of his valley was coming into view;
he was sure he would be able to see the Bag from the break over.

It was as he thought it would be! From here he had the entire
upper end of the valley within the scope of his vision. The brightly
colored yurts looked like small toys in their half circle far below
him. The animals and people he could make out resembled tiny
insects and the dying sun reflected the blue wisps of smoke coming
from the round holes in the dwellings of his people. He smiled
to himself, for no man of his tribe had ever seen a sight like this
before. In spite of the wind and the bitter cold he stood there for
several minutes watching the hues of it all change as the sun settled
lower in the west.

With a spine-shaking shiver, reality came over him; Mango
realized that he must hurry to find some protection from the fierce
killing wind he knew the night and morning would bring. Using as
much speed as he could muster, he made his way around the point,
and once more found himself upon a shelf of rock headed back into
the mountain. A few hundred feet ahead of him he thought he could
make out a break in the wall and hoped it would provide the shelter
he needed.

The gloom of evening was thick and at first he was not sure that
he was seeing right, but it was so. The small opening he had spied
led him into a cavern that was warm and dry, but so pitch-black
he could not make out his footing. He was forced to inch his way
inward, feeling with his toes. Step by step he moved into it, keeping
his hands on the wall and moving his head slowly in the event the
ceiling dropped abruptly. With each step he could feel the wind
lessen and was finally far enough inside for his comfort. He dropped

to all fours and felt the ground around him as far as he could reach. It was smooth and solid, and felt as if covered by an inch or more of dust. He unrolled his sleeping robes carefully and then smoothed them upon the floor. He loosened his pack, gently placed it within arm's reach, and slid himself between the furs. As he relaxed, the tremors of the cold he had endured so long flooded over him and he shook with uncontrolled violence. Time past and gradually the trembling stopped. His body started tingling as luxurious warmth returned.

When he was finally able, he shed the mittens; he placed them beside him beneath the robe. His fingers explored the inside of his pack as he hunted for his food and water. The water he soon found to be a solid block of ice, but the koumiss was still in a liquid state. He was thankful that he had brought along a large skin of it rather than the small one he himself had originally selected. By the time he had eaten his fill of the barley cakes and thin sliced mutton, he was comfortable and content. A steaming mug of thick tea he would have welcomed, but knew himself to be more than fortunate with what he had.

Mango wondered why his eyes did not adjust to the dark and once again brought his hand before his face, but could see nothing. For the time being he was much too tired to worry about it. He rolled onto his side, pulling the robes close about himself, and dropped instantly into sleep.

*   *   *   *   *

Outside Mango's cave the wind whipped the gray stone ledges with unabated fury. The sun was obliterated by a solid sheet of high dark clouds with patches of fog moving eerily upon the mountain. Inside his sanctuary Mango stirred, rolling first to one side then the other. Full awareness came to him instantly as he sat up in his robes to examine the rock walls surrounding him. He could see quite well in the dim interior of the cave. Light from the entrance illuminated the walls and ceiling showing them to be much higher than he had believed the night before. Once inside the cave, there had been little danger of bumping his head unless he had been twenty feet tall. The rear of the cavern was visible by a pale ray of light coming from a fracture in the roof some fifteen feet beyond him. He was amazed with the features of the cave's expanse, the flatness of the floor, and the near perpendicular pitch of the sides. He rose from his bed and ventured toward the light of the roof fissure. His surprise intensified as he saw a circle of rock nearly five feet in diameter and a little to the right side of the light beam. The stones were carefully placed and nearly a foot high, with the ones of the top tier having rough, flat surfaces. The dust of the inner circle was much darker than the rest of the floor, and without thought, he stooped and ran his index finger into it, drawing his arm to his body as he rose. The material was soft and fluffy, deeper than his finger was long, and much blacker beneath the surface, as his digit attested. He realized clearly that this was a large fire pit that had been banked many times and long ago. Examining the walls, he found they were covered with grayish soot that rubbed off on his hands.

He returned to his robes and began to eat, deep in thought as he chewed absently on the thin sliced meat. Who could have been here before him and when? Where did the fuel come from for fires? There were no trees or wood, to speak of, even in the valley of the Bag far below him. His people had occupied the valley for over six hundred years during the season it was livable and none had ever ventured upon the upper reaches of the mountain, even as far as he and Gariu. So it came to him, he reasoned, that these things must have taken place centuries before the time of Kirghiz. This knowledge did not help solve the questions in his mind and as soon as his meal was finished, he gave it up, at least for the time being. A little of the ice had melted in his water skin; he drank the cold liquid it produced, sucking noisily to get the last of it. His thirst still not sated, he allowed himself two large swallows of the koumiss, donned his packs, and went out onto the shelf.

It was only upon emerging that he realized the intensity of the wind, the coming of a storm, and the lateness of the day. He had overslept by three or even four hours! The quiet calm of the cave, its darkness combined with that of the day outside had deceived his senses. He knew that the thinness of the air and his fatigue had also contributed.

Mango was deeply disturbed by the conditions he found himself in. He normally made his plans and followed them through with very little variation. Now everything was wrong! The coming storm, no matter how slight, could be extremely dangerous up here. His late start could leave him stranded and exposed when darkness came, and the creeping fog obscured much of the route he had planned to take from here up, regardless of which way he chose. *Should I spend the rest of the day and another night in the cave hoping for better weather tomorrow, or should I use the daylight left to advance my position?* While he pondered his decision, he turned and looked back down the trail he had come up on. In his uncertainty, he decided to go back out onto the point of the ridge and see if he could still view the Bag and the people below.

When he reached the point where he had stood the night before, he could see nothing. A thin layer of moving mist spread out beneath him like a blanket. As he watched, he could see that it was not solid, but broken with large holes which would afford a look, if they came into the right line. He sat down and waited, staring into the white fluffiness, imagining that he could almost see the bright colors of the yurts. His eyes began to water, and his brown leathery cheeks turned red from the frigid wind, but the window he hoped for did not appear for several more minutes.

When it did, he could not believe the picture he observed beneath him. The gaily tinted yurts were gone and in their place were large black circles, some of them emitting wisps of dark smoke that quickly dissipated in the wind. The only figures he could see were sprawled motionless upon the green grass of the valley floor and they were not many. There was no sign of the horse herds, the yak, goats or sheep. Every living thing had disappeared and there was no movement in the entire length and breadth of his valley. Mango refused to believe the sights that were there below him. It must be the wind or the altitude affecting his mind. The window he had been looking through closed as the mist moved upward and once more he stared into its murky depths.

He closed his eyes and wiped them hard with his knuckles; the moisture instantly froze on his mittens. Mango opened his eyes and stared more intently, trying to penetrate the cover of the valley below, but his efforts were useless. He waited, the minutes dragging by, and finally once more he could see the Bag; it was just as it had been before. He wiped his eyes again, but knew it would not help.

With a jerk he sprang to his feet and started running back down the ledge shelf he had traveled so gingerly the night before. He gave no thought to his own life, the yawning chasms that stretched endlessly only inches from his thudding feet, the absence of air that burned his lungs with fire and could cause him to collapse headlong to a shattering death. The cave and its mysteries along with his fascination to explore the top of the mountain evaporated as fear enveloped him like a shroud. *What of Baikali, Menilan, Gariu and my people?* Were the only thoughts swirling drunkenly in his mind.

Mango did not even sense the terror his descent of the ledge would have caused an observer, had there been one. He did not feel the cuts and scratches of his legs and arms as he scrambled down the sheer face of the cliffs above the glacier, nor did he see the dark blood encrusting his mittens as he fell repeatedly crossing the ice floe in such haste.

Two hours before darkness fell, he arrived at the smoldering heap of ashes that had been the council house. His pace slowed with reluctance as he continued on to the Bag, for he was sure now what he would find. He had made his suicidal trip down the mountain in little over a third of the time it had taken him to go up, but this fact did not register with him either.

All that he did realize was that most of the dead were within the areas that had been their yurts. Most probably they had died in their sleep. Their bodies were covered with ash and the congealed blood of their wounds formed large brownish welts as more and more of the windblown debris would stick and build higher. Occasionally, as he went from one pile to the next, he would find a man or woman that had made it outside only to die within a few feet of their beds. Their wounds also acted as magnets to the drifting ash, but at least he could tell who they were, and the nature of their dying. So far, he had not seen a solitary bullet hole. Lance, sword and dagger were the only weapons used indicating that the attack had been under cover of darkness, with stealth and superior numbers. These facts Mango derived without thinking, for his mind was still filled with his loved ones. He proceeded from one yurt to the next identifying the corpses only as not being that of his wife, daughter and cousin. Eventually there was no other place to look beyond his own yurt, which he had purposely avoided until last.

Gariu lay on his back, within ten feet of what had been Mango's door. His entire body, from head to foot, bore evidence of the battle he had put up. His arms, neck, shoulders and legs were slashed with repeated sword wounds. The haft of a broken lance protruded from his right shoulder, two arrows stood erect from his left breast, and the handle of his shattered sword was still clutched in his right hand.

Behind Gariu, and closer to the tent, lay Baikali, also on her back. A single lance at the base of her throat pinned her to the ground and a stream of adhered ash indicated where her life blood had flown.

To the rear of the yurt, near a large boulder, Mango found the broken body of his daughter. She had been swung by her heels to snuff out her tiny life against a rock.

Gently Mango picked her up from the cold ground to cradle her in his arms. He sat beside the stone pulling her closer to his breast as the tears streamed uncontrollably down his cheeks. Low moaning sobs emerged from deep within his chest to be carried away by the whistling wind.

Mango did not know how long he sat holding Menilan. The first few flakes of snow melting on his wide nose brought him back to the present. His first thoughts were that he too should die, take his own life, for there was nothing left to live for.

He started to lay Menilan back on the ground when it came to him that he could not leave her here, nor his wife or Gariu. He would take them to the caves, out of the weather, and away from the wild animals that might molest them.

With gentle care he removed Menilan and her mother to the first room of the great cave. He laid them together on one of the flat rocks that had held food stuffs off the floor. Beneath them he placed the softest robes that he could find with the aid of the butter lamps he had lit. He placed Gariu on a robe, but in a sitting position with his back against the wall directly in front of the tunnel leading in from the valley. He crossed Gariu's hands in his lap and laid another sword from the stores across his thighs.

He had thought that with this done he would look to himself, but now his conscience began to bother him. The rest of those people out there were his too! They had given him allegiance and homage while they lived; how could he now ignore them in their ignoble deaths? Quickly he decided they too must be brought inside and once more he ventured out.

As rapidly as his strength would allow, he carried them into the cave, in most cases two at a time, for the majority of them were women, children, and old men. As he brought each of them into the cave, he wiped their faces clean so that he might know which ones he had recovered. When it grew dark, he searched the ruins with the aid of butter lamps, but could find no others. He had them all,

all except four, and he knew who they were. The snow fall had been light and the wind had slackened as he worked, but as he made his way back to the caverns the deluge increased.

Inside the cave Mango seated himself beside the body of Gariu so he could rest. It had been hard work moving so many bodies and his exertions of the morning and afternoon overtook him once he had finished. *Four people had escaped this carnage,* Mango thought as he leaned his back against the wall. *Two men and two girls, Jebtsun and his brother, Plauyat, and the two young females that had refused them. Clearly we have been betrayed! The two brothers were surely in collusion with the Uli Prang while in the service of Maleek and that is why they were dismissed. When they returned here, they were refused the brides they thought they were entitled to and an inheritance that did not exist. When I threatened to expose them and impose punishment, they again went to Tal Rashi to conspire this massacre in my absence. No, that's not true; they did not know that I was not here and so I was to have been included. How could I have been so blind not to know what they might do? How could I have been so stupid not to see the implications their return could bring? And how could they have been so idiotic to believe that Tal Rashi would allow them to keep any of the spoils once they were of no further use to him? Oh those utter imbeciles; they have delivered their people, their wealth, and their brides into the hands of a mad dog who will cut out their livers for their reward.*

Surely Tal Rashi must know by now that I am not dead, for it is my skull that he has promised to drink from. Will he return for me, or will he set an ambush for me in the narrows below, thinking that I will charge into pursuit of him in my rage and grief? He will undoubtedly do both, not knowing that my grief alone almost accomplished the deed his sword has not been able to do.

As he had gathered the bodies of his people, the thought of self-destruction had left Mango completely to be replaced by a rage and hate he had never experienced before. His first thoughts of revenge had been to charge after the murderers of his loved ones straight into any ambush or trap they might have set. As time wore on, however, he became more rational and knew that he could do nothing by himself. This only served to infuriate him all the more. By the time he finished and returned to the caves, he was quivering from an inner black wrath as well as physical over-exertion.

Mango sat for a long while beside Gariu debating what he must do. At length, he knew his only chance was to go to the Merchant of Chamdo and ask for help. He must get to him without encountering the Uli Prang as he had no doubt Tal Rashi would pay dearly for his head. The only way he could accomplish his escape was through the caves emergency exit and if he did this, he must close the entrance. As he pondered this, he wondered why the Uli Prang had not bothered any of the stores here, and then realized they did not know of their existence. Only Plauyat, Jebtsun and the two girls knew it was here and they had most likely been put to death as soon as the herds were clear of the valley narrows.

Mango rose from his seat, picked up the heavy wooden mallet, and went into the tunnel. When he arrived at its mouth, he stepped outside to reconnoiter. He saw nothing save the falling snow and heard only the low moaning of the wind. He then stepped inside and looked at the large timbers supporting the tons of rock above him. Without hesitating, he knocked the wedges from the first set jumping clear as the cap timber came slamming to the floor. Nothing else happened. He moved to the second set, then the third, and still nothing happened! Within half an hour, he had knocked out every set of timbers from the cave south of the point where the rock turned solid, fifty feet or so before entering the first room.

Disappointment flooded over Mango as he stood looking back down the tunnel he had stripped of supports. He had lit two more of the butter lamps so that he might see what would take place during a scene that had been planned over six hundred years before. He had a lamp in each hand and one by each foot as he peered anxiously at the tunnel. Here and there he could see a thin stream of dust fall from the roof, or a small pebble plummet to the floor, nothing more.

After several minutes he turned away in disgust. The plans of Kirghiz had failed and there was nothing he could do but leave the tunnel open. Mango knelt beside Gariu, taking in the lines of his blood smeared face for the last time. He then went to stand over Baikali and Menilan. When the time came for him to leave, he found it hard to break away. Unnoticed tears rolled down his face now covered with the white ash dust and a terrible emptiness filled his chest. It was then that he heard the first deep grinding rumble. He turned quickly and went back to the two lamps on the tunnel floor. He got there in time to witness the collapse of the tunnel mouth. A moving wall of tumbling stones jumped toward him like something alive and was accompanied by a terrific roar that hurt his ears. Sheer terror gripped him for the first time in his life as an unseen force hurled him backward into the wall beside Gariu and total blackness. The events that followed were dreamlike, though he knew he did not lose consciousness. His head, back and shoulders hurt unbearably. The roar subsided to a deep rumble that seemed to get farther away, then stopped and started again after a second or two. Finally, the sounds quit altogether and the dreadful silence was almost as frightening as the noise.

With a great deal of pain and effort, Mango got to his knees. He had no idea in which direction the lamps had gone when they were blown out of his hands. He tried to orient himself as to where the other lamps had been stored then crawled forward. He anticipated some trouble in finding the unused lamps and was shocked when he discovered he had only missed their location by a few feet.

When he once more had a light, he returned to where he had been standing. Tons of rock had been forced back into the solid part of the tunnel, almost to the place where his feet had been. He was so startled by this phenomenon that he would not even venture to guess what the outside looked like. He gathered a supply of lamps, some food, and a skin of koumiss, then headed into the underground channels that were supposed to lead him to its one other exit.

The knowledge that he was completely alone in this world came to Mango as he watched the weird shadows dancing on the walls of the last large room of the cavern. Fear tugged at him again as he remembered he had not been beyond this point for many, many years. "Suppose I can't find my way out now?" he said aloud for the assurance of his own voice. *Maybe I won't recall the right way it's been so long ago. The connecting tunnels could have caved in during the years that I have not been down here. The truth is, no one has been down here and anything could have happened.* He tried frantically to recall his last visit and how he had plotted the trail. Near panic seized him when at first he could not think. Then little-by-little his memory returned and he quickened his pace. Deeper and deeper into the caves he went, hoping that his memory would not fail.

The hours passed slowly as Mango walked, crawled, and bellied his way through the cavern's torturous course. The muscles of his legs ached, his neck and shoulders hurt, and he was terribly tired.

The tunnel he followed grew narrower as he progressed and the head room lowered. When he reached the dead end, he was in a half-crouched position. The passage was blocked with a pile of rubble from the floor to the ceiling. He placed the lamps and the few supplies he carried on the floor to one side. He then worked his way to the top of the heap and began to remove the rocks near the ceiling. He knew only too well that he might have made a wrong turn and this might be a cave-in that he would never dig his way through. He was too weary and broken to care anymore. Methodically he removed the rocks and slid them behind to the side opposite the lamps. The first thing he noticed was that his hands were getting cold; then he could feel and smell the difference in the air. Moving back to the lamps he blew them out, then felt his way back to the top again. He worked by feel to move more of the stones and then was momentarily blinded by a bright light hitting him squarely in the eyes.

When his eyes adjusted, he looked ahead and found the light not so bright. He peeked through the hole he had made to the outside world which was covered with snow and reflecting a brightly shining sun. He had thought it would be dark if indeed he had broken through and had blown out the lamps so that no one would see a light where it did not belong. Instead it was broad daylight and it was hard for him to accept that more than twenty-four-hours had gone by since he had overslept in the cave high up on the mountain.

Mango wiggled himself back to the floor of the tunnel. He had made it through the cavern and now had a chance to get to Maleek if he was cautious and traveled by night. He stretched out on the ground trying to relax his aching muscles. It was then that the full extent of his losses swept over him. His body rolled up into a tight knot, a stifled scream escaped from his mouth, then soul tearing sobs and moans filled the cavern with echoes rebounding from the walls.

CHAPTER 4

◆•◆•◆

At the lower end of the narrows guarding the valley of Kirghiz, two of Tal Rashi's most trusted warriors had been standing their lonely vigil for two days. The first day they had spent at the upper end of the narrows so that they could observe the approach of anyone. When the storm came in the evening, they had retreated to the lower end where the guard station was warm and comfortable. They were sure no one could surprise them there and certainly no one could get by them. Four muzzle loaded rifles lay cocked and primed on their side of the fire wall. Each of them carried a long sword and dagger, while a lance apiece leaned against the wall.

In the beginning, their watch had been zealous and exciting with the possibility that they would be the ones to bring in Prince Mango's head. Riches and acclaim would be theirs, and their position with Tal Rashi assured forever. By the afternoon of the second day their interest had worn thin. They were sure no one was coming and were rapidly tiring of each other's company.

The larger of the two men was called Carfoo. He was coarse and raw boned, dressed entirely in skins, most of the hair of these still in place. It was hard to tell where his chin whiskers ended and the tunic began. Despite his size, he was light on his feet and his movements closely resembled those of a large cat.

Bronsso, his smaller companion, was fair headed and of slender build. Chin whiskers had never arrived with his manhood and the few that did appear he plucked out to keep from looking ridiculous. His garments were made up of whatever might be at hand when anything wore out, or got to smelling so bad it bothered him. At the moment, he wore a rough woven black tunic with long sleeves and skirt, two pair of trousers, the outer ones a dirty brown, sheepskin boots that reached to his knees, and a conical fur cap he had taken from a dead man.

Most of the snow in the bottom of the gorge had melted and Carfoo regarded this as he looked up the trail for the thousandth time, seeing nothing as he had expected. He turned and spoke testily, "I'm for getting out of here! Mango is not coming, and Tal Rashi said he would return last night or this morning. I don't intend spending another night in here with you, Bronsso, you stink!"

"It's only that you're used to your own stench," Bronsso replied easily. "Tal Rashi said for us to stay here until his return and here we'll stay!"

"Don't tell me what I will do and not do," yelled Carfoo, lowering his hand to his sword hilt.

"Do what you will do then," answered Bronsso, "but don't force your luck with me at swords or anything else; because if you do, you will never leave this place." Bronsso's tone did not change, but his hand dropped to within easy reach of his own weapon.

The situation grew tense and might have erupted had they not heard the approaching horse at the same time. Carfoo turned his head to look out on the approach from the plateau. "It's Tal Rashi," he grinned, forgetting his anger instantly. "He has come back!"

"You didn't think he would?" Bronsso asked still not ruffled.

"I knew he would," snapped Carfoo, "I only wondered when."

Both men stood erect as Tal Rashi entered, stooping as he did so, "Well?" he inquired with impatience.

"Nothing," Carfoo answered quickly, "absolutely nothing."

Tal Rashi looked at them both carefully, then at the passage to the valley. He was a tall man, an inch or so more than Carfoo, but he seemed much more than that. His face was lean and long with a tapering black beard confined solely to his chin. A square fur cap covered his dark hair and most of his ears. His tunic and boots were trimmed with fur and though worn, were well kept. It was Tal Rashi's eyes that disturbed his subordinates the most. They were jet black and piercing, seeming never to stop their probing for a second. He returned his gaze to the men and both instinctively lowered their heads. "You have had no sight of him, have seen or heard nothing since you have been here?" demanded Tal Rashi.

It was Bronsso that recovered first. "We saw nothing from the time you left us here until now. However, on the first night about two hours after it turned dark and the snow fell heavily, we heard a great rumbling from the mountain." Bronsso did not know how his leader would receive this bit of news and looked to him expectantly.

"What do you mean a rumbling from the mountain?" snapped Tal Rashi.

"As he said," interceded Carfoo, "a series of loud booming noises came from the direction of the mountain on that night. The first one was long and loud, followed by several short sounds that were muffled. We could almost feel them in the ground," he finished lamely.

"What type of nonsense is this?" Tal Rashi spat. "Get your horses and arms. We will go up to the camp and see if anyone has been there." With this he turned and went to his mount.

By the time the trio of riders reached the camp of Kirghiz, the snow had melted except that which lay in the shade of a boulder or a bush. They rode directly to what had been the center of the Bag. Tal Rashi's face remained as if carved from ivory as he glanced around, but astonishment and disbelief showed clearly from the eyes of his fighting men. The dead and bloating bodies they had expected to find had vanished. There were no flocks of birds that always managed to find the sight of a massacre. A ghostly quiet prevailed, broken only by the heavy breathing of their mounts.

"We will search the area!" Tal Rashi exclaimed with confidence. "Apparently some larger animals have dragged them off." The assuredness Tal Rashi displayed was only superficial, for his mind was racing. *What could have happened to them?* He asked himself. *They could not disappear; one man could not have carried them far, or placed them in the ground.* His anxiety increased as their circles got wider; they found nothing. Tal Rashi regretted at once his haste in regard to the two traitors of the Kirghiz. He would like to question them concerning the habits of their leader and their people. He also had questions of this valley, but he knew woefully that men without tongues cannot answer. The two girls he had given to the pleasures of his warriors; he was sure they would either be dead or insane by the time he got back to them.

Carfoo and Bronsso could see the panic rising in each other's eyes every time they crossed in the ever widening circles. They were both ignorant and superstitious men. Their glances more often turned to the heights of Kula Kangri, than the ground that showed them nothing.

Tal Rashi watched them guardedly, for he knew what was creeping into their stupid hearts and minds. If either of them got back to his camp, they would spread hysteria among his people. This mountain had always been taboo to them. From the beginning of his tribe, it had been so. He had been forced to pleading, bribery, threats of torture, and all of the forces of leadership at his command to get them to attack this valley in the first place. If they should now learn of the disappearing dead, he would never be able to control them again. He was deep in thought on this matter when he discovered that he too was staring up at the snow covered heights above him.

Tal Rashi called roughly to Bronsso, "Go back to the narrows and guard the exit, lest Mango should slip out on us while we are up here. I should have left you there anyway."

"But, but," stammered Bronsso, "what of the dead ones?"

"We will find them in a few minutes," Tal Rashi replied with a hard stare, "now go!"

Bronsso wheeled his mount and rode off at a gallop.

Tal Rashi watched him ride until he vanished behind a low knoll above the narrows. He then whistled to Carfoo and motioned him to come in.

When Carfoo was near enough Tal Rashi commanded, "We'll ride over to those big rocks there near the base of the mountain. I do not recall them being that large on the day of our attack and I wish to examine them. The bodies are most likely hid among those boulders."

"I don't recall them being there at all," replied Carfoo nervously, "but then there are many things about this place I do not recall, and not sure that I care to," he finished with a whisper glancing upward.

"Don't be a damned fool!" shouted Tal Rashi. "Tether the horses here; we can't take them into those rocks." The two dismounted and Carfoo complied.

"Alright," said Tal Rashi, "we'll go in together, side by side where possible, and single file as need be."

A quarter of an hour later nothing unusual had been found. No bodies, no tracks, and in that jumble of mud and rock even a mouse could not have moved without leaving signs. As they started circling back to the horses, Tal Rashi knew he must do what had to be done now!

Two large boulders were crowded together near the spot they were passing; a small pocket lay between them where they separated near the earth. Tal Rashi bent over as they came abreast of it and stared for a moment into the small hole.

"I think I see something in there, Carfoo!" he said with excitement. "See what you think," he added as he straightened and stepped back.

Carfoo came forward eagerly, stooped, and then dropped to his knees for a better look. He did not hear the swish of Tal Rashi's sword as it was drawn from the sheath; he was too intent on seeing what was not there. He did hear the whistling blade as it sliced the air in a double handed downward sweep. He turned his head in time to glimpse the scimitar as it completed its deadly arc.

His body slammed forward into the ground, but not before his head had separated from his torso in a bounding motion. His arms and legs thrashed the earth as though he was trying to defend himself. Before the body had ceased quivering, Tal Rashi had wiped clean his blade on the fur covering of Carfoo's legs and returned it to his scabbard. He then mounted his horse and rode toward the guard station. He never glanced back at the man he had killed nor would the horse he had left be ridden.

The convulsive spasms of the headless corpse soon ceased and lay quiet and hidden between the giant stones. Less than five hundred feet away, directly into the mountain, the body of Gariu sat propped against the wall facing the violent scene that had just finished. Perhaps it was the rigors of death that had pulled his lips at such an angle, but then again it could be a smile, for one of the arrows buried in his heart had belonged to Carfoo, and the other to a robber of the dead known as Bronsso.

The shadows of late afternoon were lengthening when Tal Rashi arrived back at the lower guard station. Bronsso ran out to meet him. "Where is Carfoo?" he asked in a shaking voice, "isn't he coming in now?"

"He'll be along in a few minutes," Tal Rashi responded smoothly. "He is returning down the far side of the valley. I came down the short side and got here first. There were a couple of things we wanted to check out before leaving."

"What did you find?" Bronsso asked, still nervous.

"I'll tell you when he gets here," answered Tal Rashi. "I want to compare a few notes with him before I decide what we should do. Come on, let's go inside. It's getting cold out here."

They entered the station and immediately Bronsso started pacing back and forth across the dirt floor. Tal Rashi didn't like this. He knew Bronsso would be hard to kill if the first strike was not the lethal one and he could not be sure of a killing blow with him constantly on the move. Tal Rashi thought for a moment, but said nothing. After a short while, he removed his sword and sheath, and laid them carefully by the muskets at the fire wall. He now appeared unarmed. He went to the small aperture looking up the gorge and sat down near it. As he did so, he slid his dagger from his belt into the sleeve of his tunic.

For a few more minutes he sat perfectly still, watching Bronsso pace the floor. Then suddenly he cocked his head as if he had heard something. He looked through the aperture until he was sure Bronsso was standing behind him. Tal Rashi straightened with a smile. "He's coming now," he announced and motioned to the window with his left hand. Instinctively Bronsso bent forward and looked up the narrows, vacant and awesome; they were the last thing he would see on earth.

Tal Rashi was slow and deliberate. The point of his dagger entered Bronsso's back precisely an inch below the tip of his shoulder blade, angling upward and at the same time twisting with the motion of Tal Rashi's wrist. The direction and powerful thrust caused the cutting edge to explode the heart of a fighting man that had boasted when it came his turn to die, it would take all day and most of the night to accomplish the deed.

Bronsso fell upon the floor without a sound and hardly a twitch. Tal Rashi took only his dagger and sword when he departed. He left the four muskets, the lances and Bronsso's mount. In the gathering gloom of evening, he rode down the shallow sided canyon that led out onto the broad plateau below. Within the hour, he left the last of the hills and only then did he look back. Cold shivers shook his long frame as his eyes came to rest on the tall white peak. He cursed aloud, "None of my people shall enter upon this ground again as long as I live, and this will be under pain of death!" he swore. But in honesty he knew he would not have to threaten them to keep them away from this place. He turned his horse in the direction his people had headed with the stolen herds, then kneed the mount for more speed. The quaking that shook him would not dissipate.

CHAPTER 5

━━━━━━◆◆◆◆━━━━━━

Mango had lost count of the exact number of days it had been since he left the caves of Kula Kangri, but was sure it was more than two weeks. In most cases the days had been warm and he had been comfortable holed up in whatever hiding place he could find at daybreak. The nights, however, had been cold, especially in the many high passes he had been forced to cross. Gyangze was the closest town to his mountain home, and also in a direct line with Shigatse where Maleek would be; but he must avoid the first city, for even though he had friends there, he knew Tal Rashi also had informers there. The Uli Prang had spies in Shigatse too, but by the time they learned of his presence he would be under the protection of Maleek's guards.

His food and koumiss were used up and he sorely regretted not thinking to bring one of the old muskets stored in the cave supplies. He had not bothered to look for any of the newer rifles; he was sure Tal Rashi had taken them all before firing the yurts. Even a bow and a few arrows would have given him meat, though he would have had to eat it raw. The thought of eating raw meat was easily acceptable in his present state of starvation. For three days he had had only water taken from the small streams he came upon and these were not easy to find in the dark.

The trails he followed were precarious and seldom used. He could not risk walking into any camp; it could contain enemies as well as friends. When his strength began to ebb, he found a short stick and used it as a walking staff. As silently as he could, he made his way up the bottom of a close canyon, hoping the end of his journey would be in sight as he emerged at the top of the pass. This thought had been in his mind for four nights and he soon wondered if he had lost his sense of direction. He had never come this way before as he was always on horseback, with armed men, and never in fear of his life. Lost or not he must go on, for he had no other alternative.

Two hours before dawn he finally arrived at the top, but the winding canyon below gave him no chance to see the valley it led to. Without hesitation he started on again now that the walking was easier. As he descended, he was surprised to find a trail that smoothed and widened as he went on. The shadows of night began to fade and he thought of looking for a safe place to spend the day. His eyes searched the knolls to each side as he moved and he was not aware that he was at the floor of the valley until he looked ahead, and saw the dim shapes of many farm huts directly in front of him. Further on he could define the outline of the city. To the north the shining glint emanating from the roofs and spires of Tashi Lhunpo monastery was visible. The many tents and pavilions of Maleek would be pitched beside the long wall surrounding the sacred grounds of the Lamaists. "I have made it, I have made it," Mango said aloud and broke into a hobbling run.

Mango avoided the farm huts as best he could as he skirted the westward side of the city. He was noticed only by a few early rising dogs and they paid him little attention. The first rays of the morning sun danced brightly on the golden roofs of the monastery; the bold colored tents of Maleek's portable town nestled near the wall.

Mango had little doubt in recognizing the quarters of the merchant; they were the largest and gaudiest, adorned with metal ornaments at the roof peaks. A guard stood at either side of the main

entrance; a jeweled turban crowned each of their heads and white
tunics covered their arms and chest reaching halfway to the knees.
Their trousers were also white and high polished boots fitted the leg
calves loosely. Each man held a drawn curved sword high across his
chest and was preoccupied with the emptiness of the morning sky.

Their inattention vanished as Mango made a direct approach.
The two swords crossed abruptly when he was within a few feet
of the door. Neither spoke but stared at him expectantly. "I seek
audience with his Excellency Maleek, the Merchant of Chamdo,"
Mango stated with authority.

The sternness of the guards faces eased and was replaced by a
slight smirk by the one that addressed him, "Who might you be that
you seek to disturb the venerated Maleek at this hour of the day?" he
ask with impudence.

"I am Mango, Noyan of the Kirghiz, the people of the Blue Wolf,
and former captain of the guard you represent." Mango stated with
force.

"You don't look much like a Prince, lest it be that of the beggars;
we know our captains, past and present," laughed the other guard.

Mango's anger rose and it was evident to the first man, "Fetch Pic
Rhee, and be quick!" he ordered. "I'll keep an eye on this intruder."

The subordinate guard disappeared within the tent. A few
moments later he returned with another man. The late comer was
dressed as the other two, distinguished by a large amulet hanging
from a golden chain about his neck. His hair and eyes were brown
and his heavy beard was neatly trimmed to form double points
above his collar. He was a young man, of middle twenties, with a
curved sword hanging from his left side and a two-edged dagger
from his right. He was a fairly tall man with a tight and powerful
build. He looked at Mango with neither malice nor pleasure. His
glance took in the dirty smeared face, the tangled hair with bits of
grass and leaves intertwined the worn out boots, and the shredded
clothing. He also noted the scratched and torn hands with their

scabs and dried blood. He paid particular attention to the knife at Mango's waist.

"I am Pic Rhee Sing, captain of the guard," he stated quietly. "I give you this information as it is well known, but it is the only thing I will give you. The honorable Maleek dispenses his alms at the market place in the city each day at high noon. I advise you to depart from this place immediately and take your chances with the rest of the beggars at the proper time and place. Your insolence here can only cause you pain!" Normally Pic Rhee would have ended this unpleasant encounter by turning his back and withdrawing, but the madness he saw in the intruder's eyes, and the red flush of his face beneath the dirt, warned him not to do so now.

Mango's patience had passed their limits and he let out a bellowing roar as he reached for his dagger. All of the pent up rage and frustrations he had faced in the past weeks now engulfed his brain. The face of the captain became the face of Tal Rashi and it was Mango's turn to kill.

Pic Rhee saw the first flicker as the hand started for the dagger and his own hand flew to his sword. He brought it out of its sheath in an upward swing, turning the blade as it rose. The flat side of it caught Mango on his right cheek with tremendous force, knocking him to the ground. His own weapon came up in a defensive position automatically, but he was stunned and could not rise. Pic Rhee stepped forward to stand over him, waiting for Mango's next move that might spell his death.

From the door of the pavilion came a rustling sound that caused the two guards to turn. Maleek, the fabled Merchant of Chamdo, emerged in a flurry of purple silk robes trimmed in flaming yellow, and a small square hat of the same color perched atop his head. He was short and round, but not obese. His black mustache was thin and hung a full four inches below each corner of his small mouth. A long narrow beard extended more than a foot from the point of his chin. His eyes were brown and his skin flawlessly smooth, belying the fact that his fiftieth birthday was only weeks away. "Hold," he ordered in a soft voice as his eyes took in the scene. "What have we here?" he inquired.

"This beggar is causing a disturbance, and I was sending him on his way," replied Pic Rhee candidly.

"On his way to Allah?" questioned Maleek, eyeing the sword held firmly in Pic Rhee's hand.

"No, honorable master," Pic Rhee assured, "only if he deemed it the necessary end. He is armed and dangerous, don't get too close to him," he cautioned.

In spite of his captain's warning Maleek came closer. He glanced curiously at Mango and was about to turn away, when recognition flooded over him. "By the beard of the Prophet it is Mango Noyan! What are you fools about? Help him to his feet and bring him inside. He's critically ill can't you see that?"

The shock of seeing Mango in this condition and his own failure to identify him had caused Maleek to lose his composure. Maleek never called any of his people fools, even though some of them might be; it was only on rare occasion that he raised his voice. "Quickly, quickly now, carry him in and lay him on my couch," Maleek ordered more civilly. "Pic Rhee, bring strong wine and some light food. The Prince is in great need of it. Get help from the servants and hurry."

Pic Rhee wheeled instantly to obey, but his mind was filled with one thought only. He had struck a blooded Prince with his sword and the Prince was dear to his master. For this offense, even though in ignorance, he knew he would die!

With the sound of Maleek's voice in his ears, Mango had loosened his grip on the dagger and it slid to the ground beside him. His head was spinning and he could only discern the shadows of the people above him, but he knew he was safe and he drifted willingly into unconsciousness.

He awoke several times to the sweet taste of strong liquid on his tongue. Each time he swallowed, then drifted back into deep sleep. Later he imagined the warmth of wash cloths being applied all over his body, then smooth hands rubbing scented oil to his aching muscles; after came the gentle caress of an enveloping mantle that covered him from his neck to his ankles. Then finally, peaceful sleep that was not disturbed.

Maleek sat beside the couch where Mango had lain since early morning. Every so often he would wring his hands together so hard that the many rings on his fingers would bite his flesh. Then he would sigh a deep sound and murmur another prayer to Allah. All day he had neglected his prayer rug to be at Mango's side and his five invocations to Mecca were forgotten in his concern for his friend.

The hours grew long; the day faded as it had begun and the evening lamps were lit. When the hour of midnight neared, Mango stirred, and then opened his eyes. "Where am I?" he asked in a hoarse whisper.

"You are in my bed where you belong," replied Maleek softly, "and everything is alright now. Are you strong enough to tell me what has happened?"

"They are gone," Mango said bitterly, "all of them are gone."

"Who is gone?" Maleek implored, "I don't understand you."

"All of them," Mango repeated, "Baikali, Menilan, Gariu and the rest of my people. They are all dead! We were betrayed by two of our own clan. Tal Rashi and the Uli Prang were allowed to enter our Bag while the people slept. They did not know I was not there. They killed all of them, most without even a fight. We were betrayed and I am to blame for not knowing what would happen." Though Mango's eyes still reflected his wild madness, his voice was soft and calm. "I am to blame for not being there!"

"I need your help, Maleek," Mango stated, his voice rising. "I need men, arms and supplies. I must go after them at once. I must destroy them before they have a chance to get away. I must avenge my people, but mostly I must avenge myself." As Mango spoke he tried to rise from the couch, only to collapse before he finished speaking.

"Calm yourself, my Prince," Maleek soothed, "do not exert yourself, or you will do great harm. You are ill and you need to rest for some time. Besides, Tal Rashi is not going anywhere. This land, the mountains and plateaus, the deserts and the steppes are his home, and he has nowhere else to go. He will still be there when you are strong enough to go after him. As for my help, it is all yours, everything you need; but not until you have rested and had a chance to recover." Maleek spoke from the heart because of his great friendship to Mango and the people of the Blue Wolf; but he also felt a strong responsibility for what had happened. He had sent back to Mango the two young men that he was sure had betrayed him without any mention of what he was sure they had done. He had no proof, only intuition and circumstance; he had not felt justified in making an accusation that might prove to be false. Only now he was sure that he had been right and ruefully wished that he had acted.

Maleek clapped his hand and instantly a servant appeared. He ordered food and more wine. When the servant left he turned once more to Mango. "When you have eaten and slept some more we will talk on what things you need. I will go now and give instructions to the guards; it is possible that Tal Rashi has realized by now that you would come here."

Mango nodded weakly as Maleek left the chamber; his hands trembled noticeably.

A light wind came from the southeast feebly fluttering an unfastened tent flap. The thin crescent of a new moon arched toward its apex in a cloudless sky and the air was cold. Maleek pulled his long flowing cape closer about his neck as he made his way toward the quarters of Pic Rhee. It was a tent of medium size, pure white and distinct by its solitude against the high stone wall of the monastery.

Maleek could discern a dim light from within and heard a slight whispering sound as he approached the entrance. "Pic Rhee," he called softly, "are you awake?" He did not wait for his captain to answer but went directly in.

"Yes, master, I am awake," Pic Rhee replied. "Would you like more light?" The brazier glowing in the center of the room was the dim illumination Maleek had seen.

"No, no this is fine," returned Maleek as he extended his hands toward the warmth. "Mango Noyan has finally regained consciousness. His people were betrayed during his absence, and have been annihilated: his wife and daughter, his cousin, who was his best friend and chief advisor, and his entire clan down to the last child. Tal Rashi and the Uli Prang have very nearly accomplished what his ancestors have been trying to do for the last six hundred years. I say nearly, for Mango's life Tal Rashi desired above all things. He made an oath to his people when his father died." Maleek's eyes had adjusted to the dimness and he could see that Pic Rhee had truly not been asleep. He was full dressed with no sign of retiring.

Pic Rhee listened intently, but made no effort to comment.

"It must have been two weeks ago, or more, that this treachery occurred," Maleek continued, "and by now Tal Rashi knows Mango has escaped his trap. Tal Rashi is no stupid man, and it is only a question of time until he realizes, or is informed of Mango's whereabouts. He has many spies throughout this land and will undoubtedly increase the price he has on Mango's head. I want you to double the guard of our camp immediately and inform all of the men what they might expect."

"Yes, master, at once," replied Pic Rhee, "is there anything further you might wish?"

"Quite possibly there is," returned Maleek in deep thought, "but I will not know for a while yet. Are you tired?" Maleek inquired, eyeing his commander for signs of weariness.

"No, Excellency, I'm disturbed but not tired," answered Pic Rhee.

"Disturbed?" asked Maleek, his eyebrows arched quizzically.

"I have drawn my sword against a royal Prince!" Pic Rhee answered soberly. "I struck him and would have slain him if you had not interceded." Pic Rhee did not continue for he knew that Maleek understood the implications.

"Yes," Maleek answered slowly, "I appreciate your concern. In all of the confusion and my anxiety for the Prince, I had forgotten." Maleek remained silent for a moment in concentration then, "What is done, is done, and in full innocence. It is a matter of extreme graveness, but not for the moment. We will give thorough consideration of this when it becomes paramount to our situation. For now it is not. Do you understand?"

"Yes, great one," responded Pic Rhee, a thin note of tension clouding his reply. "By your leave I will now see to the sentries."

Maleek waved his hand absently as Pic Rhee darted through the tent flaps. In a moment he followed.

As he neared his own quarters Maleek could hear voices from within. They were soft in a low monotone at times, then rising in strength and tempo, interrupted at intervals by harsh roars. When he entered the bed chamber he saw two of his servants struggling to keep Mango on the couch.

Mango's eyes were wide and vacant. Small beads of sweat covered his brow and cheeks that were tinged with a deep red flush. Both servants were experiencing difficulty keeping him on the charpoy during his thrashing seizures. He talked and shouted endlessly, with neither continuity nor reason.

Maleek laid his hand on Mango's forehead and removed it at once. He noticed the untouched food and the full goblet of wine. He watched the lumping of the muscles of Mango's neck as his head jerked from side to side, the heaving of his body when he arched upward trying to free himself from the restraining hands. For several minutes he continued his observation deep in thought. Both servants glanced at Maleek appealingly several times, but he did not respond. He knew that he must do something or Mango would die in this state of delirium, but what could he do?

When he could stand it no longer, he walked to Mango's side and picked up the wine vessel, then left the room. In the antechamber he opened the top portion of a large carved chest, placing the glass upon the opened lid. He rummaged with the contents of the chest, and then raised a small silver box covered with rich engravings and a few imbedded stones. From the box he produced a long thin vial containing a brownish liquid. After removing the stopper, he carefully counted the number of drops he poured into Mango's drink.

Returning to Mango's side he found him wide eyed and raving, but slightly less violent. With gentle care he raised his head to his own shoulder and patiently forced the wine between his lips each time he ceased to struggle. Maleek's arm was numb by the time the goblet was empty, but the results were worth the discomfort. The writhing and tossing ceased immediately, the head moved slowly and the words were soft, though unintelligible. The servants released their holds with awed expression and in a few minutes Mango closed his eyes and became silent.

Once more Maleek touched Mango's brow to check his fever, but found the wine had not quenched the burning fires. He addressed himself to the servants still standing awkwardly at Mango's side, "You," he said to the nearest one, "prepare me a bed beside the Prince then bring your own pallets into this chamber. The three of us will spend the rest of the night watching over him." To the other he added, "Stay close by him until I return." Maleek whirled without waiting for conformation and once more made his way to the quarters of Pic Rhee Sing. The strangeness of his going to his commander rather than summoning him came to his mind. He found it neither distasteful nor amusing under the circumstances and quickly dismissed the thought.

Pic Rhee rose from his seat beside the brazier as Maleek entered.

"Do you know the Lama called Blen Adri?" Maleek queried without preamble.

"The one of medicine and black magic from the temple of Ramoche?" asked Pic Rhee in surprise.

"Yes, that one," Maleek responded with slight exasperation, "but his magic is not black and it is only magic because you do not understand his methods. He is a man of great learning and ability; and there is nothing evil or sinister about him!"

"Of course, Master, you are right," Pic Rhee answered lamely. "I only meant that I knew who he was by sight, and what I have heard the people of his land speak of him."

"Do you also know where the temple of Ramoche is located in the city of Lhasa?"

"Yes, Great One," Pic Rhee answered with pride, "through the western gate between the Potala Monastery and the Chakpori temple. Stay on the main north road and beyond the green tiled bridge is the temple of Ramoche."

"You know the city better than I had thought for one spending so little time there," acknowledged Maleek. "Take two of the best horses and go to the Lama Blen Adri. Change the horses at each of our stations and make all the speed that is humanly possible. If you arrive in Lhasa during the morning or early afternoon, you will find Blen Adri at the temple of Ramoche, but if late in the afternoon or evening, he will be at the temple of Chakpori whose location you have already mentioned. This one is easy to find, even in the dark, as it is on the ridge opposite the Potala of the Dalai Lama."

"When you find Blen Adri," Maleek continued, "tell him I have sent you and that I need his presence here without delay. Tell him also that the protector of his pilgrims is dying here for the need of him and there is nothing I can do without his aid. In addition, inform him that this is to help feed the hungry and the poor that seek the enlightenment of Buddha." Maleek, while speaking, had slipped a gold ring from his right thumb. The stone was a blood red ruby, twice the size of his thumb nail, and the enormity of the mounting had caused his hands to look small. "Tell him further,"

Maleek went on, "that I offer this in appreciation of his friendship and the many courtesies he has done me in the past."

"It will be done as you say, Great One," Pic Rhee assured him. "Have no fear that I will not find the Blen Adri. I shall return with him in five days or less, though the journey should take at least eight."

Pic Rhee turned to leave, and as he did so, Maleek laid a restraining hand upon his arm. "Do not spend your valuable time dwelling on specters of the future, Commander. Though your god, Akal, is different than mine, and I know him not, I do know that Allah smiles warmly on men of valor and integrity. He knows we are only human and therefore not infallible. His power I know to be great and I would not be surprised if it were great enough for him to have a conference with your god Akal in a very worthy cause." Maleek released his Captain's arm and patted him gently on the shoulder as he left, then called after him with a slight chuckle, "Perhaps there is just a tiny amount of black magic in some of the practices of Blen Adri."

Pic Rhee turned and faced his employer, a puzzled expression blanketing his face. Then as he saw Maleek smile it dawned on him that the Great One was trying hard to elevate his spirits and he smiled back and was on his way.

There was little that Maleek could do for Mango beyond administering the drug whenever he became violent. The servants bathed him, rubbed his body with light musk scented oil, and changed his bed several times each day. The fever remained high and sweat poured from him continually. He would not eat, and drank only water and small amounts of the wine. Maleek was aware that he needed nourishment if he were to live, and tried to force additional drafts of wine down him without the drug; but Mango would only take so much then turn his head away, or swipe the goblet from the bearer's hand. As a result, there were a few times when the drug was needed and they could not get him to take it. Maleek soon discontinued trying to force it on him and could think of nothing else to do.

He stayed at Mango's bedside day and night, and not once did he venture near the seraglio. His four wives knew only that he would not be with them until some crisis had passed. His servants and many concubines saw him only at his prayer rug facing Mecca five times each day; but he also wandered the streets of the tent city in the chilly hour of dawn, and again in the evening before full dark. His eyes frequently scanned the road coming into the valley from the northeast, even though he knew Pic Rhee could not possibly have reached Lhasa as yet, let alone started back.

The days were long and hot, as the nights were cold and lingering. Mango spoke less often and the words afforded little meaning. His strength was fading and his voice was barely above a whisper. There was nothing more Maleek could do than he had done. Each time he prostrated himself to Allah, he pleaded for Mango's life and return to sanity. His prayers did not cease when he arose from the rug, but stayed with him throughout his vigil. He dared not think of how his own faith would be shaken if Mango should die.

On the morning of the fifth day after Pic Rhee's departure, Maleek continued walking slowly even though the sun had risen. He watched the road so long in the poor light that his eyes hurt and several times he wiped the moisture from them with a silken scarf. Eventually, he decided Pic Rhee had set an impossible task for himself and was in the act of turning when he spied the dust rising from the road at the north entrance of the valley. Three riders were approaching at a hard gallop, and the tall one was leading three extra mounts. *It must be Pic Rhee,* thought Maleek, *but if the second is Blen Adri, then who is the third?*

It was indeed Pic Rhee, but the Commander remained in the background as the other two men dismounted. They were both in the gray robes of the Lamas, both small and lean of stature.

Here the resemblance ended, for it could be seen that one was young by the way he slid from his mount before it came to a full halt. The other was much older, for he sat his horse and waited to alight. As the older man came to earth, Maleek ran to meet him.

The older man released the draw string of his cowl, and then flipped his head throwing the covering back between his shoulders. Maleek stood looking at the small shaved head, the bight brown eyes with their graying brows, the thin angular face and the smooth unwrinkled skin of his neck below. The small mouth formed a grin that changed into a brilliant smile displaying nearly perfect teeth.

"Blen Adri, my friend, thank you so much for answering my plea," shouted Maleek with joy as he pulled the Lama to him in a bear hug.

"It is I who should be thanking you, old Merchant of Chamdo," answered Blen Adri in a smooth rich voice as he disengaged himself from Maleek's arms. "All my life I have wanted to do something for the people of Kirghiz, and in the last few years, especially for the young Prince Mango. Now I am told I can do nothing for his people, but that I might be able to save his life. Is it true, does he still live?"

"Yes, Learned One, he still lives, but in the valley of the wandering spirits between the two worlds. I only hope that you have arrived in time, and yet I wonder how you came so far so quickly," Maleek added with a puzzled expression.

"We had the best of guides and finest of horses, though I could have used a lot more padding," Blen Adri answered with a light smile. "We traveled day and night, and stopped only as nature bade us. I might add that your courageous Captain has not rested since he went to fetch us. You had best see to him, or I shall have two men to raise from the dead!"

"Kora, come here," Blen Adri called, and the young Lama stepped to his side. "Maleek, this is Kora, my Geshe. He is a Lama, but a student to me. He will one day take my place if I can live long enough to teach him all he needs to know. He is a bright young man and learns quickly. I am thankful for that, for he has been my shadow for the past three years. It is my fondest hope that we shall spend many more together."

Maleek scrutinized the young Lama intensely. His head too was shaved, but his eyes were deep dark pools set wide under thin arching black brows. His nose was slender with flaring nostrils and until now, his lips had been set in a noncommittal posture. He smiled briefly, and bowed from the waist slowly and deliberately. "It is my great honor Esteemed One," Kora stated with feeling as he straightened. "I have waited a long time to meet the distinguished friend of my worthy Master."

Blen Adri laughed aloud, "Three years is a long time to an impetuous youth that aspires to be a great physician and teacher. Come, come friend Maleek," entreated Blen Adri, "take us to the Prince. We have squandered too much time already."

A visible shade of crimson touched the pale cheeks of Kora, and he lowered his head slightly. Maleek was watching and suddenly he liked Kora very much. *In time, he will become the great physician and teacher you want him to be.* Maleek said to himself.

Maleek led them into the pavilion to the couch where Mango lay. Pic Rhee remained outside; he had said nothing. Blen Adri's examination lasted only a few minutes. He looked into Mango's mouth, his nose, and ears. He lifted each eyelid and peered into the vacancies. He felt the pulse at Mango's neck and noted his breathing, then went over his limbs gently with his hands. At length, Blen Adri straightened and nodded that they should retire to the outer chamber.

"Are these your quarters Maleek?" Blen Adri inquired.

"Yes, they are," answered the Merchant, "and I don't want him moved," he finished with conviction.

"Very well then," Blen Adri stated, "you and your servants will have to find a place to sleep elsewhere. Have a couch laid for myself and Kora. When this is done, I want everyone out and no one is to enter these chambers under any circumstance. Is that clear?" he stated with authority.

"If that is what you wish," replied Maleek. "When will we know?" Maleek began, but Blen Adri cut him short.

"When I send for you, and not before," he answered. "I will call for what food and other items we will need. Otherwise do not even come near that room. Now, go see to your Captain, and tend to the other needs of your business." Blen Adri turned and re-entered the bed chamber with Kora on his heels.

For a second Maleek felt as though he had been slapped for something he had not done, then he remembered Pic Rhee.

With all the speed at his command, he called servants and issued orders. He then mixed a good portion of the drug he had used on Mango with a flagon of wine and proceeded straight to Pic Rhee's tent.

The Captain sat on a large cushion near the center of the floor. The dusty clothes of his trip clung to his body. His head was erect and his eyes were wide. As tired as he was, he had keyed his mind to such a high pitch in the past five days that he now found it impossible to relax.

Maleek handed him the wine bottle, "Here, drink deeply of this. I know that you do not use strong drink, but this is for medicinal purposes, and I command that you take it!"

Pic Rhee took the bottle from Maleek without protest and did as he was ordered. Servants entered the room with jars of warm water and large fluffy towels. They went about their task of stripping Pic Rhee of his garments, and then gave him a thorough bathing and massage. During the procedure Maleek extended the wine bottle until it was empty and Pic Rhee said not a word.

When they had placed him in his bed and shaded his eyes, the servants withdrew. Pic Rhee asked softly, "Will he live, Maleek?"

The Merchant noted the familiar address, but replied in a similar vein, "I don't know, faithful one. We'll just have to wait and see."

Pic Rhee went instantly to sleep. For him the first two days of waiting were easy. He slept day and night for the full forty-eight hours. When he finally awoke, he was ravenously hungry. It took most of the morning on the day that he rose to appease his appetite. He then turned his attention to his duties; he knew there was nothing he could do to aid either Mango or Blen Adri.

*   *   *   *   *

Pic Rhee commanded one hundred and eighty-two fighting men. They were not soldiers; they were trained only in defense of the caravans. Except for those assigned to the camp of Maleek, none of the guards had a regular unit or group to work with. They were attached to the individual trains in various numbers depending on its destination, the terrain it would pass through, the type and value of the cargo, the number of animals involved, and lastly the whereabouts of the Uli Prang, or any other marauding party that might have banded together for the purpose of raiding the caravans. The number of camels and horses used could range from ten to two thousand; the distance involved could be from one hundred to two thousand miles, and the value of their goods just as disparate. The two areas most vulnerable to attack were the vast reaches of the Gobi desert far to the north and the high mountain passes and plateaus of Tibet, with Shigatse at the center. Most caravans from all over Asia converged upon this hub to be rejuvenated, refitted and redirected. A train of one hundred from India comes north through the Chumbi Valley. At Shigatse, it would pause and reform with two, three or four other units, then head northeast to Chamdo and on through the Gobi to Mongolia. It might meet a train coming to Shigatse destined to split in two, one half going to Darjeeling and the other on to Kabul.

It was Pic Rhee's duty to see that each train had the proper amount of guards. Too many would cut the profits of the venture, and too few might erase both profits and assets. The guards were human, some got sick, a few got too old for the rigors of the trail, and some were killed at their job. Their equipment wore out or was lost, their mounts became lame and some died. Supplies were constantly being exhausted. All of these items were the responsibility of Pic Rhee and since the arrival of Mango he had not been able to attend to any of it. Life and business had gone on as usual. Caravans had come in, but none had gone out and now Pic Rhee must get the whole process moving again.

It was not so easy for Maleek to return to the routine of his life. Being fabulously wealthy, he had no duties beyond making the few decisions his subordinates thought were too much for them. He made a great show of running his vast empire of trade, but no one knew better than Maleek that it could function without him as easily as any lowly camel boy. This, in itself, was the secret of his success and he found it extremely difficult to find anything that could truly occupy his mind. He had been ordered not to come near the sick room by the only man in the world that could make it stick and his only genuine concern was the progress within that chamber.

In desperation, he sought the companionship of his four wives at the seraglio only to find that their incessant questions unnerved him. He then decided that one, or possibly two, of his young concubines might prove to be the distraction he so sorely needed. To his great consternation, they aroused absolutely nothing, and in his confusion he gruffly ordered them out of his sight. He then proceeded to the counting tents where the heart of his business pulsed under the exact direction of trusted clerks and scribes. Within the space of a single morning, the entire operation was in complete chaos because of his presence, and so Maleek retreated to his own temporary quarters.

As a last resort, Maleek finally sought the company of Pic Rhee. To retain the affiliation with his Commander, Maleek soon learned that he must be constantly on the move; and so it was that the venerable Merchant of Chamdo lost twenty pounds of his girth in the next two weeks.

Pic Rhee instinctively grasped his employer's plight and worked hard at alleviating the situation. He ask Maleek for suggestions on trivial matters he normally would give little attention to himself. He engaged him in long-winded conversations that meant nothing to either of them. He tactfully avoided any mention of Mango or his condition. It became a game they played with each other knowing that the other knew it to be a game also. The bond between them was strengthened considerably.

Day and night a servant was posted near the door of the antechamber of the sick room. He supplied all of the needs of the three people within, but saw only the head or hand of one of the Lamas. Maleek questioned each one of them as they were replaced during the day, but they could not enlighten him.

Two weeks passed by and Maleek had not even a glimpse of either of the Lamas. He was therefore quite shaken to see Blen Adri as he emerged for his morning walk before the sun rose. Blen Adri stood in the center of the street watching the shadows of dawn change on the spires and rooftops of the Tashi Lhunpo monastery. He did not seem to hear as Maleek stepped up beside him.

Maleek's whole brain was burning with the questions he had wanted to ask for ever so many days, and he found that he was deathly afraid of what the answers might be. Eventually, he drew up his courage much as a naked man would dive into an icy pond. "Does he live?" he blurted.

"Yes, he lives," replied Blen Adri, "and you may see him this morning for yourself." The monk did not move his gaze from the monastery.

Fear again laid its cold damp hand on Maleek's shoulder. "Is he alright, is he sane? Will he recover fully?"

Blen Adri turned and looked at him. "He is sane, and he will recover fully," he stated but did not smile.

"You look sad, or perhaps disappointed, old friend. What is it? Can't you tell me?" Maleek queried softly.

"It is possible that it is not important," Blen Adri began, "but, I will tell you anyway. I have cured his body and restored his mind. In most senses of the word he is normal, but he will never be the same as he was before, and this is what I would like to have seen. The rage and hate were burned into him too deeply. The scar tissue of it in his brain is too thick and hard. I could not smooth it away, nor wipe it from his memory. I tried with all of the resources I possessed, but I could not. He can and will go on, but he will live for one thing only and that is revenge. It is a poor substitute for love, ambition or even curiosity; eventually it will lead to his final destruction. I wanted him to be the selfless great man I had heard that he was before and that is why I am sad."

Maleek did not reply immediately, then eventually responded, "You have done all that you could do and no one could expect more. Maybe, in time, Allah the beneficent one will find a way to change even this."

The Lamaist looked at his friend blankly for a moment, then smiled wryly, "Yes, old Merchant, perhaps he shall. At any rate, Mango is asleep right now and when he awakens, he will be in your hands. Kora and I must return to Lhasa immediately; we have our own work to do, and have been absent for some time now. Mango will need more council than care while he regains his strength. He must not be allowed to dwell in the past and his mind must be kept occupied. I'm sure, old friend you are devious enough to take care of this?"

"Yes, of course," responded Maleek with a smile. "When you have taken your morning meal, and are ready, I will arrange your transportation back to Lhasa. I trust you do not care to make the trip as rapidly as the one here?"

"Very true," Blen Adri agreed, "but I would like to get there as soon as possible in some degree of comfort. By the way, there is another thing that I ought to tell you. I did manage to rekindle the sixth sense in Mango, and I have no doubt that it will soon be put to use."

"What do you mean a sixth sense?" inquired Maleek with a puzzled expression.

"The sense animals have always had of knowing when they were in danger," replied Blen Adri. "At one time man had it too, but he outgrew the need of it in the ages past and it shriveled up within him. It still remains in each of us, of course, and can, so to speak, be brought to life with the proper procedure. Mind you, it's not a long range thing and most certainly won't stop a rifle ball, but it can warn him that someone is aiming at him, or about to plunge a knife in his back."

"That's truly remarkable," Maleek stated in awe.

"Not really," Blen Adri corrected, "I wish that I could have given him more than that. I have the feeling he's going to need it."

"I'm sure you're right," Maleek agreed. "However, I have a few security plans of my own I don't believe you have taken into account, and I think that they will see him through. Now, I want you to take this on behalf of Prince Mango." Maleek tugged at one of his fingers to remove another ring, but Blen Adri stopped him with a gentle hand.

"If ever there was a mortal man, my friend," Blen Adri began, "that walks the Noble Eightfold Path here upon this earth, it is you. I am sure that if for any reason your Merciful Allah should not be able to find a place for you in Paradise, Gautama himself would take you by the hand and lead you into Nirvana. The ruby you sent me is worth a fortune and will feed the pilgrims for a year or more; I can accept nothing more, even for them. As I told you in the beginning, I too had a debt to pay. Let us hear no more on it."

"Very well," Maleek said, glancing at the now risen sun. "Would you and Kora take the morning meal with me before you leave?"

"We'd be more than happy to," replied Blen Adri. The two men joined arms, and walked back to the large pavilion.

*   *   *   *   *

"How long have I been here?" Mango addressed himself to Maleek as the two of them sat beside the river. The sun was high and warm, the day ideal. A light breeze gently rocked the branches of the fruit trees in the field across the Tsang Po; Mango could see the tiny balls of green when they caught the light just right.

"Nearly thirty days, I think," replied Maleek. "Strange, I don't recall the exact day you came. Oh well, it's not important. Why do you ask?"

"Curious as to the time lapse," Mango answered. "I was wondering how far away Tal Rashi could be by now and what he is doing."

"One thing is certain," Maleek stated, "with all the wealth he now has, he will have a hard time getting his people to do anything. They're basically a lazy lot, and won't even steal as long as their bellies are full. That's the one good thing that has come out of this. It has given us time, and a chance for you to recover."

"You're right there," Mango agreed. "He won't be able to rouse those dogs until they have butchered the last yak. It will be next spring before they raid again; I have no doubt that he will be sending someone for me before then!"

"We're waiting for whoever it might be," Maleek grinned.

"We'll be waiting for a lot of things from now on," Mango said with certainty. "Waiting is to our advantage though, for the longer the time, the stronger I shall be and the better my plans."

"What exactly are your plans?" Maleek asked looking up from his hands.

"I can't say exactly," Mango returned seriously. "First I will have to work for you to supply my needs. Secondly, I will have to assemble and train a force capable of tracking them down and destroying them. When I came here, it was in my mind to ask you for a hundred men with arms and supplies, and start after them immediately. I can now see the madness of that!"

"Where would I have gotten one hundred men of the caliber needed on such short notice?" Maleek questioned. "I have only eighty or so more than that in my whole guard compliment; and they are scattered over half the continent. Besides, they are trained only in defense, and on the roads and trails they know."

"I realize that now," Mango smiled. "Going after the Uli Prang with those men would be like chasing the tiger with a band-of-sheep. He would eat them at his leisure and spit the bones back in my face. No, I will have to hand pick my followers and train them in the ways of these mountains and of the Uli Prang. More than twenty would be too obvious; and each of them will be worth ten average fighters when I am through with them."

"It may take years to find, equip and train that many superior people," Maleek stated with mock surprise.

"I have no doubt that it will take that long," Mango said wistfully. "The longer it takes, the more certain Tal Rashi will be of my purpose and the less he will sleep at night. Before it is over, he will be praying that I come sooner."

"Will it always be so important that you destroy him and his people?" Maleek ask hopefully.

"It will always be so," Mango stated, staring at the distant mountains. "There is nothing left for me than this. It is what I would die for, and what I now live for."

Maleek was about to pursue the point when he recalled the parting words of Blen Adri. If the famous man of medicine and so called magic had not been able to free him of this with two whole weeks of treatment, surely a simple-minded merchant could not talk him out of it. He switched to a new tack, "What of Tengri and Kirghiz?"

"What of them?" Mango asked bitterly. "If the spirit of the Blue Sky ever existed, would it have permitted such a thing as this to happen to those few that followed him so faithfully? If Kirghiz had been so far sighted, and so loving of his people, could he not have warned us of this?" Mango's voice rose considerably and his fists were clenched tight.

"Maybe he did warn you and you misinterpreted the meaning," Maleek suggested.

"No, no, that is not so," Mango objected fiercely. "I have read the words of the Yassa many times myself as did the Shaman. If it were there, one of us would have discerned it."

"The ways of Allah are sometimes mysterious to mortals," Maleek quoted from memory and regretted it almost instantly.

"Don't speak of your scriptures to me!" Mango shouted. "You are Chinese and a Muslim; Blen Adri is Tibetan and a Lamaist; and I am a Mongol and an apostate! It is gone, I reject all of it; I will do what I have to do without any divine help from gods that do not exist! You are my dearest friend, and Blen Adri has saved my body and my mind; but I implore both of you not to force this thing of religion on me anymore."

"Very well," Maleek agreed with a note of sadness he could not suppress, "but there is one more delicate subject I would bring up at this time merely for the point of clearing the air for good. I swear to you that I do so in my sincere concern for you and not to grind the broken pieces of your heart."

"Speak out then," Mango said in a milder tone, but acting as if he was expecting a spear thrust. "What is this subject of such delicacy?"

"A woman," Maleek said with simplicity.

"A woman," Mango repeated in startled surprise. "What in the world . . . ," his voice trailed off as though he could not believe his ears.

"The days ahead of you will be long and arduous, and the nights lonely and cold," Maleek murmured almost to himself. "I am aware that no one will ever fill the great void of your loss. Further, that now, and in the near future, it would be impossible for you to even consider it. But, if the time should come that you feel this need, and any of my servants or concubines be appealing to your eye, you have only to ask and they will be yours. I would include my wives, but it is forbidden," Maleek's sincerity was obvious.

The lines of hardness relaxed in Mango's jaws and the fires faded from his eyes. He reached out and placed his open hand gently on Maleek's forearm. "Thank you, dear friend," Mango replied. "Your offer is befitting only one of your great heart and I shall not forget it. I do not believe I will ever be able to bring anyone close to me again. If it should happen, I promise I will accept," he finished with a lame smile.

"Good," Maleek responded with a wide grin. "Now, where shall we begin?"

"I must first find employment," Mango stated.

"Why, you are my Commander, of course," Maleek blustered at being taken by surprise.

"What of Pic Rhee?" Mango jabbed once more.

"Yes, Pic Rhee," Maleek said, his eyes clouding. For a moment he remained in thought, and then added, "He has been waiting to see you for some time now and I didn't know exactly how to handle it."

"What does he wish to see me about?" Mango asked with new interest.

"He thinks you will have him executed!" Maleek stated bluntly.

"He what?" Mango exploded as he rose from the ground. "Why should I want his life?"

"He used his sword on your person, remember?" Maleek admitted hesitantly.

"As any right minded man would have done under the same circumstances," Mango stressed positively. "I also recall that, in my madness, I drew my dagger on him first and intended to use it."

"He doesn't see it that way," Maleek explained. "In his land if one raises his hand against a person of noble birth it is an automatic death sentence, regardless of the situation."

"Not so, according to my way of thinking," Mango stressed. "I think we had best inform him of this immediately. This good man has lived under this threat for the past month?" Mango asked incredulously.

"Yes, he has," replied Maleek, with a relieved warm feeling inside. "As you say, I think he should have his mind put at ease. Let us return and I will send him to your quarters."

Without further conversation the two men set off for the compound at a rapid pace. The quarters Maleek had provided Mango were new. The tent was a blue and white sectional design with eight sides. Within, the floors were covered with heavy mats and rugs on top of these. A pale pink drapery divided the interior into a sleeping chamber and a receiving room. Large cushions and pillows, handsomely decorated, were scattered about the front chamber, and a low teakwood table stood at its center. Mango had been assigned two male servants, both of which were on housekeeping errands when Pic Rhee arrived. He announced himself at the entrance and Mango bid him to come in. Mango was seated at the table finishing a bowl of tea. Pic Rhee came to attention a few feet in front of him, then said in precise and measured tones, "My Master, the Great Merchant of Chamdo, has said you would see me now, Excellency Mango Noyan."

"Yes, Pic Rhee Sing," Mango replied, as he rose and made his way around the table to stand before him. "The most honorable Maleek has told me that you have been laboring under a misconception since my arrival. Is this true?"

"I know the truth Mango Noyan," Pic Rhee replied, "that I raised my sword against you with violent intent and that I struck you to the ground. There can be no recourse from this." His eyes remained straight ahead; his voice without emotion.

"That is true, but you struck me with the flat of the blade. Was this an accident?" Mango queried.

"It was no accident, great Prince," Pic Rhee replied. "I take no man's life without just cause."

"What of Tal Rashi and his followers?" asked Mango. "Have they earned the cutting edge of your blade?"

"Many times over, Mango Noyan," Pic Rhee answered with slight bewilderment, "but that has naught to do with this."

"It may well have a great deal to do with this," countered Mango. "Had it not been for them I would not even have been here, and even if I had been here on a mission, you would have recognized me as what I am, rather than a beggar from the streets."

"This does not alter the law, Mango Noyan," Pic Rhee argued even more puzzled than before. "It has been so always and it will always be so. My life is forfeit and yours to take as you see fit, when and where you so desire. It cannot be otherwise." With this final statement he drew the heavy curved sword from his side very slowly. He took it next by the blade with both hands, and extended its grip first toward Mango.

Mango looked Pic Rhee squarely in the eyes, then at the set of his facial muscles and his stance. He took the weapon in his right hand, held it close, and then smoothly tested the weight and balance of it, stepping back slightly as he did so.

"Very well, Pic Rhee Sing," Mango said with gravity, "I shall take your life as you insist, and by the law," he emphasized. Purposely he allowed a long silence then continued. "But I shall take it in the manner I deem fit, and how I desire. These are your own words. Do you still agree to them?"

"Yes!" Pic Rhee answered with finality. He pursed his lips which were slightly blue and a ghastly pallor covered his face.

"I take your life to serve me for so long as I shall live," declared Mango. "You shall do my bidding and will be my personal protector. You will be my own Captain and my shadow, and will answer to me above all others. You shall, as I have, dedicate your life to the complete destruction of Tal Rashi and the Uli Prang. You will be my champion, but not my slave; you will be my friend, but not my conscience; and you will be my people, though not my brother. You yourself gave me the means to make this so. Will you abide by it?"

For several seconds Pic Rhee could not answer. He was struck dumb. He could not comprehend what was happening, nor why. He had entered this tent prepared to die, but would leave with his life, and a purpose to it which he had never had before. It was true that he was fond of Maleek and dedicated to his service. He knew he was free to leave it at any time, or be relieved at any moment. To be the personal Captain of a Prince was a thing he never dreamed of. To rid the land of Tal Rashi was in his mind most of the time, but he knew he could do nothing by himself. His composure returned and he spoke, "Yes, my Prince, I shall abide by it for so long as there is breath in my body and blood in my veins."

"Then it is done," said Mango with warmth. "Take your sword and use it well. We have a long road to travel, you and I. We have a tremendous job ahead of us, but it will be accomplished!" He handed the sword back to Pic Rhee in the manner it had been offered him.

Pic Rhee took the weapon and returned it to the sheath then looked at his new sovereign with admiration and a shortness of breath.

Mango grinned broadly then grasped Pic Ree's forearms as he would his own people. "Let us tell Maleek and then get on with it. Agreed, Pic?"

"Agreed," laughed the Captain, and a wide smile split his beard.

BOOK TWO

The Legacy, 1910, Year of the Dog

Chapter 6

The waters of the channel approach to San Francisco Bay lay dark and flat beneath the heavy hand of the gray misty blanket that covered everything, the water, the land and the sky. Fog horns of varying pitch and depth had been blowing from all directions throughout the early morning hours. Not a breath of air stirred, and the clipper ship, *Westphalia Lady*, lay dead in the water. The anchor lights were lit, and muffled voices could be heard coming from below decks, but there was no movement of any kind. The pilot had been aboard since early the night before hoping for a break in the murky weather so that he might bring her in. The ship was twenty-four days out of Salina Cruz, Mexico; a beautiful run up the coast, and now this. It was, however, the expected thing for this time of spring rather than the unusual, so no one was disappointed.

The changing of the fog from dark gray to yellowish white announced the fact that the sun was shining somewhere far above; and the incessant cry of the sea gulls blending with the fog horns said the struggle was on and another day was born.

It was impossible to tell precisely when the air began to move. One moment the fog was still and clinging and the next it slowly swirled and gyrated as though it had found life of its own. The dim outline of other ships lying in the channel formed, and then disappeared, only to reshape with more clarity and soon the shoreline became visible on both sides.

The harbor pilot uncoiled from his seat beside a life boat, stood erect and spoke loudly, "This is it Captain, best have your crew look alive. We might not get another chance till late afternoon."

"Very well, Mr. Plover," a deep voice answered. "The command is yours, take her in, Mr. Constantine!" the voice roared, and pandemonium broke loose.

Out of the deceptive confusion many things happened almost instantly. The anchor came miraculously aboard, sails bloomed from bare yards, the anchor lights were snuffed out; the *Westphalia Lady* moved toward her berth. She looked very much out of time and place amidst the coal burning steamers on all sides and did not pass a single vessel without turning all eyes upon her.

*   *   *   *   *

It was afternoon when Cameron J. Hewitt began his homeward climb up the narrow street on Telegraph Hill. Halfway to his house the sea bag he was carrying began biting into his boney shoulder and seemed much heavier than when he first picked it up. He lowered the bag to the ground, then wiped the sweat from his high forehead and ran the damp fingers through his nearly straight brown hair, pushing it upward out of his eyes.

He looked back down the street to the bottom of the hill and out onto the wharf. The *Lady*, as he had called her, was snuggled into the dock, her three tall masts bare and reaching for the sky. She was a beautiful sight, at sea or at anchor, and he wasn't the only one that thought so. A crowd had gathered round and he could see them pointing out the trim lines and sweep of her. There were no tender glances at the smoke belching obesities that filled the bay; once more he was thankful that he had been aboard her on his homeward journey. It wouldn't be long until there were no more ships like her.

Without thinking, Cameron squatted his lanky frame upon the sea bag; and for the first time he really looked at the rest of the city. It wasn't at all like he remembered it. The piles of rubble, the gutted building and other scars of the quake were gone. In their place were new buildings, larger and more permanent in appearance. Four years had passed since that terrible day, but even two years ago, when he had left, a person needed no imagination to see what it had done. He found it remarkable that so much could be changed in such a short period of time.

The sky above was almost clear and the sun shone brilliantly. The harbor pilot need not have worried about the fog settling back in.

Cameron shook his head in disbelief and again ran his fingers through his hair. The first thing he would buy, now that he was home, was a hat. He shouldered the bag once more and made his way on up the street.

He sat the bag down on the porch of a small white cottage that boasted a trellis by the front window, with a red rose bush using it to good advantage.

The key was atop the door case where it always was and after unlocking it he went inside, hauling the bag with him. He stood in the center of the kitchen and looked around. The linoleum floor was fresh mopped, both kindling and coal sat beside the cook stove, everything was dusted and clean and it smelled so fresh. "Yes," Cameron said aloud, "I'm really home."

Cameron made a pot of coffee and was having a cup when the drayman delivered the rest of his things from the ship, five large cartons in all. The drayman helped him carry the things into the house and after being paid, he left. The balance of the afternoon he spent unpacking and storing all the articles he had brought back. By the time all that was done he felt tired and decided to take a nap.

Later, when he woke up he would walk to a restaurant and have something to eat. *Nothing exciting to be done this night*, he promised.

Half-awake he heard the door being banged, but thought he was still on the ship and the noise nothing more than a loose block. The sound stopped. Someone was calling his name and gently shaking his shoulder.

He looked up into the round ruddy face of Harry Clayborne; the bushy mustache it supported tickled his nose. A light fragrance of pipe tobacco and good brandy filled his nostrils. He pushed Harry back from him and sat up. "How the hell did you know I was here?" Cameron exploded, and at the same time began pumping Harry's hand.

"Didn't you know?" Harry grinned. "I've got spies all over the world and they keep me posted on your every move. They told me of your thousand mile trek through the bloody jungle, how you saved the white queen from the savages, and of your bare handed battle with the great cats!" His brown eyes twinkled and the trace of cockney he always tried to hide lay uncovered.

"Harry, you're still a confirmed idiot," Cameron managed to get out between laughs. He clung to Harry's hand and playfully slapped him on the shoulder. "It's grand to see you Harry, honestly."

"What the blazes, Cam," replied Harry, "it's good to see you too! I'd begun to worry you might have set up housekeeping with one of the brown skinned maidens of our neighbor to the South. After all, you were only supposed to be gone six months or so and it's been a full two years."

"I liked it down there, Harry, I really did," Cameron replied. "You know how it was; we went out with a limited amount of money to work on and a confined scope to the project. We did so well that the foundation came up with more money and we got involved in a broader area than we had planned on. The entire expedition was a success; and everyone came away happy, including the backers. That doesn't happen very often, you know!"

"Tell me Cam, what was it you liked best," Harry smiled, "the country, the work or the women?"

"Hells bells, Harry," Cameron began seriously, "where I was there wasn't a woman within three hundred miles." He was going to go on but Harry held up his arm.

"I know, I was only being funny," Harry interjected, "and don't tell me about the part you liked, because I have no interest in thousand year old bones, musty and broken relics that are better off buried, and theories of our ancient ancestors. Once in a very great while you do come up with things I like such as diamonds and emeralds, gold vases and statues, and some carvings or such that some rich person might want."

"Harry," Cameron ask mockingly, "did anyone ever tell you that you possess all of the qualifications of a professional grave robber?"

"Yes," Harry replied playfully, "My father did and he should know," he chuckled. "In truth though, and no insult or slight intended, I can't see the difference between what you do and what I would like to do."

"There's a world of difference, Harry," Cameron assured, "and you know it but are to Limey stubborn to admit it. We do it for enlightenment and improvement; and you would do it only for personal greed."

"This Limey doesn't see any of you chaps giving away any of that gold and booty." Harry squirmed. "What say we scuttle this conversation? I'm getting goose bumps. Besides, we're going out to dinner and a night on the town. There's something new I want to show you; so put on some fancy clothes and let's get at it."

"Harry," Cameron objected, "I haven't had a bath in anything but salt water for almost a month; I'm not going anyplace until this is rectified. Also, I'm not budging until you tell me how you found out I was home."

"Get your clothes together and you can bathe at my hotel. There's always hot water there." Harry said impatiently. "Alright, I'll confess.

I've been in touch with your landlady since you've been gone. She told me about your letters and when she expected you. Then it cost me a dollar to bribe one of the boys in the harbor master office. Nothing so sinister about that, huh?"

"I'll accept that," Cameron laughed. "What about this something new you're dying to show me?" He went to the closet and started selecting the clothes he would wear.

"I'll only tell you this," Harry teased, "it's called *Margo's* and it's sensational. Now hurry, we're wasting precious time."

Cameron stood before the full length mirror in Harry's apartment making the final adjustments of his bow tie. The dark blue suit was the only one he owned and it felt tight across the shoulders. The pants looked a trifle short too, but they would have to do for the night. It didn't surprise him much for it seemed to him he had been growing out of his clothes most of his life; and was sure he had added a few pounds since the last time he'd worn this.

Harry peeked into the mirror over his shoulder, only the upper half of his jovial face reflecting from the glass. "Aren't you satisfied as yet?" Harry asked tauntingly. "You can only do so much with a stone pile like that for a face."

Cameron looked into the mirror again, but for the first time at his own face. He stared intently for a moment and decided that his features did appear somewhat craggy. He turned and smiled. "I guess you're right," he admitted, "what say we go?"

"I've been waiting on you," Harry said as he turned to display the gorgeous brown tweed suit he wore. The tiny flecks of red in the material were more pronounced by the reddish cast of his brown wavy hair.

Cameron noted that the shoulders of the coat needed a little more padding to disguise Harry's true form, but could not decide what could be done about the slight bulge at his middle. "You look like a dashing Philadelphia banker. Very impressive," Cameron replied with sincerity.

Harry beamed outwardly. "We'll arrive at *Margo's* in style too," Harry announced. "How would you like to travel, by coach or motor car?" he asked with a gesture.

"The only sumptuous ride I've had in two years was on the back of a fat burro that didn't bite me for the liberty," Cameron laughed. "I think I'd best stay with the coach until I become more civilized."

"As you wish," Harry bowed mockingly. "This is your night!"

The exterior of *Margo's* was impressive, three stories of new red brick with high arching windows and a broad oaken portico. The stairway from the street was marble with wrought iron balustrades at least ten feet apart and heavy double entrances at the top. In the upper half of each door was a small diamond shaped slot; at one of these a face appeared when Harry slammed the knocker.

The right hand entrance opened and the sound of soft music floated out into the night air. Harry announced himself in a low voice. The huge man in severe black evening dress let them in, nodded his head slightly and led them to the dining room where they were met by a beautiful brunette woman in a deep rose full length gown that took Cameron's breath away.

"Margo," Harry said formally, "I'd like you to meet a very dear friend of mine. This is Cameron Hewitt, Cam this is Margo. Isn't she divine?"

"My great pleasure, Margo," Cameron stammered slightly, not knowing exactly now he should address her. He had noted the strange omission of her last name. Almost at once this slipped his mind as his gaze floated from her glistening long hair to the deep depths of her green eyes, the arching lines of her chin and full mouth, the tapering white throat dipping into a high bosom straining at its confinement. Her waist was small and accentuated by a black lace belt knotted neatly to the side. Cameron found himself staring down below the belt trying to visualize what her long slim legs really looked like. He glanced up to find her smiling at him with a knowing gleam in her eyes that made him feel like a naughty little boy with jam on his hands.

"Your companions are waiting at your table, Mr. Hewitt, Mr. Clayborne," she said in a slow easy voice. "Will you follow me?"

Cameron steered in closely behind her as she made her way around the immense dining room. He was too busily engaged in watching her every motion to notice the almost concealed orchestra playing softly at the rear, the large and lavish dining booths screened off from prying eyes and the closely intertwined couples swaying on the dance floor.

In his enchantment he almost bumped into her as she came abruptly to a stop and turned. "Your table, Gentlemen," she announced, drawing open a curtain. "Harry, I'll let you take care of the introductions since you're acquainted with both of the ladies. It looks like you'll need more champagne. I'll send a waiter right away." She gave Cameron the benefit of a wide smile and a slight inclination of her head, then left.

Harry looked at Cameron with forced gravity, and then laughed. "Meet our ladies for tonight, Cam. This picture of blonde loveliness is Lolly, and she's mine. The exotic damsel with raven locks is Amy and she is yours. I purposefully arranged it this way so we wouldn't get them mixed up," he chirped.

"Good evening, Lolly, Amy," Cameron ventured while twisting his head for a last glimpse of Margo. He eased himself into the seat Amy offered and really looked at her for the first time. She was exactly what Harry had said, young, pretty and with a splash of lightening in the dark depths of her eyes.

She took the bottle from the ice bucket, filling his empty glass and her own. As she handed him the goblet she slid closer to him along the curved seat of the booth. "May I call you, Cam?" she asked pleasantly.

"Why not?" he smiled. "If his lordship there can get away with it, anyone should be able to."

Amy giggled; the sound was like a small bell ringing.

"I can see where you two are going to get along fine," snorted Harry. "She's got a warped sense of humor like you."

The girls laughed heartily as Lolly moved in close to Harry's side. She looked up at him tracing the outline of his ear with her finger. "I've missed you, honey," she purred. "Where have you been the last two weeks? It's been real lonesome without you."

"Busy, busy, busy, darling," Harry replied. He looked her up and down with an appraising scan, and then added, "It'll be a long, long time before you're ever lonely, and I'd bet on that."

"I meant I was lonely for you," Lolly answered forcing her childlike face into a pout.

"I missed you too," Harry replied candidly, "but I honestly couldn't do anything about it. There were some things that had to be done and I had to take care of them myself. That's the truth!"

Amy casually laid her hand upon Cameron's thigh and asked, "What have you been doing all this time he's been so busy?"

The shock of her intimacy brought to mind all the other odd things he had experienced since entering; he suddenly realized the true nature of this establishment and felt like a fool. "I've been on a boat," he blurted out.

"Is that all you've got to do, sail around on a boat?" she asked easily.

For a moment Cameron was angry at being taken in, then he fathomed that this was precisely the reaction Harry was looking for. *I'll be damned if I'll give him the satisfaction of knowing just how dumb I was*, he thought to himself. Aloud he said, "Good lord no, girl, I've been on one of the most exciting adventures you've ever dreamed of for the past two years and I'm dying to tell you all about it." He drained the wine glass in two large gulps and added, looking sharply at Harry, "And that's the Gospel truth."

For several seconds Harry looked at him quizzically and then erupted into a loud booming laugh. "Let's us nice people all have a party," he said and began refilling the glasses.

By the time dinner was over and all traces of it removed from the table, Amy had made quite an impression on Cameron. He found her to be charming as well as desirable, and the same applied to Lolly, but in different way. Amy was mysteriously seductive, while Lolly was warm, comfortable and compelling.

The ladies excused themselves to the powder room and Harry could hardly wait until they were out of earshot. "Well, what do you think of it?" he asked, his eyes sparkling.

"I'll say this," Cameron replied, "I've never seen anything like it in my life. That Margo is something special in a woman!"

"Yes," Harry intoned with gravity, "I noticed the way she affected you when we came in; I'm not going to give you the usual word of advice, I'm just going to tell you her ground rules. There isn't a thing that any man in the state of California has that she wants beyond what he might like to spend in this establishment. The entire spread is hers; she has no assistance, and needs none. She has no husband, lover or pimp and needs none. She has only one love in this world and that is money. She already has a lot, but wants more, with no strings attached. She can get what she wants without becoming personally involved and that's the way she's going to play it. Now, if there are still any wild ideas in that head of yours I'll tell you the capper. She is a hell of a lot older than you think she is and has the brains to go with the years."

"Just how ancient is she?" Cameron asked with a hint of a sneer.

"She's forty and that puts her about eight up on you," Harry replied frankly.

"Incredible," Cameron replied still not serious. "I'll bet she could spot me that eight years and still give me one hell of a run."

"No doubt about it," Harry admitted, "but if you're smart you won't even try it, or entertain the thought. She'll put you in your place proper, and fast, and after she does you won't even dare show your face around here again. There have been a lot try it with more class, looks and money than you; and it always ends the same. Take my word and just enjoy looking."

"Are you really serious?" Cameron asked soberly.

"Dead serious," Harry answered. "What say we forget it? The girls are back."

"If you say so," Cameron agreed lamely.

Harry popped the cork of a fresh bottle of champagne and the party renewed in earnest.

An hour later, Cameron was on the dance floor with Amy nestled closely in his arms. He had been thinking of Margo and what Harry had told him. He admitted that with all Harry's antics and clowning he was a very shrewd and knowledgeable person. He had to be to own the business he did and have it function so well. At length he finally talked himself into putting Margo from his mind. He pulled Amy's body closer to him and lightly touched his lips to her forehead.

Slowly she tilted her head back to peer into the grayness of his eyes. At first she didn't speak, then softly whispered, "You know, we can go upstairs any time you like."

"That would be nice," he answered in the same key, "and I think I'd like right now. What about Harry and Lolly?"

"They know their way up, silly," she giggled as she led him toward the stairs.

From sheer habit Cameron awoke shortly after daylight. He opened one eye and saw the heavy drapes were visible at the window and felt the warm smoothness of Amy, tight against his back. He smiled briefly, then closed his eyes and went back to sleep.

The next time he opened his eyes Amy was gone and Harry was shaking his shoulder again. "Hey, this is getting to be a habit with you," he said good-naturedly.

"Yes, it is," Harry concurred, "And all because we got things to do and places to go."

"Where are we going at this hour of the morning?" Cameron yawned as he sat up in bed. "Where's Amy?"

"Amy's gone about her business like any good girl," Harry said flatly. "We are going on a picnic out in the country to a very secluded private spot I'm sure you'll like. Now, come on, get your clothes on and make your face pretty," he added.

"Just the two of us going on this picnic?" Cameron inquired with a raised eyebrow as he wormed into his pants.

"Not hardly," Harry answered with a smile.

"I'd like to have asked Amy to come along," Cameron said as he put on his shoes.

"You know, Cam," Harry replied, "I've been told that just a little bit of variety keeps a man at his peak. What do you think about it?"

"Well, I don't know. I believe I'd still like to have." Cameron started to reply.

"Come on, Cam," Harry interrupted, "indulge me. You won't be sorry, I promise. After all, I've made all these plans especially for you as a home coming. Just trust me, and I'll show you the time of your life."

"Okay, Harry," Cameron laughed, "but, only because I know you're crazy, and I like you. I've got to buy some clothes sometime today."

"We'll do that when we return," Harry agreed. "Right now we've got a beautiful lunch and two lovely ladies waiting for us at the foot of the stairs. Hurry up and shave, I put the gear over by the basin."

A few minutes later the pair of them walked down the hall and then to the stairs. At the bottom landing the two women looked up, the taller one steadfastly at Cameron. She was fair, with flaming red hair that hung below her shoulders and caught the light whenever she moved her head. Cameron had expected her to look nice, but nothing as incredibly dazzling as this. "This is going to be some kind of a day, Harry!" he exclaimed in a hushed tone.

"We're only getting wound up," Harry stated with assurance.

Cameron gave him a sidelong questioning look, but Harry ignored it and started down the stairs.

*　　*　　*　　*　　*

"Harry!" Cameron exploded with exasperation from the tub, "it's been three nights and three days since we started on this lunatic assault on wine, women and song. Why in the name of heaven do we have to go out again tonight? I'm tired and worn out. I've drank enough to last me the rest of my life, and I've hopped so many beds that I'm starting to feel like a professional."

Harry listened from the bedroom, but didn't reply.

"Look, Harry," Cameron continued, "it's all been grand. I do appreciate all your plans and preparations, but there is a limit to what I'm capable of. How did you dream all this up anyway? The day of the picnic, the boating trip yesterday and the beach today? Who did that beach belong to anyway? It must have been guarded. I didn't even see a seagull. Those girls, different ones for the days and still other ones for the nights. You just don't find girls like that standing around on street corners, Harry. What in the hell are you up to anyway, Clayborne? I know you, and this not your loveable self. You take out an insurance policy on my life or something like that?" He finished washing his feet, then stepped out of the tub and began to dry.

"No, I'm not planning to kill you," Harry stuck his head through the door and glowered. "I'm only trying to show you a good time and let you know I missed your ugly face," he finished sheepishly.

"Alright, alright, I believe you," Cameron sighed. "It's just that tonight I'd like to sleep in my own bed. And alone. I'd like to get up in the morning and pick up my life where I left off. I've got notes that need transcribing and some reports to write. I haven't seen my landlady and there are a dozen other things I've got to do. You promise tonight will be the last of it?" He wrapped the towel about his middle and followed Harry out into the bedroom.

"Yes," Harry agreed without hesitation, "I promise tonight will be the end of it," as he smiled inwardly.

"Good enough then," Cameron beamed. "Where are we going, and what will her name be tonight?"

"Oh," Harry said as though collecting his thoughts, "I had in mind going back to *Margo's*, where we started that first night. Is that acceptable? Her name is Madeline and I'll have to admit I saved the best for last."

"I don't see how there could be any best applied here," Cameron said. "Sure, *Margo's* is fine as long as this is the end of it," he finished with no enthusiasm, nor thoughts of Margo.

Harry watched him closely, then thought to himself, *The party's over.* Aloud he said, "We'll have a grand finale."

Cameron didn't feel much like eating the breakfast of ham and eggs that sat before him. His stomach still churned from the night before and his temples ached in a slow tempo. He took several sips of the black coffee and made up his mind that he had to eat if he were to feel better.

Across the table from him, Harry ate with relish. "Don't you ever have a hangover?" Cameron asked in disbelief, while gingerly chewing a piece of ham.

"Not very often, I'll have to admit," Harry responded between bites. "I don't know why, but that's something that doesn't seem to bother me. Oh, I feel a little squeamish when I first open my eyes some mornings, but it goes away in a few minutes. You ailing this morning?" he grinned.

"Yes, damn it," Cameron flung, "and I wish you were too! I think you should suffer just as much as I because you're responsible for it."

"Eat your breakfast," Harry laughed, "then you'll feel better. I've got a surprise for you when you're through."

"I don't believe I can stand anymore of your surprises," Cameron replied without interest.

Daylight had brought with it a misty drizzle of rain that showed no sign of leaving. Cameron idly watched the people on the street hurrying for shelter as he finished his last cup of coffee.

Harry methodically filled and lit his curved stemmed pipe, then between puffs of smoke and sips of coffee, scrutinized his friend in leisurely anticipation.

Realizing that Harry was waiting for him to make the first move he asked, "Now, what's this big surprise?"

"I've got a job for you," Harry replied smoothly.

"What the hell do you mean; you've got a job for me?" Cameron asked in amazement. "What kind of a job? I don't know the first thing about the import-export business and I haven't the slightest desire to learn!" he finished with emphasis.

"The job is heading up another expedition with a healthy sum of money involved," Harry replied without emotion.

"Since when have you started sponsoring archaeological ventures?" Cameron asked with a noticeable sneer.

"Not me," Harry stated with a smile. "The United Federation of Theological Research and History. They want you to take out a party into some part of Asia to look for some religious relics. They want you and they're willing to pay damned handsomely."

"Who are they?" Cameron demanded. "And, why have you waited until now to tell me about it?"

"There are several people involved, I guess," Harry replied soberly. "The only one I have talked with is the curator of the museum, Dr. Edmond Felix. He seems to be in charge of getting the thing set up. The reason I didn't tell you before now is that I didn't want to spoil your homecoming until you had a chance at a little fun."

"Harry, damn you!" Cameron swore, "You've been up to something ever since the night you walked into my house and woke me up. Come on now, lay it on the line. How soon is this project supposed to be worked up, how many months have we got to prepare for it, where is the area of investigation and just what are they looking for?"

"I think," Harry said evasively, "it would be better if you ask those questions of Dr. Felix. He's got all the answers and it would save us all a lot of time and repetition."

"Just when do I get to meet this mysterious Dr. Felix?" Cameron asked suspiciously.

"We have an appointment with him and some others within the hour," Harry replied with a slight tremor in his voice.

"Well I'll be double damned!" Cameron exclaimed from shock. "You look here, Harry Clayborne, I've been out there in the brush, jungle and desert for two years now. It's my line of work and I like it. But that's two years without letup; if you think for one minute that you're going to give me a guided tour of civilization for a few days and then ship me out again, you've lost your mind! I'm entitled to a rest and some leisure time of my own choosing. I've not even finished the records and reports of the last project." He had spoken so rapidly that he was out of breath.

"At least you'll go with me and have a talk with the good doctor about it, won't you?" Harry pleaded. Cameron was about to continue in the same vein when he noticed the grim set of Harry's mouth and the deep troubled look of his eyes. It came to him that there was a lot more to this affair than showed and he began to suspect that Harry's every move of the past four days had been leading up to this moment. There must be some definite purpose to Harry's actions and he wasn't going to find out about it if he withdrew in a huff. Besides, he was more than a little uncomfortable about all of the money and time Harry had spent on him since his return. Friendship should only be allowed to run the gamut so far in one direction if it were to flourish. "I'm sorry, Harry, I didn't mean that," Cameron said. "We'll go see him alright, but I don't see how anything can come of it."

"If we hail a cab we can make it with minutes to spare," Harry replied with renewed enthusiasm.

Cameron watched closely as the handsome cab made its way up and down the many hills of the city. He was trying to orient himself, but gave it up at the end of half an hour. The only thing he could be sure of was that they were headed up the peninsula in the general direction of the Mission Dolores. The rain continued and there were few people on the streets.

"I can't get over how much the city has changed in such a short while," Cameron stated. "I don't even know where I am!"

"You should have seen how much it changed in less than a minute on that day four years ago," Harry answered with a faint belying smile. "Of course, the greater damage was done by the fires; they burned for days."

"I sometimes wish that I had been here," Cameron said sincerely. "Standing off at a safe distance, naturally."

"Be damned thankful you weren't," Harry replied with equal seriousness. "It was a ghastly experience for me even though I lost nothing from it. Sometimes I can still hear the rumble of the buildings collapsing, the frightful screams of the maimed and dying, and the roar of the thousands of fires that followed." He pulled his coat about him at the middle and shuddered.

Cameron commented, "It's hard to see how it could cause such complete devastation in one area and little or none close by, that one brought complete destruction and extended the damage to such great proportion. What you say is true, though. Neither my office nor warehouses were disturbed, but would have been a total loss if the flames had gotten that far. The wind was blowing right and I was lucky that the street behind me was so wide. Otherwise, I would have been wiped out like all the rest. I don't believe you ever did tell me what your personal losses amounted to at the Palace Hotel."

"I didn't tell you because there was never an applicable value established," Cameron replied absently. "The insurance company paid me two hundred fifty dollars for the things I had stored in the basement of the hotel. In one sense, they overpaid me. The clothing

I had left there wasn't worth that much and other than time, the other things hadn't cost me a nickel. Like you said the other day, 'Old bones, broken pieces of pottery and the like are better off left in the ground.' Well, that's where they wound up again, along with my records and notes of every expedition I had ever been on up to that time. There were some other papers too. A wedding certificate, my college diploma and a writ of divorce. There were a few other knickknacks from my childhood, but nothing of great value. All of the discards from my previous employers might one day have proved to be of great worth; but right now I guess they are just the debris the cleanup crews thought they were. If I had gotten back even a month sooner I might have salvaged some of it, but that's life."

"I imagine you've started collecting again, haven't you?" Harry asked with genuine concern.

"Oh sure," Cameron replied. "There's no problem there. The backers won't pay the return freight on a lot of the artifacts that are turned up such as duplications, fragments and in some cases materials of questionable origin and authenticity. It's a blasted shame; at the present time I'm afraid there is a lot more discarded than brought home for study and display. It won't always be this way though. One day there will be properly trained people in the field to do the job and ample funds for them to do it right."

The hansom pulled to the curb and stopped. Harry got out first and Cameron followed.

The building was two stories of gray stone, the rocks old and the mortar new. A large sign with gold lettering, UNITED FEDERATION, hung over the double doors. Harry proceeded toward them after paying the cab.

They entered into a small foyer with a wall desk and register. Harry walked straight through into the main gallery. The floors were of new hardwood covered by rows and rows of tables displaying icons of every description; paintings, carvings, sculpture and molds. There were single pieces of parchment and paper enclosed in glass cases, holy books of dozens of religions printed and copied in a hundred different languages; gold and silver ornaments, plates, belts and rings. Gems cut and polished or in the rough. Each had a printed card telling of their individual religious significance.

Cameron was instantly intrigued and slowed to a stop, but Harry grabbed him by the arm and pulled him on to the rear of the room. He was so entranced by the quantity and quality of the collection that he failed to see the two men waiting for them. He jumped inwardly when he realized they were there.

"Dr. Felix," Harry smiled, "this is the man we've all been waiting for. May I present Mr. Cameron Hewitt? Cam, meet Dr. Edmond Felix and his assistant Mr. Norman Clyde."

"How do you do, gentlemen?" Cameron inquired as he extended his hand first to the doctor and then to his assistant. For some reason, unknown to himself, Cameron had expected Dr. Felix to be a little old man slightly bent with age and responsibility.

To his surprise he found him to be a powerfully built man in his early forties, surpassing his own height of six feet by an inch or more. His face was squarish and pleasant to look upon with large blue eyes, a high nose and jet black hair with a single streak of gray running from front to back. "I understand from Harry that you're planning some sort of trek and would like to consult me about it." Cameron said trying to avoid involvement from the beginning.

Dr. Felix's laugh was easy and soft, "I'm afraid we require the sum total of your many talents, Mr. Hewitt, or there shan't be any trek, as you put it, at all." He noted Cameron stiffen ever so little at this remark. "There are other people involved and they are present, so I think it would be best if we adjourn to the conference room. After you've met them I'll give you a complete run down on our objective and the reasons for it." He looked thoughtfully at Cameron for a moment, and then asked, "Mr. Hewitt, do you have any reservations about going out on another trip so soon after your return?"

"Yes, I'm afraid I do," Cameron said simply. For some reason he found himself wanting to be completely honest with this man.

"Mmmm, well in that case, I would like to ask one simple favor of you before we join the others," Dr. Felix said. "I realize it's presumptuous of me, having just met, but I would appreciate it greatly." His gaze was steady and warm.

"I'd like to oblige you Doctor," Cameron returned somewhat ill-at-ease. "Wouldn't that be like buying a bat in a box?"

"To be sure," the Doctor agreed with a smile, "but it's nothing of a serious nature. I would merely like you to defer a decision until tomorrow on what we discuss today. Would that be too much to ask?"

"Not at all, Doctor," Cameron offered eagerly before he realized he had committed himself for at least another day.

"Excellent, excellent!" exclaimed the Doctor taking him by the arm. "Now let's go meet the other folks."

The conference room was small and narrow running at a right angle to the gallery. A large mahogany table and a dozen chairs nearly filled the extent of it. Three of the inner walls were white and bare. The fourth was nearly all window and at the opposite end from the entrance. Three people sat at this extreme side of the table, two young women and a man. The two women both wore large capes of gray with hoods still covering their heads as though they had just come in from the rain or were chilled by it. The man was in his middle twenties and of medium build and height as he rose. He had a full head of blond wavy hair and a sensuous face with eyes of pale blue. He too still wore a long coat; open at the front displaying an expensive brown suit of English cut. He nodded his head, but did not speak.

"Mr. Cameron Hewitt, Mr. Harry Clayborne, May I present Miss Constance Crawley, Miss Penelope Rutledge, and Mr. Roger Tibbs," the doctor paused long enough between each name for each of them to acknowledge briefly.

Miss Crawley's, "Gentlemen," was barely lukewarm Cameron noticed.

Miss Rutledge was friendlier with, "My pleasure indeed, Mr. Hewitt, Mr. Clayborne," her eyes responding and her hooded head tilting like a small bird.

Once more Roger Tibbs nodded his head, taking his seat with apparent boredom.

"Miss Constance is the daughter of the late Dr. Emmett Crawley," Dr. Felix stated addressing the remark toward Cameron. "I presume you were acquainted with him, being in the same field of endeavor?"

"Why, yes, I did know him," Cameron stammered, "but I didn't know he was dead," he replied. "I'm terribly sorry to hear of this, Miss Crawley. His contributions to the field of archaeology are formidable and widely known. He will be greatly missed and mourned by all quarters," he finished lamely trying to recover from the shock.

"Thank you, Mr. Hewitt," Constance replied placidly. "My father suffered a series of strokes that began shortly after his return from Greece a year and a half ago. Five months later he died in his sleep. I do appreciate your sympathy, Mr. Hewitt, but he passed on with a minimum of suffering and all his affairs were in order according to his standards. It has been over a year and all my tears are dry. We are here now to instigate his final wishes and Dr. Felix is the administrator." Her speech was directed solely to Cameron and though he knew the words to be sincere he could not help but sense the icy crispness accompanying them.

Cameron scrutinized her carefully trying to decide if the hostility he felt was toward her father's wishes, or to himself. She had not lowered the hood of her cape, as had Miss Rutledge, and there was no hint as to the color or length of her hair. Her eyes were large blue green orbs that gave no hint of her emotions. What he could see of her brow was narrow and smooth, underscored by a small mouth and nose. Her chin was rounded with a slight jutting appearance that might have been his imagination. To the left side of her mouth he could see the indentation of a dimple that would have been pleasing if she were to smile. High on her right cheek, an inch or so below the eye was a pale crescent scar arching downward like a frown, and about the width of a man's thumb nail. He looked at the whiteness of her throat, but could only see a small portion below her chin; from there down she was concealed completely by the raincoat, though it did not hide the square set of her small shoulders.

"Yes," Dr. Felix stated as if he had been asked a question, "I was appointed administrator directly by Dr. Crawley. He took me into his confidence several years ago and I presume it was only natural that he chose me to execute his final wishes. You are all no doubt aware of the many, many years Dr. Crawley devoted to his field, to the worldwide travel that this involved, and to the great number of significant discoveries that he is personally accredited. The field of archaeology was his entire life, from the time he was a young man in his early teens, until he passed on. During the course of his years of service he represented the major foundations of three great nations. His work took him to nearly every corner of the globe and encompassed every phase of history from war to religion." At the start Dr. Felix addressed the table at large, but as he continued he slowly focused solely upon Cameron.

"As you are probably painfully aware, Mr. Hewitt, people like yourself and Dr. Crawley are the life blood of your profession. However, it is not you that make the decisions as to where you go and the nature of your quest. It is understandable that the financing of such undertakings are beyond the means of most individuals, and therefore are the responsibility of groups such as ours. Many times a man of Dr. Crawley's acclaim is convinced that his personal dreams are sound and would be fruitful, but is unable to convince those with the money of this truth. The sad fact is that the foundations do not have the wealth needed to investigate all of the things they would like to. As a result of this, the monies they do have are doled out on what they think are the most probable and rewarding ventures. Dr. Crawley accepted this fact. That is why he set aside a good portion of his estate toward an expedition he himself had longed to make for a number of years. The amount Dr. Crawley left for this purpose will be matched by the United Federation, but only if all of the conditions of his will are met," Dr. Felix finished softly.

"That's not hard to understand," Cameron replied with honesty. "I'd probably think the same way if I were financially able. I know of several sites we were forced to evacuate before they were thoroughly examined. The reasons were always the same."

"This is undoubtedly true, Mr. Hewitt," Dr. Felix concurred, "but not the case with Dr. Crawley. He wanted to go to a new place for a very unusual reason! Do you read the Bible much, Mr. Hewitt?" he asked.

"Not as much as I'd like to or should," Cameron replied uneasily.

"Do you recall the part in Genesis where Noah's Ark landed on the mountain after the forty days and nights of rain?" Dr. Felix inquired pointedly.

"Yes," Cameron laughed with relief that he should know the answer. "It was on Mt. Ararat. It's located somewhere in the remote part of northeast Turkey as I recall."

"That's quite true, according to the Scriptures," Dr. Felix responded with a slight smile. "However, during his travels in Asia and the Near East, Dr. Crawley became aware that there are a great number of people that contest the name of the mountain and its location."

"That's hard to believe," Cameron replied incredulously, "I've never heard this before. Where then is this mountain supposed to be and what is it called? Who are the people that believe this and what are their reasons? Are they Christian people?" Cameron asked in disbelief.

"Yes, some of them are Christians," Dr. Felix replied seriously. "Others are Moslems and Buddhists basically and there are some Brahmans. The mountain is in the lesser Himalayas. It has many names, depending on the country you are in. In this country it is generally called Kula Kangri and is located in Tibet near the Bhutan border. There is no current physical evidence to prove their belief, but strong legends from widely separated parts of the world led Dr. Crawley to believe there must be something to it."

"Do you mean," Cameron asked in apparent shock, "that this is the expedition Dr. Crawley wanted to fund?"

"Precisely," Dr. Felix answered intently. "It was not a decision of the moment with him. For many years after he first heard these stories, I guess you'd call them, he discounted them completely as native hearsay and superstition. As time went on and he heard the same things from other parts of the globe, his interest kindled. For the last five years of his life, he was convinced that there was some truth to the tales of this mountain he was told of, and that there were things there that would be of great importance if they were brought to light. Naturally, he could not be sure they would be of Christian religious significance, but he was positive it would be both beneficial and enlightening to the point of justifying his involvement. Dr. Crawley was not a frivolous man and if you had known him well, you would now second this opinion."

"I met and talked with Dr. Crawley on several different occasions. I liked and respected him without reservation for his work, but as a person, I couldn't really say that I knew him well," Cameron replied.

"As I said before," Dr. Felix repeated evenly, "Dr. Crawley's work was his life. If you knew and respected his enterprises, then you had to be close to him. The reason I am pursuing this point, Mr. Hewitt, is that you are mentioned directly and decisively in his will!"

From the time Cameron had entered the building, he had been assailed by one shock laid upon another. Dr. Felix's last statement was the gut shattering blow that caused him to reel back in his chair. For a full minute he sat staring at Dr. Felix, momentarily forgetting there were other people in the room. He opened his mouth to speak, but the right words would not form. Finally, from sheer embarrassment he managed, "I don't understand!"

"I'm sure this has come as a complete surprise to you," Dr. Felix answered evenly, "but I can explain. I said you were mentioned in his will. You are not a direct recipient, however. You were named to head up the expedition that he would like to have made himself. Furthermore, you and you alone are to be the director of this venture. If for any reason you cannot be prevailed upon to do so, there will be no expedition. The money so allotted will revert to his only living heir, Miss Constance Crawley. The amount to be paid you for your services was left to the joint discretion of Miss Crawley and the Federation. For my part this would be a flexible sum that could be worked out to your satisfaction. Dr. Crawley expressed the greatest faith in you, both in his will and verbally. If you decline, that will be the end of it. I personally wish you would accept. Even though we only met this morning. I know a good deal about your accomplishments and believe Dr. Crawley made the right choice for the job at hand. I further believe in the convictions of Dr. Crawley regarding this trip. Don't ask me why, for I know very little about it except that he believed in it. Perhaps that's all I need to know. What do you say, Mr. Hewitt?"

For another long while Cameron remained silent, then replied, "To tell you the truth I'm afraid to tell you what I think for fear of offending all of you." He noticed Miss Crawley stiffen visibly, glancing at the others, remembering they were there. Again Cameron hesitated before he began, "As I said, I have no desire to affront anyone. I did and do admire Dr. Crawley for all that he has contributed. He was a pioneer in our field by introducing logging, cataloguing, cross referencing, grid procedures on site, and most of the other scientific advancements of the last fifty years that differentiate us from the ghouls our predecessors were thought to be. He possessed skill and imagination, coupled with the courage and energy needed to succeed. And yet, with no disrespect in mind, I cannot conceive how he could propose such a preposterous operation without any concrete evidence to support these legends he was influenced by. Beyond that, there is the inaccessibility of the region of his destination. Tibet is the land of the Forbidden City, Lhasa. Only a few foreigners have ever been allowed to enter the country. There are no charts or maps; the terrain is physically the most impossible of any place on earth, barring the poles. And lastly, you don't even know what you would be looking for, nor for that matter how long it may or may not have been there. Oh, yes, and with all the trouble the British are having in India they wouldn't allow you near the border, let alone cross it. To be very frank, and I regret to say this, I think it is fantasy."

Cameron had directed his remarks to Dr. Felix, but he turned at the scraping of a chair. Constance Crawley leaned toward him, her face white with anger. She was about to speak when Dr. Felix raised his hand, "I too thought it fantasy when I first heard of it!" he interjected rapidly. "But, when Dr. Crawley finished telling me of the many different places he had gathered this information over the years, the pinpoint accuracy of all accounts including the location and description of the mountain itself, I soon changed my mind. I only wish that he could have talked to you personally as he wanted; but you couldn't be reached and time ran out on him. I know that he could have convinced you as he did me. In regards to the way the place could be reached, he did not plan to go through India at all. China was to be his means of entry into Tibet and we do have connections there. We have made a great number of inquiries over the past year and I am pleased to report we have made a great deal of progress regarding transportation, guides and the like to the very borders of Tibet. Also, we have been promised assistance by some very important people. They seem to feel that with the proper escorts and certain conditions we could enter Tibet with government permission.

None of this is cut and dried, you understand, but what things in life are?" Dr. Felix spoke rapidly trying to avert a confrontation, halting momentarily to take several deep breaths.

During the conversation Roger Tibbs had gotten too warm. He stood up to remove his coat, flopped it carelessly over the back of the chair, and then dropped back to his seat. His eyes wandered aimlessly about the room and his fingers drummed softly against the table, then noiselessly against each other as he brought the palms of his hands together. His boredom was plain and he made no effort to hide it.

Miss Rutledge had also shed her cape, but she did so with grace and attention to the conversation. Her round cherubic face moved from one speaker to the next; her dark eyes reflected her approval, or discontent, with each statement that was made. Her long brown hair made a rustling sound against her high lace collar each time she moved her head.

Constance's face was still framed by the cape she wore. The light pink color had crept back into her cheeks and she settled back into her chair, but the coldness of an iceberg still glistened in her eyes.

"To continue with the rebuttal, so to speak," Dr. Felix went on, "it is like you said to a point. We have no maps or charts, but we do know the location of the mountain in question. We do not need a map to chart our course from here to Shanghai, nor up the Yangtze River to where we will acquire our guides. They will be the ones to take us to the mountains and if they do not know themselves, they will know someone who does. What you said about the objective is also true. We don't know precisely what we are looking for. Of one thing I am sure. If it's there we will find it and recognize it for what it's worth. Your friend, Mr. Clayborne, has been most helpful with the contacts in China and other places. I'm sure he'll fill you in on the details later in the day."

"There's one thing I'm certain of, Dr. Felix," Cameron countered, "that there is no one in Shanghai that knows what to expect in the interior of that vast country. No one, including the Emperor, has known for the last thousand years. Why should it be any different at this time? The present Emperor is a mere baby ruling through his mother, and she through her ministers. Their power along the coastal regions and the larger cities is a fact, but in the distant provinces of the north and west, where travel is tedious and communication next to nothing, the war lords rule with open contempt for the Emperor and a downright hatred of foreigners. How do you propose to deal with them?" Cameron finished shooting his query directly to Harry Clayborne.

"The winding roads of trade seem to find their way through the war lords and the river pirates as well, Mr. Hewitt," Dr. Felix proposed. "We will follow them."

"When you say we, Dr. Felix," Cameron responded, "do you imply that you will be part of this expedition?"

"Yes, indeed, Mr. Hewitt," the Doctor responded with a smile. "Both Mr. Clyde and I shall represent the Federation. We are, supposedly, especially equipped for a mission such as this don't you think?"

"I truthfully don't know what to make of the whole affair," Cameron answered. "As I recall, though, I made you a promise and I'll hold with that. I'll sleep on it!"

"Miss Constance," Dr. Felix inquired, "do you have anything further to add that I may have overlooked?"

"Nothing you've overlooked, Doctor," she replied easily in her deep soft voice, "but there are some details I'd like to add on my own."

"By all means," Dr. Felix agreed, eagerly nodding his head several times.

"The first thing I would like to make absolutely clear to Mr. Hewitt," she continued, "is that I am wholeheartedly in favor of this expedition even though it will bring no personal honor nor profit to me whatsoever. If this mission should fail to materialize, my father's bequest will revert to me; and for that reason alone most people would be against it, but I am not. I believe in my father's judgment and I happen to know that this is no simple minded whimsy of his. I know that he spent a great deal of time and money tracing out each and every lead he came upon. He had gone as far as he could without actually making the trip. If time had allowed, he would have done this also. He had a great deal of information at his disposal and his intuition told him that this would not be in vain. I have seen his intuition at work over a period of many years. I accompanied him on many of his field trips and was with him constantly when he was not. I knew him better than any person alive and I believe his judgment was sound and will prove to be productive." While she spoke, her chilling stare never wavered and Cameron could feel it penetrate his vitals.

After a few moments pause she went on, "The second thing I should like him to know is that I am, and always have been, personally opposed to his command of this party. However, according to my father's will I cannot accomplish one of his wishes without fulfilling the other wish. If he does accept, I will place no obstacles in his way to make his job more difficult. One other point I would like to make is regarding the commission. The entire project, if handled properly, shouldn't take over six months, a few weeks one way or the other. At first I thought six thousand dollars would be an adequate sum, but now in view of all the objections he has raised, perhaps eight thousand would be a more appropriate figure." Her facial expression remained passive. She looked straight at him and yet spoke as though he was not there. Neither venom nor malice was evident in her tone, but the chill was unmistakable.

Miss Rutledge's eyes grew wide with admiration as she stared amazed at her friend's disclosures.

Roger Tibbs remained oblivious to it all. His fingers returned to their senseless drumming of the table.

There was no longer any doubt in Cameron's mind as to the direction of Miss Crawley's frigid feelings, but he could not imagine why. He knew that Dr. Crawley had a daughter and that his wife had died many years ago. Beyond that, Dr. Crawley's family was a complete mystery to him. He had never seen the girl before and he couldn't imagine why she disliked him so. But she did and there was no question about that now.

Cameron's thoughts were in utter confusion. The whole morning had been like a grotesque nightmare; a mixture of a small amount of sane reality, and an overwhelming dose of delirium. There were too many questions with no perceivable acceptable answers. The only thing he was sure of was that he had no intention of getting mixed up with a senseless mess like this. The question was how to withdraw gracefully?

Not knowing quite how to reply to such an onslaught, Cameron turned to Harry Clayborne. Harry's natural ruddy complexion had turned to a light crimson. Small beads of sweat stood out on his forehead and he squirmed nervously in his chair. For a moment he met Cameron's gaze, then looked away.

Cameron pulled himself together, glanced about the table, and then addressed himself to Dr. Felix, "I suppose, Doctor, the best thing to do is have Mr. Clayborne bring me up to date on the entire matter," he said as he lowered his pointed stare to the top of Harry's head. When Harry didn't look up he went on. "We'll spend the rest of the day going over it and I assure you I'll give it my fullest attention! As we agreed earlier, I'll sleep on it and give you my answer in the morning."

"We can't ask any more than that," Dr. Felix replied sincerely. "What time would you like to meet?"

"Whenever it's convenient for the rest of you," Cameron replied, once more surveying the group.

"I'm sure the same time and place will be convenient for all concerned," Dr. Felix responded, glancing at Miss Crawley for conformation.

Constance acquiesced with a slight smile and a nod of her head.

For all his apparent indifference Roger Tibbs was aware of his surroundings. Her nod, to him, was a signal; and he lost no time getting to his feet and donning his coat. "Are we finally through?" he ask, his voice deep and rich.

"For the moment," Constance replied as she and Miss Rutledge rose.

"Thank the Lord for that!" Roger exclaimed. "I thought you might go on for the rest of the day."

"That's enough, Roger," Constance rebuffed, but the words were soft and indulging. Once more she nodded to Dr. Felix and Mr. Clyde and then started toward the door.

They had barely left the conference room when the chiding words floated back. "Connie, how could you be so calculatingly rude to a person you had just met? Lord above, dear, he's not some ignorant lackey, you know? How can you expect him to cooperate if you treat him like that? If it were me, I'd never want to see you again!" The voice was that of Penelope Rutledge and her tone was pleading.

"I don't care to talk about it right now," Constance answered, "and I mean it, Penny, so just hush!"

"I'd be willing to forget the whole damned thing," Roger said with a slight chuckle.

"What I said to Penny applies to you too," Constance added.

The pleasant sound of Roger's voice could be heard, but trailed off as the street door opened.

*   *   *   *   *

"How the hell could you ever get me mixed up in a mess like this, Harry?" Cameron exploded when the cab was a full two blocks away from the foundation.

Harry sat slumped in the far corner of the seat, staring at a rain drenched window he could not see out of. His coloring had returned to normal, but his attitude remained downcast. He didn't reply immediately and when he did, he continued staring at the rain soaked pane. "I didn't think it would be a mess when it first began," he answered blandly. "I honestly thought I would be doing you a big favor. If you recall, this started a year ago. I thought you'd be back from Mexico in a few months and deal with it yourself. There would be plenty of time to check it out and do as you liked. When you didn't return, Dr. Felix kept coming back to me to help him with some of the preliminary work. Things just kind of built up by themselves over the months. But, I didn't commit you!" Harry said with emphasis as he turned to face Cameron for the first time.

"Well, thank God for that!" Cameron snorted in exasperation. "That slip of a girl, Lord, what a prig she is! The very least you could have done was warn me about her!"

"I didn't know about her," Harry replied flatly. "I mean, I knew about her, but we never met until today. I do know that she's no girl. Maybe she is a prig, as you say, but she's twenty-four years old, and that makes her a woman."

"Why in hell is she so down on me?" Cameron asked, cooling off a few degrees. "I've never seen her before either and I'm certain I never did anything to harm her or her father."

"I can't imagine either," Harry replied. "She was as much a surprise to me as she was to you." His expression initially serious, then a slight smile peeked through.

"What the hell are you grinning about?" Cameron barked. "I don't see anything remotely funny about that little bean pole."

"I was laughing at myself," Harry admitted. "Like I said, I hadn't seen her before and imagined she would be very different, or at least I hoped so. I thought, knowing her age, that she might be pretty, and even influence your decision about this trip. That just shows what a fool I am doesn't it? About all I can do is laugh at it now."

"No, Harry, you're not a fool. An idiot at times, but never a fool," Cameron offered, his attitude softening even more. "This whole situation wasn't sour for you right from the start, so you need to know how I feel about it at the moment."

When Harry didn't answer, Cameron went on, "As a rule, I never drink before the sun goes down, but today I don't think the rule applies. Let's go to Margo's. I could use a glass or two of good brandy!"

"Margo's will not be open for hours yet. Her business is strictly a nocturnal operation," Harry quipped with rising spirits. "The only place you are liable to find any quality brandy at this hour is in the bottom drawer of my desk at the office."

"That's better yet," Cameron responded. "You can give me a complete rundown on everything relative to this proposed fiasco. I've got to give them an answer in the morning. Even though I know the answer is no, I want to know what I'm talking about."

"I guess it might as well be now as later," Harry replied with some reluctance.

*   *   *   *   *

CLAYBORNE & SON IMPORT-EXPORT covered two full city blocks, fronting the Bay with its private pier and dock facilities. The general office was on the street facing landward and Harry's private sanctum was on the second floor. The entire decorum was one of permanence, with paneled walls, heavy furniture and deep rugs that muffled their footsteps as they entered.

"I just don't see how you manage a business of this size and not spend any more time than you do here," Cameron marveled as he sank into a deep cushioned easy chair. "You must have a hundred people working for you, Harry."

"If you mean altogether, it's closer to two hundred," Harry corrected matter-of-factly. "Most of them are full time, others on a commission basis. I have people working for me in the Orient that I've never seen. Some of them worked for my father and a few worked for my grandfather. The secret of running any business is to hire the best men in that field and then keep a careful eye on them, but don't be obvious about it. All of the responsible parties of this operation have been with me for years and I can safely say it could run without me for some time if the need should ever rise."

"That's a unique situation," Cameron observed as Harry filled two glasses. "Now, I'll try not to interrupt. Fill me in on everything you've done so far."

"Well, as you know," Harry ventured, "our entire business is concentrated in the Orient and Near East. In most of the larger cities we have one or more permanent agents. Most of them are engaged with other firms of various origins, but their main function is to serve us. The majority of these agents was contracted before my time and as a result has been in the trade business for a great number of years. They have contacts with places you couldn't even imagine."

Harry leaned back, savored a sip of brandy, continuing, "Our representative in Shanghai is the House of Te Chien, an ancient, and I must add, honorable firm. One of our agents there is a moderately young gentleman by the name of Jo Lung. At least that's the way he signs all correspondence. He reads and writes the English language flawlessly. Marvelous isn't it? Well, to get on with it Mr. Lung informs me that there are weekly river packets plying the Yangtze from Shanghai to Ipin, which is nearly three quarters of the journey across China. From Ipin to Chengtu overland is scarcely over one hundred miles and Mr. Lung says we should have little difficulty obtaining transportation. From there to Chamdo it is a simple matter of following the trade route. We could probably join a caravan and share their protection. Also Mr. Lung points out that if the water is high we might be able to continue by smaller boats up other rivers, which I have momentarily forgotten the names of. We would arrive much closer to Chamdo or even all the way if we are extremely lucky. The latter, of course, is pure chance and he could not speculate on it."

Harry stopped for a breather and a sip, then proceeding, "In Chamdo there is a very powerful merchant. Mr. Lung reveres him almost as highly as a king of some sort. Anyway, he reports the merchant rules the trade with an iron hand. His caravans extend north, west and south for hundreds and in some cases, thousands of miles. He has access to all of Tibet, including the Forbidden City, and the ear of both Lamas. This merchant instructed Jo Lung that he would have little difficulty arranging our journey into Tibet, if certain conditions were met. He did not elaborate on these conditions, saying only that they would not be impossible. In addition, a certain amount of trade goods from our own country should accompany us." Harry stopped abruptly, breathing hard and in need of refreshment.

Cameron sat fully relaxed, nursing his glass. At times he shot an inquiring look or raised his eyebrow, but never spoke. When Harry finished he sat silently reviewing and sorting all he had been told.

"I almost forgot," Harry added as an afterthought. "The merchant also said that if we were to make the trip this year we should be on our way right about now; the summer is very brief in the land of the Lamaists. Well, what do you think?" Harry asked now aglow with enthusiasm.

"Just like I thought an hour ago," Cameron replied without heat. "The more I hear, the more impossible the whole affair becomes. Just how do you propose to be on our way right now?"

Harry squirmed visibly, "That's the rub chum. The only ship headed that way in the next two weeks is a tramp steamer, Greek registry. She was due in port three days ago, but hasn't made it yet."

"Well, that fits," Cameron laughed cynically. "What sort of trade goods was specified?"

"Things that are typically American," Harry replied. "First class bourbon whiskey, high proof dark rum, new weapons of the latest design with proper ammunition, and one other item that doesn't make any sense to me. This merchant would personally like rattles from several of our desert vipers plus one large size stuffed rattle snake. I could scarcely believe my eyes on that one!"

With Harry's final statement Cameron broke into real laughter, both to Harry's dismay and the climax of their situation. When his humorous spasms subsided he said, "With your nose for spirits I don't think you'll have much trouble with the first part of that order, but I'd be a little touchy about the rest of it. For shipping arms illegally you can go to jail, and those snakes could make you wish you'd stayed there. Seriously now, Harry," Cameron asked with new light in his eyes, "you haven't gotten involved in any of this have you? I mean financially?"

For a moment Harry was tempted to lie, but he thought better of it. "I'm afraid I've done exactly that! I came across some good buys in the past few months. I bought a few cases of rum and bourbon, and some guns." His head drooped ever so slightly with the mention of the guns.

Instantly Cameron knew there was more to it than a few guns. "Just how many guns did you purchase, Harry?" he asked keenly.

"Twenty-two," was Harry's nearly soundless reply.

"What kind of guns are they, Harry?" Cameron prodded.

"Oh, hells blazes, Cam, I'll show you," Harry conceded. He rose and went to a large closet behind his desk. After a few seconds of fumbling in his pockets he produced a key and unlocked the door. Without looking he reached inside and retrieved a rifle; the blued barrel and highly polished stock reflected the light from the window. He handed it to Cameron without a word.

Cameron possessed a great deal of knowledge in weapons because of the nature of his life and work, but he had never seen a rifle quite like this one. It was obviously a military piece from the design of the stock, the bayonet mount and sling. The barrel was long, a magazine fed repeater with a positive smooth bolt action, a receiver sight with windage and elevation adjustment, but the amazing features were its compactness and light weight. "Where did you get these?" Cameron snapped after reading the print at the barrel base.

"I bought them from a dealer of sorts," Harry responded with apparent agitation.

"I'm sure he was a dealer of sorts," Cameron exhaled. "And, how much ammunition did this dealer of questionable merchandise sell you at his undoubtedly bargain prices?"

"A thousand rounds for each rifle," Harry replied with difficulty. He hurriedly filled both glasses and downed his own in one gulp.

"My God, Harry," Cameron asked incredulously, "What are you planning to do, start your own civil war?"

"Hell no, I'm bloody well not!" Harry spouted indignantly. "I was merely trying to look ahead and I got these at bargain prices."

"You bet!" Cameron shouted, "A bargain that could land you in a federal prison for as many years as you've got guns. Don't you realize that all these are property of the United States Army? That no matter who has them they're still property of the Army? It's stamped right on them if you'd care to look. Hell, Harry, this is the latest thing they've got and it's still classified secret. I heard about them before I left, but never dreamed I'd see one this close. Where are the rest of them?"

"Right there in the closet," Harry answered visibly shaken. "They're still packed in the sticky stuff they put on them for shipment, I guess. Honestly, Cam, I didn't give it a second thought. To me they were just guns and they looked like good ones. You know, I'd never fired one in my entire life until I bought these."

"The ammunition is not in there too, I hope?" Cameron prayed.

"No," Harry brightened somewhat, "I did know enough about it to store it in one of the concrete sections down next to the water. I also had it put into sealed containers marked machine parts," he finished with a smile.

"No doubt some of your grandfather's logic seeping through," Cameron suggested sardonically.

"He was rather a slippery old codger, wasn't he?" Harry beamed.

"From the little you've told me about him, I'll agree with that to say the least!" Cameron conceded. "Well what's done is done," Cameron proffered philosophically. "After we get this other mess straightened out in the morning we can figure out some safe means of disposing of this stuff. I've just about reached the point where I wish I had stayed in Mexico for another six months," Cameron concluded desperately.

"I guess you know we've missed lunch and it will soon be time for dinner," Harry observed, changing the subject eagerly.

"Yes, I know," Cameron agreed. "We'd best go get cleaned up a bit, however, there are a few things I want you to get straight right now. The first one is that tonight I'm picking up the check. If you reach for it, I'll break both your arms with a great deal of relish. The second one is that tonight I'm going to bed early, alone and in my own house. The third is that when we meet those people in the morning my answer is going to be no! A big fat unmistakable no! So don't you get any more of your persuasive brain storms or I'm liable to forget we are in a civilized country. There is a good market here for fish bait, you know?"

"Alright, Cam," Harry agreed, "I promise to mind my own affairs and not to mention anything relative until tomorrow morning. You do want me to attend the meeting with you?"

"I wouldn't have it any other way, seeing it was your brain child." Cameron mocked.

*   *   *   *   *

The rain entered its second day without letup, slow and methodical. As Cameron and Harry made their way up the stairs from the street to the foundation offices, Harry touched his companion lightly on the shoulder, "By the way, I stopped by the office on my way to pick you up this morning. There was word for me from the Harbor

Master. The Greek freighter, Petros, came into port late yesterday. They had encountered a severe storm off Baja and lost two days steerage, but suffered no damage."

"Well hurrah for the Petros," Cameron replied with no enthusiasm.

Dr. Felix met them just inside the foyer; he had apparently been waiting for them. Mr. Clyde was nowhere in sight. "Right on time, gentlemen," he greeted them in his deep pleasant voice. "I do hope you had an enjoyable evening since we last met. This rain makes the days somewhat dismal. The others haven't arrived as yet. Shall we wait for them in the conference room? Here, let me take your coats. It's considerably warmer in here today and I'm sure you'd soon find yourselves uncomfortable."

"Thank you very much, Doctor," Cameron responded passing his rain coat. "Yes, we did have a pleasant evening, although a short one. The conference room will be fine."

When they were seated at the familiar table, Dr. Felix addressed himself to Harry about some triviality of his business. Cameron didn't bother to listen for his mind was troubled and he was thinking of himself. For the tenth time that morning he wished it were over and done. He liked his life style tranquil, proceeding from one stage to another in easy measured and deliberate strides. More than anything he could think of, he disliked animosity and preferred to avoid argument. There was no way out of this one and he knew it. Nervously, he ran his finger through his hair and for the first time realized that he still hadn't bought himself a hat. He tried to pick up the conversation between his companions, but at that moment he heard the street door slam shut and footsteps crossing the gallery.

Constance entered first, followed by Penelope, with Roger bringing up the rear. They each said good morning as they passed and went to their respective chairs, much like practiced school children. Roger slipped out of his great coat en route; Penelope lowered her hood, and unfastened her cape after being seated. Constance, however, made no such motions. She sat in her chair pert and erect, her hands placed firmly on the table before her. A tight lipped smile came alive on her face as she addressed the assemblage, "Well, I hope everyone is as refreshed this morning as I am. I'm pleased to see you looking so well this morning, Doctor. And you, Mr. Hewitt, did you get a good night's sleep?" her tone was cheerful as she addressed him for the first time.

"Yes, I did, Miss Crawley," Cameron replied easily, "thank you." He noticed that her smile did not fluctuate and her arms were rigid. *She's forcing herself to be nice to me*, he thought. "I guess I have Miss Penny to thank for that."

"How are you this morning, Mr. Clayborne?" Constance asked turning her attention to Harry.

"Tip top, Miss," Harry beamed.

"Did you manage to go over the plans and preparations you've already made with Mr. Hewitt?" she inquired.

"Yes, I did that, completely," Harry responded with a considerable loss of vigor.

"Well then, Mr. Hewitt," Constance switched back, "inasmuch as you're here and have about all of the information available, I surmise that you have arrived at a decision?" The close smile held and her blue green eyes probed his for his thoughts.

"Yes," Cameron said softly without rising, "I have made a decision." He looked fleetingly at each person sitting around him so that they would know that he was speaking to all of them, not anyone in particular. He took three deep breathes and thought to himself once more, *The only way out is to cut my way there with one clean stroke.*

Aloud he said simply, "I believe this to be an anomaly of misplaced ardor from start to finish," There was an audible silence filling the room as though everyone had stopped breathing. Not knowing what else to do he went on, "The idea of Noah landing on this Mt. Kula Kangri you might call a legend; I call it a myth, or more likely a pipe dream. From everything I have heard, no one has ever come up with even a single piece of paper professing this had happened, let alone any direct evidence that it had. The whole idea runs contrary to every historical record of thought that we possess. This biblical event took place thousands of years ago, just how many is anybody's guess. At least Mt. Ararat has the backing of the Bible and that record has been around for a long, long while. The plans you have made aren't plans, they're wishful thinking and grasping at straws." Cameron stopped for breath.

"The agent in China says this trip, to be successful, should have been started weeks ago. The ship you planned to take from here is two days late on a short trip up the coast and probably won't be ready to sail for a least a week. The river boat in China is supposed to get to a place called Ipin or farther! Maybe it will, and maybe it won't, depending on how high the water is. Then we're supposed to round up horses and pack animals! Have any of you every tried to buy horses in a foreign country? I'll bet not! It's not like it is here. They're damned scarce and plenty expensive if they can be had at all. If you should be lucky enough to get clear to Chamdo, you're only three quarters of the way there. At this point you'll be placing your very lives and property in the hands of some greedy merchant that might very easily slit your throat for the shoes you wear. Barring all this, it's on into Tibet where few white men have ever entered and returned to tell about it. I'm sorry, but I believe its madness!" Cameron finished nearly shouting. He sank back in his chair and closed his eyes.

While Cameron spoke, Constance sat in stunned silence. As he finished, she loosened the draw string of her hood, then stood up, pushing her chair backward. Cameron heard the scrape, but did not see her through his closed lids. He should have.

When she dropped the hood of her cape, a marvelous transformation occurred. Her hair was not the dingy brown that Cameron was sure it would be and it was not done up in a tight knot at the top of her skull. Instead it was a close cropped mass of large curls clinging loosely to her head. The hair was a burnt golden color that had the unusual ability of attracting light that was not there and illuminating each coil with a brilliant gauzy perimeter. Slowly she removed the cape, folded it neatly and placed it on the back of her chair. All eyes at the table, save Cameron's, followed her every move. She leaned forward against the table, placing her clenched fists on its top. Only a few seconds had elapsed, but it seemed much longer.

"Mr., Hewitt," she said in a loud clear voice, "You've had your say; now damn it, I'll have mine!"

Penny Rutledge winced at the severity of her words but it went unnoticed. Roger arched an eyebrow in her direction then shrugged his shoulders.

Cameron didn't want to open his eyes; this was the sort of thing he so disliked. He wished that she would melt and disappear into the floor. Slowly he raised his lids; then his eyes snapped open as he reared backward in his seat. She was smaller than he had thought her to be beneath the cape. He was also not prepared for the dark green dress she wore with its V-neck and clinging cut. Through her leaning against the table, the material of the dress was stretched taut across her bosom and abdomen. It left little doubt as to the shape of the real Constance Crawley. For the first time in his life Cameron was totally speechless. He couldn't have uttered a single word, but his mind was racing, *This can't possibly be the same woman. My God, she's absolutely the most beautiful creature I've ever seen. If I close my eyes she'll vanish, but I don't want to close my eyes.* He saw the sunlight sparkling in her hair and there was no sun; he saw the green fire dancing in her eyes and the tension of her knuckles thrust against the table top. He saw the fullness of her breasts each time she took a breath, the clear white glow of her throat, and the exquisite tapering of her waist. He saw her lips moving before the words slammed their way into his brain.

"There is no truth to many of the things you have said," He heard, "and you yourself are the reason for no better planning." Her words affected him like a hard slap across the mouth, but he recovered enough to listen attentively.

"There is a great deal of writing on this subject in other parts of the world. They are sacred materials and have not been duplicated so that every skeptic may have a copy. My father examined many of them and declared they were authentic." Her words were crisp and sharp. "He went to every conceivable length to rule out the possibilities you have mentioned. How dare you say you respect and admire him and deny his credibility at the same time? How could you malign the Merchant of Chamdo, when he has been vouched for by one of the largest and oldest companies in China? You speak of the improbability of reaching Ipin by river, when it's being done every day by hundreds. No one said it would be easy to acquire transportation as easily as it is here; but it can be done and we have the money to pay for it."

"As for the ship from here, how were we to make any plans other than a week or two in advance?" she went on, not giving him a chance to interrupt. "The will says that you are the only one to lead, God grant me why, and you were supposed to have returned nearly a year ago. How could we have done anything other than what we did?"

"Now I'll tell you the real reason you decline, Mr. Hewitt," Constance spoke more softly. "From the very start of your career you've been an opportunist! You've never gone out on an expedition that there was any doubt about. You wanted a sure thing each and every time. This is how you gained your fame; you wouldn't gamble on a thing unless the odds were all in your favor. My father saw you as a great organizer, a tireless worker and a true believer in our field. I see you as a man that wants only glory where there's no risk involved. You're not worried that this mission will fail in regard to my father. You're worried that it might put a black mark on that precious record of yours. You don't really care how much money we offer you; because if this didn't add to your personal image, it wouldn't be worth it. I came here this morning prepared to offer you ten thousand dollars so that I might see my father's dream fulfilled, even if you didn't find a single thing to prove him right. The fact that he might not be right didn't bother him at all, but you wouldn't understand that, would you?" Connie sat down in her chair feeling suddenly very weak. She felt sick inside knowing that she was beaten, knowing that what she wanted to do for her father would never be done. After what she had said, there was no room for a change of heart on Cameron's part.

Cameron heard her words, each and every syllable. He felt them too. He felt them stab into his belly and his conscience; for most of them were true and he could not deny it. He had wondered why she disliked him so and now he knew. Without ever meeting him, she had seen through him like he was made of glass. For the first time in many years, he realized he really cared what someone thought of him.

He looked at her forgetting there were others present. He could see the deep hurt in her eyes and the pride that held her head high, even now. In his mind a thought was forming, *I can't let it end like this. I can't have her think this of me; besides, I want to see her again, and I never will this way.*

Cameron squared his shoulders, sucked in his breath and said aloud, "Miss Crawley, most of the things you said about me and the reasons for my declining are embarrassingly true. I'm sorry that things are that way, and I can't change how I have lived and been; but I can and do change my mind on what I will do. If you'll still have me, I'll accept the position you offered me, but at the figure you stated yesterday!" His tone was soft and pleading.

All heads jerked in unison at Cameron's statement and several gasps were heard. Constance could scarcely credit her ears with words she had never expected. A great flood of joy swept through her and then she remembered from whence it came. "Do you honestly mean that, Mr. Hewitt?" she questioned with gravity.

"Yes, I mean it in all sincerity," Cameron replied, "and I won't, for any reason, go back on my word."

For a long while Constance remained in deep thought. Several times she glanced questioningly at Penelope who responded equally. At length Constance replied, "In that case, Mr. Hewitt, I'd like to make an announcement that I have given a lot of thought to. I want you to know that I'm not taking advantage of your pledge and have been thinking along these lines for the past several months. To state it point blank, I've decided Miss Rutledge and I shall accompany you, all the way!"

It was strange that this revelation did not surprise Cameron. He had almost sensed it from the moment she had started speaking. Yesterday he would have objected most violently to such a proposal; since his wife, he had never allowed a woman near his camp, let alone become a member of his crew. In a way he did not entirely comprehend, he had subconsciously hoped that she would join them. The extra and unique responsibility of the two new members would be a trying task, but somehow he would manage. It was at this particular moment that Cameron had a startling, and somewhat humorous inspiration. "Very well, Miss Crawley," Cameron said pleasantly, "I'll accept that if I may be allowed to make one stipulation of my own."

"And, what might that be?" Constance asked guardedly, fearing it would be something she would not like.

"Only this," Cameron revealed with a full and genuine smile, "that since Harry Clayborne is the only expert we have on the Orient, who has direct access to those people important to us there, I suggest that he accompany us to Shanghai, or better yet, to the end of the river voyage at Ipin!"

They didn't have to wait for Harry's answer; he was on his feet instantly. "Now I say, Cam," he blurted indignantly "as you bloody well know I'm a business man and know nothing of this sort of thing, absolutely nothing! After all, I have my own affairs to look after." To Harry, this seemed to be all the explanation needed to excuse himself.

"Harry," Cameron began explaining very patiently, "if you'll recall, you're the one that involved me so deeply in this matter in the first place and without my knowledge or consent. I believe you owe me a little more than, by your leave. And, if my memory doesn't fail me, it was only a few hours ago you were telling me that this fantastic business of yours could run itself for a year if need be. Dear boy," Cameron added with a knowing grin, "there are some things that you're going to need some assistance in disposing of! I'm in charge of this enterprise and my first order is that if you don't go, your equipment items don't accompany us! Is that clear, Harry?"

"Damn it, Cam," Harry snorted, "that's out and out blackmail! I'll, I'll . . . ." he trailed off for lack of words.

"Call it what you like, Harry," Cameron replied gleefully, seeing the small beads of sweat pop out on his friends face. "Take it or leave it, right here and now. You gave me about the same choice, remember?" Cameron's logic was threefold. If Harry went along, he would be gaining some companionship he knew he was going to need. He would also acquire a watchdog for the ladies who would take some of the load from himself. Lastly, Harry and Mr. Jo Lung would be invaluable in dealing with the Chinese authorities and the mysterious Merchant of Chamdo.

"Alright, Cam," Harry acquiesced, "I'll do it, but I want you to know it's under duress and I don't think it very sporting of you."

When Cameron had first began to speak, what now seemed a long time ago, Dr. Felix had leaned back in his chair and folded his hands in his lap as a play spectator might do. The lines of his forehead deepened and his blue eyes were troubled. His anxiety increased when it was Constance's time, but long before she had finished, his countenance changed to one of knowing pleasure. He had seen the depths of Cameron's soul exposed in his eyes, though no one else had. The doctor's face blossomed into a rich smile with

Harry's acceptance. *The Lord works in mysterious ways,* he repeated to himself silently. Aloud he said, "This is just wonderful, wonderful," and he meant it as a prayer.

Roger Tibbs sat immobile throughout the entire episode. He seemed neither depressed nor elated at any turn of events. His entire attitude was passive. In the quiet that followed Harry's ceding, he opened his mouth for the first time. "I don't want to be an outsider at this gathering of the famous and the would-be," Roger said with eloquence, "so if no one has any strenuous objections I'll come along too!"

Cameron started to refuse. He could see no earthly advantage in the presence of Roger; he might even cause trouble when the novelty of it wore off. His second thoughts told him, however, that he should leave this up to Constance. Roger was her friend, or whatever he was to her and it was her money that would be spent on him. "I don't see any reason why not," Cameron stated with a twinge of doubt.

"Why, Roger," Constance said turning to him, "I'm flabbergasted. You've never shown any interest in this in your entire life. Why on earth do you want to go now?"

"That's the crux of it," Roger answered with some gravity. "I just realized that I might be missing something. Do you mind, Connie?"

"Not at all," Connie answered, "I'm pleasantly surprised that you've changed your mind."

"This is marvelous," Dr. Felix interposed, "we're in complete agreement. Well, Mr. Hewitt, it's entirely up to you now. We'll be at your disposal day or night. I suppose you have things you'd like to do right away?"

"A great number of them, Doctor," Cameron concurred. "So Harry and I had best be on our way. I'll send a list to you of the items I think each of us should take. The important thing is that we should travel as lightly as possible and still have some degree of security and comfort. Harry, would you get Miss Crawley's and her companion's address? What about Mr. Clyde, Doctor, will he be here later in the day?"

"Yes, he will be," Doctor Felix answered. "He's out doing some errands for the two of us, Mr. Hewitt. You see, I rather fancied that your answer might be in the affirmative after some negotiation." His warm smile and gentle voice made Cameron wonder just how well he had hid his feelings.

"Let's up and at it, Harry," Cameron ordered. "We've a lot to do and a short time to do it in."

As they were leaving the conference room he turned once more to Constance, "I'm glad it worked out this way," he said.

"I am too," she admitted, but she did not smile.

CHAPTER 7

━━━━◆·•◆•·◆━━━━

The misty rain of San Francisco was well into its sixth day without let up and it was beginning to get on Cameron's nerves. "Isn't this weather ever going to ease up?" he ask of Harry seated at his office desk.

"You'll get used to it," Harry replied without looking up from his supply checklist.

"I didn't ask if you thought I'd get used to it!" Cameron returned sarcastically. "I wanted to know if it were ever going to quit!"

"Sure it will," Harry raised his head, "when it's damned good and ready, just like always at this time of year. You've lived here long enough to know that."

"I've been gone so long I forgot," Cameron said simply. "How's your supply inventory working up?"

"It's finished as of this minute and the bulk of it already aboard the Petros," Harry answered with a sigh of relief. "What sort of chap is the Captain?"

"Stavros Demetrius is his name," Cameron replied searching his mind for a proper description. "He's in his late fifties or so, stout build with no flab, speaks English with a strong accent, but handles a conversation well enough. He's affable, intelligent, and has the usual amount of salt in his craw. From what I saw, he runs a tight ship."

"And the Petros?" Harry inquired with one brow raised.

"About what you'd expect of a tramp," Cameron replied with obvious disgust. "Of course, you know I'm biased when it comes to steamers. Our quarters are unbelievably small, directly over the engine room and with only one small porthole; the air is bound to be foul. In spite of the captain's obvious attention, the whole ship smells of smoke constantly and there is soot in every cranny and crack aboard. The captain, by the way, is the only one of the ship's compliment that speaks our language."

"Sounds as though it's going to be a pleasant voyage," Harry remarked without humor.

"The only thing pleasant I'm able to think of at the moment," Cameron jeered, "is that it will terminate sometime in the future and that might be anyone's guess. However, there's not another ship going our way for at least another two weeks, so we have no choice in the matter."

"And the final question," Harry inquired while producing two glasses and the brandy from his desk, "when do we sail?"

"Day after tomorrow at first light," Cameron returned, as he sipped his drink with relish. "How did you manage to get those guns and ammunition aboard?" Cameron quizzed.

"I'd really like to tell you, Cam," Harry snickered, "but it's one of my grandfather's secrets and I don't think he would approve. The only thing I'll tell you is that you don't have to worry about them. They won't be discovered!" he finished adamantly.

"If you say so," Cameron replied with little interest, "I'll leave that up to you and your sneaky ancestor."

"He wasn't sneaky!" Harry countered. "Sly, devious and clever, yes, but never sneaky."

"I'm sorry," Cameron apologized good-naturedly. "I guess I formed a wrong impression of the old scamp."

"He wasn't one of those either," Harry demanded, "He was a Captain in the Third Indian Rifles in the service of his Queen. If you'd like I'll tell you all about him," Harry added in defense.

"Not right now, Harry," Cameron begged. "It's been a long day and I'm tired. I'm sorry I slandered your lineage, so let's discuss him another time. How long will it take you to round up the balance of our needs and get them stowed?" Cameron asked closing his eyes.

"My people can get most of it tonight and the rest in the morning," Harry said simply. "By early tomorrow afternoon we'll be able to board, if everyone else is set."

"They assured me they were ready to go yesterday," Cameron stated. "I'd just as soon postpone the boarding until the last minute, if you don't mind. We're going to be damned sick of that floating furnace long before we're ever able to get off her," Cameron said with conviction.

"I don't doubt that," Harry agreed. "What's the quartering arrangement?"

"You and I will share a compartment we'll both have trouble getting into; Dr. Felix, Mr. Clyde and Roger will have a cabin slightly larger, and the two ladies, by comparison, will have a suite with scant leg room. We'll all take our meals with the captain and I'm sure he suggested this in the way of a concession. Speaking of eating, aren't you hungry?" Cameron asked hopefully.

"Come to think of it, I am," Harry replied. "I'll give these lists to my manager on our way out. He'll see that the details are taken care of. Do you want him to take care of moving your things on board tomorrow?"

"Why, yes, Harry, I'd appreciate that," Cameron accepted. "That will leave me free to catch up on any loose ends I may have forgotten. Let's be on our way."

The two men rose and passed into the outer office.

*   *   *   *   *

The skies were clear and the western horizon visible on the morning the Petros steamed through the Golden Gate and headed for the open sea. Harry was amazed at how rapidly the coastline sank below the curvature of the waters as he and Cameron stood watching from the fantail of the ship. He had never been at sea though his livelihood depended on it. They watched for a full two hours as the sun grew warm, until finally not a single craft was visible in the vast expanse of blue sky and water.

"I don't know what your plans are," Cameron ventured, "but I'm going to turn in for some sleep. In spite of what you put me through recently, I'm not used to staying up all night."

"I find this fascinating," Harry replied in childish eagerness. "It's so awesome and makes me feel so insignificant in the scheme of it all. I don't believe I've ever felt so alone before in my life. Did it affect you the same way the first time?" he asked gravely.

"It does everyone to some degree or another," Cameron replied with a yawn. "Stay up here and enjoy it as much as you like. I'm going below and catch a few winks. If you'd like another new experience I suggest that you go forward, up to the prow of the ship." Without further words he turned and headed for the companion way and his much needed bunk.

For a short while Harry remained watching the receding skyline, the scattered white puffs of low hanging clouds and two screeching gulls that seemed destined to follow the Petros on its long journey. Eventually, Cameron's final remarks got the better of him and he made his way forward.

Throughout his life Harry imagined that the deck of a seagoing ship would be alive with activity. He was astounded that he saw no one topside other than himself. Glancing upward as he passed the superstructure mid-ship, he saw two men in uniform watching him from the bridge. He was slightly startled by their attention; in his momentary confusion, he waved to them, but they did not respond. Immediately, they became preoccupied with their charts or whatever they had on the slanted desk before them. Sheepishly, Harry lowered his gaze and continued ahead.

As he neared the prow, he felt the slight quickening of a soft warm breeze upon his cheek. When he could go no further, he looked downward along the knife-like edge of steel. A silvery arch of water splayed outward in a receding line as it traveled back along the plates. With each bound of the ship, the design of it increased or diminished, forming a multitude of outlines in his imagination. A feeling of enchantment came over him like he had never experienced before and he realized a finite fraction of the lure of the sea that had beckoned to men from the beginning of time. He looked outward across the slow rolling waters ahead and tried to visualize the vast distance they must traverse, the depth of the swells beneath and what lay below them. His brain reeled with the immensity of it and in desperation; he returned his thoughts to the shimmering outlines of the spray below.

Harry hadn't heard, but rather felt the presence behind him before he turned. Captain Demetrius stood near his shoulder, smiling lightly. "Good Morning," he boomed from habit. "You are Mr. Clayborne?" he asked, squinting his eyes with emphasis.

"Why, yes," Harry beamed, "I'm Harry Clayborne, my pleasure indeed. Captain Demetrius?" he ventured.

"That is true, I am Stavros Demetrius," he replied in slow measured words. "Strange," he continued, "my ship has your name on its manifest many times, but we have never met."

"You mean you have hauled goods for me?" Harry inquired with interest.

"Both for you and for your father," he answered, amusement sparkling in his dark brown eyes. "I have been plying these waters many years."

Harry observed him with growing curiosity; the near six feet of him, his thick neck, proportions of arms and legs, and the close cut gray hair at his temples, the squareness of his jaw and long line of his nose. "Yes, it's odd that we've never met, but then I don't suppose that my consignments to your ship were very large in contrast to your cargo," Harry advanced.

"True again," agreed the Captain, "but then many ships would not sail if their holds were to be filled by only one shipper. I see the motion of the seas doesn't seem to bother you as they do some," he changed the subject. "Have you spent much time sailing?"

"None," Harry admitted grudgingly, "this is my first time out, I'm sorry to say. I never imagined it would lift my spirits so. How far is it to our first port of call?" he inquired using what little he knew of seaman's jargon.

"Near twenty-four hundred miles to Honolulu in the Sandwich Islands," Demetrius responded.

"You mean the Hawaiian Islands, I presume," Harry corrected impulsively.

"They have always been the Sandwich Islands to us," the Captain answered positively.

Harry stood the reprove gracefully by asking without hesitation, "How long do you suppose it will be before we make port?"

"The soonest would be two weeks with perfect conditions; the longest would be three, short of severe adversity. I do not crowd my ship under any conditions; and for this reason you and others have always received your goods, and will continue to."

"And from the islands," Harry omitted naming them, "how long to Shanghai?"

"A direct run will take three to four weeks under favorable conditions," the Captain replied watching Harry keenly.

"That's quite a long while, isn't it?" Harry asked stupidly.

"You wouldn't think so if you knew the early histories of the sailing ships. This same cruise could take as long as six months."

"I'm certainly happy that we shan't be that long!" Harry exclaimed.

"So am I," laughed the Captain. "Will you take the noon meal, Mr. Clayborne?" he asked.

"I don't believe so," Harry smiled, "I was up all night having a final fling and I believe my sleep is catching up with me. I'll take a nap and join you for dinner this evening."

"I shall look forward to it," Demetrius replied in his slow manner. He touched his cap momentarily, then strode back in the direction from whence he came, rolling easily with the deck.

Harry returned his attention once more to the scene before him, then said aloud, "Seems I'll have plenty of time to admire the view later on, think I'll join Cam for a few winks."

As he entered their quarters, he could feel the dull thrum-thrum of the engines directly below. Cameron lay soundly asleep on the lower of the two hard bunks fastened to one wall. Harry removed his shoes and then climbed cautiously to the upper berth, pushing himself the final way by placing his foot against the opposite wall. He rolled onto his back and stared at the ceiling only inches from his nose. *It is rather compact, isn't it,* he thought as he closed his eyes and dropped instantly to sleep.

In the other men's cabin, Dr. Felix and Mr. Clyde were fully occupied seeing to the needs of Roger Tibbs, who lay prone on one of the two lower bunks. His face was ashen and his entire body oozed small beads of sweat. Periodically Dr. Felix changed the damp cloths on his forehead, while Mr. Clyde tried to anticipate the most beneficial position of the bucket on the floor. The small confine reeked of Roger's first explosive failure to make the rail outside. Every few moments Roger emitted a low, nearly soundless moan, hugging his writhing stomach.

"Norman," Doctor Felix speculated, "I believe if this room were sweetened up a trifle he wouldn't be quite so nauseated. Do you suppose you could get another bucket of salt water and mop the floor once more?" His eyes were mildly imploring.

"Certainly, doctor, certainly," Mr. Clyde replied instantly. "Do you think he's finished vomiting for the moment?" he asked.

"I doubt if there's anything left down there to come up," Dr. Felix answered hopefully. "I'll keep one eye on the bucket all the same," he added with a smile. Norman nodded and left the room.

"You'll be alright, Roger," Dr. Felix said soothingly. "Just concentrate on some pleasant experience you've had in the past. It happens to a lot of people, you know? Doesn't mean a thing and it's nothing to be ashamed of. Norman and I will both stay with you until you're on your feet again."

Roger was so deathly ill he could neither answer nor open his eyes. In grateful response he rolled his head from side to side and instantly began retching, trying desperately to locate the bucket.

The ladies cabin claimed the luxury of steel cots, bolted to the deck, complete with springs and mattress.

Constance and Penelope showed little interest in their departure from the mainland. They proceeded directly to their quarters after coming aboard and after arranging and storing their belongings went to sleep.

It was early afternoon when Penny awoke to the scratching of a pen. She raised her head from the pillow to see Constance busily engaged in writing; a large hardbound notebook rested on her knees. "What on earth are you doing, Connie?" she ask in surprise.

"I'm beginning a diary of this expedition," Connie replied, looking up, "and you're going to help me keep it. I want everything we do entered in here, including the kind of soup we have for dinner. I mean everything, Penny! Each thing we do from the time we wake up to the time we go to sleep and this includes the rest of our party."

"How are we to know what they do during all that time?" Penny asked a mischievous look in her eye. She kicked both feet up over her back displaying long shapely calves and tiny bare feet, contrasting sharply to the white linen shift she wore.

"Don't be coy with me!" Connie snapped in mock severity. "You know what I mean. Just the things you know about will do nicely and don't let that imagination of yours run loose." Connie returned to her writing.

For a long moment Penny lay contemplating her bare arms from her shoulders down to her fingers, a pensive look gradually formed on her face. "Why do you dislike Mr. Hewitt so, Connie?" she ask thoughtfully.

Constance jumped as though she had stuck herself with the pen. "I don't dislike the man so," she stated after collecting herself visibly. "It's just that I don't care for him."

"That's a contradictory statement if I ever heard one." Penny retorted with a toss of her head. "It's plain to everyone that you work at giving him the cold shoulder and I just don't understand it. He seems awfully nice to me and he certainly has made a name for himself."

"That's part of the reason I don't like him," Constance reasoned, "the manner in which he made his name. He doesn't even have a doctorate in archeology. He's a geologist that just happened to fall into this field through a lucky set of circumstances and he's been lucky ever since, plus he is calculating and scheming. I think he has a lot of undue notoriety that should have gone elsewhere."

"What else don't you like about him?" Penny asked softly.

"I don't like his easy going cocksure attitude about everything that comes up," Constance replied with some irritation. "I don't like the way he evaluates people with his naked stare; and I sincerely distrust the manner in which he changed his mind about coming on this mission!"

"He told you why!" Penny objected.

"Did you believe that?" Constance sneered. "He's got an ulterior motive of some kind and since it wasn't money, I'm beginning to believe it might be some kind of a side trip of his own that he had forgotten about and suddenly remembered."

"I don't think so," Penny argued. "I think he changed his mind because you found his 'Achilles heel' and he had almost forgotten he had one."

"Don't be silly, Penny." Constance replied emphatically, "he hasn't got a conscience, or he wouldn't have accepted honors that rightfully belonged to someone else."

"Who do you think those honors belonged to, your father?" Penny asked before realizing the importance of the question.

"A lot of them, I do," Constance agreed, the green fires kindling in her eyes, "and the rest probably to someone else."

"I don't think you're being fair, Connie," Penelope stated quietly. "You're prejudiced because of a lot of the setbacks your father had suffered. How can you judge the man on his other accomplishments that have no bearing on your father? Do you honestly know that much about him?" Penelope's eyes were wide and her tone serious.

Constance nearly flared in her response, catching herself. "I'm sorry, Penny, I guess I'm not being fair. I let my temper get the better of my judgment again. I just can't help it, the man's character and personality rubbed me the wrong way the first time I ever heard of him and now that we're in direct contact it's even worse. Why is it that you never disapprove of anyone I like, and yet seem to like the few people that I don't?"

"I would say it's because you have such flawless taste," Penelope answered with a hint of her smile returning, then added, "most of the time."

Constance giggled openly at the last remark, suggesting, "Let's get dressed and take a couple of turns about the ship. It will soon be dark and time for dinner."

"That sounds like a splendid idea!" Penelope exclaimed hopping from the bed.

The sun was less than an hour from setting when they finished their third round of the ship and stopped at the rail on the starboard side forward. The atmosphere slowly changed from a golden yellow to a bright orange, tinting each wave crest with its delicate hue.

"Isn't it beautiful, Connie?" Penny asked in wide-eyed admission.

"It is breathtaking," Constance remarked trying to take in the entire dimension of it. "Oh, look, Penny," she said excitedly, "there's a school of porpoise out there!"

Penny didn't answer, instead focused her entire attention upon the exposed fins, then the graceful arches of their bodies as they cleared the water in gigantic leaps.

From directly behind them came a strange male voice, "They are dolphins."

Both women whirled in unison to face the captain of the ship. "I did not want to correct you, but they are not porpoise. I am Stavros Demetrius, your Captain, at your service," he said with a slight bow.

Each of the young women introduced themselves and then all three returned their attention to the acrobatics being presented.

"How do you tell the difference?" Penelope asked without turning her head.

"The dolphin is much larger," the Captain replied, "and he has a beak like snout. Watch and you will see! There, did you see his nose? A porpoise is less than half the size of those fellows."

"They are big, aren't they?" Constance queried.

"About ten or eleven feet long," the captain agreed. "They're a good sign too!"

"How do you mean?" Penelope asked intently.

"According to legend, their presence is supposed to indicate a safe voyage and fair weather ahead."

"Do you believe it?" Penelope asked, squinting her eyes as she turned to face him.

"Sometimes I do," the captain admitted with a smile as he warmed to the delightful company he had not expected. "It's time for dinner," he said glancing at the watch he produced from his trousers. At that precise moment a series of bells sounded from above. "May I escort you ladies to our table?"

"It would be our pleasure," Constance replied relishing his rich accent and his slow deliberate choice of each word.

He extended an arm to each of them, guiding them to his quarters and the evening meal.

*   *   *   *   *

It was well past midnight and Cameron hadn't been able to go to sleep. The compartment became stuffier with each passing hour and the continuous noise of the engines seemed to increase as well. He lay there in the darkness, his eyes open, staring up at the blackened bottom of Harry's bunk. He thought back to supper in the captain's cabin and vaguely remembered what he had eaten. He did remember that Constance sat on the captain's right and was in a gay mood. Penelope sat on his left and the three of them had monopolized most of the conversation. Everyone was polite, and even though no one ignored himself or Harry, the captain was definitely engrossed with his female passengers. *Little wonder*, Cameron thought, *the poor guy hasn't had anybody like those two on this tub since it was commissioned.* Harry had said little, which was unusual for him, and was satisfied mostly to listen and enjoy his food. Dr. Felix and Norman Clyde had eaten in shifts so that one of them could be with Roger. The doctor had been more than a little concerned for Roger's condition and was relieved slightly when the captain recommended a potion he thought would bring him around in a day or two. His thoughts rambled on; he flinched involuntarily at the sound of Harry's voice.

"Why don't we take a couple of blankets and find us a nice breezy spot out on deck?" Harry pleaded softly. "Neither of us is going to get any rest in here."

"I thought you were asleep," Cameron whispered.

"Hell's bells, no, I'm not asleep," Harry swore. "Your breathing in here sounds like a freight train. I've been laying here counting each breath you take and trying to figure what you're thinking."

"I wouldn't advise you to get involved in anything that deep," Cameron laughed aloud. "Let's go, it can't be any worse out there than in here."

The two of them wrapped their blankets about themselves, making their way out onto the deck.

"There's a good spot over there by that hatch," Cameron exclaimed nodding his head. "We'll be out of the way here in the event someone should come barging through."

Harry grunted his approval.

They settled down to the cool hardness of the deck. The air was clean and balmy and the noise from the engine room barely audible. It was only a matter of minutes before the pair of them was soundly asleep.

With the sun's first light Cameron awoke, nudged Harry in the ribs and made a suggestion. "I think it might be a good idea if we gather up our things and get back in our cabin. The captain might object to our sleeping out here, and I don't want to take a chance on losing a good thing."

"I'll go along with that," Harry chimed as he rose to his feet. He looked at the railing only a scant few feet from where he had been lying. There was a yawning gap below the bottom rail and the deck. "I believe it might be a good idea if we appropriated a cargo net or something to put over that before one of us makes a detour in the night," he added pointing a not too steady finger."

"I see what you mean," Cameron said uneasily, "that could be embarrassing."

"To say the least, dear boy," Harry grinned.

Inside the cabin they replaced the blankets and made up their bunks.

"What do you have in mind to occupy our time between meals?" Harry asked lightly.

"Don't worry about it!" Cameron said with emphasis, "you're going to help me fill out all those reports I'm supposed to have been working on. I'll have to get them mailed at our first stop or I'm going to be in some serious trouble back home."

"I don't see how two of us can work on it at the same time," Harry replied hopefully.

"I'll tell you how," Cameron replied impishly. "I want a copy of the whole thing for myself. As I finish each sheet I'll be submitting, you'll make a duplicate for my use. That will keep us both busy for quite some time."

"I should have known better than to ask a question like that," Harry mumbled.

"You'll be wishing you had something else to do long before we ever reach Shanghai," Cameron stated with emotion. "Let's go see what the morning meal is like."

*   *   *   *   *

It was late on the morning of the fifth day when Roger Tibbs made his first appearance on deck supported on each side by Dr. Felix and Norman Clyde, His steps were slow and uncertain, his face gaunt with sunken eyes underlined by dark splotches.

Each person in the party, including the captain, had visited him on the first days of his illness, but he made it all too plain that he did not want to see anyone until he recovered. He even wished there was some way he could do without the services of his two billet companions. Never in his life had he been so sick or so humiliated; the irony of it was his own physique that he was so proud of, had let him down.

A chair had been provided so that he might sit in the sun. After he was seated, a blanket was placed about his waist and legs. Constance hadn't seen him brought out, as she was busily and noisily engaged in a game of volley ball with Penelope.

Harry had miraculously produced two long pieces of battered netting; one he had used for his own protection and the other he had erected for the ladies entertainment and exercise. Just where he had acquired them and the soft lumpy ball he would not say.

Penelope saw them first and finally got the message to Constance, who then hurried up to Roger's side, with Penny close behind.

"I'm so glad you're feeling better, Roger!" Constance said taking his limp hand. "We've all been terribly worried about you."

"Well, you can stop worrying about me," he said with open irritation, "I'm going to be alright now!"

"I'm sure you are, Roger," Constance answered apologetically. "Is there anything we can do for you, something I could get you?" "You can stop patronizing me!" Roger snapped with all the force he could muster," and don't mention food of any kind. Just go back to your game, and leave me alone," he finished out of breath. "Sure, Roger," Constance answered with the hurt showing. "Whatever you say," she finished lamely, letting go of his hand. Penny's round face was beaming as she ran up to stand beside him, but it faded as he looked at her and didn't even nod. Norman whirled and walked to the rail obviously shaken; but Dr. Felix stood his ground, a light flush creeping over his striking features. He placed his hand gently on Roger's shoulder, but never said a word. Cameron witnessed the entire episode from his perch a-top the hatch as he and Harry worked on the reports. He watched the two women as they returned to their game, listless at first then picking up tempo as their spirits revived. He shook his head, returning his scrutiny to the neat ciphering on the page before him.

It was several minutes before he realized that the faint rhythmic sound of Harry's scratching was missing. He looked up at his friend expectantly.

Harry's gaze was fastened on the bounding forms of the two women at the net. At least this was Cameron's first impression. He soon discovered that it was only on one of the women. Harry watched each move that Penny made, his eyes wide, and with a wistful smile on his face.

"What have we got building up here?" Cameron asked himself, and didn't know if he were pleased or disturbed.

*   *   *   *   *

The high dark outline of Hawaii was on the starboard side aft when they awoke early on the morning of the fifteenth day out. Cameron and Harry stood at the rail watching.

"We'll run up on Oahu tomorrow," the captain said as came up behind them, eyeing the blankets they had forgotten.

"That's great!" Cameron said sheepishly, as he stood there in his underwear and followed the captain's glance.

"We'll meet at breakfast?" the captain asked, as he turned and left without waiting for an answer.

Harry looked to Cameron, feebly exposing his teeth, "I guess we'd best get those put away," he said pointing his finger to their sleeping gear.

The following day, within an hour after lunch, the Paulos reduced her speed and began luffing her way into the city harbor at Honolulu. The prominent landmark of Diamond Head was to starboard, with Punch Bowl Crater near dead ahead.

Roger stood erect at the rail, his glance taking in the extreme length and less than a mile-width of the city, with its rolling hills rising to the rear, and the Koolau Range forming a picturesque background. The sun-drenched beauty made no impression on him, and he made no sound amid the "oohs" and "ahs" erupting from the rest of the party flanking him on either side.

Roger's color had returned and his facial features were more pronounced through his weight loss. His total lack of enthusiasm would have indicated to a stranger that he had been here dozens of times in the past; but this was his first visit. He was back to normal, and able to fend for himself.

"Are you sure you won't change your mind, Roger, and join Penny and me for a couple of days in town?" Constance repeated for the second time since lunch. "There's so much to see and do. It will probably do you good to get on dry land for a while."

"I'm positive I'll be fine right here, Connie," Roger stated tersely. "You go ahead and see the sights. I don't feel that I'm up to it. I believe two days of rest here with peace and quiet will do me more good than chasing you two around like a bird-dog." He gave her the benefit of his most convincing smile, while thinking to himself that he didn't dare leave the ship for fear that his sickness would start all over again when he came back aboard and they put out to sea. He reasoned that if he stayed with the Paulos and never left until they reached Shanghai, he would have no more embarrassment. That he knew, he couldn't stand!

"We feel guilty running off to have a good time while you're left here alone," Constance said taking both of his hands.

Penny nodded her head in agreement and shot him an imploring look.

Roger smiled at her briefly, "What are your plans?" he asked, purposefully altering the course of the conversation.

"We're going to find a nice hotel with plenty of hot water and soft dreamy beds," Penny began excitedly. "Then we're going to take in all the sights that we can in the two days we have. We're also going to take in all the marvelous shops they have and see the Kings Palace."

"But," Connie cut in sternly, "we're not going to buy anything that we don't absolutely need right now."

Penny knew the restriction was for her benefit. A tiny pout formed at the corners of her mouth. "Maybe just a ring or small pin?" she asked hopefully.

"Maybe," Connie laughed. "Penny, you're impossible. Do you know that?"

Penny answered with a broad smile and a warm squeeze of Connie's arm.

"They call Erin the Green Isle," Cameron stated thoughtfully, "but I don't see how it could be any greener than this."

"I think you're color blind, Cam," Harry chirped, "those mountains are black!"

"I was speaking of the lowlands," Cameron replied as the Paulos bumped gently against the pier and the hawsers were played out to lash her snug.

Within minutes the gangplank was in place and Harry watched as Penny and Constance hurriedly made their way down it.

From the corner of his eye, Cameron watched his friend with deepening interest.

Captain Demetrius met them too as they were about to debark. "Remember," he cautioned, "we sail at noon day after tomorrow. Don't make me come looking for you!"

Why, Captain," Harry said playfully, "whatever made you think that might be necessary?"

I know a couple of would-be rakes when I see them," Captain Demetrius winked.

"We'd be honored if you could join us," Cameron intoned seriously.

"I'd like that very much," the Captain replied wistfully, "but I can't get away until this evening. We've got coal, water, fresh supplies and some cargo to take on board; some to be discharged, and some authorities to meet with. My first officer can't handle it all." "Perhaps later, then," Cameron implied. "That would be good," the Captain agreed, knowing full well that he would never get beyond the first waterfront saloon with a good stock of Greek brandy.

After a delightful meal at their hotel, Harry and Cameron began making the rounds of the city. The newness of their surroundings, and the strange quality of the different drinks they sampled added an exciting spice to the tour. Harry's mood was bubbling. Shortly after midnight, however, he seemed to lose some his excitement.

"I thought we might bump into Miss Crawley and Penny," he said as he listlessly nursed the drink before him. "I think we've covered just about every place on the island."

"Not hardly, Harry!" Cameron exclaimed. "Besides, I don't think they travel in the same circles that we do."

"Perhaps you're right," Harry admitted. He raised his head and scanned the dozens of people standing at the bar, those seated at separate tables and the couples on the dance floor. The revealing costumes of the native girls that had caused his blood pressure to rise early in the evening, left him cold and unmoved. The soft strumming music that filled the air no longer buoyed his spirits.

"This is a new experience for me," Harry stated dolefully. "I feel like I want to quit the party before it even gets started," he said looking Cameron straight in the eye.

Cameron was now sure what the matter with his friend was, but knew better than to tease him about it. It was a weird phenomenon that Harry should be brought down in this fashion by a woman like Penny. A few weeks ago he would have thought it an impossible feat for any woman to make an impression on Harry beyond a good time, and a one or two-night sortie. *Poor Harry*, he thought, *now that it's happened, he doesn't even know how to begin to cope with it, much less make it grow.*

"Yes, that's it," Harry replied dejectedly.

"Suites me," Cameron answered, wishing there was something more he could say that would make his companion feel better, "Let's go," was all he could think of.

Harry's first full day in Honolulu was a long and tiring one. He followed Cameron on a ten hour sightseeing jaunt that left him with burning feet, sweat soaked clothes, and a throbbing headache.

The historical lectures that Cameron enthusiastically rendered with each new site they visited were wasted on him. His eyes probed the picturesque sweep of Waikiki Beach, the venerated rooms of the Lolani Palace, and the sparkling halls of the new University, but never came to rest on the small figure that dominated his mind.

The following morning he remembered only bits and pieces of where he had been and what he had seen. More vividly than anything else, he recalled the luxury of his warm bath before dinner, and the fresh clothes he had donned.

It didn't seem possible to Harry that the two women could be so elusive since leaving the ship; but by the last morning, he had given up all hope of seeing them before leaving port. He wanted desperately to do something for Penelope! To take her somewhere or buy her something, he didn't know what or why, but was sure now that it was too late.

Throughout the morning of their last day in town, he followed Cameron like a hound from one shop to another in search of a hat that didn't exist in this part of the world. They had exhausted all of the possibilities of finding anything new, and in desperation turned to the local pawn shops as a last resort.

After Cameron finally made his purchase Harry exploded when out of earshot of the store, "You mean to say I've spent the whole morning, and walked another five miles for that: The damned thing is wore out! Look at it! The top of it has been flattened down so long the creases are shiny, the brim of it's so weak, it sags down over your face, and that leather thong looks like it was some logger's boot lace. I'm not sure if that ghastly brown is the natural color, sunburn or old age. I wouldn't be caught dead in a thing like that," he finished in disgust.

"You might change your mind about that in the next couple of months," Cameron answered humorously, his eyes dancing below the dipping water-stained line of his hat. "Personally I consider it a bargain at a dollar. It fits perfect, and I'll bet there's a lot of wear left in it yet.

"Probably got lice!" Harry stated with a grimace.

"You heard the man tell me it was steamed and blocked since he bought it," Cameron snorted as he removed it from his head, folded out the sweat-band for close examination, then replaced it. "If there are nits in there, you wouldn't be able to see them anyway," Harry chuckled impishly.

"Oh, shut up, Harry," Cameron snapped. "Let's gather up our gear and get back to the ship. The Captain is a nice enough fellow, but I believe he could be damned nasty if we gave him a good reason."

"I've been ready since breakfast," Harry replied with new vigor. "As for your inference that I might need a hat like that, forget it! When I get you safely on that riverboat headed up stream, I'll be booking passage on a decent ship for home. I won't mind if I have to wait a few weeks for a comfortable one."

"Okay, okay, that's fine with me," Cameron agreed visibly, but couldn't help wondering if that was the way it would be.

Captain Demetrius, Constance and Penelope were standing on deck at the head of the gangplank as the two men came aboard. They were all smiles and laughter, with Penny dominating the conversation, "I think it's the most beautiful place I've ever seen, and I'd almost sell my soul to live here!" she finished as they approached. Her eyes and engaging face were radiating the truth of her statement. "Don't you think it's heavenly here, Mr. Hewitt?" she asked. "Indeed I do," Cameron replied with a loose smile. "I'm thoroughly fascinated, and hope that someday I can spend some time here. I'd like to ask a favor of you ladies," Cameron said changing the subject. "We're going to be in close proximity for some time to come, so I wish you would call me by my first name, or even Cam for that matter." "I think that's practical as well as pleasurable," Penny bubbled. "Does that apply to you also, Mr. Clayborne?" she ask turning her full attention to Harry.

"Why, of course, of course," Harry stammered at a total loss for words, and the sparkle returned instantly to his face.

"I don't like to interrupt these pleasantries," Captain Demetrius picked his words carefully, "but since everyone is aboard, there is no reason to delay. If you will excuse me, I'll get us under way." Without waiting for their reply, he turned with a slight bow and left.

"Where did you get that ridiculous hat?" Constance queried with a genuine laugh that made her face glow.

"It wasn't as easy as you might think," Harry answered devilishly out of turn. "That piece of felt you mistakenly called a hat cost eight man hours of searching this morning. I'm sure of at least two more blisters on my feet," he stated moving closer to Penny.

"Don't you think it was worth it?" Penny laughed.

"Not to me," Harry responded lightly, "but there's no accounting for taste," he laughed, oblivious to all but Penny, and not sensing that Cameron had maneuvered the two of them to the initiation of this new relationship.

"Harry forgot to mention that it also cost a dollar," Cameron added to keep the tempo of the mood going. It was the first time he had a glimpse of what lay beneath the mask of dislike Connie always wore when he was around and he wanted earnestly to see more.

"A whole dollar?" Connie asked in mock astonishment. "You wouldn't think anything as stylish as that would be quite so dear. Did you really search all morning?" she asked with gravity and a smile. "I'm afraid we did," Cameron replied with a sheepish grin. "In the first place, I have to own up to having an unusually large head. Secondly, I found that most people on these islands don't wear hats, so they don't stock many. Lastly, those they do stock are woven straw things that are fine in this climate, but won't stand a lot of dampness or freezing."

While they spoke, the throbbing of the ships engines became more pronounced; the wispy streamers of smoke that emitted from her stacks developed a rhythm, and the hawsers were lifted clear. Once again the Paulos began searching her way to the open sea.

As they gained the center of the harbor channel, Connie stepped to the rail for a better view, and Cameron followed leaving Penny and Harry to themselves.

"I'd never stopped to think about it, but I guess it would be hard to find something like you wanted out here," Connie went on pleasantly.

"Well," Cameron confessed, "I'd planned to buy a lot of new clothes and a couple of hats in San Francisco, but then those last few days were a little hectic. Before I knew it we were on our way, and I had forgotten the hat. I'll admit this one is pretty dilapidated, and looks somewhat silly, but it's all I could get, so it will have to do the job."

"I didn't mean to laugh at it," Connie said. "You'll have to agree it would give anyone a shock after seeing you without one for weeks. You look so, so," she stammered for the right word, "different."

"How so?" Cameron asked warming to her sincerity.

"Well," she answered slowly, "for one thing, you don't look quite so formidable. I don't really know how to explain it. Before you looked so dead serious all the time, like you were competing in some grim game. The hat gives your face a comic twist, it reshapes the granite features of your face, if you don't mind my saying so."

"Lord no, I don't mind," Cameron laughed easily. "Harry says my face is a rock pile, a stony cliff he calls it sometimes, so I guess it must be true." He watched her closely, waiting for the first signs of withdrawal, not wanting it to happen.

She turned to face him directly, and met his gaze head on. "I would say it was distinctive, a very personal face, never to be confused with someone else's; one that won't change much with the passage of time." Unconsciously, her eyes traced the outline of his nose and mouth, the set of his jaw, and she blushed slightly as she confronted the questioning look of his eyes. "You think a great deal of Mr. Clayborne, don't you?" she asked, purposely changing the subject and looking back to shore.

"We've been friends a long time," Cameron replied. "He's a good man in all respects, though a trifle wild at times. Like everyone else he has his faults, but I don't see them most of the time. He's a rare mixture of a lot of things, that one, and most of them good. Yes, I do like him very much!"

"It shows," Connie said candidly. "What's going on over there?" she ask pointing toward the shore.

"That must be the dredges deepening the harbor of the Navy installation Harry was telling me about when we came in the other day. We were too far away for me to see well then, but I'm sure that's it. He says it's going to be a permanent facility, and a big one," Cameron stated following her pointing finger.

"Why would they build a big Navy base clear out here?" Connie wondered idly.

"Harry say's this is the crossroads of the world, and that in time shipping here will double, triple or quadruple. He's most likely right too," Cameron said softly as his gaze returned to her.

"He could be right," Connie laughed, "but it certainly seems like a long way from anywhere. Have you any idea how long we will be before we reach Shanghai?"

"Four weeks, more or less, from what I gather," Cameron replied. "It's going to be a long haul, no doubt of that. If you have any hobbies or activities that will occupy your time, I suggest you break them out. I understand that when we get into the Horse Latitudes we're liable to have some squally weather each afternoon, and have to spend a lot more time in our quarters."

"How soon will that be?" she asked.

"A week or ten days I would imagine," he answered.

"I've wondered several times why they call them the Horse Latitudes. Would you know?" she asked attentively, cocking her head.

"It comes from back in the days of the sailing ships," he said with a smile, thankful he knew the answer. "There are no steady winds in these areas. Sometimes when they were transporting cargoes of horses, they would become becalmed. If they stayed in those circumstances very long, they would run out of water, and the horses would have to be disposed of. There must have been a lot of them that never finished the trip, because the name stuck."

"That's horribly fascinating, isn't it?" she replied with a grimace. "I'd like to go on a sailing ship someday, but I think I'll pick a trip that doesn't cross there! Have you ever been on a sailing ship?" she asked with renewed interest.

"I came from Mexico to San Francisco on one a few days before we met," he chuckled, "and I enjoyed it immensely."

"Oh, I'd just love something like that," Connie said wistfully. "Could you tell me about it? What it feels like, I mean."

"Well," Cameron began slowly, trying to recall the sensations he had enjoyed most, "it's cloud-white clean all the time, and you can sense in your legs and chest each time the wind quickens even a little and you pick up speed. It gets to where you can almost feel the pull of the canvas against the spars and the masts; like the tension of a green stick when you bend it across your knee. You get to where you can read different things from the squeaking of a block, the whirring sound that comes from the wind feathering off the rattling and the roll of the deck beneath your feet. It's nothing like this, believe me," he went on.

The last visible portion of Oahu had been swallowed by the sea a full hour before Connie noticed the emptiness before her. She turned abruptly to speak to Penny, and was surprised when she found both them gone. "I guess I let my imagination carry me away again, Mr., er I mean Cameron," she said, once more turning pink. "Penny's probably wondering what happened to me, and I haven't even said hello to Roger yet. I'd best go now. Thanks so much for indulging me. See you at dinner?"

"Yes, of course," Cameron replied. He almost thought that she didn't really want to go, and then decided that she was trying to cover her embarrassment at being with him so long.

CHAPTER 8

———◆·◆·◆———

The delicate balance of Roger Tibbs's digestive tract flatly refused to attune itself to the motion of a ship at sea. Even with all his precautions, he still became violently ill within hours after leaving port. The severity of his condition was perhaps only half of what it had been previously, but his mind would not admit to various degrees of seasickness.

More than a week passed before he could retain even a light diet, and except for emergencies, he never left the confines of his bunk.

The afternoon squalls that Cameron had predicted began in less than a week, and were accompanied by a blanket of heat that increased every day. Confinement in their compartments during these periods became increasingly uncomfortable for all the passengers, and doubly so for Roger. Other than grunts, moans and groans Roger would not communicate with Dr. Felix or Norman Clyde. This day, however, Dr. Felix had ordered a large wooden box brought from the hold to their cabin. The box had returned with him from his visit to his missionary friends in Oahu.

Lying on his back with his eyes closed Roger tried to ignore the other two men's excitement as they opened the carton, and began a thorough examination of several dozen artifacts relative to the pagan religion of the islands. At length, his curiosity got the better of him and he sat up. "What's that hideous looking thing?" he ask ogling a foot long carving Norman held in his hand.

"This one is a bad-luck Kapu," Norman replied with a smile as he handed it over. "Supposedly, if you didn't like someone you could secret this little devil in his house, or near his person, and all sorts of bad things would happen to him."

"Feels like iron wood," Roger remarked hefting it. "He's certainly ugly enough to cause a lot of trouble."

"It's made from the wood of the Lehua tree. I guess that's a form of ironwood," Norman answered. "They also made their war clubs from it. Here, feel the weight of this."

"Wow!" Roger exclaimed, "You could really bash someone's skull in with this!" he added swinging it over his shoulder several times.

"I wouldn't doubt that it has been used for exactly that purpose more than once," Norman laughed. "This one is for good luck," he said offering Roger another figure. "And, this one is to insure fertility." "Except for this one with the fat belly and the back pearl eyes, they all look about the same to me," Roger chuckled feebly. "Are those pearls real?"

"The particular function of Kapu, or taboo, was denoted by the priests. In most cases, appearance didn't enter into it," Dr. Felix interjected. "Yes, the pearls are real and probably worth a small fortune in some circles today. When this was made, however, the owner probably had dozens of them, and still lacked the price of a young fat dog." The doctor ran his finger over the protruding abdomen of the figurine. "I'm sure the designer had fertility in mind when he carved this one though!"

"You mean to say they eat dogs?" Roger asked incredulously. "Next to pork it's their chief delicacy," Dr. Felix said smoothly. "If you'd like to see something priceless, look at this," he stated while unwrapping a robe made of yellow, red and black feathers worked into an intricate diamond design.

Roger took the garment to examine it closely, noting the netting and how each tiny cluster of feathers was fastened individually and durably. "It would take months to make something like this. I'll bet there are a million separate feathers in this whole thing!" Roger gasped.

"There are surely several thousand," Norman agreed, "and just think how long it would take to collect them. Each one is select and rare. I'd venture it took a large number of people several years to make this set," he added extending the matching headgear.

"Who wore them?" Roger inquired as he continued his scrutiny.

"Only the great chiefs and certain high priests at ceremonial occasions." Dr. Felix enlightened. "Not too long ago I am told there were several hundred of these on the islands, and thousands of Kapus, but now most of them have been destroyed."

"But, why?" Roger asked wide-eyed.

"Over-zealous missionaries that believed the only way to insure the teaching of the Gospel was to obliterate everything from the past." Dr. Felix replied sadly. "A considerable amount of history has been lost throughout the ages for this same reason I'm afraid. Manuscripts and tablets burned, sculptors smashed, paintings touched up or obliterated, hieroglyphics defaced, temples razed, and it goes on and on. It is a shame!"

"Sickening!" Roger concurred, and the emphasis could be seen in his face. He handed back the robe and headpiece, then lay back on his berth and closed his eyes once more, swallowing intermittently and with great effort.

"Well, Norman," Dr. Felix exclaimed after appraising the situation, "the first thing we've got to do is catalogue these items with a detailed description; then pack them properly for shipment home when we reach Shanghai. Do you suppose the captain would have some smaller cartons and wrapping materials available?"

"I'll go ask him right now, Sir," Norman returned. "It's going to be well into the night before the inventory is complete, and these things are back in the hold."

"Most likely," Dr. Felix agreed mildly.

Roger wondered idly if the distraction they were creating could help. Time passed so slowly when he was here by himself. In a moment he forgot them completely as he struggled to control the retching that started deep in his stomach.

*   *   *   *   *

"This damned heat is stifling!" Harry exploded. "It takes my breath away." He sat on the edge of his bunk, stripped to the waist, with large beads of perspiration glistening on his soft white skin. "I just don't see how a civilized man could ever get used to it," he added.

"Your grandfather must have if he lived in India as long as you say he did," Cameron reminded Harry.

"He spent nearly twenty years there!" Harry exclaimed, bristling ever so slightly.

You never did tell me why he left the service," Cameron said trying to make conversation.

For at least two minutes Harry did not reply. He remained motionless on his bunk staring into space. Finally he broke the silence softly, but did not alter his gaze, "He left at Her Majesty's convenience; he was cashiered!" Another long pause, then he went on, "He was one of those black sheep you often hear about in England; a full-fledged bastard, if you will. His commission was purchased for him by a guilty conscience and the rampant ambitions of his sire. The best place for him was naturally halfway round the world, which is about as far as you can get. It worked out quite well for the scamp that fathered him. My grandfather wasn't that fortunate. In India they knew who he was, and the reasons for his being there before he reached his post. They assigned him the duties of a mess officer in some dreary spot where he would cause no one any annoyance.

He would be doomed to spend the rest of his life without the prospects of relief or promotion. The Crown's first mistake was in letting him know this; their second was in giving him more and more responsibilities without increasing his rank. Their third was in allowing him to handle large sums of monies that his duties required. He was in mess procurement, by-the-by. He apparently inherited a good many of his own father's traits, but predominant was his ambition. His shrewdness, I think, came from his mother. At any rate, by the time his superiors figured out what was going on, the poor little chap had amassed a fortune. He invested it where only he could put his fingers on it, and had made several contacts throughout the Orient that would be the springboard of his new enterprise in America."

Harry paused, took a large towel close by and wiped the sweat from his face, neck and shoulders. He swung around glaring toward Cameron, but when he saw the sincere interest Cam displayed, his own features mellowed. "Well," Harry continued, "that's how it came about. He had been so clever in his planning that they couldn't prove a thing without getting a lot of their own people in the soup; so, he got away clean, tuppence and all."

Harry stood up, took a long drink of warm water from the pitcher on the chest, then sat again. "He spent the next year setting up his agents and so on, then went directly to San Francisco where he bought up all the property I now own. Six months after his arrival he married a prostitute from one of the better establishments and set up housekeeping. I'm told, or was, that she was an exceptionally beautiful woman as well as a competent one. I don't believe either of them expected my father; her being from the cribs and him being past middle age.

It happened anyway; and my own father told me they were a very devoted couple and wonderful parents. I never knew either of them. They died of natural causes long before I was born."

"That's quite a tale, Harry," Cameron said with surprise. "How have you managed to keep all of that bottled up inside of you all these years we've been friends?" he asked.

"Every word of it is the solemn truth!" Harry insisted. "The only reason you haven't heard all of it is that every time I mentioned him you would give me the impression you thought I was procrastinating."

"I'm sorry, Harry," Cameron allowed, "I didn't mean for you to think that. The last thing in the world I'd accuse you of is making up a story. You've had enough real life escapades to fill a book. No need for fantasies with you, my boy." He noticed the frown start to deepen in Harry's brow, adding, "Seriously, Harry, I recall your father, a true gentleman. He died two years after we met, didn't he?"

"Thereabouts," Harry concurred. "Everyone always liked him, especially me. But, you know, he never was the same after Mum died. Fifteen years, I think it was. He lost most of his gaiety when she went away. Too bad people have to live like that after they've lost someone dear. I guess it's like that with real love. I've thought about it a great deal, but I don't believe I'll ever know what that's like. You know the way I am, Cam," Harry stated with slight discomfort.

Cameron eyed his friend quizzically. After a moment's thought he said, "I know the way you have been, Harry; but that doesn't mean you're going to continue that way. You seem to have a different gleam in your eye lately when you come near Penny. Is there something you're not telling me about?"

Harry stiffened visibly at the mention of her name, forcing himself to relax. "I just don't understand it, Cam; I didn't believe she'd be exciting, and I know she isn't overtly pretty, so I don't see why I should be drawn to her, but I am!"

"She's probably just different than all the other women you have known," Cameron tried to explain. "Different background, different breeding and different goals. The kind of girls you've always insisted on were fun partners, running from one party to the next; not wanting to think that someday the parties would end, and there would be nothing left. You just never have wanted to be around females like Penny before; so it's more than likely the newness of her being that attracts you. It'll wear off once you're back in your own element, or meet other girls like her." He wondered how Harry would accept this last bit of reasoning, but he didn't wonder long.

"I'm not sure I want to get back into my own element or for that matter if it really was my element, as you put it," Harry blurted out. "I've been doing a lot of thinking since we left the islands. Seen lot of time for it . . ." he trailed off.

"Well," Cameron cautioned, "don't get too upset if you don't come up with any startling answers. Things like this can take a lot of time."

"Just thinking about her bothers me considerably," Harry conceded, "and there's no cure for that."

"That's an age old statement of fact," Cameron chuckled. "At any rate, old friend, I want you to know I'm on your side, and if you believe I can help in anyway, let me know."

"Thanks, Cam," Harry replied softly, "I appreciate the thought. While they had spoken the sun had set, and the gray shadows of evening stealthily invaded the room. "Soon be dark enough for us to move outside. Shall we gather up our night clothes?" Harry asked in a whisper. "Sounds grand to me!" Cameron boomed as he rolled to his feet.

*   *   *   *   *

Connie could feel the cooler night air coming through the two open portholes. She wished she possessed the courage to open the cabin door and block it too, but knew her own modesty as well as Penny's prevented it. Both of them had on the thinnest nightgowns they owned; and even in the dim light, she could see the pinkish glow of her thigh through her own. It took only a few minutes of lying in one spot before the material under her became damp. *It's like roasting a chicken on a spit,* she thought, *you just keep turning.* She switched positions again, and welcomed the chilling sensation that ran along her hip and side. She listened to Penny's irregular breathing and knew she wasn't asleep either. "What are you thinking about, Penny?" she whispered.

"A hundred pound block of ice, and a big shade tree with lots of grass under it," came the soft dreamy reply.

"Oh, you silly," Connie said impatiently, "I mean really!" "That's honestly what was on my mind," Penny assured her. "I've been trying to figure out how to keep the ice from melting, but without success."

"I give up," Connie replied, as they fell silent for a moment "Is there some kind of a romance building up between you and Harry Clayborne?" she ask point blank when she resumed.

"Not that I know of," Penny giggled ever so little. "He's just a real nice man, and a passenger I couldn't avoid even if I wanted to." She let it hang there.

"Don't you play dumb with me, Penelope Rutledge," Connie snapped playfully. "You might make other people believe that act of yours, but I know you better. You know what other people are thinking before they know themselves, especially men," she added.

"Well," Penny answered after slight deliberation, "I'm sure he likes me a lot even though he hasn't said so in so many words. I believe he's kind of mixed up about girls in spite of his years, but I don't know why. He hasn't told me much about himself other than a few isolated incidents and about his business. He talks a lot about Cameron, and things they do together. He told me he had to hoodwink Cameron about this trip; and that he wasn't very proud of some of the things he did. He didn't go into detail about it, and for some unknown reason, I'm glad he didn't. Anyway, I think he's very nice, and I enjoy being with him. That's all I can tell you. If there is any romance in his mind I don't know it yet, but unless I'm badly mistaken about him, I'd welcome it."

"What did he have to say about Cameron?" Connie asked, trying to sound nonchalant.

"Oh, the usual things that men talk about," Penny teased, "you know."

"No, damn it, Penny, I don't know or I wouldn't be asking!" Connie exclaimed forgetting herself.

"He told me that Cameron had been on his own most of his life; that he spends the majority of his time out of the country doing his work, that he lost just about everything he owned in the earthquake, that he enjoys good food and fine wine in moderation and that he sleeps buff," Penny said without taking a breath.

"Anything else of importance?" Connie inquired guardedly. "Nothing that I can think of at the moment," Penny replied feigning a yawn. After a long silent pause she added with indifference, "Harry did say that he had been married for a while, but I think he's divorced now. Goodnight Connie.'

"Goodnight, hell!" Connie bellowed. "Now you stop that, Penny, do you hear me? Who was he married to, and for how long? Is he or isn't he divorced, and if so when and why? I want the truth now, Penny, I mean it." A long pause, then, "Please."

"I'm sorry, Connie, I didn't mean to make you angry," Penny implored. "It's just that you're so fascinating when you get upset enough to curse. You seem to come by the right words so natural. I know some of the words, but I invariably use them in the wrong place, and then I feel so foolish."

"Alright, Penny," Connie coaxed in a softer tone. "Now get on with it."

"Honestly, Connie, I don't know her name," Penny said. "Harry didn't tell me. It happened years ago when Cameron first got into the limelight. She was some spoiled society deb from Denver. Her father had more money than an Indian Rajah, and the poor girl never knew from one minute to the next what she really wanted. She swept Cameron off his feet before he knew what it was all about, and divorced him less than a year later. He never even got used to being married. Harry said they didn't live together more than three months of that time. That was seven years ago, and the lady is on her third husband since Cameron held the place of honor. Harry also says she isn't truly a bad person, just terribly confused. How come all of a sudden you're so interested in Cameron's past? A couple of weeks ago you couldn't stand for me to mention his name," she finished suspiciously.

"It's only that I've realized since we've got to trust our very lives to him, I should know a little more about his background, so I'll know what to expect of him under pressure. Don't get any funny ideas, Miss Smarty-pants," Connie stated firmly, I still don't like the man and never will. You said yourself that I couldn't expect the man to do his best if I continued to treat him with such open hostility. I've merely come to the conclusion that you're right, and from now on, I'm going to work at it."

"If you say so," Penny agreed lamely

"Don't you worry your pretty little head about it," Connie assured her, "that's the way it's going to be and nothing more to it. Now, go to sleep, goodnight, Penny."

"Goodnight, Connie dear," Penny replied. But the wheels that were racing in her mind repeated, "This might bear watching too!"

None of the passengers needed to be told when they began making the final approach to the port city of Shanghai. Early in the morning they sighted their first junk. It was only a small fishing vessel and not very impressive. After six full weeks at sea, the sight of the strange shaped sails and hull sent a ripple of excitement through all of them. Before the day had ended, they passed six more of them of varying sizes and conditions.

The next day they soon lost interest in the count as they became so numerous; and on the following day the junks were interspaced with the smaller sampans that ventured out from the Yangtze River.

The large number of crafts they had witnessed did not prepare any of them for the vast armada they encountered as they slowly progressed up the river and into Soochow Creek, the heart of Shanghai, where they docked on the west bank.

Dozens upon dozens of ocean going vessels from every nation filled the miles of wharfs and peers on both sides of the channel. It was impossible to count the junks that were everywhere a person could look; and the sampans were so numerous they reminded Cameron of water skippers that collect by the thousands on the stagnant pools of a marsh, darting here and there without purpose while others wait motionless for some silent signal that would tell them it was their turn to play the pointless game.

An equally impressive sight, however, was the modern European city that stood before them. All the way up the river and part of Soochow Creek they had noted the shanties and hovels that people appeared to be living in. Rafts and small barges clustered along the banks also doubled as homes. It was unbelievable, and now this.

Between the bellowing of ships horns, the shrilling of whistles, the high pitched squawk of the gulls, the hum of a thousand or more human voices, and the clanging of bells it was impossible to localize any one particular sound. Add to all of that the smell of it: coal smoke, dead fish, rotting timbers, incense, sour sweat, oil of sandal wood, human excreta, burning joss sticks, a light touch of jasmine and the scent of rain that was on its way; the odors of both the living and the dying, joined together to form the overpowering undefinable aroma.

Shanghai was too awesome for them to take in all at once, and it left them speechless.

When the gangplank was lowered into place, the Captain came forward and addressed himself to Cameron, "Well, Mr. Hewitt, what are your immediate plans, and may I be of assistance in any way?" he asked with a pleasant smile. "Clayborne and I must first make contact with his agent," Cameron was forced to speak loudly. "We would greatly appreciate it if our people could remain on board until suitable quarters are arranged for them on shore."

"Of course, of course," Captain Demetrius boomed. "Anything else?"

"Yes," Harry said stepping forward. "Would you happen to know the location of the House of Te Chien? That's where I'll find my agent, Mr. Jo Lung."

"That won't be difficult at all, Mr. Clayborne," the Captain laughed. "This must be your lucky day. Their offices are located on this side of the harbor, only five blocks further up that way," he said pointing ahead.

"That's fine," Harry breathed a sigh of relief. He had envisioned walking around in this huge city looking for a firm he did not know, and not being able to utter a single word of the prevailing language. "Thank you ever so much, Captain."

"It's nothing," the Captain replied. "I'll be here when you return, and I'd like all of you to have dinner with me this evening before we part." Being used to giving orders he did not wait for a reply, he turned, waived his hand and walked away.

"I hadn't counted on that," Cameron said, "but maybe it's just as well. I'd like everyone to get their baggage and belongings assembled, ready to go, then wait on board until we return. For God's sake don't get off this ship and get lost before we establish some kind of a base."

Cameron looked around for their approval, and noted everyone nodded except Roger, leaning heavily against the rail. For a fraction of a second he thought he detected a note of resentment in those pale blue eyes, but then it was gone and he nodded indifferently.

"We'll be back just as soon as we can then," Cameron said as he took Harry by the arm. "Let's be on our way, your Lordship!"

"Enough of that!" Harry snapped.

The office of Jo Lung was not an office at all, but instead a small work room secreted deep within the honeycomb forming the House of Te Chien. The cubicle was compact and neat, displaying the qualities of the man seated at a low table in the center. He was in his early thirties with a waxy complexion and small piercing eyes. Except for the black plaited queue, dangling behind his silken cap, his face was hairless. Neat piles of papers covered his work desk, leaving only enough space for ciphering. On the floor to his right and left stood an abacus, and the beads of both were clicking sharply when Harry and Cameron entered guided by a young barefooted boy.

Jo Lung extracted himself and stood erect as they came in. The lad bowed deeply, directed several rapid fire sentences at him, bowed once more to him, twice to the strangers and left.

"Could it be," Jo asked in flawless English, while looking steeply upward to Cameron's full six feet, "that you are my benefactor, Mr. Harry Clayborne?" His smile was genuine, his tone soft and friendly, and his accent decidedly aristocratic British.

"Only a slight mistake," Cameron laughed extending his hand, I'm Cameron Hewitt, this is Mr. Clayborne."

"My greatest pleasure, Gentlemen," Jo assured as he bowed first to Harry and then to Cam. "Please be seated," he added indicating heavy cushions resting against one wall.

Jo clapped his hands briskly, then in one deft motion stacked the papers he had been working on and placed them in one of several pigeonholes arranged on the far wall. As he was seating himself another boy entered the room. "Would you Gentlemen care for some refreshment? Some tea, brandy, scotch, gin or perhaps some rice wine? We have nearly everything you might desire, so don't hesitate to ask," he added.

Harry looked to Cameron, who in turn nodded. "That would be delightful," Harry replied with gusto, "we've had a long dry spell since we left the islands. To satisfy my curiosity I'll try some of your rice wine."

"I'm equally inquisitive," Cameron joined.

"In that case," Jo smiled, "I must warn you that it will not be what you think. The European given name of wine is a misnomer. It more closely resembles whiskey and is quite potent."

"That should make it all the more interesting," Harry laughed. Jo gave instructions to the youth, and then turned back to his company. "I trust that your trip was as pleasant as it was expedient. I didn't expect you for a least another week or two."

"It seemed like an eternity at times," Cameron replied, "but I guess comparatively we did make fairly good time."

As the refreshments were served, Jo smiled his reply. "I don't suppose you have arranged for lodging here in the city as yet?" he inquired.

"No, we haven't," Harry conceded. "Having no notion of any arrangements you might have made, we thought it best to confer with you before doing anything"

"Here in the Bund, the international part of Shanghai, you have a wide selection of accommodations," Jo informed. The English have always been noted for their insistence on refined comfort, so I would suggest the Carlton, or one of their other establishments."

"After spending so many weeks cooped up on the Paulos it won't take much to satisfy any of us," Harry chuckled. "The Carlton, as you call it, will do nicely. Could you have someone take care of our luggage?"

"I shall do better than that," Jo said with sincerity. "If you'll tell me how many there are in your party and their needs, I'll send someone to get them settled and look after them."

"Wonderful, wonderful," Harry bubbled, then proceeded to inform Jo of the others, and how they would like their rooms arranged. Cameron sipped gingerly at the aromatic drink in his hand, and decided it didn't taste much like whiskey.

Jo excused himself and left the room for a few minutes, returning with a white bearded old gentleman dressed entirely in black.

"This is Li Po, an associate of mine," Jo explained making introductions. The old man bowed low with grace and nimbleness belying his age, his eyes friendly though keen and alert.

"Li Po has been working with me on your behalf," Jo continued. "He has friends and relatives in the interior, and although he speaks only his native tongue, I'm sure you will find him invaluable. He personally will see to most of your requirements, including your quarters."

At some unseen signal from Jo, Li Po bowed once more then left on his errand, his slender form rustling his silken robes. Without summons the young boy once more entered the room and silently filled their small cups as the trio resumed their seats. "Not knowing your time of arrival it has been impossible to make definite plans," Jo began. "Your ultimate destination is another world from here; and we can only plot the beginning. Intelligent speculation will be the rule as we proceed up river. There are boats leaving in that direction almost every hour, most of them making innumerable stops you can ill afford. Therefore we must select one whose entire cargo is destined far inland. Beyond Chunking, the river may be too shallow for the ship we start out in. We may reach Ipin before encountering this condition. At any rate, at this point we will either have to find a smaller craft or continue overland. Wherever the waters become difficult and the boats smaller the river pirates become more active. The final stage of your journey will have to be on horses anyway, so it might be wise to acquire them at this point. Horses of any kind are hard to come by in the interior. The provincial military take most of them. However, if we are fortunate enough to arrive in the general area of Ipin, Li Po should be able to procure us some sort of transportation. He and our small assistant, Chu Chuer will accompany us that far. Their presence up to then will be a dual purpose as the House of Te Chien has interest in that area that requires attention."

Both Harry and Cameron listened intently as Jo outlined the plans he had in mind.

"When we leave the river it would be best to strike north to the caravan route from Chengtu. We might even be lucky enough to join one of the caravans going directly to Chamdo. This would be gratifying, for there are many bandits and robbers in that area. Also, in that province there is a general known as Cheng Wu. Since the death of the Emperor, he has assumed a great deal of power locally. He is a very cruel and aggressive man, with a deep hatred of foreigners, and open contempt for the edicts of the Hsuan-T'ung. You must understand that all of China is in a state of turmoil and change. Our present illustrious Emperor is a mere babe of less than five years. His father, Prince Ch'un is Regent in his place, and has inherited a task far beyond his capabilities. The Hsuan-T'ung, the Prince's government, is fast losing control in the remote regions, and General Cheng Wu is one of its most notorious opponents. It is my most fervent hope we shall not encounter him or his Army," Jo Lung stated.

"Thinking positively," Jo continued, "when we reach Chamdo the great merchant Maleek will arrange for your further progress, and I shall return here by the best available means. If you gentlemen have a better plan, or any other ideas, I should be pleased to hear them."

For several moments there was silence, then Cameron spoke, "For the most part we'll be playing it by ear, I guess. The only thing we can definitely arrange is the initial stage of our trip up river. How long do you think it will take us to find the right ship?"

"Not more than three, possibly four days," Jo replied.

"In that case," Harry said jubilantly, "we'll have some time to rest and get acquainted with the city."

"I agree with enjoying your rest, Mr. Clayborne," Jo said, "but I strongly caution any of you against leaving the area of the Bund. The native sections of Shanghai abound with every type of thief and cut-throat, beggar and prostitute that ever existed. Sentiment is high toward all foreigners, and you shouldn't venture from your hotel after dark. Be sure to advise the rest of your people in this matter!" he added adamantly.

"Is it really that bad?" Harry asked slightly irritated.

"Indeed it is," Jo admonished. "Dozens of people die violently here each month, and very few of them are Chinese. I'll send Chu Chuer along as your guide, and he can act as liaison while we are waiting, if you don't mind having him under-foot. He speaks enough English to get along, and it undoubtedly will improve, the more time he spends with you."

"We'd be glad to have him," Cameron said rising. "I'm sure we'd all be hopelessly lost within the hour without someone. His name has a rhythmical sound, what does it mean?"

"You would doubtlessly find out in time, when he loses his shyness," Jo laughed heartily. "The literal translation would mean Cricket, and it fits him aptly."

"That's an odd name, isn't it?" Harry mused.

"Yes," Jo grinned, "odd but appropriate. I'll need to know the size and weight of the supplies you brought with you to determine our space needs on a river boat. You can make up a list later and send it to me. I should have some word by tomorrow concerning our departure. In the meantime, Li Po and Chu Chuer will see to your comfort. Enjoy yourselves, I'll visit you not later than noon." Jo rose and bowed solemnly to each of them.

Cameron returned the bow with some awkwardness, as Harry caught himself extending his hand.

The Crawley expedition found the Carlton Hotel to be the culmination of luxury even in the far flung reaches of Shanghai. Each group of the party had its own suite, but only the one occupied by Dr. Felix, Norman and Roger had a drawing room; and it was only natural that it soon became the group meeting place during the four days of their stay in the city.

In the long days of waiting everyone concerned had ventured farther and farther out into the Bund, until at-last they had even penetrated the native quarters, discretely ignoring the warnings of Jo Lung. Luck and divine protection stood a joint guard on them, for they encountered no trouble, and only a few glaring stares of hatred. The merchants of all the shops they visited treated them with respect and a degree of fairness in their dealings.

On their last night in the city they held a banquet in one of the private dining rooms the hotel boasted. It was supposed to be a lively affair celebrating the halfway point of the journey, and the last place they would have accommodations for any type of gaieties. The party started with gusto, but the sobering fact that morning would thrust them into a vast and unknown land few western men had ever returned from began preying on each of their minds. By the time they returned to their meeting place the conversation was forced, and they looked at one another questioningly.

On the way back upstairs Harry grasp the opportunity to speak to Cameron alone. "I've been talking with Jo Lung, and he thinks it best that I accompany you to the end of the river voyage.

Something in Harry's expression wasn't right, and Cameron sensed that at least some part of this, or all of it, was a fib; but he did not express his suspicions. He would have been disappointed if Harry hadn't made some excuse to stay with them to the rivers end. "I think Jo is right, and that you should give it strong consideration," Cameron retorted blandly.

"I've already decided to go along that far," Harry said aglow, "but then I'm positively returning home!"

"I'm glad about your change of heart, we can use you and your company, especially me," Cameron smiled as they entered the drawing room.

When everyone was seated, Dr. Felix addressed them collectively, "I sincerely hope that all of you enjoyed this meal as much as I did," he began smiling warmly. "It will undoubtedly be remembered for quite some time to come, as I don't believe we'll dine that well for the next few months. Now, has each of you packed and delivered to Te Chien your recent purchases, and anything else you wished to send home? Remember, from here on we must travel as lightly as possible, and now is the time to take stock of it. Your packages will each have your own name on them, and will be placed in one large carton which will be shipped to, and stored at Harry Clayborne's establishment."

"I didn't buy half the things I wanted to," Penny pouted while wrinkling her nose at Connie, "but everything I managed to get is on its way."

"I don't believe I've forgotten anything," Connie stated ignoring Penny for the moment.

"Anyone else think of any last minute things to be done?" Dr. Felix inquired at large, glancing from one to the other. "How about you, Roger, you look as though you have something on your mind?" During the four full days ashore Roger had gradually regained his old composure of complete indifference, but this evening he was sullen and remote.

"The only thing I might have neglected to ship home is myself'." Roger replied faintly.

"What do you mean by that?" Connie asked with concern, thinking his illness had returned.

"I mean that I'm damned sorry that I ever became part of this affair. I think the whole thing is a mistake from start to finish. I wish there was some way I could ship myself home in a carton without experiencing that damnable ocean trip. I have deep foreboding about the outcome of this fiasco, and I hope you will all reconsider just what you're committing us to," Roger finished without heat.

"Oh, Roger," Connie soothed, "we all understand. You've been very ill for a long period of time. It's bound to have left you weak and unnerved; it will get better for you, wait and see. A large river boat like the one we've got isn't anything like being at sea. You'll actually enjoy it." As she spoke, she rose and went to his side and gently placed her hand on his shoulder.

"I'm not worried about the goddamned river or the boat," he replied coldly, "It's the rest of it! No one knows anything about where we are going or what we'll encounter. I have a feeling that we'll be damned lucky if any of us come out alive. I think it's only sensible for us to forget the whole stupid scheme, and get back to civilization as quickly as possible!" The tone of Roger's voice rose as he spoke, and Connie realized he was serious.

Still caressing his shoulder she replied softly and with conviction, "There isn't one single reason for you to feel this way, Roger. Nothing has changed since we first agreed to come. Nothing bad has happened, and in truth we've been extremely fortunate. Our crossing was made in record time, considering, and we've been treated much better here than Mr. Lung thought we would. I'm not the least bit superstitious and I didn't know you were. If I were, I would take everything that has happened to be good signs. I honestly believe, Roger, your illness has completely exhausted you, and left you in a state of anxiety that is causing you to feel this way. A few days of rest, warm sunshine, and fresh air will make you more like yourself again, and you'll laugh about the whole thing." Connie looked at him intently, "We've come too far to turn back now Roger dear!" she concluded emphatically.

As Connie talked, Penny rose from her chair and came to stand in front of him. "I think she's right, Roger, you've probably been having some bad dreams and with good reason. If there was anything to be frightened of I'd be the first one to show it, and I'm not."

With resignation Roger looked up at her, "Penny, you don't have brains enough to be afraid of anything that really matters. A spider or a mouse will set you squealing, but that's about the extent of your fear. With me, this is something I can only feel, and I don't like it. After my past performance, however, I don't expect anyone to pay any attention to me, so forget it." He looked around the room defiantly.

Harry withdrew his large gold watch from his vest pocket. After staring at it for several seconds, he feigned surprise and interrupted the conversation, "The river boat will leave in just a little over five hours, and unlike Captain Demetrius, it won't be waiting for us if we are even a little late. I propose we all try to get a little rest before we depart as tomorrow will be a long day. Li Po will be here shortly for your luggage, and you should keep only those items you intend to carry yourself." He smiled pleasantly as he gained their attention, "Jo says our state-rooms are all on the top deck, very spacious and will provide and excellent view."

Throughout the discussion Cameron sat back in his chair and refrained from comment. He had decided that as long as Harry's people were arranging things, Harry should be the lead man, and make the few decisions necessary. His own turn to take the reins would come when they left the river and commenced the overland part of the journey. For the present he was enjoying his leisure, and only now and then did he nod his head to show he was listening. He was so relaxed he caught himself dozing off.

"Most of our ship's cargo is destined for Ipin and some of it beyond, but it might have to be transferred to smaller boats at Chunking," Harry was saying. "We won't know this until we get there, and only then can we decide what we will do; so don't waste time or sleep worrying about it now. At the moment I believe we would do well to get our things together," he concluded.

The light scratch of Norman's pen could be heard whenever he decided something of interest to Dr. Felix's journal had been said or done. He was still writing when the last of the visitors left the room and only he, Dr. Felix and Roger remained.

*   *   *   *   *

At two o'clock in the morning the temperature had dropped to seventy degrees; but the hot sticky hand of the humidity still gripped the city. A full moon shone brightly, outlining the twin stacks, the huge paddle wheel, and the hundred or more people sprawled about the ship's two lower decks. The Crawley party was the sole occupants of the top deck, and they lined the rail, avidly watching as the ship made her way to mid-channel. Above them stood the small square wheel house, occupied by the three men directing the withdrawal.

The hum-drum noise of the great harbor during the day was only slightly diminished even at this early hour. Dozens of lighters plied between ships anchored mid-stream and shore, ships loading and others unloading at the many pontoon piers, some coming into dock and others, like themselves, making ready to sail.

Sang Chow Te market, the center of Shanghai, had remained nearly deserted for six hours; now anxious farmers and merchants started setting up their stalls in anticipation of today's trade. The windows of the many trading and banking firms remained dark, but even they would come to life before the sun broke free.

The task of threading the river boat through the mass of anchored and moving shipping was a slow and difficult maneuver belonging to the pilot. At various times his voice could be heard above the din surrounding them. Ever so slowly they picked up momentum; and the international settlement receded from view as they gained steerage way in the Whangpoo River.

They traversed the main silt bars of the Yangtze at a point called Shen Van an hour before dawn. Much later Cameron was to learn that Shen Van was known to the Europeans as Fairy Flats, and he could never get a proper explanation of the significance. To the pilot, this area was his only immediate concern for many a ship had run fast aground in the constantly changing silt bars of the mighty river.

By the time the sun had risen they were so far out into the vast expanse of the Yangtze estuary that it was impossible to see the far shore, and too far to observe the scenery of the near one in any detail. Within the hour they had encountered a fleet of junks and sampans, barges and open rafts, a large number of steam river boats, and at least three seagoing vessels.

Jo Lung and his associates were the first to lose interest. They retired to their quarters with sincere apologies, and the proper amount of bowing. They were followed by Dr. Felix and Norman with a great deal less formality. No one really knew when Roger left, he was beside Connie one minute, and gone the next.

"I'm getting terribly tired," Penny yawned as she dabbed at her left eye with a clenched fist.

"There really isn't much left to see now, is there?" Connie asked in agreement. "Let's go find out what our beds are like. Will you excuse us, gentlemen?"

"Of course," Cameron and Harry chimed almost in unison.

"I believe I'll have to go along with the girls," Cameron stated as he once more scanned the still morning waters. "We've seen at least half of all the junks and sampans that there are in the world; so I don't think we'd miss much if we went to bed too."

"I shouldn't be too sure about seeing half of them!" Harry exclaimed. "This is one hellishly large river. Looks more like a small ocean at this point."

"It will neck down as we go upstream," Cameron assured him. "We're out in the delta now."

"I wouldn't know which way is upstream if my life depended on it." Harry sighed in awe.

"I wouldn't either," Cameron concurred with a grin. "What say we let the pilot worry about it? Let's catch a few winks before it gets so blasted hot we can't." With that he took Harry by the arm and led him toward their cabin.

The immense vastness of the Yangtze did not neck down as Cameron had supposed it would. Instead the opposing banks merely inched closer to one another as the miles fell behind. At sundown land was visible on both sides, but Cameron had to use his binoculars to determine individual activity.

Early in the evening of the second day they entered the fabled and sprawling regions of Nanking. Here the ship dallied only long enough to discharge a few of the lower deck passengers and take on fuel. The temptation was on all of them, including Roger, to leave the confines of the ship and seek the adventurous lure of the ancient narrow streets; but Jo Lung was adamant in forbidding their desire. He knew that even the slightest incident could prove disastrous to the entire venture.

At noon on the following day they passed the city of Wuhu, and were informed by Jo that they were now on a static river; the tides of the East China Sea had no effect beyond this area.

To the delight of all concerned they discovered that their deck had retractable awnings to shade them from the sun, and allow the full thrust of the slight breeze that prevailed each afternoon. The heat was so stifling that no one could stay in the cabins after ten in the morning, nor return much before the same hour in the evening.

The entire company spent this time of day collapsed in the many bamboo deck chairs scattered about. It greatly amused the profound Li Po to watch Cameron's reaction to the living drama constantly taking place about them, just as it had done for thousands of years.

Both banks, with their forty-foot high earth dikes, and the many small inlets they passed were clearly visible without the aid of glasses. Men, women, and even some children, were constantly at work repairing the earth works; their twin baskets arching the shoulder pole when full, and giving it a bouncing effect when empty. Had the party been on either of the lower decks they could not have seen the endless vista of the rice paddies extending beyond the levees on either side. Each day in these inundated fields they saw thousands of people toiling in the ankle deep water, preparing the soil, transplanting the foot long shoots, thinning or meeting other demands of this life giving crop.

The small wooden plows pulled by human draft animals came as a shock to Cameron; but it did not prepare him for the sight of a beautiful young girl, of perhaps sixteen, with the harness strapped about her delicate shoulders and waist. His eyes went wide in amazement, and he turned to expound his disbelief, but found himself trapped in the scrutiny of Li Po. He saw the gray hairs of wisdom of the old man's beard and mustache, the chiseled lines of care that etched his face, and the soft caress of understanding that flowed from his eyes. Without a word being spoken he understood that here in this land of great need, beauty and charm in themselves earned nothing; only those that produced would survive, and though at times it was harsh, there was at all times a harmony in it. He turned his gaze back to the fields and dikes and for the first time gave his full attention to the countenance of the multitudes close at hand. He saw determination without anguish; he saw pride without vanity, and a hint of happiness without futility.

For the remainder of the afternoon Cameron refrained from joining the conversation that flowed to either side of him. He was drawn solely to the people of this strange land. At one time he thought he must be looking for some flaw that he had missed earlier, but soon gave it up. He sensed that Li Po somehow approved of his thoughts, and it gave him a curious sensation of comfort. He was so aware of this feeling that he knew without seeing when Li Po retired in the darkness.

Jo Lung remained seated on his left and Cameron turned to him to ask, "How many times have you made this trip before, Jo?"

This is my third trip," he replied. "I must confess I am more impressed each time."

What is the farthest you have gone up river?" Cameron persisted.

"Ipin," Jo answered, "that is the location of the final House of Te Chien. We trade beyond there, but it is conducted through local agents and independents."

"I've been meaning to ask you," Harry interrupted from his chair in the shadows, "what is the exact meaning of Te Chien?"

"In your language it would translate to the Gold Coin," Jo responded.

"Very appropriate for a commercial establishment," Harry mused.

"What's the name of this ship, and who does it belong to?" Cameron inquired with interest.

"It is called Shi Shen, or deep water," Jo stated.

"Rather a strange name for a boat, wouldn't you say?" Harry queried.

"Not if one knew the history of it," Jo chuckled. "You see, it came across the deep water from your own land. It was one of the last boats built for the trade on your big river; but by the time it was completed, there was little use for it. The owners found they could ship cheaper and faster by rail; so this ship was sold for less that it cost to build. She was brought to the House of Te Chien by an American crew, and they instructed our people as to her operation and care. She has paid for herself many times in the past thirty years."

"I thought her lines looked familiar," Cameron ventured, but decided it was only a copy made by some fanciful world traveler of yours."

"No," Jo laughed with pleasure, "she is the genuine article on a new river."

"How did you come to learn English, Jo?" Cameron asked hesitantly, not knowing if this might be impolite.

"My esteemed father was a very talented young man; one of those natural linguists," Jo answered eagerly. "His services were traded to the British early in his life by the Te Chien; and he served them in Shanghai, Hong Cong and in Calcutta where I was born. I grew up during his office with the East Indian Company; but the language did not come as easily to me as it did my father. Perhaps you have noticed I speak with a slight English accent?"

"Not English," Harry objected, "British! There are many different English accents, but only one that resembles yours."

"When did you leave India?" Cameron asked curiously.

"When my father's ancestors called him, and he knew that he was going to die," Jo answered solemnly, "he gathered up his entire family and took us home. He knew almost exactly how much time he had; for he managed to get all of us established before joining his honorable forefathers."

"Does your mother still live?" Harry wanted to know.

"Yes," Jo answered smiling, "she is hardy like bamboo; she will survive many more years, and I am thankful for that! She keeps my house, and manages my family," he added proudly.

When Jo Lung started speaking of himself, Connie and Penny had ceased their chatter to listen. Then Penny broke the momentary silence, "I'm famished, when are we going to eat?"

"You're a bottomless pit," Connie teased. "You eat more than any two men of our party, and I can't see where you put it. You should be fat as a walrus, and look at you, little more than skin and bones."

"There appears to be more than that to me," Harry vouchsafed without thinking, flushing with embarrassment. "At any rate, I'd like something myself," he added to cover his confusion.

"Good idea," Cameron ceded coming to Harry's rescue, "It's cooled down some now, let's all go inside and see what we'll have." The hours flowed into the days much as the water beneath them drained toward the sea, without sound or apparent motion. The daily tableau so much resembled yesterday's that Cameron began to wonder if this mighty river did not run in a circle; and they were seeing the same thing over and over again. The brief fueling stops were the only realistic signs of progress, but once they fell behind they too assumed an abstracted quality.

They passed the city of L'chang in the late black hours of the night, and when they emerged on deck shortly after sunup, they could scarcely credit their eyes. Sheer rock walls, near vertical hillsides, towered hundreds to thousands of feet above them, blocking out all view save the sky above. Beneath the left bank, and still in the morning shade, they could see a broad path running beside the river.

The current had increased considerably, and their speed slowed markedly. At various spots white water could be seen. It was plain had the water been a few feet lower, they would have had some problems with rapids. At one of these spots they were amazed to see a junk being dragged upstream by a half-mile long bamboo rope with at least fifty men pulling on it from the path.

"That's a hard way to earn a living," Cameron remarked shaking his head sadly.

"Not so difficult if there is no other way, and you do not believe there ever will be." Jo admonished from directly behind him.

"I guess you're right there, Jo," Cameron admitted. He looked upward idly, then whistled sharply. "Does the water level really get up that high?" he asked in astonishment.

"Nearly every spring," Jo said flatly.

The water marks Cameron had referred to were at least two hundred feet above the present level.

Sometime during the morning, the monotony of the gorge was broken periodically by the deep right angle ravines cut over the centuries by feeding tributaries.

Since the inception of their river journey, Harry had always managed to find some excuse to visit Penny not later than the noon hour, and this day was no exception. His sojourns grew longer each day, and now generally lasted until the late evening meal. Since leaving Shanghai, Roger had shown no sign of recurring seasickness. The pair kept the ladies entertained most of the time. A slight twinge of resentment gnawed at Cameron because of this development; but he soon allowed he was thankful, for it gave him time to question Jo Lung, and through him Li Po.

Cameron wondered aimlessly how this proximity romance would survive when it came time for Harry to make his farewells, and head back down river. *Too bad*, he thought, *Penny might really have done something for Harry had she been given the time.* Aloud he addressed himself to Jo, sitting beside him, "Before we started you mentioned something about some safe conduct papers you had acquired."

"Yes," Jo responded sleepily, "I have four of them signed by the Regent, Prince Ch'un himself. Don't get the wrong impression, however, they don't mean much, and were not made out for us specifically. They are really a form sort of thing, if you follow me, and know where to get them."

"They wouldn't do us much good then if we needed them, is that right?" Cameron asked slightly disturbed.

"They could," Jo countered, coming fully awake. "For most people in this area the throne of the Emperor is in another world, and these papers do have the official seal. They might be very impressive under the right circumstances. Two of the four copies I have are addressed to whom it may concern, one to the Merchant of Chamdo, and the other to General Cheng Wu.

With this bit of information Cameron brightened somewhat. "Do you think we'll need them?" he asked hesitantly.

"I certainly hope not!" Jo exclaimed, his deep thoughts reflecting in his eyes.

Cameron did not reply for several moments, then asked, "Tell me what you know of the general and the Merchant of Chamdo." "No one knows much about the early life of the general," Jo began. "He was a common soldier, of humble beginnings; and his real name was Moy, his entire name I do not know. He adopted the name Cheng Wu when he pronounced himself general; and his new name is as deceptive as he is, translated it means something like 'upright military.' He possesses two chief characteristics: one is his strong ambition, and the other, the intelligence to curb his desires to the situation at hand. He is cruel and greedy, but smart enough to know all things worthwhile take time; and his sadism must, for the most part, be directed in people's interest." Jo caught his breath, then continued. "He came up through the ranks to a point on his unusual abilities. From then on, his superiors died off or were killed in the line of duty, supposedly. Had they understood his ingenuity and his ambition, most of them would be alive today!"

"I don't believe I'd care to encounter that rogue," Cameron shuddered. "What about the merchant?"

"In truth," Jo replied in a different tone, "he is even more powerful than the general. His financial and political power is felt throughout all of China and most of her neighbors. He is a Moslem, has many wives and concubines, but is now an old man. He is as good and respected as the general is evil and feared."

"That sounds encouraging," Cameron sighed. "Where will we find this gentleman of commerce?"

"Until recent years that could have been a problem in itself," Jo confided. "He was known for decades for traveling with his caravans, and establishing all his foreign ties personally. His age has curtailed most of this, and he now has a permanent headquarters in Chamdo. I'm praying that he will be there. He knows that we are coming."

"What do we do if he is not?" Cameron inquired with a cocked eyebrow.

"We either wait or make other arrangements on our own," Jo said simply.

Cameron mulled this over in his mind for several minutes, deciding not to pursue the subject further. Instead he asked, "Do you think this General Cheng Wu is strong enough to stay in power here, or will the Throne eventually oust him?"

For a long while Jo did not answer, small lines formed on his forehead, and the troubled look returned to his eyes. At length he replied slowly, "There has always been isolated power within the interior and undoubtedly, in time, others will replace him. My main concern is for the Throne of the Emperor. It has been waning for many years now, and all of the trouble with the foreigners has not helped. The whole country is in quiet turmoil. There are many new and powerful voices speaking for a different kind of government, and they are receiving a good deal of support."

"From what little I know," Cameron speculated, "and what I saw in Shanghai, I would say that foreign trade interests are milking the country dry!"

Jo gazed upward at the rim of the gorge, and the last rays of the dying sun. He answered quietly, "The sleeping dragon suckles and nourishes only her own offspring; when the time comes she will clean her nest of their droppings."

Cameron looked at Jo sharply, but detected no heat or emotion. He decided it was a simple statement of what Jo believed would happen, and his blood lines had shaped its utterance.

With the setting of the sun, the light breeze funneling down the canyon stiffened a bit, but it still bore the heat of the day. Late the following morning they emerged from the gorge, and passed the city of Wanhsien without making the usual fuel stop. The earth banks of the river were fairly low, and there was no more diking.

The following day, at mid-afternoon, they reached the city of Chunking where the captain, pilot and one other officer left the ship to confer with authorities to determine if they could proceed, or must now transfer the cargo. They returned before dark and gave their decision to Jo, who in turn related it to Cameron and Harry.

"At the far end of the city," Jo exclaimed, "the Chia-ling Chiang leaves our river and goes northward. This in itself would not trouble us, but beyond there are two more tributaries that will lower the water level considerably. There is no way we can have precise information, for it is still over two hundred miles to Ipin. The pilot feels that we can reach the last of these feeders with no difficulty; and that by anchoring there overnight the water will rise high enough to complete the journey before the level falls again in the afternoon. They are willing to gamble on the pilots plan, but the decision for us to accompany them is yours!"

Instinctively Harry looked questioningly to Cameron, and he knew it was time for him to take over. "The captain and pilot both have a lot at stake in making their decision, and I doubt that there is any gamble to it. If we remain here, I understand it might take a week or two before we could assemble enough animals to proceed. We're going to have enough setbacks without manufacturing them, so we shall go with the ship!" His voice was firm and positive.

"The captain," Jo expounded evenly, "advised me that if this was your decision he would be fueled and ready to leave within three hours. He is anxious to be on his way, so that he might reach his anchorage before dark tomorrow night."

"Tell the captain that we are equally anxious and that no one will leave the ship to cause him a delay," Cameron replied.

As Jo scurried away on his errand, Harry watched until he disappeared. "It won't be long now, will it?" he asked, his features forming a frown.

"No, it won't," Cameron agreed sympathetically," but I believe I'm actually beginning to look forward to it."

"So am I," Harry replied, but there was the unmistakable sound of confutation in his voice.

* * * * *

Li Po was indeed an influential man at Ipin; his friends and relatives were many, and he had little adversity procuring suitable quarters within an hour after their arrival. The horses, he assured Cameron, would be forthcoming also, but would take slightly longer.

For three days Li Po and Jo scoured the environs of the city, and the near country side, before securing enough animals suited to their purpose. They obtained twenty three of the small ponies native to the area, and after seeing them, Cameron rejected one of them out of hand saying, "That pitiful thing wouldn't last the first day."

The business of Jo Lung, here in the city, was short and to the point, but not completed as he explained to Cameron and Harry. "Ipin is one of our principle suppliers of lacquer, and we are interested in larger amounts than we have been able to obtain in the past. Two of the men we must have agreement from are in Chengtu, and are not expected back for several weeks. I had not planned to go there; but it is not far out of our way, for we must travel in that general direction to pick up the Chamdo caravan route. It might even prove to be beneficial, for once there we should be able to join a larger train and gain their protection."

"I can't see that it makes any difference then," Cameron shrugged.

"The difference is that Li Po and Cricket, as you call him, will have to accompany us so that they might take the documents back with them." Jo answered.

"That should make the ladies happy," Cameron chuckled. "They've been monopolizing Cricket as an interpreter, supplier of delicacies from the galley, and personal procurer when there has been something they wanted from the Captain or his crew. Will we have enough horses?" he asked as an afterthought.

"Yes, I believe so," Jo replied smiling. "There's an excellent chance we may be able to pick up a few more before we reach Chengtu."

"That's good!" Cameron commented. "I have a psychic feeling we're going to need them," he added thinking of the animals he had seen.

The captain says that he will depart at daybreak in the morning," Jo continued. "He does not dare take on any heavy cargo until he reaches Chunking; but he has taken on some lighter goods, and wants all of the advantage he can get."

"I believe that last message was for you, Harry," Cameron said seriously, turning to face his friend. "You've done all that you agreed to do and more. I want you to know that I truly appreciate it; and

I've been grateful for having you along. It wasn't nearly as bad as you thought it would be, was it?"

"I'm not going!" Harry answered emphatically.

"What do you mean, you're not going?" Cameron asked in amazement. "You didn't want to come this far, remember? You told me coming up river that as soon as our land transportation was arranged, you would be on your way home! I don't understand, Harry, you have no responsibility in this thing now, and I thought you would be glad to be out from under it." It took Cameron several moments to realize the full impact of Harry's decision, then he proceeded softer. "Hell, Harry, this has been a picnic so far; but from here on out it's going to get rough, and I mean damn rough. You'll be putting ten to twelve hours in the saddle every day. In a few weeks you'll be freezing your tail off, and God knows what kind of trouble we're liable to run into." Cameron finished.

"Those are precisely the reasons I've decided to go on with you, Cam," Harry answered looking him straight in the eye. "I'm foolish enough to think that even though I'm out of my own class out here, I just might be able to help if given the chance."

"My God Harry!" Cameron exploded, "I didn't mean that I didn't want you any longer, and if you think you're up to it, I'll be damned glad to have you along, fact is I'd love it. Are those the only reasons you have for wanting to continue, Harry?"

"You bloody well know all of my reasons for going on with you, Cam," Harry bristled slightly, and a light blush crept up on his face. "You've been watching me for weeks like a cat with a mouse, so I'll not make a fool of myself trying to explain. You don't have any objection, then?" he finished studying Cameron's shoes.

"Lord God, no!" Cameron exclaimed, "Just the opposite. I simply never dreamed you would change your mind, but I'm damned happy that you have, and I'm sure the rest of the party will be too." With these last words Harry blushed even more, but raised his eyes and spoke in a stronger tone, "Cam, you know what I am, no Nimrod or adventurer I mean, so you're going to have to help me a lot if I'm going to make it at all. Will you do that for me, Cam?" His gaze was unflinching, and there was a note of urgency in his voice Cameron had never heard before.

"Hell, Harry," Cameron snorted, "you know I will without asking."

"It's not that I'm worried for myself, even though it sounds like it," Harry went on. "It's just that if I got my leg broke or got myself killed, I wouldn't be able to do anything for anyone else that might need me. I er, uh . . ." he began to stammer in confusion.

Quickly Cameron went to his friend's side, wrapping his arm about his shoulders in a bear hug. "I understand what you mean, Harry, and I give you my solemn word I'll watch over you like a mother hen until you get the feel of it. But, don't think for a minute that you're by yourself. We're all of us going in blind, so to speak, and all of us will need each other's help. Even Jo here has never gone beyond this city, and this is the real beginning of our expedition. Up to this point we were nothing more than a group of tourists. I don't know what we'll encounter out there anymore than you do, so I can't be any better prepared for it. But I'm quite sure whatever materializes we can handle by helping each other, and that's the only logical approach."

"Thanks, Cam," Harry responded with new composure. "If you don't mind, I'd like to go tell the others that I'm going on with them."

"Hop to it," Cameron smiled as he watched Harry leave the room. He shook his head several times in bewilderment, chuckling in delight at this sudden turn of events. "What about a guide?" he asked Jo when he sobered.

"I have a man from Loshan to serve in that capacity," Jo replied quickly. "He is old, but very capable, and brings with him two of his sons to tend the animals, baggage and any other required services."

"Is he trustworthy?" Cameron asked directly.

"According to Li Po's relatives he is a man to be relied upon, and his sons are their fathers." Jo answered.

Cameron reflected on this statement for several moments before he understood, then asked, "Can we start in the morning, then?"

"They are already arranging the pack loads for each animal, and will be ready whenever you say," Jo smiled his anticipation.

"Very well," Cameron said softly, "tell them we shall leave as soon as it is light in the morning." His eyes held fast on Jo's small face while his imagination soared out across the river to the distant hills, and then the mountains to the north.

The road north from Ipin to Loshan and on to Chengtu, for the most part, was a wide trail winding beside the Min Chiang River. There were many places where the bamboo glades were impenetrable, or the river flowed through a rocky ravine, and in these spots the road narrowed to a path barely wide enough for a cart, and the distance from the water could be miles. The rolling hills and valleys were of dull red sandy soil, rich in crop yield, worked through an intricate system of terracing and irrigation; only the sheer rock wall of the mountains and the dense bamboo forests were left.

The Min Chiang, like all rivers of China, served as the main artery of transportation, and swarmed with the usual assortment of junks and sampans. They were there with the first light of morning, and their slow moving silhouettes could be seen long after it turned dark.

During the day the temperature clung near the one-hundred mark, though they never saw the sun, and at night the heat remained as a hot clammy blanket. The afternoon rains were misty and unpredictable, giving relief from the heat only while they lasted.

For the first three days, after leaving Ipin, Cameron tried vainly to keep their small company bunched together so that he might keep his eye on all of them but finally gave it up. The differences of each animal, their loads and the terrain kept them spread out for a quarter mile most of the time; and it was seldom he could see the lead horse and the rear one at the same time. As much as he hated to, he finally placed the slowest beast at the head of the small caravan, and it was none other than the horse he had wanted to be rid of in Ipin.

From the fields several hundred pairs of eyes would glance up curiously each day, but never acknowledge their presence with a wave or smile.

Norman Clyde had spent most of his youth on a farm in Iowa. He adapted most easily to the crude saddle, and the chopping gait of his pony. "I wonder just how many centuries these people have farmed this way?" he asked of Dr. Felix riding by his side at the moment.

"I would imagine it began many centuries before the birth of Christ," Dr. Felix replied as his eyes took in the complexities of the irrigation system, and the total utilization of all but the near vertical mountainsides. "Yes, it must have been that long at least," Norman agreed in awed appreciation. "Can you possibly imagine how it looked when they first started?" he queried.

"No," Dr. Felix smiled, "but you may rely on the fact that it was a very humble beginning in the easy bottom lands. Countless generations, each adding his own small contribution of his life toil, amalgamated what exists here today. As in most other fields of endeavor, necessity is the mother of invention, and these people's needs have always been very great."

"They are fortunate that the soil is so rich, the water so abundant and the climate so mild," Norman offered. "I wonder how long the winters are here?"

"Through Jo Lung, I questioned Li Po about the country," Dr. Felix related, "and he informed me that the growing season is eleven months out of the year, and it never really freezes as we know."

"Did you also ask him why it is always clouded over?" Norman grinned.

Dr. Felix smiled knowingly and responded, "Li Po's answer to that was something to the effect that when the sun shines in

Szechwan Province, the dogs bark; which I took to mean it didn't happen very often."

Norman laughed aloud, "Li Po is certainly a graphic old gentleman, isn't he?"

You're right on both counts," Dr. Felix replied as he hunched forward in an effort to readjust his large frame to the smallness of his saddle. "The Chinese possess a picturesque and poetic manner of speech that I would dearly love to learn if we had the time."

"Yes," Norman agreed, "that would be an interesting undertaking, but far too extensive for the time we will have here, I'm sure. How long till we reach Chengtu and the caravan route?"

"I couldn't say," Dr. Felix answered, "but we're supposed to be in a place called Loshan tomorrow, and that's about half way, I'm told. Not much point in getting anxious though; we've got a great many weeks of this sort of travel ahead of us, and this stretch is supposed to be one of the best parts," he concluded as he squirmed once more for a softer seat.

"Are you terribly uncomfortable, Doctor?" Norman inquired with concern.

"Not so much so that I can't endure," Dr. Felix responded good-naturedly. "Each time I arrive at the intolerable point I focus my attention on Li Po, and remember how old and delicate he is. I look at the straight line of his back and the tilt of his chin, and I know that if he can be so regal, I must at least survive!"

At this point the trail narrowed, and there was no longer room for them to ride abreast. Norman reined his mount and fell back, putting an end to the conversation. For the next fifteen minutes or so he caught only occasional glimpses of the shaggy graying head, and the broad shoulders of the man in front of him. Eventually it came to him that though Dr. Felix and Li Po were born at the opposite sides of the earth, and they were different in almost every aspect, yet they were very much alike.

Near the noon hour of the third day past the city of Loshan, they were threading their way through the vastness of the largest bamboo glade they had yet encountered. It was impossible to see into the gloom beyond fifty feet at either side. Trunks as thick as a man's thigh rose straight up for a majestic hundred feet or more, and the space between these giants was choked with smaller plants and shoots.

They had proceeded for a full hour under these conditions when they miraculously came upon an open meadow with a sparkling ribbon of water bisecting it neatly in two.

The guide and his sons had started across with scant attention, when Cameron called a halt. "This would be an ideal place to have a lunch break, don't you think, Harry?" he asked as the latter rode up beside him.

"Excellent, excellent," Harry chirped as he took in the secluded beauty of the spot. "Not only am I famished, but my ass has blisters on its blisters, and they are begging for relief," he said, rising in the stirrups to gently massage his backsides.

"You've a lot of company, Harry," Cameron grinned as he kneed his mount closer to the tiny stream. "I've got a collection of my own, and I'm beginning to wonder if I'm ever going to callous," he added.

"I've been a mite too shy to ask Penny how they are faring in that respect," Harry blushed, "but I know they must be having a worse time of it than I am."

"If they are, they're concealing it beautifully," Cameron answered, while his eyes gently caressed Connie's trim form as she dismounted. "What do you think of those ladies trousers and shirts they picked up in Loshan?" he asked eyeing his friend guardedly.

"I don't believe you would be quite so entranced if the fit of them were a little less precise," Cameron laughed softly as he tethered his animal. "Those outfits were made for young boys, not full-blown women!

"As usual," Harry beamed, "you're probably correct, but I'm certainly thankful the girls don't realize that!"

"Oh, I think they knew what they were about alright," Cameron countered. "That's one of the few things I know about women; they are always anxious to try on some new type of clothing. When they do, they will use it to their best advantage. All women like to be looked at," Cameron asserted, "and I don't mean by other women."

"I'm in complete agreement with you, old chum," Harry sighed softly, "let's not spoil a good thing; they can wear what they want, and I'll cooperate by doing the watching. Besides, I think their choice most practical. Riding in those long skirts could get them killed in this terrain!"

"I had no intention of asking them to change back, you stiff necked Englishman," Cameron chuckled as he lowered himself to the ground, and the rest of the party came up.

"What an exquisitely beautiful place!" Connie gasped as she looked about. "Did you order this up especially for our luncheon, Commander?" she asked playfully of Cameron.

"Exclusively for our charming hostesses," Cameron returned in a similar manner, "meaning you and Penny have the honor of serving our meal." He smiled at her with warmth he couldn't hide, but she returned only a small grin.

"It's just like something out of a fairy tale," Penny said as she helped Connie with the two canvas bags. "I wish we could camp here tonight, it's so enchanting."

"I know what you mean," Cameron smiled, "but that would mean we'd lose half a day, and we can't afford that!"

Penny bit her lip in a gesture of disappointment, giving him the benefit of a radiant smile, "It was only wistful girlish fantasy. I know we can't delay even an hour unless it's critical, but I can still pretend, can't I?"

"Of course you can," Harry assured with open affection.

"I'm certainly thankful we were able to upgrade and enlarge our horse herd," Cameron said to no one in particular, as his eyes once more surveyed their mounts.

"You've paid a damned dear price for them, I'd say," Roger spoke for the first time. "You also use the term horse rather loosely in referring to them;" he nodded his head. "I should think they were more closely related to the burro family." It was hard to tell if his tone was his usual aloofness of veiled sarcasm. He looked directly at Cameron as he nibbled on a rice cake with obvious disdain.

Cameron was momentarily startled by his statement; his mouth was full of food, and he chewed vigorously to clear it before giving an answer. He felt as though Roger had slapped him.

Before he was able to speak, Connie broke in, "I'm afraid we're one hell of a long way from the polo fields, Roger, and I believe we have about the best there is to be had," her tone was soft and accompanied by a definite sparkle in her eyes.

"I didn't mean it that way, Connie," Roger blurted, himself now taken back. "I guess it was just some wishful thinking on my part, like Penny, you know?" he finished lamely.

Cameron watched in a mild state of awe and turned to Connie. He was sure she would have something more to say, but it never came.

Penny had finished her meal, and had risen to ease her sore spots. She scanned the perimeter of the clearing trying to avoid the thought of the unpleasantness that would soon be here, then suddenly she forgot about it completely. "What on earth is that?" she shrilled, pointing her finger to the lower far side of the meadow.

Her voice was so shattering that everyone rose, and looked to see what she was pointing at. They beheld what they thought to be an oddly colored black and white bear and her cub. The mother was oblivious in her feeding on tender bamboo shoots, while the curious cub stalked cautiously toward them a dozen yards or so, then dashed back and concealed himself behind his mother's bulk.

"That," laughed Jo Lung, "is the Beishung, or as some say, the white bear. They are not truly bears, however, but members of the raccoon family."

"Are they dangerous?" Penny asked, her voice still quavering. "Only if threatened directly, or handled foolishly," Jo assured her and the rest of them. "In captivity they are quite playful, and display the comic side of the animal world. Except for their huge appetites, they make excellent pets."

"I'd just love to have that little cuddly thing for my own!" Penny exclaimed. "It looks so soft, and fluffy, and cute with those two black eyes and ears. And those black leg stockings, it's adorable!"

"If you must have him," Jo teased, "then it would be better if you would stay here with him, for it will be a full-time job to gather feed to keep him alive."

"No," Penny replied, "I have better things to do. We'll just leave him here with his mamma. They sure don't pay much attention to us, do they?"

"Nor we to them" Jo answered pointing to a tall tree not fifty yards behind them. There another large panda was rolled into a ball, sound asleep in the fork some twenty feet above their heads.

"Well I'll be darned," Harry exclaimed, "and we didn't even see him until now!"

They watched the different pandas for several moments in silence which Cameron finally interrupted, "I think we'd best pack up and be on our way." He looked directly at Roger anticipating some sign of remaining hostility, but found only the same old indifference. He then looked to Connie, but her back was to him and he could not see her face. He could remember the sparkle that had come to life in her eyes, though, and the strange feeling it had kindled back in San Francisco. That same sensation now swirled inside him, and he knew there was nothing he could to about it.

He swung up and into the saddle hard, forgetting the tender blisters he was nursing. A sharp burning sting and the sticky feel of the saddle told him he had burst most of them. He headed back out onto the road without a word, nor turn of his head.

In another three days or so we should reach the city of Chengtu, he thought to himself, *and Jo Lung will be able to complete his business. Then we can say that we are really on our way, with no side trips, and I can look forward to the end of this job, and all of the foolishness that has accompanied it.* He shook his head in self-disgust, and seconds later found he was looking back over his shoulder to see if Connie was in sight.

*   *   *   *   *

They emerged upon the Chengtu plain early in the morning. The road widened and they made much better time, but the evening stars were in the sky before they arrived at the ancient city of Chengtu itself.

They pitched their tents and lighted fires in the huge section near the outer wall reserved for the caravans, and were delighted to find they were not alone in their journeys.

After they had eaten a late evening meal and all the tasks were done, the entire group gathered round one large fire to listen as Li Po told them about this famous city, and the fertile plain around it. Li would speak in his rich musical tones for several minutes without interruption. When he fell silent, Jo Lung would make the translation into English, telling it in the first person as though he himself were Li Po.

"I came here first with my parents when I was a boy of six or less, and though that has been some time ago, it's only as one short breath to the age of this city. The canals and irrigation systems for the plain, and areas beyond, were accomplished by the great Li Ping fifteen-hundred years before the Mongol barbarians overran our land, and the city was here even before that time. Seventeen-hundred years ago it was the capital of the Kingdom of Shu, and has since been the home of many Emperors, and the refuge of still others. It has also been the home of some of our most illustrious heroes, poets and historians. The finest silver thread work in the world is made here. The famous embroidery work of Shu Chin originated here, along with the purest of silks and the best grade of cotton. The renowned prostitute, Hsueh Tao, took her own life here, and a large tower was erected in her memory. The tomb of the General Liu Shiang is not far distant."

"The city is actually three cities, one within the other, surrounded by their own walls. The Imperial City is the center, then the New City and finally the Outer City. Nearly three hundred years ago more than half of the population of the metropolis, and the crowded plain surrounding it, were massacred during a rebellion. There are some today that believe it was this terrible atrocity that turned the soil red for all the land around it. That is not so, for the color of the earth was explained a thousand years before that happened."

"One hundred years after the massacre, all of the vacant land had been settled by immigrants from the south. That is why one hears Cantonese spoken even today in this remote northern country." "The trade tentacles of this city reach out in all directions for two thousand miles and more. Her works of art and hand crafts can even be found in the distant lands across the seas and her many temples are in themselves a work of skilled genius."

It was plain to all those listening that this was the city Li Po loved the most and with good reason. He had spent a good part of his youth here, married and buried his wife within its walls. He went on to describe the gardens, streets and tea houses in detail, and the evening was well spent when his praise ran out.

"I believe I'd best be getting some sleep," Cameron said softly after Li Po failed to continue with Jo's silence. "There's a lot to be done in the morning, and I'd like to get an early start."

"What you say is true," Jo acknowledged. "It has been a most pleasant and enlightening evening," he went on, bowing to Li Po, "but we must all rest."

Still seated, the old man nodded silently to each of them as they departed to their tents, a warm smile framed his mouth; his face was ecstatic, with a tiny sparkling tear hugging the corner of each eye.

Cameron's tent had been designed for one primary purpose, to allow him to sleep protected from the elements regardless of what they might be. It embraced the ground closely with barely enough room to sit up and raise him arms, if he were directly in the center. The material was of lightweight water repellent canvas; the top of it was also the sides, and though it could be opened from either end, it featured a tight overlap closure that secured him from any type of weather. It also boasted a floor which kept any dampness from creeping into the double down comforter that he used mostly as a mattress. There was enough room at each end of his bed to store all of his gear, with space left over.

Normally, when he retired, he would drop off to sleep instantly; but this night he lay awake for more than a full hour listening to the stomp of the horses in the rope corral, the muffled voices coming from the other tents, the grunting of the camels of the other two caravans, and the distant sounds of people from within the city.

It vexed him that he could not sleep. He pretended that it was the excitement of their locations, the expectations of the next several weeks, and the mysterious mountain they had traveled so far to find. He tried to visualize the caravan route that they would follow westward to Lhasa, and the Forbidden City itself; but his thoughts would invariably drift back to Connie, and the first time he had witnessed the fire flashing in her eyes. Throughout the ocean voyage, and the trip up river, he had been able to control his mind concerning her; but now in her tight fitting peasant costumes he was reminded of his inner feelings a hundred times a day, and he began to regret changing his mind. He didn't like his personal life being complicated; and he wished that he were back in San Francisco, or even Mexico, doing the work that he knew and loved without the emotional conflict that he experienced during his brief marriage, and he now felt throbbing in his vitals.

"Damn it all, anyway!" he breathed, "I've been a stupid impulsive idiot again, and there is no way to back out."

The simple admission of the fact seemed to have eased his mind, if not his conscience, for not long afterward he floundered into troubled sleep. The nights were slightly cooler here, but the damp stickiness of the day remained.

Two days passed and both of the other caravans had left, one due north to Lanchow and on through the Gobi, the other northeast to Peiping. Except for their own small unit the great caravan square was deserted.

As was his custom, Cameron had pitched his tent slightly apart from all of the others. He didn't like to admit it, but he enjoyed a certain amount of solitude, especially at night. To him, being by himself offered nearly as much rest as sleep. He liked company also, but at the proper place and time of his choosing.

He and Harry had wandered the narrow picturesque streets of Chengtu all of the first day until their feet gave out. They saw the colorful gardens, the Taoist and Buddhist temples, and many of the other wonders of which Li Po spoke. One day, however, was as long as he could keep Harry from Penny's side, and he spent the second day with Dr. Felix and Norman.

The sun was setting when Jo Lung approached him as he sat alone before his tent. Jo's face was warm and radiant, but Cameron knew by now that this did not reflect the young man's inner thoughts. "What news do you bring, friend Jo?" Cameron asked hopefully. His inactivity was gnawing at his nerves.

"Some good and some bad, as the saying goes," Jo replied with amity. The first good news is that my business here has been terminated. Li Po and Chu Chuer will be able to undertake the return trip to Shanghai tomorrow."

"How do they plan to make the trip?" Cameron asked with interest.

"They have the same alternative as we coming here," Jo reminded. "They can take a junk down the Min Chiang to the Yangtze, and thence to Chunking where they will have no difficulty obtaining passage on one of the larger river boats. Or, they could take the southeast caravan route overland direct to Chunking."

"Which way do you think is the wisest?" Cameron inquired once more.

"There is a certain amount of danger either way," Jo responded, "but I believe their best chance to be the overland route. As the water lowers in the rivers, the pirates become more daring, and it is said that during these times some of the timid fishermen change professions to one of greater rewards. There are always bandits along the trails, but their numbers do not vary during the year," Jo said while squatted on his heels in the dirt by Cameron's side.

"Very well," Cameron said. "We shall give them a horse a piece and one to carry their belongings. Naturally they will have to take the poorest of the lot, but that's not too bad in our present circumstances. Do they have any other needs?" Cameron asked.

"None whatsoever," Jo announced exceedingly pleased with himself. "What will you have them do with the animals when they reach Chunking?" Jo queried as he regained his composure.

"Sell all three of them to the highest bidder," Cameron said after several moments of serious deliberation. He allowed several seconds of silence to follow, then added, "Divide the dividends into two equal parts, and put it in their pockets," he finished with a wide grin. When Jo Lung came to talk with Cameron it was with the hope that he could convince the latter of the necessity of the overland trip. Not that he greatly feared the river pirates, but instead, he knew this would be Li Po's final trip to his native land that he cherished so dearly. To send him away on a junk would be like leading him away with a blindfold over his eyes. Jo knew how valuable the horses were, and he had presumed Cameron would want them sold and the monies credited to Harry's account with the Te Chien. His wildest dreams for Li Po's happiness never encompassed this.

Jo's eyes grew wide, his mouth dropped open and his hands flew high in the air as he left the ground in one bounding leap. When he lit, he began clapping his hands together, and loosed a bellowing squeal that stung Cameron's ear drums. Then he stopped abruptly, and tears of joy streamed down the young man's cheeks. What can I say?" he asked. "My happiness for Li Po is so great that words are beyond me."

"Don't even try, friend Jo," Cameron gently soothed." "We are in their debt for all they have done for us. Besides," Cameron added, cocking his head with a wink and a smile, "the animals I shall select would not make it from here to Chamdo anyway. They will be three of the same Li Po purchased for us in Ipin, so I feel he deserves to be stuck with them. Now, what other good news do you have for me?"

Jo returned to his squatting position as he gently, and self-consciously, wiped his cheeks with the back of his hand. His dark eyes reflected a new kind of admiration. "It is only rumor, and a stale one at that," he began, "but it is said that General Cheng Wu and his army are operating far to the north of the city in the vicinity of Sining. If this is true he will pose us no problems."

"Yes," Cameron answered hesitantly, "if it is true, but there is no way we can be sure. Nothing we can do about it anyway, so, what's the bad news?"

"Two items," Jo replied with seriousness. "There will not be a caravan in from any direction for at least three days. News travels ahead of them that fast. It could be we must wait ten days or more to join a train going in the direction we desire. Also, I have not been able to find a reliable guide and two young tenders; but no guide that will venture westward more than three days. What shall we do?"

Cameron's thoughts began racing to meet the problem at hand; he sat in complete silence, weighing the probabilities, one against the other. "What of the two tenders?" he asked finally. "Are they young, strong and trustworthy? Is it possible that when a three-day guide turned back, we might find another at that point who would take us three days beyond there, and so on until we reach Chamdo?" Cameron's eyes were searching, his expression hopeful.

"The tenders are merely overgrown boys, strong and willing, and I believe too young to be corrupted," Jo answered. "As for the three day guide, I begin to see what you mean. Most men know the area within three days of their home, and will not hesitate up to that point, but refuse to go an inch beyond. Yes! I do believe we can work it that way. Would you like to start tomorrow?"

"It would be my greatest pleasure!" Cameron snorted.

"We'll need some fresh supplies, meat, vegetables and the like. It's too late to start rounding up that stuff tonight. We'll do that after we see Li Po and Cricket off in the morning. Is that agreeable?"

"To be sure," Jo smiled. "Also we should pick up extra warm clothing and blankets for everyone. They will be plentiful and cheap here at this time of year, but these conditions will change drastically as we progress."

"Good thinking!" Cameron stated as he gently slapped Jo on his scrawny shoulders, and rose. "I'll go tell Dr. Felix and anyone else that's in camp. Harry and the ladies are probably still within the city." He moved briskly as he strode to the Doctor's tent; there was purpose and meaning to his gait, and he was glad that he was able to do something positive at last.

That night when he retired, he fixed his vacant stare where he thought the "V" of the canvas should be in the blackness directly above his head. He would lay that way for a while and contemplate a few other maneuvers that might help in the days ahead. Within five minutes he was sound asleep, and did not waken until the morning sky had turned pale. The first day out they could have done without a guide, for they merely retraced their steps of the trip in for most of the day. By late afternoon, however, they left the trail and later took a crude ferry across the Min Chiang River.

Their guide seemed anxious to earn his pay, and he kept them moving long after the sun had set. The tenders erected camp by the light of camel dung fires on which the cooking was also done. When the meal was finished everyone went to bed with a minimum amount of conversation. The day had been a long, hot and tiring one.

They were off to an early start again the following morning, and within four hours the plain of Chengtu was behind and below them. The familiar rolling hills and low mountains with the bamboo glades and a few conifers were much like the ones they had encountered a few days earlier.

On the evening of the third day their guide came for his pay, and he disappeared before daylight of the following morning. They were about halfway to the city of Yaan and there was no chance of finding a replacement, so they went on without one. The trail was broad, for the most part, and always well-defined with an abundant supply of camel dung. The two young tenders had declared themselves to Chamdo, and it looked as though they meant it.

At Yaan they resupplied themselves on victuals and after some delay, retained an old man that said he would show them the way to the small city of K'angting, three or four days ahead.

The changes of the countryside were so gradual they hardly noticed them at first. The large forests of bamboo got farther apart and smaller in size. Eventually there were no more of the Pandas to be seen, and the steep slopes of the mountains were covered mostly with birch and conifers. The mountains themselves become more frequent and appeared a little bit taller.

There were many other changes too. Though the days remained hot, the nights cooled off to allow comfortable sleep. Different types of flowers and grasses were observed, and now and then, a dark robed pilgrim of Buddha would be seen standing or sitting beside the road spinning his prayer wheel. High up on the taller peaks they could see glistening banks of snow and ice that lay in the shady crevices.

The heavy cloud cover and misty fog banks melted away as the days past. The dogs of Szechwan would have set up a terrible din had any of them been present in this remote corner of the province.

They forded innumerable small creeks and large streams, some that would be classed as rivers elsewhere. They crossed from one mountain valley unto the next by slow easy gaps and passes, but these too were becoming steeper and longer with the passing of each day.

They discovered that K'angting was really a large town and not a city at all. Also, that one more day to the west was another river they must cross by ferry, its name the Yalung Chiang.

They were told that from this town to Batang it would be a full ten days march, and that they should prepare themselves for much more difficult terrain.

"From what Jo has learned from the local inhabitants this afternoon, I think it might be wise to rest here for one day before going on to Batang," Cameron addressed the group in masse as they finished their evening meal. "I don't like the idea of losing a full day, but I think we will be better for it in the long run. The animals are losing strength, we are getting tired, and the altitude is increasing with every mile we gain. A day of inactivity would allow us to acclimate and freshen up. We also need a new guide from here on, and this will give Jo a chance to find someone. Does anyone have any objections?" Cameron looked first to Connie, then to Dr. Felix and on to the others.

When only Connie nodded her head in agreement, Penny grabbed her golden opportunity. "I think it's a fabulous idea! I need a bath, a real bath I mean. I'm so sticky I can hardly get down from my horse." Her eyes glowed and the tinkle of her voice detracted from the sincerity of her thoughts. A round of laughter was her response. "It's not funny," she stiffened as much as she was capable of. "I used to think a person would die if they went this long without bathing." No one laughed in reply, but several smiled their understanding.

"We all realize the inadequacies of our circumstances as far as you ladies are concerned," Cameron said to her, but meant it for Connie's benefit. "If there is anything we can do in addition to screening off a toilet for you each evening, I'm sure every man here will cooperate. It's been very difficult for you, we all know that, and applaud you for your courage and tenacity. But, we would like to make it easier if there is any way that does not consume too much time." He wanted to say more about how he admired them for the way they had responded without complaint, but felt the subject too delicate.

"We shall manage just the way things have been," Connie stated sweetly while looking him straight in the eye. "As Penny says, a good warm bath and one day of rest will be welcome, but I don't think we should have any further delays."

"Good," Cameron replied. "There shouldn't be any problem getting enough hot water for bathing for all of us that want it. We can erect a special tent. You ladies will use it first, naturally!"

"It would be greatly appreciated," Connie assured him with sincerity and a warm smile.

"Now, anyone else have any special needs at this time?" Cameron looked first to Roger who shook his head in the negative.

"I desperately need some type of cylindrical container for my charts and drawings," Norman offered hesitantly. "I don't know exactly what it would be in this neck of the woods, but it must be waterproof. That's the one thing I forgot before we left Shanghai; and I meant to do something about it in Chengtu, but again my memory failed me," he finished lamely shaking his head.

"I'm sure we can take care of everything in some fashion," Jo replied to Cameron's questioning glance.

"The first thing we'll need is some large pots to heat the water in, and something in the way of a tub. Bring the two tenders, and we'll go into town and see what we can scrounge," Cameron suggested.

"Harry, maybe you'd best come along too. The rest of you folks would do well to sort through your belongings, and discard anything you don't actually need. We won't have any use for light clothing in the future, so we'd better dump it now. Before we leave here tomorrow a committee will be formed to go through everything, including my gear. Anything that isn't absolutely essential will be disposed of. Save yourselves the embarrassment of argument, and get rid of it today!" he finished with authority.

By late afternoon the bathing had been completed, and the bath tent struck. Fresh provender had been added to their dwindling supplies, and the animals were given all the grain they could eat.

Cameron was last to utilize the tent, and was standing by his sleeping quarters drying his hair when Jo returned from town for the fourth time since dawn.

"I have found a guide that claims he can take us all the way to Lhari if we so desire, but I'm not sure you'll approve of him," Joe stated minus his usual exuberance.

"Where the hell is Lhari?" Cameron asked ignorantly, lowering his towel.

"About one-hundred-fifty miles this side of Lhasa on the caravan trail," Jo responded.

"I thought we only required a guide as far as Chamdo. What makes you think I won't approve of him?" Cameron asked squinting his eyes. "Any guide at all should be better than none in this country, right?"

"I'm not sure," Joe answered looking away. "This man is Tibetan, a seller of hides supposedly. Little is known of him in town except that he has been here for a week waiting for someone to travel with. There is something in the man's appearance that I do not trust, and no one else here seems to either. We do need a guide only as far as Chamdo, providing Maleek is there; but we do not know this to be a fact."

"That's true enough," Cameron concurred. "What did he say when you talked with him?" Cameron asked, his curiosity aroused.

"The man isn't strong on conversation. Perhaps this and the fact that he is a Tibetan have contributed to my feelings," Jo replied. "He claims to be returning from Chengtu where he had accompanied a shipment of hides his own people had consigned to him, so they might get a better price. The hides were sent as part of a larger caravan two months ago, and he went along as supercargo. He has come this far much the same as we have, but fears to go further on his own because of the gold he carries. He didn't say gold, but implied he had the returns from his consignment. He would be justified in his fears for we are in the border area, and there are renegades, from both sides, that have no compunction about whose throat they cut, if there is booty to be earned.

"That sounds reasonable enough to me," Cameron intoned. "Is there any chance you might be just a little bit prejudiced against Tibetans, Jo?" Cameron asked smiling.

"I asked myself the same question," Jo admitted, "and did not arrive at a conclusive answer. A point in this man's favor is that he does not seem overly anxious to join us. He says that he would prefer to wait for a larger party that could afford more protection."

"That in itself would seem to substantiate the fact that he is what he says, and is concerned for his own wellbeing," Cameron observed.

"Perhaps," Joe mused, "then again, if he is a decoy he may think we are too small to possess anything of value beyond a few trinkets. If he should be one of a large group, he must be sure the trap is not wasted on mice when fat sheep may follow."

"I see what you mean," Cameron replied. "Is there any way we could be more sure about him? Do you think it might help if I went to see him?"

"There is no way that I can think of," Jo answered. "You may go see him if you believe it will do any good. He, and two horses of good lines, is camped by a creek the other side of town. I doubt that you could learn anymore of him by your presence. I have told you all he said, but not what I observed. He is a small man in his mid-thirties, and wears the garb of a mountain herdsman. He seems of average intelligence for his station and a devout Buddhist. The latter I could tell by his charms and prayer wheel. His clothes and equipment are of good quality, though showing signs of wear. He could be genuine; I know of nothing to say otherwise. Only there is this feeling I have, and I'm sure you will agree there is something wrong about him, or else he is so nervous for his safety that it exudes from his pores." "That could be it," Cameron accorded. "But, let us suppose for a moment that he is not what he claims to be. When we leave, he could readily get word to any allies he might have and his position here would remain secure for any caravan following us. Might it not be wiser to test him and see if he will join us; then if he does we can keep an eye on him?"

"It could be inviting disaster to ride with us; but at least we would know by his actions when to expect it, if he were with us," Jo contemplated aloud. "Yes, I agree, that is the safest way."

"Very well," Cameron said. "We'll not approach him until morning, and then one of us will keep an eye on him until the time we leave. What he does then should tell us something. What about the old man that brought us here? He's never come by to pick up his pay!"

"He did not wish to trouble you when we arrived. He understood you would have many things needing your attention. He will stop by after the evening meal. He has two nephews that live here, and he is visiting them. He told me he would remain with them until the next caravan goes east," Jo explained.

"That was very considerate of the old gentleman." Cameron said honestly.

"It is the way of his generation," Joe said simply.

"Not in all parts of this world, I'm afraid," Cameron objected.

"I am glad that it happens where and when it happens," Jo stated.

For a moment Cameron looked at him obliquely, then, "So am I," he admitted.

*   *   *   *   *

There was no moon, and their encampment at the outskirts of K'angting lay engulfed in cool darkness. From one of the small straight sided tents the tantalizing scent of lilacs filtered through the door flap, even though it was securely fastened. Inside the blackness was dense, and the aroma much stronger. Penny lay on her stomach, her head resting on her crossed arms. "I never dreamed the simple pleasures of living could seem so dear," she breathed softly.

"Yes," Connie answered wistfully, "a good hot bath, clean clothes, and a little perfume and powder do a lot for a girl's spirit when she's been denied them for any length of time. When I was younger, and accompanied my father, I tried being like him, and did without all feminine needs, but I soon gave it up. I found out quick that I was a woman, and I liked being one."

"So do I," Penny giggled. "I wouldn't want to be a man for anything in the world."

"Oh," Connie speculated, "there are lots of things that men do that I would like to do also, but not if I have to stop being a woman! A lot of girls I've known actually resented the fact they were not born boys, but not me. They were so silly, wasting their time wishing they were something they were not, that they didn't have time to appreciate and enjoy what they really were. That doesn't make much sense, does it?"

"No, but then there are a lot of people that don't make any sense either," Penny replied as though in deep thought.

"Are you thinking about other people or one in particular?" Connie inquired, the gloom concealing her smile.

Penny didn't reply immediately, blurting out, "It's Harry I'm referring to and you know it. He makes me so angry! He's a man of the world, in a manner of speaking; he has to be very bright and competent to run the business he owns, and I'm reasonably sure he's had some lady friends in his life. I'm certain that he thinks a good deal of me, but do you think I can get him to tell me so? Not on your tin-type he won't"

"I believe he told you quite a bit when he changed his mind at Ipin and came on with us," Connie stated, not waiting to be asked. "He didn't want to come on this trip at all, remember? Then, under duress he agreed to come only so far, but gave that up because he felt so strongly about you. I would say that's quite a declaration myself!"

"He hasn't told me those were his reasons," Penny pouted, hoping to hear more.

"Maybe he doesn't know the right words to tell you," Connie intoned with slight impatience. "Maybe he's never been around a girl like you before, or never met one that affected him as deeply as you do. You also have to remember that he's an Englishman. They are a strange breed when it comes to reserve, especially where romance is concerned. Now Latinos, they are altogether different!"

"I don't want to hear about Latinos," Penny interrupted. Besides, you don't know any more about Latinos than I do," she laughed.

"I'm just telling you what I've read, silly," Connie chuckled. "I haven't had any personal experience."

Neither have most of those writers that pretend they know so much," Penny continued. "They just imagine most of those things, put them down on paper, and everyone takes it for the gospel truth. I hope you're right about Harry though, Connie; because if it should turn out in the end that he doesn't really care about me, I think I'll just die!"

"You won't die, dear, because he does love you," Connie assured. "I can see it in his face, hear it in his voice, and it shows in his every action. Whenever he thinks you might need him he's always there, and would be at your side constantly if it weren't conspicuous."

"How come I can't see all those things?" Penny asked thoughtfully.

"Because you're so blinded by your own feeling for him you can't see anything else." Connie stated flatly.

"I guess that's true," Penny agreed dreamily. "Whenever he's near me I get all slushy and warm inside; and I'd like to do things for him the way he does for me, but most of all I'd like to take him in my arms and squeeze and kiss him."

"Why don't you?" Connie asked smiling again.

"Don't be crude!" Penny snapped indignantly. "I don't want him to get the impression that I'm a wanton and a harlot!"

"Don't worry your pretty head about that," Connie intoned. "Nothing you could do would change his mind about you now, he's too far gone!" she finished confidently.

"Oh, I hope you're right, Connie. It's such a wonderful feeling I don't want to lose it." Penny sighed. She turned over on her back and stretched languidly, intoxicated by the heady thoughts spinning in her brain. This lasted only for a short while, however; the silent darkness chilled her happiness with a pointing finger of guilt, for Penny must share everything to be truly content. "Do you think you and Roger will be married when we return from this trip?" She asked timidly, breaking the stillness.

It was Connie's turn to be reticent now. It took her so long to answer Penny thought she might be asleep. "I don't know what to think anymore, Penny dear," Connie confided.

"From the time we were children Roger was always distant and hard to communicate with; but now he's retracted into a shell where I can't reach him at all. He's an entirely different person than he was a few months ago, and the worst of it is I don't know what caused it, nor when it started. There never was any declaration of love between Roger and I, it was more of an understanding. We just took each other for granted, and everyone else took us the same way. I've had several beaus besides Roger over the years, but nothing that lasted and I always came back. But, I've never felt about any man the way you feel about Harry Clayborne. I'm deeply troubled, Penny! Had Roger wanted to marry six months ago I would have agreed instantly. But now I'm not so sure, and I just don't know what to think." The tone of indecision was evident in her voice, and it was a side of her Penny had never seen.

"Oh, honey, I'm so sorry," Penny soothed. "Why didn't you tell me before? What can I do to help, or make you feel better?"

"I don't believe there's anything anyone can do, Penny," Connie replied with gratitude, "but thanks for asking. I did want to talk to you about it before, but it never seemed like the right moment. It's one of those things that only time will provide the answer to. Right now I know we'd best get to sleep? We're supposed to be having breakfast before daylight in the morning, and that's not many hours away. Goodnight, dear, and thanks again for trying to comfort me." Goodnight, Connie," Penny replied, rolled over on her side and drifted instantly into sleep.

It was not so simple for Constance. She lay there wide-eyed for a long time trying to decide if it was really Roger that was causing her to feel so uneasy, so apprehensive. *Perhaps the altitude has something to do with it*, she thought, *we are pretty high up*. The idea did not give her the comfort she thought it would, and it was another hour before she joined Penny in slumber.

*   *   *   *   *

Norman Clyde munched silently on his breakfast of cold sliced mutton, hard biscuits and two large fresh pears. These items he had hurriedly gathered when he was awakened in the darkness, and informed he was to accompany Cameron and Jo Lung to visit a possible guide. He was both surprised and shocked to learn his role in this mission would be as a spy; but after a hasty explanation he accepted it with the enthusiasm of a novice.

He sat well concealed in a clump of trees near the creek, and slightly above the camp of the Tibetan. His vantage point afforded him a clear view, but he was out of earshot. He watched closely as Cameron and Jo drew near the small circular tent below. It seemed only seconds before a small man dressed entirely in black emerged wearing high loose boots, a tunic that came far down over his trousers and a long coat of heavy felt. Atop his head perched a tall tapering conical hat that had flaps for covering his ears. Norman listened closely, trying to catch a word or two, but it proved impossible. There was much gesturing of the hands by all concerned, and several times the Tibetan pointed both westward and straight up. The man in black reentered his tent momentarily, reappearing with two steaming leather mugs which he offered his guests. The three of them then sat, and the conversation continued.

After ten minutes, or more, they reached some kind of agreement Norman observed. The empty mugs were returned, and there was a good deal of bowing. Cameron and Jo retired to their own camp without glancing in his direction.

Norman waited patiently after the Tibetan reentered his tent for the second time and did not emerge. At the end of twenty minutes he was almost sure the man had gone back to sleep, and wondered what he should do now. Cameron hadn't made any provision for this eventuality. The thought vanished as his quarry appeared, then rapidly began to strike his camp and load his animals. "All I can do now is wait and watch until he leaves with or without our group," Norman said aloud softly.

Norman's wait was not nearly so long as he thought it might be. Cameron had apparently had the rest of their people doing things also; for an hour had barely passed when their small retinue passed by, and the seller of hides fell into the lead.

Dr. Felix brought up the rear of the procession, leading Norman's mount. The good Doctor had been well briefed, for he lagged a good hundred yards behind the two camp tenders. When Norman ran to his horse from his concealment, the Tibetan was already out of sight.

Dr. Felix handed him the reins with a curious nod of his head and his usual smile. "Have you had something to eat, Norman?" he asked with concern.

"Yes, thanks, I had a filling breakfast," Norman replied. It seemed strange to Norman that the Doctor showed no more interest in his activity than to inquire about his morning meal, but he left it at that.

An hour later Cameron managed to drop back along the train until he rode at Norman's side.

"Did he do anything at all that seemed suspicious to you after we had left?" Cameron asked softly.

"Nothing," Norman answered in disgust, "nothing at all. He went back into that round thing immediately, and didn't come out for quite a spell. I guess he was having something to eat. When he did come out he started packing and loading, and was ready to go more than half an hour before you returned. When he was finished he sat down with is prayer wheel. The only things he did were to spin the wheel and watch the sun rise until you arrived. He never looked to the trail or the mountains during all that time. Is that good or bad?" Norman asked curiously.

"I don't know, Norman," Cameron replied, "We'll just have to wait and see. Keep a sharp eye on him whenever he's in sight; and also keep watch for anything else you might see, anything at all!"

"Sure will," Norman agreed. "Do you want me to stay here at the rear or somewhere else?"

"I believe this would be the best spot for both you and Dr. Felix." Cameron answered. "Would you tell the Doctor about watching too? I've got to get back up front with Harry."

"I'll take care of it," Norman assured with renewed interest, now that he was taking a part again. He watched Cameron make his way toward the head of the column, moving up beside the doctor to relay the message.

Dr. Felix listened attentively, and without any show of emotion replied, "I understand, I'll let you know if I see anything unusual."

Norman waited for him to continue the conversation and when he did not, he himself fell back in line, for the trail was narrow and rocky at this spot.

As the day wore on, Norman noted the severity of the surrounding mountains on his scratch pad. He would transfer it all to proper sketches and charts that evening when everything else was done. He marveled at how rapidly the country had changed in the last few days. In the passes they crossed they were above timber line, and it was not unusual to see clouds lying below them in the wide and fertile valleys. Though the remaining banks of ice and snow were still above them, the icy chill was carried on the perpetual light wind.

At ten the next morning they crossed the river on a tiny ferry that had all the earmarks of calamity in waiting. It took four trips to transport the entire party; and Norman held his breath several times before he was safely landed on the far side.

From their contiguity to the timber line, he noted in his memory that they were constantly gaining altitude from one valley to the next, and the trees that remained were becoming much smaller. The emerald luster of the bottom lands faded perceptively. They passed through a handful of small hamlets that had no names, as far as Norman could find out, but he marked them on his charts all the same. More and more he noticed that the attire of these villagers resembled that of their guide; on the sixth day, he sighted a large lowland lake some twenty miles to the north of the trail.

The following morning, much to everyone's dismay and apprehension, they discovered their guide had disappeared sometime during the night. He neither collected his pay nor had he taken anything with him that he did not own.

"Now what the hell do you suppose this means?" Cameron exploded when Harry informed him of the absence of the guide.

"I don't have the foggiest notion," Harry admitted, "but I can't say that I like it, whatever his reasons. I didn't tell anyone else. Thought you'd like to know first!"

"That's good, Harry," Cameron applauded. "I'll go around and tell them individually, that way we might avoid a panic. I just can't imagine why he would lead us this far and then sneak off. If he were setting us up he could have done us considerable harm by sabotage. Why don't you start checking our supplies and gear while I tell the others? And, Harry, be nonchalant about it, huh? Oh, yes, put your side arm on!"

"Right-O," Harry quipped as Cameron spun on his heels. *I don't like any of this,* Harry muttered to himself, *and most of all I don't like wearing that bloody pistol. Hope I don't have to use it for anything,* he prayed as he made his way to the supply pile and pulled back the tarp covering.

He found Cameron with Dr. Felix, Norman and Jo standing near the cook fire. "Nothing has been tampered with that I can see," Harry announced as he came up to them.

"Thank God for that, anyway," Cameron breathed a sigh of relief. "What do you make of it now, Jo? He asked.

"I wish I knew," Jo responded. "It is difficult to imagine his line of thought when we knew so little of him. He could have merely gotten tired of our company, remember, we are all foreigners to him. The only thing I am sure of is that the man was frightened of something from the very start. I have no idea of whether this was a personal thing with him, or something that could affect all of us. What do we do now?" Jo addressed himself to Cameron.

"Have something to eat and get moving as fast as possible!" Cameron replied positively and without hesitation. "Does anyone have a hand gun besides Harry and me?" he asked. When he received no affirmative reply, he swore, "Damn it! I wonder if Roger has one.

Would you ask him, Doctor, and tell him to put it on if he does? He isn't too well disposed toward me, you know, and might take this kind of order the wrong way."

"Certainly, I'd be glad to," Dr. Felix obliged.

"Do you think maybe we ought to break out some of the rifles?" Harry asked with a shudder.

After several seconds thought, Cameron replied, "Yes, let's clean up and assemble about eight of them. Make them ready for service, and then put them back in the crate so they can be brought out quickly. Also, some ammunition, but let's do this in one of the tents in case we're being watched. Take your time. Act like we had decided to have a leisurely breakfast; I'll tell Connie and Penny to slow down on the cooking, and we'll do just that. I'll be in to help you with the rifles in a couple of minutes."

When they departed their bivouac area nearly two hours later, Cameron cautioned each of them to act casual; talk, laugh and grumble, just like they had on preceding days. He also asked them to be especially alert to anything that varied from the normal of the past week.

The day passed without incident, much the same as any other day had transpired. The road narrowed sometimes to no more than four-foot wide in the mountains, and spread out to fifty, and even one hundred yards, in the valleys. Each of them strained their vision to see what lay behind each bush, tree and rock; and the effort proved to be wasted. The total absence of apparent danger, however, did not allay their fears and tension.

"It is strange," Connie stated to Roger riding by her side "how difficult it is to act natural when you are told to do so. If you stop to think about it you find you really don't know how you act most of the time. Everything comes spontaneously; you don't even think about it, much less recall precisely how it was. Silly, isn't it?"

*   *   *   *   *

Throughout the day Roger sat bolt upright in the saddle, his back and neck rigid; his eyes darted from one shadow to the next, and small beads of sweat formed about his mouth. "Who cares whether it's silly or not? Just do as you're told and shut up about it!" He snapped nervously. He slapped the trailing ends of the reins back along the horses flank, and the startled animal nearly jumped out from under him. When a good three lengths separated him from Connie he leveled off. Roger didn't want to talk himself, much less have to listen.

In their haste to make up for the time lost that morning they marched for two hours past the usual halt. It was full dark by the time the cook fires were lighted, and they began to erect the tents for the night.

"We'd best set up a guard for the next few evenings," Cameron addressed the men as they finished with the tents. "There are enough of us to handle it without the tenders. An hour and half apiece should do it. Just so there will be no argument we'll draw straws for the time. Long straw takes the first watch, and so on down the line to the shortest one and the last period. Anyone have a better idea?"

"Why can't we have two sentries on for three hours?" Roger asked quite calmly.

"Because we're going to push for a full twelve hours tomorrow, and I want everyone to get as much rest as possible. If we are in any kind of danger out here, the best thing to do is get to Batang as quickly as we possibly can. We're not sure how far that is. We were told back in K'angting it would take ten days, and that would make it day after tomorrow. But, how do we know we've made a daily average to total that? The only assurance we have will be to make up for any time we might have lost; and that's what we're going to do, whether we've lost any or not. It's going to be a damned tough haul, and we're all going to need every bit of strength we can muster. Agreed?"

Roger didn't like the notion of being on guard alone in the small hours of the morning, but he needn't have worried. He drew the longest straw of all, and although everyone else was in their beds, he was sure none of them were asleep.

Jo Lung drew the worst possible shift, the next to the last one. When he awakened Cameron for his turn he had only an hour and a half to get to sleep and wake again. It was hardly worth the effort, but he decided he would try anyway.

It was shortly after ten in the morning when Cameron glimpsed the first rider traveling abreast of them, about one mile north on the rough valley floor. At first he thought it must be their vanished guide; but a few minutes later he saw a second rider trailing behind the first. Within half an hour he became aware of at least three riders to the south of them, matching their speed, and about the same distance away. He put his glasses on them for several seconds each time one of them breasted the horizon. Finally he handed the binoculars to Harry saying, "Have a look at our outriders, and tell me what you think." He was aware that Harry had seen them too, and was watching him intently without comment.

"It's beastly hard to tell how many there are the way they keep bobbing up and down. I'd guess their number to be five or six to each side," Harry replied as he handed the glasses back. "Whoever they are they're keeping pace with us, and trying to stay out of sight as much as possible. Do you think they are bandits?" he asked without emotion.

"I don't know if they are or not," Cameron answered putting the glass on them again. "It looks to me like they're all wearing the same kind of clothes. A uniform, maybe? They're certainly not dressed like our Tibetan guide was.

"I wonder just how long they've been out there before we caught sight of them?" Harry speculated as he glanced from one side to the other.

"Hard to say," Cameron retorted still watching, "but I wouldn't be surprised if this was the reason for the hasty departure of our guide."

"If that's true," Harry mused, "we've had uninvited guests for the last two days at least!"

"I'm afraid so," Cameron concurred.

It was the noise of a fast moving horse that caused Cameron to lower the glasses and look behind him, just as Norman came along side. "Did you see them?" he asked excitedly.

"Yes, just a few minutes ago," Cameron replied. "When did you first spot them?"

"About the same time, I guess," Norman supposed. "Who and what are they? Where did they come from, and what do they want with us?" Anxiety was plain in Norman's tone, but he seemed to have good control of himself Cameron noted.

"I don't know any more about that than you do," Cameron admitted, "but apparently they mean us no harm for the present, or we'd know about it by now. Harry and I think they've been with us two days or more. We'll just have to continue on like they weren't there and see what happens. There's nothing else we can do!"

"Maybe they're an escort sent out from Batang," Norman speculated hopefully. In a few moments he rejected the thought with, "They would have reported to us if that were the case, wouldn't they? Maybe our guide was some kind of criminal, and they think he's still with us," Norman went on grasping for straws.

"That Tibetan stood out among us like a giblet in a rose garden!" Harry spat. "There's no way they could miss his absence, especially if they were after him. I'll wager it's an escort of some kind, but one we're not likely to appreciate. If we were to veer off the trail or turn back, I'm sure we'd find that out in a hurry!"

"You're probably right, Harry," Cameron said as he felt rather than saw Norman's questioning glance, "but I have no intention of doing either. There's only one road we can follow without getting hopelessly lost, and that's straight ahead. As for turning back, we knew we were going to have problems right from the very start, and this is the first real test we've encountered. We'd have been better off to have stayed at home than to come this far, and turn back at the first sign of trouble. Besides, we don't know that they mean us any harm at all. They might be just curious, and when they make up their minds, they might merely want to do some trading. We'll wait and see!" His voice was sure and steady. "Pass the word along to continue as though they weren't there, Norman. Here, take my pistol, and return to the rear with the Doctor. If they should start to close in fast, fire one shot in the air, but only if their movements are explosive, and it looks like they mean trouble! Do you understand?" Cameron asked leveling a cold hard stare.

"Yes, I understand," Norman responded soundly. "Their sudden appearance did startle me; but I'm not the type to lose my head, Cameron. You can count on me!" he exclaimed.

"I never had a single doubt that I couldn't," Cameron smiled his answer and motioned him to the rear.

"What about the rifles?" Harry asked as Norman rode away.

"I think we'd best leave them hidden until we absolutely have to use them," Cameron said thoughtfully. "In this part of the world those rifles and ammunition would be worth a king's ransom, and might even tempt honest and well-meaning people. I don't like the looks of this any better than you do, Harry, but I don't know any other way to handle it. Do you have any suggestions?"

"I'm afraid not, unless you'd like to ride out there and have a parley," Harry ventured.

"If they had talk in mind they would have come in some time ago. Let's just hold to our course and see what develops," Cameron concluded.

"Fine with me," Harry answered vaguely as his eyes swept their surroundings. "I hope the girls don't get too upset with this turn of events," he added looking back over his shoulder.

"They'll manage," Cameron said with certainty. "They've both got a lot of sand in their craws, or we'd have had a lot of complaining by this time. Those two are really something, you know? I was fully against either of them coming along at the start. Now I'm glad they did. They turned out to be an asset rather than a liability. I'm genuinely surprised."

"You needn't sing their praises to me, old boy," Harry sputtered. "I've been sold on the pair of them for quite some time."

Cameron looked at his friend with an open grin, and a sudden warm glow inside lifted the icy sensation that gripped his guts.

The warm sun reached the pinnacle of its arc then began the downward plunge as they left the valley to enter a long narrow pass leading steeply upward. They saw two riders enter the narrows before them, the remainder vanished, presumably to fall in behind. They made camp in the near foothills of a new valley when the evening stars appeared. Five miles further on another mountain range rose formidably in their path. They looked for the light of other campfires, but saw nothing. Their aloof companions either ate cold rations, or concealed their whereabouts well.

The guards each stood their lonely vigil and the night passed without incident. When the march began next morning, the distant figures materialized almost instantly and in larger numbers.

All eyes of the expedition watched them constantly, expectantly. As they began the ascent of the new range an hour before noon, the strangers had closed to within half a mile; it became evident they were indeed in some type of uniform with slight variations. The mounts they rode were fine animals without exception, and in good condition. Each man was armed with a rifle and saber, and at least three of them carried side arms as well.

As they made their way up a broad winding canyon they caught glimpses of a party of ten or more not far ahead of them, and at least another dozen behind. The newcomers made no effort at concealment now; and at times were close enough for the sound of their voices to drift back.

When they reached the summit, they could see the next valley was wide and long, with an abundance of rice paddies surrounding a city of moderate size. The green velvet floor looked out of place in the desolation of the country they had passed and it lifted the spirits of the entire party.

Eagerly, they began the downward sloping trail, thinking the city of Batang would offer sanctuary from any harm that might be intended. They did not reach the plain, much less the city, before they were brought to an abrupt halt.

Where the mountains joined the foothills, the road left the canyon and emerged out onto a shallow bench. As they topped this last rise, they ran head on into a city of tents straddling both sides of the road. Several hundred uniformed men on foot lined both sides of the caravan route; just beyond the largest tent of all, they blocked their path with ranks twelve deep. On a tall pole above this largest tent flew a double pointed purple banner with two large gold stars in the center of it.

Cameron didn't need to ask Jo Lung what it meant. He knew now the purpose of the uniformed men of the past few days; just as he knew they had been herded directly to the center of an army encampment. There was only one army in this part of China, and it had to be that of Cheng Wu.

As Dr. Felix came to a stop beside his friends the ranks closed in behind him, hemming them into a rectangular box of human flesh.

A young officer with a caustic eye stepped out from the tent doorway, and then stood scrutinizing each of them, their mounts and pack animals. At last he spoke, rapidly and with the bite of a whip. "He says we are to dismount in the presence of the Governor General Cheng Wu," Jo interpreted, "and he wishes to know who is in charge."

"We'll oblige him," Cameron said forcing a smile. "Everybody down and come up front together. Don't be frightened, everything will be alright. Introduce yourself, Jo, and tell him that I am in charge."

Jo had barely finished complying when another figure stepped out of the tent. By the gray showing beneath a billed military cap, the man was in his fifties, a good five-feet-eight, tall and slender in build. His face was handsome and clean shaven, save the hairline mustache that adorned his upper lip. His skin was dark tanned, without wrinkles, and in his left hand he carried a soft pair of leather gloves. He wore tight-fitting boots that glistened in the waning sun; his riding breeches, shirt and tunic were pale green with several medals on both breasts. In contrast to everyone else, he was unarmed.

He too looked for several moments before speaking, and when he did he addressed himself to the young officer, apparently his aide, in low monotones. The officer in turn relayed the questions to Jo in his original style.

"The general wants to know by whose authority we are traveling in his domain, where we come from and what is our mission." Jo related.

"Tell him that we travel by the authority of the Emperor granted by the Regent himself; that we come from across the ocean from the land of America, and that our mission is peaceful in search of religious relics in the land of the Lamas. Tell him also that we bear trade goods that belong to the Merchant of Chamdo, and that he is expecting us. You can embellish on that any way you believe might help, and show him the safe conduct addressed to him. Whatever you do, don't let them know you are afraid of them."

"I'm not at all sure how I'll manage that," Jo replied, "but I'll try." He began his translation, and Cameron watched him closely to see how he would hold up.

As though the general hadn't heard a word Jo said, the aide repeated it all again; and it came to Cameron that only certain people were allowed to speak directly to this great man.

Again the aide turned to Jo, barking more questions. "He is not satisfied that we are here for the purpose stated," Jo related. "He thinks perhaps we have ulterior motives. He alludes to knowing of our progress since leaving Ipin, and strongly wonders why we detoured to Chengtu. I explained that, but don't think he believed me. He's not impressed with the papers, although he thinks them genuine. I can't tell if mentioning the Merchant of Chamdo has helped our cause or not. What shall I tell him?"

Cameron's mind raced, trying to form the words that would convince the general of the credulity of their mission and their intent.

He was never allowed to speak, for the aide's voice sliced through his thoughts. His words were loud and clear so that all of the assembled troops could hear; and the rapidity of his speech resembled the staccato bark of a machine gun. He continued talking more than a minute and it was evident, even without translation, that he was addressing the entire assemblage.

When he finally finished, Jo translated barely above a whisper, and without turning his head, "He says that our untimely arrival has interrupted a formation called for the fulfillment of justice, and he does not plan to keep his troops in discomfort while the validity of our presence is decided. Therefore, the executions that had been scheduled will take place now, and matters concerning us will be attended to later. It seems that two notorious bandits are about to witness their last sunset. He went on to praise his men for the capture of this pair, but I'm sure you're not interested in the rest of his propaganda."

"Not in the least," Cameron replied.

The aide gave a sharp command of several words, and two bound figures were dragged from behind the large tent. Both were tied with their arms behind their backs, and ankles lashed together so that they were literally carried to the open space a few yards in front of the general. There were barely enough rags upon their bodies to cover their nakedness, and their emaciated frames plainly showed they were near starvation.

The older of the two condemned men was roughly forced to his knees; and a rifle-armed soldier planted a heavy boot in the small of his back, causing his torso to lean forward at a steep angle. A low moan escaped the man's lips as the boot made contact with his spine; but he made no other sound, nor did he attempt to struggle.

Cameron noted the fact that the queue was missing from the man's head, the vacant stare of his eyes, the slackness of his jaw, and the small stream of spittle dripping from the corner of his mouth. He judged the poor creature to be near forty; but realized it would be hard to tell in his present state, he might be only half that old. A surge of pity flooded Cameron's mind, but was cut short by a sudden roar from the assembled troops.

Cameron looked up to see a huge man standing directly above the crouched figure. He was well over six-feet tall, bare to the waist, with neck and arms as thick as most men's thighs. Proportionately, his head was as large as the rest of him. The set of his mouth and the light in his eyes revealed that he clearly enjoyed what was happening, and what was going to happen. His arms were crossed above his naval as he stood contemplating the wretch at his feet; and a heavy Indian Talwar hung from the sash that supported his crimson trousers. His feet were bare, and Cameron noted that his toes continually arched as though trying to get a better grip on the soft dust beneath them.

In one swift motion the executioner slipped the knot that held the Talwar to his side; and it miraculously jumped into his double-fisted grasp. He took one step forward, while slowly extending the heavy weapon above the nape of its intended victim. Then he stepped back, and an unbearable silence smothered everything.

When the roar of the soldiers had first erupted, the people of the expedition had instinctively moved closer together. Without either of them realizing it, Harry had slipped his arms around Penny's shoulders, and drew her tightly against his chest. Somehow Constance had moved slightly in front of Cameron; as the executioner made his final measurement, she lurched backward pressing herself firmly against him and at the same moment, began groping for both of his hands. Having found them, she brought them tightly about her waist.

The exorbitant silence was broken by the swishing of the heavy blade as it came upward from behind, flashed blindly in the dying sun as it came to the zenith of its arc, and down!

This time the roar from the soldiers was thunderous. The head of the condemned man literally catapulted from his body and landed more than twenty feet away; then rolled again to bounce off the boot of an unsuspecting trooper. The headless form slammed into the dust with such force it actually shook the ground where Cameron stood.

Twice the torso and legs arched upward as it tried to rise, the arms and feet bulging against the restraining ropes. Two bright streams of scarlet spewed outward with each contortion, then slowed as the twitching of the body began to ebb. The soldier at whose feet the head had stopped gave the member a vicious kick and sent it back, though far short of its owner. Another roar of approval went up from the uniformed men and then silence, as the aide held up his hand and issued a command.

Two men with rifles slung across their backs stepped forward and grasped the headless corpse by each ankle, then dragged it back behind the tent from where he first had come. A third man gingerly rolled the head into a piece of tattered cloth with his foot, and followed. The giant with the sword watched with gleaming eyes and slight smile as he wiped the blade clean upon his pants.

When the three soldiers had taken their places back in ranks, the aide once more barked a series of orders, and the second culprit was dragged to the center of the awesome stage.

"He isn't much more than a boy," Cameron perceived instantly, "not more than twenty, if that, and his physical condition is no better than his companion's." His eyes were wide with terror; but he was not mute, for he cried, moaned and screamed with each inch that narrowed the distance between himself and the glistening blade that hung beside the crimson clad leg of the smiling one. For a small man, and being bound, he fought like a tiger, but to no avail. He was, in the end, picked up bodily by four soldiers, and dumped into the blood soaked dust where his companion had gone so resignedly a few minutes before.

Two soldiers raised him to his knees, and bowed his back to the proper position; but the second they released their hold on him he fell forward and clutched at the ground with his shoulders and toes as though somehow he might wedge himself to where he could not be raised.

Cameron lifted his eyes from this pitiful scene and looked squarely into the appraising stare of the general. There was a strange quizzical expression about the general's mouth, as though he would like to ask a question; his gaze was cold and calculating. The aide standing next to him was watching the condemned man with open contempt, and his hand nervously went to and from the butt of his side arm.

As revoltingly ill as Cameron felt himself, he became more and more conscious of the quivering figure of Connie that he held even tighter in his arms. Her whole body shook against him and she pulled the palms of his hands even tighter against her abdomen. Through his fingers he could feel the rapid thudding of each beat of her heart and he expected at any moment for her to collapse, but she held her head high.

Once more Cameron looked to the ground in time to see the two soldiers raise the condemned to his knees. The soldier closest to the headsman looked up at him with a questioned look.

The large man's reply was only a few words and two more soldiers stepped from the ranks; each of them taking hold of the victim's legs to pin him to the ground. Each of the other two took hold of an elbow behind his back and bent him forward. This time he was powerless to move, or so they thought.

Perhaps it was because the headsman prided himself in the swift precision of his work, and was irritated by this lack of cooperation; or maybe the young man's screams of terror for so long had unnerved him, and he now only wanted to get it over. Whatever the reason, the man wielding the sword did not take his measuring thrust this time; but instead brought the blade directly from his side, over and around. Though he was pinned on all four sides, the boy somehow managed to find the strength to shove both he and his captors away from the oncoming blow, though only a few inches. The very tip of the steel sliced through the near side of his neck, exposing the vertebra and spraying blood in all directions.

Each and every animal becomes dangerous when wounded, regardless of its docility in normal living; and its strength can become tenfold with the realization that beyond this last effort there is nothing. A terrifying roar burst from the young man's throat, and though he was bound hand and foot he managed to toss his captors to and fro regardless of their efforts. The smile vanished from the headsman's lips, and grim determination radiated from his eyes. He watched the struggle below him knowing that this strength could only last so long, and his wait was shorter than he thought.

Once more the broad, heavy Talwar split the air in the back hand swing, but it landed a split second after the boy made his final and supreme effort. Again he pulled away from the arc of the blade with a mighty surge of power, but the swordsman had compensated for this and the shimmering steel neatly did the job it should have done long before. The applause went up from the gathering of troops, and for several moments no one noticed that the near guard, holding the boy's elbow, had shared that lethal blow. The last effort of the youth had pulled him directly beneath the rear section of the descending edge; and it had severed his collar bone and shoulder, and stopped only as it touched the fifth rib. His scream of pain was drowned by the tumultuous sounds of the troops. He reeled backwards away from the sword and the headless form. Instinctively he knew that he too was dying.

The smile returned to the headsman's lips, but it remained only briefly. He alone understood what had happened. He watched as the soldier oscillated backward, dropping flat on his rump in a sitting position, but not before the rifle slung over his left shoulder had incredibly swung around, and pointed directly at his huge chest.

A bellow of rage burst from the big man's lips as shock and hatred formed strange lines in his face. *I am the executioner*, filled his mind, *no man has the right to point death at me!* Again the Talwar started its upward swing as he bounded toward the fallen soldier. The blast of the rifle in such close confinement sounded like a cannon! The Talwar never completed half of its upward swing, falling to the ground as its bearer was blown backward, a neat round hole in the center of his breast plate and shattered pieces of vertebra protruding from his back.

The soldier that had fired the shot remained in a sitting position, the rifle lowered and resting on his legs. He stared in shocked amazement at the executioner lying dead a few feet in front of him. He was so mesmerized by these last few seconds that he even forgot that he himself was doomed. He did not take his eyes from the great Talwar that had not been wiped clean; nor did he see the aide of the general walk up behind him, slowly take his revolver from its holster and place the muzzle behind his ear.

The report was muffled and sounded like a toy compared to the earlier rifle shot. It seemed strange to Connie that there should be so much difference in the two sounds and it was then she heard another unusual sound. She managed to tear her eyes away from the horror she had witnessed and looked down to her side, and slightly behind her. Roger was there in the dust on his hands and knees, brownish yellow vomit spewing from his mouth and nostrils. Whimpering sobs and moans emerged from his throat between the whistling noises of him trying to catch his breath. It was at this moment, that she felt the blackness closing in on her; the bones of her body were turning to jelly, and her heart seemed to have stopped, for she was icy cold all over.

Cameron sensed what was happening to her even before she started to slip in his arms, but he was numbed and his reflexes slow. Her legs gave way completely, and her head rolled forward. Automatically Cameron tightened his grasp, and her downward plunge halted as his hands firmly cupped her breasts. The unexpected intimacy with which he was supporting Connie's body brought Cameron out of the nightmarish state of hypnosis he had been in since the executions first began. Trying desperately not to injure her, and yet not let her fall, he tightened his grasp on her left breast, and swiftly regained his hold about her waist with his right arm.

Slowly he inched her form upward until he was able to put both arms about her middle. He then leaned backward as far as he dared, and let her head roll back beside his own. He wanted to lay her down, to open the tight collar of her tunic so she might breathe, and bath her face with a cold towel; but no one except himself knew that she had fainted, and he did not want them to know; especially the general and his aide. He said a small prayer of thanks when he felt her take a deep breath, and then another. She jerked slightly as she regained consciousness and he felt her begin to support her own weight. "Are you alright now, Connie?" he whispered with concern. "Can you stand on your own? If not, I'll help you a little longer, but I'm afraid our very lives depend on a show of strength," he added.

At the full realization of her position, she stiffened instantly and then just as quickly relaxed against him. "I think I'll be alright in just a few more seconds, Cam," she whispered also. "Just give me a few more moments, and I'm sure I can make it."

Still holding her firmly Cameron turned to check on Harry and the rest. He was almost afraid to look, not knowing what to expect from his English friend in this first terrible time of stress. It startled him beyond belief to see the white hot rage that filled Harry's eyes, the deep reddish hew of his face and the tightly clenched fists behind Penny's back as he held her up on his shoulder completely off the ground. Harry must have felt his gaze, for he turned to face his friend and gave him a solemn nod, as if to say he agreed with any plan of action Cameron might have.

Next Cameron scrutinized Norman Clyde and was relieved to find that though Norman was visibly shaken, he too was angry, and could be counted on in what might come next. Dr. Felix was a different matter; there was neither fright nor anger in his expression, only a great pain and sadness, but he stood firmly erect and not even a hair of his head was out of place.

The two young camp tenders stood close by the doctor holding on to each other; it was obvious they were scared stiff, but there were no tears or crying and Cameron was grateful for this. He was aware that Roger had not yet risen to his feet and was afraid that if he were to look down at him he would be sick himself. He turned once more in time to see Penny flutter briefly, and put her lips to Harry's cheek before he set her on the ground.

Cameron could scarcely credit his senses, when he again faced the General and deduced that none of them had witnessed the fainting of the two women, or even Roger for that matter.

Cameron turned slightly, bent his head and in as loud a voice as he dared, he addressed Roger, "You get that gutless, yellow-bellied, jellyfish carcass of yours up out of the dirt in the next three seconds and stand up like a man, or I'm going to do it for you. If I have to, I'll kick your ass all the way through the general's tent and tell him we got one of our own that could do without a head since he doesn't have a backbone to support it!" Cameron's words stabbed out like a lightning bolt.

Roger's hideously stained face looked up in surprise, which quickly changed to anger, then hate, just as Cameron had hoped it would.

"And, clean up you face," Cameron snapped, "You look a mess."

Throughout the whole episode, Jo Lung's countenance had remained impassive. His hands had trembled one or twice, but even Cameron would not have noticed it had he not been watching him.

The general's anger was so intent that Cameron was sure he could feel it, yet it only showed in the general's eyes. Once more he spoke to his aide for several seconds, waiting for the orders to be carried out. A few harsh commands from the aide and the three bodies that lay between them were removed; buckets of sand were spread to hide the blood.

The aide then addressed himself to Jo Lung and when he had finished, Jo translated slowly, "The general does not believe that we are only passing through on our way to the land of the Lamas. He believes instead that we come as spies to scout the land for the purposes of commerce, just as the foreign devils have done in the coastal parts of China. He believes that our purpose is to set up trade outposts, and that once this is accomplished, hundreds or even thousands of others like you will follow. He says further that he is the law here, and will not allow it. His rule is absolute and his justice swift, as we have just witnessed. He wishes to know if we have any further evidence in our behalf."

"Tell him once more that we are only passing through his domain," Cameron said exasperated. "Tell him that we go beyond Lhasa to seek an ancient city for religious artifacts, perhaps gold and jewels. I don't know anything else to say Jo; do the best you can," Cameron finished lamely.

Jo spoke for quite some time and Cameron guessed that Jo was doing some improvising on his own, but he could tell by the general's glances, that it wasn't doing any good.

When Jo repeated the aide's latest words, his face was pale, "They're going to search our pack animals!"

Instantly Cameron grasped the full impact of Jo's words, "My God, if they find the rifles we'll all be dead in a matter of minutes," Cameron whispered to himself. He felt the terror and panic he had seen in the boy's eyes as the guards dragged him out to lose his head. He saw the aide motion four soldiers toward their mounts and pack animals. Flashes of the past hour went through his mind; only it was not the poor wretches he saw under the sword, but Connie, Penny, Harry and the rest. His blood began to boil, and the scalding anger he tried so desperately to control most of his life erupted like a volcano.

Cameron eased Connie aside, and took five quick steps forward to the exact spot where the headsman had died, before the aide responded by drawing his revolver again. Cameron drew himself up to his full height and extended his arm, his finger pointing into the face of the general, "Cheng Wu, you slant eyed sadistic son of a whore," he roared with a voice like thunder, "if you so much as lay a hand on any of my people or animals, you'll die by the garrote before the Emperor himself, you and your officers. I had this promise from the Regent before leaving Shanghai. If you think for a moment he won't know what's happened to us, you're wrong as hell! When we left the river packet at Ipin, I sent messages back to inform the Regent of our progress and that we were entering your province. When we left Chengtu, I sent two more envoys back overland to inform the Regent that we were safely in your territory and under your protection. All three of these people have long since arrived in Shanghai and reported to the Regent. He will now be expecting a coded message from the Merchant of Chamdo, who is also expecting us. When that message does not arrive, they will know what has happened to us and by whose hand. You may believe you're a big man here in the interior and this is probably true; but have you ever before directly gone against the wishes of the Emperor or the Regent? No, you're damned well right you haven't, because you're too smart for that. If you think for a moment that you can start going against them now, you're wrong. Maybe a few years from now, but not at this time. They'll hunt you down and give you the same treatment you gave those two poor devils you saved long enough to put on a show for us. The least you could have done would have been to feed them a little, while you were waiting for us to arrive. They both damned near starved to death before you got a chance to cut their heads off and even that backfired! That's a hell of a good sign as to what will happen to you if you even as much as touch one of my horses. Now, you dog-eared son of a bitch, chew on that awhile!" Cameron finished as ferociously as he began, his finger still pointing between the general's eyes and addressing him face-to-face.

When Cameron had started to speak, the startled aide had raised his revolver and pointed it directly at Cameron's head, but he lowered it at a single word from the general. The four soldiers that had started to their mounts stopped dead in their tracks, as did everyone else.

For a long moment Chen Wu stood looking silently at Cameron, a puzzled expression replaced some of the cruelty of his features. Eventually, he turned to the aide to ask what had been said.

After the aide had spoken to him, Jo turned to Cameron and asked with grave seriousness, "Just how much of that recital do you think I should convey to the general?"

"Every single word of it Jo!" Cameron exploded, lowering his arm at last. "And if you can think of a few indignities regarding his birthright in Chinese that I haven't covered, throw them in too!"

"Do you think this wise under our present circumstances, Cameron Hewitt?" Jo inquired somberly. Cameron did not fail to notice Jo's use of his full name signifying the gravity of the situation. He had not done this since they first met. "Friend Jo," Cameron answered softly, "we haven't got any circumstances. Our only chance now is to bluff our way out of this. You told me yourself that he was a very greedy and cruel man, but that he was wise enough to curb both if it suited his purpose in the long run. We've already planted the notion of gold and jewels in his head; now we must imply that he will be coming into greater power soon, and at the same time make him doubt the absolute power he holds here now. The more we abuse him, the more he will doubt himself, I hope. At any rate it's our last and only chance Jo. Say it all just like I said it, and say it like you believed it!"

When the aide had asked for an interpretation, Jo had come up to Cameron's side. Now it was Jo's turn to act boldly and he did not falter. Without hesitation, he walked directly to the aide, stopping a scant three feet in front of him. As he began repeating Cameron's words, the aide's face grew livid and his eyes nearly bulged out of his head. Once more his hand flew to his side, but again the general stopped him. When he had finished, Jo bowed slightly, then returned to stand beside Cameron. "Like you said, I never left out a word, and did add a few of my own." Jo stated loudly.

"Good man," Cameron breathed softly.

The aide turned and began his translation to the general, but Cheng Wu waived him aside. Though the general had no knowledge of English whatsoever, he understood the portent of Cameron's words and gestures. He listened attentively to Jo's translation and there was no reason for him to hear it the third time. For a long moment the general looked at Cameron, then at each of the rest of them. He then called the aide and spoke to him sharply. The aide was gone for a full five minutes, then returned with three civilians; merchants by their appearance, one old and two middle aged. The general put several questions to them through his aide.

Jo listened attentively for some time, whispering to Cameron, "He is questioning these people about our departure from Ipin, our stay in Chengtu, and Cricket and Li Po going back overland. These men are terrified, but seem to be telling the truth so far."

"I hope it will be to our advantage if they do!" Cameron sighed. Jo listened for another five minutes, then spoke to Cameron, "They have been trying to figure out who you sent messages back from Ipin with, and since they have no idea, they are quite sure he got through. As for Li Po and Cricket, they thought they were merely going out into the country for a rest, and expected them to return, so they too got away. The general is very angry, but I believe your strategy is working."

A few minutes later they sent the merchants away; then the general and his aide spoke in low tones for several more minutes.

Finally the aide wheeled about and came to where Cameron and Jo were standing. He bowed low before Cameron and then Jo Lung. When he spoke, his manner was apologetic and cordial; as the last rays of the dying sun splashed across his hand, he pointed west and finished speaking. He then waited very politely for Jo to extend this information to Cameron.

"The esteemed General Cheng Wu begs you to forgive him for a grave error he has made through misinformation supplied him by his subordinates. There is another party journeying in this direction with plans to cause serious trouble for his people. Unfortunately, we were mistaken for them and the general wants to make amends. He is providing us with an honor guard of thirty mounted soldiers to accompany us to the very door of the Merchant of Chamdo. These men will guard us day and night; we need have no fear of bandits or other marauders. Further, from here to Chamdo they will supply our victuals as well as the needs of our mounts and anything else we might desire. He also said to tell you that when we return to Chamdo from our mission, you are to send word to him immediately, so that he may provide you an escort back to Ipin. You will have no repetition of the discomfort you have suffered here today."

"Anything else?" Cameron inquired with a flood of relief.

"Not that was relayed to me by this animal," Jo smiled sweetly, "but I did hear the general tell him that we are to encamp on the far side of the city of Batang. He says he can neither stand the sight or the smell of us any longer."

"Well," Cameron mused, "I'm sure that goes more than double from all of us! Now thank this slimy viper here, Jo, and let's get the hell out of here!"

Jo and the aide bowed to each other several times, said a few more words, and the aide returned to the tent just as darkness began to fall.

Cameron and Jo walked back to where the rest of their party was standing. "Well, it looks as though we've survived this crisis at least. Everybody mount up, we'll be leaving in a few minutes, and we'll camp on the far side of town. The general is giving us an escort for the remainder of the trip. That ought to make everyone sleep easier," Cameron finished flatly.

By the time they were mounted and ready to leave, the formation of soldiers had been dismissed except those that were to escort them. Apparently the troopers had no love for the foreigners either, for they formed two groups, one way out in front of the party and the other lagging far behind "I don't like this business of the escort one iota," Harry spat, when he was sure they were out of earshot.

"I don't either," replied Cameron, "but I much prefer it to laying back there with my head twenty feet from the rest of me!"

"God, I'm sorry, Cam"," Harry blurted, "I didn't mean it the way it sounded. I realize better than anyone else here that you saved all of our lives back there. It's just that I'm afraid some of these blighters might go berserk, and forget they're supposed to escort us safely to Chamdo."

"Not very likely," Jo interrupted cheerfully, "I overheard the general's aide telling the officer in charge that if anything at all happened to any of us, his whole detail would lose their heads, and he meant it!"

"Yes," Cameron agreed, "that old wolf wants us back for his fun and games, but also loaded down with booty. We'll have to see what the Merchant of Chamdo thinks about this! The one thing we are going to have to be damned careful about," Cameron added as an afterthought, "is those blasted rifles. They could still cause us a lot of trouble if any of those soldiers find them."

"We'll just have to sleep with the bloody things," Harry concluded without thinking.

"That's precisely what I had in mind," Cameron concurred.

"Really?" Harry asked with a startled expression.

"I think we'd best move up, and see how the girls are managing after this ordeal," Cameron suggested. "Fact is we had better ride beside them until we make camp.

"Splendid thinking for a damned Yankee," Harry quipped, sounding a little like his old self.

BOOK THREE

Chamdo, The Morning Wind

CHAPTER 9

"There is no way in the world," Penny murmured, "that I could ever get used to the idea of at least a dozen pairs of eyes watching while I take a bath. What am I saying, watching, they won't even let me touch myself. I feel so embarrassed and helpless."

"You had best relax and enjoy this luxury while you can Penny dear," Connie replied dreamily. "We've been here a week, and I don't think it will be many more days until we're back on the trail, and you'll only be able to dream about the way we've been treated by Maleek's household."

"You're probably right," Penny chirped, "I haven't forgotten the long days we spent getting here when all we could afford was to wash our hands and face. All this attention still unnerves me though."

Connie didn't answer, for she too was recalling all of those long hot days in the saddle with the sweat oozing from every pore of her body; the sticky feeling that her thighs were cemented to the leather between her legs, and the ugly sensation of the small rivulets that would periodically run down the small of her back and sides of her chest.

Both girls were lying face down on huge fluffy towels that had been laid out on the thick rugs of their quarters, after the bathing gear had been taken away. Two young female servants began drying each of them with small down-like pads. The operation was delicate, thorough and time consuming.

When the drying was completed, the servants applied light scented oil to their entire bodies, massaging softly so that it might be absorbed into the skin. The servant's hands were skilled and gentle and they talked incessantly among themselves while going about their chores.

Connie let her mind go completely blank, as much as she could, during these morning ministrations so that she might enjoy every second of it. She even slightly resented the effort required on her part when her attendants indicated she should turn over; but she always cooperated, for she knew that her peaceful contentment would continue another half hour.

It was peaceful, that is, up until the last few minutes when the hands began to apply the warmed oil to her belly and her breasts; then the terrible day at Cheng Wu's camp flooded back into her mind, and there was no room for anything else. Though she had lost consciousness part of that time, she could still feel the strong pressure of his hands on her abdomen, and then her breasts as she fell, and again as she started to revive. She could not understand her emotions; only a few weeks ago she could hardly stand to be near the man and now each time she thought about him holding her as he had, a warm tingling glow enveloped her entire being.

"I'm being childish," she told herself. "The man was only doing what he had to do under the prevailing conditions. He had to make us all look strong or we would never have gotten out of there alive. He said so himself, remember? Look what he did to poor Roger to get him back on his feet; I'm sure he didn't want to treat Roger that way. Everything he did during those crucial moments there was a good reason, and none of it was personal. He was just doing the job he was supposed to do and I can certainly see now why Father would have no other man in his place. I'm nothing but a silly goose, and somehow I've got to get the whole matter out of my mind." But the matter she referred to would not leave her thoughts and each day she looked forward to her bath more eagerly.

Just how long Penny had been rambling on she had no idea.

"Connie," Penny shouted, "are you listening to a single word I'm saying?"

"I'm sorry, Penny dear," Connie replied somewhat shaken, "I guess I was just daydreaming. Would you start over again, please?"

"Oh, forget it," Penny answered slightly ruffled. "As soon as they finish dressing us let's go for a stroll in the city again. I just love it there, don't you?"

"Not especially," Connie replied candidly. "It was fun the first couple of times because of the newness. Now it's just another big pile of rock with a lot of people running around. If you want to go though, we shall, for there's not much else to do. Remember the orders we have to take along at least two guards!"

"After what nearly happened at the hands of that General, how could I forget?" Penny sobered. "I'm still having dreams about that awful day, aren't you?"

"Yes, I am," Connie replied nostalgically, and a strange new light was glowing in her eyes.

*　　*　　*　　*　　*

The audience compartment of Maleek's private quarters was a spacious affair with heavy rugs, sitting mats, low tables, and an innumerable amount of pillows and cushions scattered about. Tapestries of every conceivable design formed a double wall to the tent, to retain the heat in the winter months, and the coolness of the shade in the summer. The beauty and worth of these works of art were beyond calculation.

Maleek sat upright amid a large pile of spongy cushions, several of them piled high to support his back. His hair, mustache and beard were white as snow, the skin below his eyes and jowls sagged slightly. Over the past twenty years, he had lost a few pounds at the continued insistence of his wives, and at least three of his favored concubines. The twinkling lights still danced in his soft brown eyes and his mind was as sharp as any scimitar of Islam.

He addressed himself to Cameron, Harry and Dr. Felix sitting before him in a semicircle. "I have news that the caravan from the Gobi will arrive either late tonight, or in the early morning hours," he declared. "Then you can talk with Prince Mango himself." His English was flawless, and there was no hesitation in his search for the proper words. "As I told you upon your arrival, I doubt that he will be willing to assist you in the venture you have in mind. He has waited twenty years to take vengeance for the massacre of his people. He told me before he left that he knew his time was growing short, that he had waited much too long already!" Maleek paused momentarily to catch his breath, and then continued. "I do not agree with him, and this he knows. Allah, in his pure wisdom, has already extracted several terrible judgments against the people of the Uli Prang. The plague of cholera has visited them seven times in the last twenty years and there is not a young man or woman left to the entire tribe, only the older people and a few small children. Tal Rashi, I am told, has gone mad with the obsession that Prince Mango still lives. Twelve times he has sent assassins to finish what he started so long ago in the valley of Kirghiz and twelve times they have failed. I tell Mango Noyan that justice will be served if he lets Tal Rashi die of his madness and the Uli Prang perish out of their inability to reproduce, but he will not listen. He must have their blood on his hands before he can rest in peace."

"Is there no one else that can guide us to this mountain?" Cameron asked politely.

"There are many that could take you to the place where the mountain is located, but none that will venture even close to it, let alone guide you to the top." Maleek responded seriously. "Even I could take you to the point where you could see it, but I have never been any closer than perhaps twenty miles. For countless centuries Kula Kangri has been sacred taboo to everyone except the people of the Blue Wolf. The King Priest of Tibet knew this when he deeded it to Kirghiz as part of his Hoshun. I would not even guess the Lama's reasons for this action; perhaps he thought no one else would contest them for the land, or maybe he did not believe the legends of the mountain, or it may have been his way of evening an old score. Remember, the Mongols invaded this land many times and though Kublai Khan embraced Buddhism and decreed it to the religion of his dynasty, there were many indignities heaped upon the people of Tibet long before any of this happened. I prefer to believe that the Lama had the best of motives, for the Hoshun of the Blue Wolf was a happy and prosperous one for more than six hundred years."

"Forgive me for interrupting," Dr. Felix said, "but you keep using this word, Hoshun, and I do not understand its meaning."

"You will pardon me, Doctor," Maleek explained, "though the word was foreign to me a great many years ago, I have been using it so long I didn't realize it would mean nothing to you. The word Hoshun came with the Mongols, and it has several meanings. In this case, it refers to the domain of any given tribe or clan of people. It has boundaries just like a country, though it may be very irregular in shape, and within a country or state. Anyone with peaceful intent may cross it or be a welcome visitor, but only those of the clan may live there and graze their flocks and herds. As is the case of most nomadic people, the Hoshun has high and low country for winter and summer sustenance and Allah help the poor devil that allows his herd to graze on another's land. The word also means banner or flag, especially the lance banners carried by the cavalry of the great Khans as they went into battle. But, it has other meanings as well. Pride mostly I would guess: pride in themselves, their background, their integrity and their beliefs. Do you know that for six-hundred years the Lamas tried to convert the people of the Blue Wolf to Buddhism and never gained one convert? It is true! They worshiped the spirit of the blue sky called Tengri and nothing was ever able to sway them from it! Remarkable, wouldn't you say, Doctor?"

"Remarkable indeed," Dr. Felix agreed, "when you consider the nearness of their land to the Forbidden City, the fact they were here by the will of the Lamas, and that Buddhism spread like wildfire throughout most of Asia after the time of Kublai Khan. Does this Prince Mango still believe in Tengri?" the Doctor inquired curiously.

"No, he does not," replied Maleek, "he renounced it when his people died."

"People have renounced their faith with much less reason, from what you have told us of his past," Dr. Felix observed with strange sadness.

"That is true, Doctor," Maleek responded, observing Dr. Felix with new interest. "Do you think it unusual that though I am full blooded Chinese, I should be dedicated to Islam?"

"Not at all," the Doctor smiled now, "from what you have told us of yourself and your ancestors, your reasons are very practical ones; but the important thing is that you truly believe, and you live by those principles."

"Ah," Maleek beamed, "I am very happy to hear that. I thought perhaps before you left you might try converting me to Christianity."

"My days of converting are in the dim and distant past, dear friend," Dr. Felix replied, and the note of sadness returned to his voice.

Maleek clapped his hands twice, and a male servant appeared instantly. "Let us have some refreshments, gentlemen. What would you like?" he asked. "We have everything your heart could desire: more than two dozen different wines, brandy, scotch, gin, several types of beer, and thanks to your dear Mr. Clayborne, we also have bourbon. What is your pleasure?"

When each of them had told their host their wants, he gave the order to the servant, adding, "I thought you might also like some cheese and small cakes."

"Mr. Clayborne," Maleek smiled broadly, "I must again thank you for the beautiful specimen of the serpent you brought me, and the extra rattles. You see, very few people in this part of the world believe that such a snake exists and thought it to be one of the tales the people of the West are famous for, if you will excuse my candor?"

"Certainly," Harry laughed, "we do have a habit of stretching the truth a bit now and then, but there is one hell of a lot of dead people in America that could testify to the validity of this one."

"Is there any chance," Cameron began after the refreshments had been served, "that some of your own guards have no fear of venturing to this mountain, and that a few of them could be engaged by us for a short while."

"You would need more than a few," Maleek replied between sips of his wine. "Decimated though the Uli Pang may be, they are still a formidable threat, and a small party such as yours would be made to order. I do have some men that would be willing to accompany you, but they do not know the country. If nothing else can be done, we will find someone to take you there most of the way, and the people I have will act as your guard. The elite of guards are the men that follow Mango Noyan, and they are so dedicated to him that it would be useless to even think of them."

"The Prince has personally hand-picked and trained his men for the sole purpose of exacting his revenge on the Uli Prang, and Tal Rashi in particular. Each of them love him as a brother, and it is said that they now consider themselves to be his people. Even though the Prince does not know it, they secretly have had made, and carry, the fighting banners of the Blue Wolf. It is impressive how devoted the men that get close to him become, especially since all of them are from the countries to the south." Maleek concluded.

"There are a few men born each century with that unique characteristic," Dr. Felix observed. "Had he lived at another place and time, he might well be in the history books of the world."

"Very probable," agreed Maleek, "for he is a blood descendant of the two great Khans."

"It's getting quite late," Cameron noted, "and I doubt that the Prince would feel much like talking to us at the end of such a long day, even if he did come in tonight. Perhaps, it would be best if we were to retire for now, and see him in the morning. With your permission, of course!" he bowed slightly to his host.

"I believe you might be physic, Mr. Hewitt," said Maleek with a grin. "I was about to suggest the same thing. It has been a most pleasant evening, gentlemen, and I thank you for sharing it with me." The Merchant did not rise, but bowed to each of them as they rose and left.

An extraneous transformation had taken place within Roger starting at the moment he raised himself from the dust at the camp of Cheng Wu. From that time on he avoided all contact with both Constance and Penny; and he shied away from Cameron like the plague. With Dr. Felix and Norman Clyde it was the opposite. He went everywhere with them, joined their conversations in earnest and gradually began absorbing more and more of Norman's work.

At first Norman did not know what to make of it, and then gave up wondering as to the why of it all. He was not one to look a gift horse in the mouth, as the saying went, and he needed help desperately. He was weeks behind in his work; and was delighted to find that Roger possessed a beautiful hand with a pen, and turned out to be an exacting map maker.

They toiled together several hours each day in the spacious tent Maleek had assigned them and the Doctor. Norman was genuinely surprised to find that Roger remembered, in detail, many of the incidents and landmarks of the trip up river, as well as the overland ride. It wasn't long before an honest friendship began to develop between the two.

For the first time in his life, Roger tasted the inner sense of achievement, and he decided he wanted much more of it. There was another first that accompanied this sensation, the one of hate, and it was reserved exclusively for Cameron.

It was near ten the following morning when Cameron, Dr. Felix and Harry were summoned to the tent of Maleek. Within stood the man they had waited more than a week to see; and by his side stood another man, with turbaned head and a double pointed beard. It was apparent that the pair of them had only recently arrived, for they were covered with dust, and a rifle hung from the shoulder of each of them.

Maleek made the introductions to Prince Mango first, and then Pic Rhee Sing. He then asked them all to be seated, and informed the group that strong refreshments were on the way.

Cameron knew it would be highly impolite to broach his business with the Prince immediately, and decided to wait until the social amenities were at an end. While he lightly sipped his own brandy he turned his full attention to Mango as he was giving a detailed report to Maleek.

For some reason, unknown even to himself, Cameron had formed a picture of Prince Mango in his mind; and the person he was watching possessed not even the slightest resemblance to what he had imagined. He had thought Mango would be taller, with more delicate features, and have a certain amount of grace to his movements. This man with the thick neck, the wide-set eyes, and the barrel chest was quite a disappointment to him. He noticed the spattering of gray at his temples, the lines forming beside his eyes, and the bulging of the muscles of his forearm even at the simple effort of raising a glass to his lips. *He must really be a powerful brute,* Cameron thought to himself.

To Cameron's astonishment, it was Mango who introduced the subject of his desires. "My benefactor, Maleek, has informed me of your strong wish for me to guide you to the mountain of Kula Kangri and my former home. He has also told me of the great distance that you have traveled, and of what you hope to accomplish there. I am aware that you have invested a great deal of money, time and even placed your lives in danger of fulfill your goals, and that what you set out to do is not a thing of whimsy," Mango's voice was soft, and his use of English perfect. "I truly wish that I were in a position to cede to your needs; for I too have always felt that there was something to be discovered at the top of that mountain, and I almost got there once. But I cannot make myself available to you, or any of my men. I have a mission of my own that must be done, and it is long overdue. I cannot spare a week or even a day; for within the next two months the winter snows will come, and my own objective will have to be postponed until next year. My intuition tells me that next year will be too late; so I must regretfully deny your request. Further, to save time and disappointment for you, I will tell you that no amount of money or other riches will change my mind. I am already moderately wealthy, and when I die everything I own will be divided equally among my men," Mango stopped speaking and sipped his wine, his eyes went from Cameron to Dr. Felix as they had done several times while he spoke.

The stillness that filled the room grew longer, and Cameron's mind raced frantically to think of some way to convince this man how desperately they needed him. His mention of the oncoming winter snows reminded Cameron of how little of their own time remained. *Somehow, someway I must win him over!* Cameron thought as he watched how fascinated Mango seemed to be with Dr. Felix.

It was Mango that broke the silence, "There is some small assistance that I may offer you, although I realize it won't really be much help," he paused, and again glanced at Dr. Felix. "All of the information that I have points to the fact that the Uli Prang, since early spring, have been raiding the caravan trails far to the West, near Gartock. My information on these people has, for the most part, been accurate in the past, and I believe it to be so now. Therefore, my men and I will head in that direction at sunrise day after tomorrow. We shall follow the main caravan route beyond Lhasa to a point where you should strike south, so that you might skirt the Yamdrog Tsho. You are more than welcome to accompany us to there, because it would only leave you a little over one-hundred-fifty miles to reach Kula Kangri, and it is the easiest route I know of. Once again I say that I am truly sorry, but I can do no more!" There was a flat finality to Mango's closing statement.

As Cameron listened to him speak his eyes came to rest upon the rifle that lay across Mango's legs. He studied the piece closely, and was sure he recognized its make, and he further noticed the one Pic Rhee was holding to be identical. A plan, born of desperation, began forming in his mind.

Instead of accepting or rejecting Mango's offer he asked, "Just how many men do you have at your disposal, Prince Mango?" His tone was smooth and easy, as though prompted by curiosity alone.

"I have, not including myself, twenty of the finest mountain fighters in this part of the world," Mango answered with pride.

"And," Cameron continued in the same vein, "How many men do these people you call the Uli Prang have?"

"No one really knows now," Mango admitted. "Twenty years ago they had close to three hundred; so many, in fact, that they sometimes split up into two or three groups, forming the impression that they could cover vast distances in very short periods of time. At the present, it is hard to say; many have died by the cholera and others were killed in desperation encounters they would not have engaged in had their leader's judgment been sound. I have thought on this many times recently, and I can only guess. I would say somewhere between sixty and eighty!"

"You are quite confident that you and your twenty men can track them down, and annihilate that many foes without being wiped out yourselves?" Cameron purposefully made his inquiry sound incredulous.

"We do not believe that all of us will return," Mango replied without heat.

"Is it not possible also, that an equal number of your enemies will get away, or at least part of them?" Cameron spoke softly.

"No!" Mango replied with vigor, "we are in much better physical condition and we are better supplied. We know the country as well as they do, we are better trained to fight as a coordinated unit, and lastly we have superior weapons!" Mango's voice had risen as he spoke and red flashes of anger darted from his eyes.

May I see the rifle you are holding?" Cameron asked politely.

"Certainly," Mango responded, and instantly tossed it to him in a double-handed pitch.

Cameron had anticipated Mango's reaction, and caught the rifle expertly in midair. It was an old breach loader Sharps, one of the first repeating rifles ever made; and it had seen a great deal of use. He ejected the shells from the magazine, then fitted the lead from one of them to the muzzle. It was as he suspected, the muzzle was terrifically belled. Next he examined the firing pin, and saw that it was so badly worn it would not be long before it would no longer make contact. He checked the breach lock and found it to be significantly loose and dangerous. He then replaced the cartridges in the magazine, and tossed the piece back to Mango. "Is that one of the superior weapons you spoke of?" he asked evenly.

"Why yes," Mango replied somewhat startled, "it is a good rifle, one of the finest in this part of the country."

Both Harry and Dr. Felix had a suspicion Cameron was up to something, and Harry had a pretty good idea what it was. Neither of them took their eyes from Cameron's face for a second.

"That rifle was made about fifty years ago," Cameron stated matter-of-factly. "If you'll be honest with me you'll admit that from a dead rest, firing six shots at one hundred yards, you'll get a pattern more than a foot wide. Finally, that breach lock is so worn out that in a very short time the whole damned thing is going to blow up in your face, and Tal Rashi won't have to worry about blasting your head off!"

"It's still a lot better than those the Uli Prang have," Mango said defensively.

"How do you know?" Cameron shot. "He may have gotten lucky in the last six months, and come by some new weapons much better than this one."

"I doubt that very much in the area he has been working," Mango insisted.

"You doubt it, but you don't really know, do you?"

"No, I don't!" Mango admitted, getting slightly angry. "These are what we have, and they are what we will use!"

Cameron looked Mango straight in the eyes and asked, "How would you like to see a real rifle? One that was made less than a year ago, and has never been fired; one that can shoot five times as far as yours, and hit the target every time."

"There is no such weapon!" Mango blurted, forgetting his manners.

"Harry!" Cameron almost shouted. "Go fetch one of our rifles, and about forty rounds of ammunition."

Without a word Harry jumped to his feet, and almost ran from the tent. He returned in less than five minutes with one of the new Springfields, and the ammunition jingling in his pockets. He handed the piece to Cameron who worked the bolt twice to make certain it was unloaded, tossing the rifle to Mango who had risen from his seat when Harry reentered.

Weird flickering lights began to radiate from Mango's eyes as he put the rifle to his shoulder, tested the weight and the balance of it;

then he cocked the bolt, and pulled the trigger twice. Pic Rhee's own rifle slid to the floor unnoticed as he stood, and moved in closer for a better look at this fabulous piece. He stood close to Mango, shifting his weight from one foot to the other, anxiously awaiting his turn to hold such a gun.

After another five minutes of examination by both men, Mango turned and asked in disbelief, "Will it actually shoot that far accurately?"

"Indeed it will!" Harry replied avidly. "Let's all go out where we've got plenty of room, and I'll give you a demonstration."

Maleek rose to his feet without help from his servants, "I'd like to witness this myself!" he squealed with glee. He turned to the pair of servants attending him, and gave them several rapid instructions in Chinese. "I told them to get a cart, and gather up about three dozen of the large clay water jars. They should make good targets, being about the width of a man's chest."

"I certainly hope you've had some experience firing one of these damned things," Cameron whispered to Harry once they were outside. "I've stuck my neck out pretty far here, and it's up to you to bail me out."

"Did you ever see me buy anything that I didn't try out, and find to my own satisfaction, before I paid for it?" Harry asked.

"Yes," Cameron replied instantly, "a couple of those girls at Margo's."

"Don't be cutting now, chappie," Harry snorted, "I mean business wise."

"Well, I sure hope you know all about them, because I sure as hell don't," Cameron responded.

"Don't worry, I tell you," Harry spoke louder now that there was some distance between them and the others. "The sergeant, I mean gentleman, that sold me these spent one whole day teaching me how to load, fire, dismantle and assemble them. He taught me how to adjust the sights, the proper technique of firing, and we practiced from one to five hundred yards until I had it down pat. I couldn't hear a blasted thing for a week after," Harry recalled.

When they were well clear of the city and tents, with only emptiness before them, they had the servants set up ten of the clay jars at a paced off one-hundred yards.

"Which of you is the best shot with your own rifles?" Cameron inquired of Mango. Without hesitation, Mango indicated it was Pic Rhee.

"Very well," Cameron said, "have him use his best shooting position, and see how many of those pots he can break with ten rounds."

Pic Rhee chose a sitting position, and out of ten shots he broke four of the jars. The rest were near misses.

When the four jars were replaced it was Harry's turn and he chose the prone position. He checked the wind, but there was not enough to compensate for. Then very slowly he squeezed off five shots, and five jars disintegrated. He then reloaded and did a repeat performance.

"Now!" Harry exclaimed jubilantly, "have them set the next ones up at three hundred paces!"

"It would be a waste of precious bullets," Pic Rhee replied. "If I were lucky I might hit one or two out of ten."

Harry didn't answer. Instead he elevated the sight for the increased distance, then once more lowered himself to the prone position. He was very careful this time to make sure there were no small pebbles under his elbows and legs; that he was perfectly relaxed and comfortable. In rapid order he demolished the first five jars, and turned to Mango to ask, "Would you like to try it Prince Mango?"

"Indeed I would!" the Prince replied.

Before Harry would let him fire he drew a picture of the target in the sand, then a picture of the front and rear sight showing them precisely how they should be lined up. He explained to them the advantages of the prone position, holding one's breath at the proper time and to squeeze, not pull, the trigger. When Harry was sure they had it all straight, he loaded and handed the rifle to Mango, made sure that his position was good, and told him to proceed. Five times the rifle barked, and the remaining five jars burst into shreds.

Now it was Pic Rhee's turn, and Harry went through the same procedure, with identical results. Pic Rhee looked up at his master from his firing position, and he had never seen such a brilliant smile on the Prince's face.

"It's magnificent, positively magnificent!" Mango shouted with glee. "I never dreamed such a thing was possible!"

"I'm not through yet," Harry informed them. "How many targets do we have left?"

"Fifteen!" Maleek shouted like a happy child from his seat on the cart.

"Have them set the rest of them up at five hundred paces," Harry instructed.

"You're pressing your luck," Cameron whispered nervously.

"Have as much faith in me now, old Sport, as I had in you at the camp of Cheng Wu, what say?" Harry responded.

When the last of the targets were in place, and the servants in the clear, Harry double checked the elevation setting on the sight, then lowered himself to his shooting position. This time, however, he didn't try any rapid fire; and twice he withheld his fire, and started his sequence over because he felt off balance. When his five rounds were spent, five of the jars had disappeared. "Once again it's your turn, Prince Mango, only this time center the front sight about three inches higher on the jar."

Mango had been watching every tiny move that Harry made as he fired, and when he stood upright only five of the jars remained. "Pic Rhee," Mango laughed, "finish-off the remaining five enemies."

Pic Rhee was as methodical as his master, but on the final shot he missed, ever so slightly, but he missed. Cameron had a growing suspicion that the miss was on purpose, but did not care to question Pic Rhee's reasons.

The faces of both men radiated with pleasure as they once more passed the rifle back and forth for further inspection. Finally Mango looked up at Cameron standing nearby. "A weapon like this is worth a fortune," he said with longing in his voice and in his eyes.

"Oh!" Harry exclaimed, "There's one other little thing about this beauty I forgot to show you. Let me have her for a second. He took the rifle as Mango extended it, and at the same time drew five more single cartridges from his pocket. "Now watch," he said, "and count slowly to yourself as I begin." One at a time he loaded the shells into the magazine, closing the bolt. "How long did it take?" he asked.

"About eight or nine seconds, I'd say," Cameron replied. "Why?"

"I'll show you why," Harry snorted. He ejected the five single shells from the magazine leaving the bolt open.

From his left pocket he produced five cartridges held together at the cap end by a brass clip. In one swift motion he placed the clip in front of the bolt, forced the rear of the top shell downward with his thumb. With a loud snap all five cartridges dropped into the magazine at once, and the brass clip fell away. With the same exacting speed he slammed the bolt home, and fired all five shots into a hillside as rapidly as he could.

The eyes and mouths of the men were wide open in astonishment.

"My God, it's like lightening!" Cameron exclaimed breathlessly. "You loaded and fired all five of those shots in less than half the time it took you to only load the other way."

Pic Rhee was too stunned even to speak, he could only stand and stare in wide-eyed amazement.

Mango walked to where Harry stood, and extended his hands without a word. Harry handed it to him with a grin, "That's some fine piece of machinery, isn't it?"

Mango did not answer because he did not hear. He was so deep in thought and admiration, nothing came through to him. He sat down in the dirt cross legged, and laid the rifle on his legs very gently, then began to stroke it softly as he would a woman he cared for very strongly. He sat in this manner for a long time, then finally looked up at Cameron and stated simply, "I must have this rifle whatever your price is."

"You already know what my price is, Prince Mango," Cameron replied barely above a whisper. "Take us to your mountain, and guide us to the top."

"Then that is as it will be," Mango replied and there was a great sadness in his voice.

"That's not quite all there is to it, Prince Mango," Cameron said as he seated himself beside him. "You see, we brought along enough of these rifles so that each of your men will have one, with enough ammunition to teach them all to be experts, and still have enough left over to blow the entire Uli Prang to hell and back three times. It's all yours if you'll just help us do what we have come here to do."

With each word that Cameron spoke the light in Mango's eyes glowed brighter. When Cameron finished, Mango jumped to his feet and held the rifle high. "Yes, we will do it, we will take you to the very top of Kula Kangri, and then with these there is no doubt that we shall succeed in our own mission." He looked around at the other men, then shouted, "Quickly, quickly, we must hurry, I have changed my mind. We leave in the morning at dawn, for we cannot afford to lose a single day!"

For the remainder of the day, and well into the night, the tent city of the Merchant of Chamdo was alive with activity. Darkness fell and the lamps burned brightly in the more than one hundred pavilions that formed the compound.

The entire compliment of Mango's men was crowded into his personal quarters, and each man issued one of the new rifles. For the next three hours Harry instructed them in the removal of the heavy wax-like protective covering, the thorough cleaning of the bore and bolt, and lastly how to disassemble and assemble the new weapons. He then informed them, through Pic Rhee, as to the care, the oiling and maintenance of their rifles. He remembered that the sergeant had told him that a man should be able to strip, clean and put his piece back together in total darkness before he was ever allowed to fire it; and this was precisely what Harry planned to achieve. He would not allow any ammunition to be passed out until this feat could be accomplished by every man, and that would take more than one evening he was sure.

"For the first few days of our march we'll have to stop early enough for the men to spend an hour or more familiarizing themselves with these new guns. When I believe they are ready, and not before, they can begin shooting, but that too will be under supervision, just as I showed the two of you. That way we shouldn't have any wild firing or waste of ammunition. A week from now I expect each man here to be an expert marksman, and not just from a prone position," Harry concluded.

"You will find them to be exactly that in less time than you expect," Mango countered. "These men were each chosen because of their unusual abilities, not just their courage and fighting spirit."

"You know them better than I ever will," Harry answered. "I will leave the training in your hands, and that of your Captain. I'll be around to help as much as I can. Right now, I must leave and find Jo Lung."

"As you wish," Mango returned. "I'll keep them at this for another hour, but then they will have to be given time to assemble their gear and see to their mounts. Also, they must have rest if we leave at dawn."

"Absolutely," Harry agreed as he turned to leave.

He found Jo in the tent of Maleek along with Cameron. When he entered, he heard them talking of how the great camel caravans were slowly disappearing. They were being replaced by river boat and steamship, railroads, and in some parts of the world, the new undependable motor car.

Harry acknowledged each of their greetings, and accepted a tall tumbler of scotch and water that was handed him. After a few moments of light conversation he turned to Jo Lung and asked bluntly, "What are your plans now, Jo?"

"I shall return to Shanghai, and the house of Te Chien where I belong," Jo answered with a smile.

"I presumed that," Harry said amiably, "but how do you plan to travel?"

"Within the week," Jo responded, "three junks of the venerable Merchant here will be loaded and proceed downriver to Ipin. From there it will be a simple matter for me to take a river packet home."

"What about all those damned river pirates I've heard so much about?" Harry blustered.

Maleek cut in without apology, "I have been shipping my goods up and down that river for a great many years, and with only two minor exceptions have never lost a ship or cargo. The two exceptions I mentioned were not by pirates, but by men forced into an occupation they neither understood nor wanted. Unfortunately they never lived to regret their mistake. My ships all bear special markings, and the real pirates make sure nothing happens to them. I pay them an annual protection fee, and in the long run it is more profitable for both them and me. I also donate a moderate stipend to General Cheng Wu; and he also guards, rather than molests, my goods. But there is more to it than just the monies with the General. As you are aware he is very ambitious, and he knows that I have very powerful connections throughout the land. One day he thinks he might need my help, and well he may!" Maleek chuckled.

"I don't approve of tribute in any form!" Harry stated vehemently.

"Believe me, friend Clayborne, I'm the one who receives the most benefit." Once more Maleek laughed loudly, then grew serious. "Getting back to the General, you must not return through his territory. I know the scoundrel well, and he will not let you escape a second time. When you have finished your business at Kula Kangri, you must leave through India. Pic Rhee and Mango know the way well, and will see you safely there."

"I thought the borders were tightly closed," Cameron interjected.

"Oh, they are to be sure," Maleek assured them, "to anyone trying to come into this country, but not to those that are leaving. The only response you will get from the border guards will be a great amount of astonishment. I would like to be there to see their faces when you show up."

"Well, that's certainly a relief," Cameron breathed, "I've been worried about that for sometime now. Once in India it will be no trick at all to get back home."

"Absolutely," Maleek grinned, "General Cheng Wu is going to have a long and painful wait, isn't he?"

"That suits me fine," Harry ventured, then turned once more to Jo Lung. "Jo, I don't know the proper words to thank you for all that you and your people have done for all of us." He reached out and grabbed Jo by the arm, pumping his hand vigorously.

"There is no need for thanks," Jo smiled. "Am I not still your agent here in China, and being paid handsomely for my efforts?"

"You certainly are, Jo," Harry beamed, "and will be until I die, or some worse catastrophe overtakes me; but I hardly think I need worry about that now," he laughed. A reddish hue of frustration crept into Harry's face and he fumbled with the huge gold watch and chain fastened to his belt. He handed it to Jo, and his next words came out haltingly. "I want you to have this Jo. We might be partners in business for the next forty or fifty years, but will probably never see each other again." He wanted to say more, but was so choked with emotion he could not continue. He pressed the gift into Jo's small hands, and held them tight for several moments.

Jo had it in mind to refuse such an extravagant offer immediately, then he gazed into the deep brown pools of Harry's eyes. "I do not need anything to remind me of our friendship and our experience together; but I shall cherish this as long as I too live and when I die, it will go to my children and then to theirs."

Harry turned then to Maleek, "Your hospitality great Merchant of Chamdo is only exceeded by the greatness of your heart, and as with Jo Lung, there are not enough words to tell you of my gratitude."

"It is I who should be thanking you friend Clayborne," replied Maleek while holding firmly to Harry's hand. "Your coming here will surely lead to the complete end of the Uli Prang; of this I have no doubt. With the new weapons you provided, I am also sure that most, if not all, of my valued guards will return to me. When they do they will be the finest equipped unit in all of Asia. For all these things I am humbly in your debt." Maleek concluded.

"May I come to your quarters and help you pack your gear?" Jo inquired of Harry.

"I would really appreciate that, old friend," Harry answered and the two of them departed, Harry's arm firmly about the shoulders of the frail Jo Lung.

"I guess it's time for us to make our farewells also," stated Cameron as he rose to his feet. "We are to leave with the first light, and might not see you that early in the morning."

"Very true," Maleek acknowledged. "It has been many years now since I rose before the sun. I think you will find that my servants have taken care of your needs well. I myself took the liberty of exchanging most of your mounts. I left you the best of your own for pack animals, and you will find your riding stock stronger and more suited to this country.

I really don't see how several of your horses made it here at all." Maleek said mystified.

"There were quite a few that didn't," Cameron responded. "We were fortunate in being able to replace them when we needed. Harry pretty well summed up the feeling of all of us for the kindness and help you have given us, so I won't prolong the agony of goodbye any longer." He extended his hand and Maleek took it warmly, and then that of Dr. Felix.

Maleek stood looking at the two men for several seconds, then spoke his final words, "My only regret in life now is that I won't live long enough to meet anymore men like yourselves." With that the old man turned and went to his sleeping quarters.

Cameron and Dr. Felix left the room without speaking, their emotions charged.

I think," Cameron said once outside, "I'd best look in on the girls and see how they are coming with their preparations."

"Good idea," Dr. Felix responded, "and I'll check on Norman and Roger. The pair of them have been so busy lately that they might not even know we're leaving."

Cameron called loudly at the door of the ladies quarters, and it was Connie's voice that bade him enter. He was genuinely shocked to find both of the girls clad in tight fitting silken kimonos. They lay stretched out on the floor with two of the servant girls, playing some sort of game with large wooden cards. When Cameron entered the chamber all four of them rose to their feet.

"I sent word to you earlier this afternoon that we would be leaving at sunrise in the morning," Cameron said, a tight sensation closing on his throat. "I just wanted to make sure that you had received the message, and ask if there was anything I might do for either of you?" To himself he thought, *I don't believe I've ever seen two more beautiful women in the world.* Then he shook his head slightly as if to clear it. "I think I've been out here too long," he mused.

"Yes," Connie said as she walked toward him, "we were told; we're packed and ready to go." She couldn't help notice the way his eyes traveled up and down her figure. "These native dresses were given us by the youngest wife of Maleek. Do you suppose it will be alright if we take them with us, or should we still travel as lightly as possible?" She was playing with him, hoping for some sort of compliment.

"There's not enough weight to a dozen of them to make any difference." Cameron replied regaining full control of himself. "Take them, by all means," he added. "You girls really should have a few souvenirs to remind you of this trip. Is there anything I can do for either of you before I say goodnight?"

"No, I think not." Connie replied, her spirits dropping appreciably.

"In that case I'm going to get a few hours of rest myself, and suggest you do the same. Goodnight." he added and disappeared through the door.

For a full minute after he left Connie stood looking at the spot where he had been. The fluttering of her heart as she approached him was now a dull aching whack, and a tight agonizing knot formed in her belly. Her hands gripped each other and she squeezed so hard her fingers turned white.

Behind her Penny gave the servants a long hard stare, and they gathered up the cards and left silently. Penny waited a short while longer, and then without preamble asked directly, "You love him, don't you Connie?" her words were soft and gentle.

"Yes, damn it, I love him," Connie shouted as she whirled about, "and I wish to hell I didn't, and I don't know why I do . . ." She ran to the pile of cushions that was her bed and threw herself down, sobbing softly before her head ever touched her pillow.

Penny came and sat beside her, then began stroking the short soft curls embracing her head. In all the time the two girls had been together this was the first time she had ever seen tears in Connie's eyes.

She let her cry for a few more minutes, and then tried consoling her. "I'm sure it will all work out in the near future, darling, I know that he thinks a great deal of you."

"No, it won't work out, Penny, because I ruined it all from the very start. He could never forget nor forgive the things I've said and done to him since the moment we met.

That's where it all started, Penny. I know now that I loved him from the first moment I laid eyes on him, but I was too stubborn to admit I was wrong in my preconceived notion of him. I fought him and insulted him every chance I got just to prove I was right, and all the time I knew in my heart I was wrong, but wouldn't give into it. Oh, Lord, Penny, what am I going to do now?" and she began to sob once more.

"The first thing you're going to do, dear, is have a real good old fashioned cry," Penny said as she pulled her to her bosom. "When you're all through we're going to dry your eyes, and make you all pretty again like your natural self. In the morning you're going to mount your horse just like you have before; only this time you're going to stay as close to that man as possible, and in the days that are to come you're going to convince him that you're not really the witch you tried to make him think you were before. When the proper time comes, which I'm sure it will, you are going to let him know exactly how you feel about him. Remember, dearest, it wasn't too long ago that I had the same feeling about Harry that you're experiencing right now. It has worked out just as you told me it would, and I'm the happiest woman alive."

"But everything is different in this case," Connie countered, the tears still wet on her cheeks. "Cameron was hurt terribly by his first wife, he's been a loner most of his life, and then I hurt him even more."

"When the time comes, you'll make up for all the hurts he ever had in his entire life, and he will love you all the more for it." Penny said. "Now, dry your eyes and let's both get some sleep, it's not long until daylight."

Much later, when Connie heard Penny's deep and regular breathing she said aloud, "Dear God, I do hope she's right. I want to make everything up to him so desperately!"

*   *   *   *   *

The first rays of the morning sun exploded on the fortress wall of Chamdo a good mile behind them, and the multicolored tents of the Merchant stood out vividly against the brown stone walls.

Pic Rhee had already sent out his point men and flankers. The men still carried their old weapons with the new ones lashed securely to their saddles. A quarter of a mile behind the point men rode the advance guard, four men riding abreast though slightly staggered. Behind these four Mango and Pic Rhee rode side-by-side followed by Cameron, Harry and the two girls. This wasn't the way Mango had wanted it, but this was the way it worked out according to Penny's desires. Mango had wanted the ladies farther to the rear with the pack animals; but Penny would not hear of it, and Harry looked at her with new wonderment. He had never seen her so determined.

The total compliment numbered more than fifty horses. The morning was cool and brisk with only a slight breeze, and the sun would have some heat to it before the day was over.

They made excellent time the first day, covering near forty miles, and had an exceptional campsite beside a small stream that evening. The rifle practice started as soon as the cook fires had been lit, and the stock taken care of. Tonight it was only mock firing to get the feel of the pieces; but they all knew the next night would be the real thing, and they worked hard to achieve perfection in the eyes of the man who had brought them the rifles.

Constance and Penny had very little, if anything to do; for all of the camp chores, including the cooking was done by Mango's men, and as it turned out, they were most capable. To Penny this was an ideal situation; for it gave her ample time in the evening to help Connie with her toilet, and make her look her best when she presented herself for dinner.

The men of the guard pitched their tents on the far side of the stream near the horse corral, but Mango insisted that his shelter be next to the one occupied by Dr. Felix, Norman and Roger. He also took his meals with them; by now, everyone in the party had noticed his strange fascination with the Doctor.

By the time their supper was finished and the remains cleared away, darkness had settled in with permanence. The group sat huddled about the embers of the cook fire, for the evening chill had arrived with nightfall.

Dr. Felix looked across the fire to where Mango sat, and their gaze met and held. "Since first we met, "Dr. Felix began, a soft smile upon his lips, "you seem to have found some strange attraction in my appearance, Prince Mango. I am curious to know how I am different from the rest of us here." His tone was amiable.

"I apologize for being so rude,"Mango said without lowering his stare, "but you look so amazingly like someone I knew a long time ago that it's hard for me to believe you're not the same man. In my mind, I'm sure that he is dead and buried many, many years ago and yet his memory keeps coming alive each time I look at you."

"Who was this man?" Dr. Felix asked simply, "and how long has it been since you last saw him?"

"As unusual as it may seem"Mango replied, "I never did know his name. He was a Nestorian priest traveling from India to somewhere in Russia. It was when I was a small boy of eight or nine, and he was brought into the camp of my father more dead than alive with some grave illness. He remained with us for nearly two months, until he had fully recuperated. I remember him vividly. Once he started to mend he would set by the campfires each evening and tell us stories from what he called The Book. He did not preach to us, nor try to convert; but the tales he related were strange and sometimes very exciting. All of us, especially the children, grew to love him very much; and when it came time to him to go, we begged him to stay on with us."

"What was his answer?" Dr. Felix asked in a low whisper.

"He thanked us profusely for saving his life and allowing him to be our guest; but he said that he had been called to another part of the world, and it was there that he must go. Then, he did a very odd thing; he laid his hand upon the head of each man, woman and child of the clan, and blessed us in the name of his God. The following morning he was gone, and no one saw him leave, though the camp was heavily guarded."

"Do you still recall any of the stories he told you?" Dr. Felix asked with keen interest.

"A great many of them," Mango replied, "but not in detail. He told us of his God, and how he had created the world, the heavens, the moon and the stars. He also told us how this God created man and then woman, and all of the other things we know here upon this earth. He told us of strange lands that came into being with great kings whose names were impossible to remember; of many wars and battles, and of a simple man that was supposed to be the son of this great God, yet his own people nailed him to a wooden cross and left him to die. I remember him saying that after this man died he was taken down from the cross, and placed in a sealed tomb, and that he arose from the dead, and went to join his father who was God. He also said that after this man was gone many people who had not believed his teachings changed their minds, and spent the rest of their lives traveling through the world telling of his man, and that one day he would be savior of all mankind."

"Do you remember the name given to the one that died upon the cross?" Dr. Felix asked gently.

"For a long time afterward I did," Mango answered, "but then I forgot, and did not know it again until Maleek instructed me in the English language, and explained what little he knew of their religion. He was called Jesus Christ, was he not?"

"Yes," Dr. Felix replied emphatically, "that was his name, Prince Mango." For at least two minutes the Doctor sat contemplating the glowing embers of the fire, then raised his glance to Mango's face one more. "Perhaps I am wrong, but I have the feeling that there is something you would have me do for you."

"Your intuition is correct, Doctor," Mango replied frankly. "There is something Pic Rhee and I would ask you; but first I must explain. After I lost my people, and went to Maleek for help, it was he that taught me your language, and reminded me of what I knew of your religion. In turn it was I that taught Pic Rhee, for we have spent thousands of nights together by the camp fires of the caravan trail, and there is really very little to speak of once the day's work is done. In teaching Pic Rhee I learned even more myself, and after many months we decided that to become proficient in our new tongue we would converse in nothing but English once the camp was established each night. But in all our travels we never found anyone that could, or would, explain your religion, and unless we understand that, we feel we can never fully comprehend your people or your language. We would like you to teach both of us what the stories meant that the Nestorian Priest told so many years ago. Is this possible, Dr. Felix?"

Once again Dr. Felix's eyes returned to the fire and he did not reply. His hands trembled as he placed them upon his own thighs, and his face grew pale. His soft gentle smile vanished, and his lips compressed to a thin hard line. His vision clouded momentarily, then cleared and his frame relaxed. "It will take a great deal of time, Prince Mango, but I shall be honored to oblige you if this is your desire." The Doctor answered humbly.

"The nights are long, and we have a large number of them to spend before we reach the valley of Kirghiz," Mango responded eagerly. "Would you care to begin tonight?"

The Doctor was visibly startled by the suddenness of Mango's request. "Yes, yes, of course if you wish," he replied, his voice shaking. "Go fetch Pic Rhee and we shall begin immediately."

Mango bounded to his feet and nearly ran to the camp on the far side of the stream. Dr. Felix returned his gaze to the fire and did not look up.

* * * * *

Penny was angry. She had done everything in her power to make Connie more attractive. She had argued until she had won her point of the two of them riding directly behind Cameron and Harry, and she had spent a good hour grooming Connie before coming to the evening meal. Beyond the usual inquiries of their well-being and needs, Cameron had said or done nothing. The complete attention of all the men around the fire was directed toward Mango and Dr. Felix, and probably would be for the rest of the night. In disgust Penny rose to her feet. "I feel extra tired tonight," she feigned, "I think I'll go to bed early. Will you all excuse me?"

"I think I'll join you," Connie said without feeling as she rose.

"Of course," Doctor Felix replied raising his head.

"Roger and I still have a great deal of work to bring our charts and log up to date," Norman said hesitantly." Could we be excused also?"

"I'm fully aware of the enormity of your task Norman," Dr. Felix answered seriously. "I was beginning to wonder why you dawdled here so long. The two of you have your work cut out for you, now get along with it."

When Mango and Pic Rhee had returned, and taken their seats beside the Doctor, he did not begin immediately; but instead looked toward the heavens and the brightly twinkling stars. When he finally spoke his words were soft and clear, "In the beginning God created the heaven and the earth. And the earth was without form, and void; and darkness was upon the face of the deep. And the spirit of God moved upon the face of the waters. And God said, let there be light, and there was light. And God called the light Day and the darkness he called Night. And the evening and the morning were the first day." The Doctor's voice went on with clarity and without hesitation.

Cameron looked at the Doctor in genuine surprise, for he was sure these were the precise words from the first chapter of the

Scriptures, yet there was no Book within the Doctor's hands, and his eyes still scanned the heavens as though it was from there he was reading the words.

With a blank expression on his face, Harry turned questioningly to Cameron, who merely shrugged his reply.

Dr. Felix continued on for more than an hour without visual aid of any kind. Cameron and Harry listened with total fascination until at length Mango interrupted to ask a question. Dr. Felix turned to look at the Prince and patiently explained, then continued.

A short while later Cameron felt Harry's eyes upon him again, and after observing his friend's countenance he nodded silently. The two of them rose and went to their respective tents. The remaining trio never noticed them leave.

In his usual propensity, Cameron had pitched his shelter off to himself; a good two-hundred feet from his closest neighbor, Harry.

Tonight, especially, he appreciated his solitude, for he was extremely tired and deeply disturbed. The perpetual nearness of Connie throughout the entire day was something he had not had to cope with in the past and he found this new situation almost unbearable.

When she emerged from her tent, and sat beside him for the evening meal he was so upset he could not touch his food for several minutes.

He closed and lashed the flaps of his tent, removed his boots and clothes, then snuggled into the warmth of the comforter. "Somehow, someway," he said aloud softly," I've got to get her out of my mind. Nothing, absolutely nothing can ever come of it, and if something doesn't happen soon, it's going to drive me crazy!"

He shut his eyes and his mind as best he could, but sleep did not come for a long time. He could still hear the faint droning sound of Dr. Felix's voice when at last he dropped into fitful slumber.

Each day thereafter went much the same as the one before. The raw jagged starkness of the mountains, the narrow valleys with icy cold streams and a carpet of grass and low brush remained. The passes were steep and narrow, with many sheer drops that took one's breath away without getting close to the edge.

At the crest of each pass Cameron had noticed many strange conical piles of small rocks. "What is the meaning of those," he asked pointing as they stopped at the summit to give their mounts a breather.

Mango smiled broadly, displaying his perfect teeth." Though all of the people of this land are Lamaists, and worship Buddha, they still have other Gods. Those are monuments of thanks to the mountain Gods for allowing former travelers safe passage."

"Well, I'll be damned," was all Cameron could think of to say.

"Perhaps you had best dismount and build a monument of your own to make sure that you are not," Mango laughed in jest.

"As you wish," Mango laughed again, "but don't say I didn't warn you."

"Did you ever build one, Prince Mango?" Harry asked, with mischief in his eyes.

"Never!" Mango snorted as he kneed his horse to move out.

In the ten days since leaving Chamdo, they had passed through two tiny hamlets, each a collection of small low roofed houses made of stone, held in place with a hard clay substance. Most of the residents stayed within their dwellings as their entourage passed through. Mango did manage to purchase some fresh supplies at the last settlement they passed through.

They met few travelers on the trail, mostly tenders of the flocks that fed beside the road and a driver of some heavy laden yaks on their way to a market somewhere. They encountered one small caravan of loaded camels headed east, and moved off the trail to let it pass. There were perhaps two hundred animals in the lot, and it was not of Maleek's so they moved on without formal greeting. Occasionally, they would pass one or two of the gray clad lamas with their cowls pulled far up over their head; once they passed a small mounted group of four young women. Connie and Penny were fascinated by their ornate headdresses, and the gold and silver coins threaded into their hair.

When evening came, they camped at the foot of a low mountain range beside a large spring that bubbled out from beneath the base of a huge black rock. It was plain to see that this campsite was used frequently, for the ground was littered with dried animal droppings, and there was very little grass or other forage.

"We'll have to picket the animals some distance from here, and set up a separate guard as soon as they are unloaded," Mango said as he dismounted. "There will be nothing for them to eat for perhaps a half mile. This campsite is a favored one because of the purity of the water, and is used a great deal. We'll have no trouble rounding up fuel for our cook fires though," Mango laughed.

"Well, we can't have everything," Cameron agreed as he too alighted. "That's a strange colored boulder, isn't it?" he observed.

"Yes, it is;" Mango agreed, "it's the only one like it I've ever seen in this part of the country, so it's naturally a landmark." Mango gestured to the low range before them. "Beyond those mountains is the city of Lhasa. We will not be allowed to go through it, but there is a trail that cuts through the hills to the south of the city. Maleek instructed me that this is the route we are to take. He tried to get permission for us to pass through the city, but the Dali Lama would not hear of it. Few foreigners have ever been allowed to enter its gates. We are lucky though, being able to pass so close. You will have an excellent view from the trail we will follow."

"Have you ever been there, Prince Mango?" Harry asked with aroused curiosity.

"Many times," Mango replied, "and so have all my men. Though we are no Lamaists, we are not considered aliens."

"Then you will be able to tell us about the temples, and all when we are able to see them?" Harry asked anxiously.

"Most certainly," Mango responded, "I know the city well."

"Would it be possible for Norman to make a drawing of the city?" Cameron inquired. "He's very talented in that direction you know."

Mango hesitated only slightly, replying, "It will be possible if we are not caught in the act. As far as I know there is no law against anyone drawing a picture of the city, but then maybe no one ever thought of it before. You are among the first strangers to ever get this close. We'll see how much company we have when we arrive above the city in the morning.

During the past ten days Penny had been doing her best to bolster Connie's spirits, but knew that she was fighting a losing battle. Though she still smiled, and was polite to everyone, it was easy for Penny to see that it was only a front. Day-by-day she sank deeper into a state of lethargy from which Penny could not arouse her. She ate very little; the music was gone from her voice, the bounce from her step, and shadowy clouds seemed to be forming over her eyes. Penny was becoming alarmed, and decided she must speak to someone and soon. "Maybe tonight, after dinner," she thought, "I had best have a talk with Dr. Felix.

The opportunity for Penny to speak with Dr. Felix never presented itself. The nightly rifle practice and the Bible instruction for Mango and Pic Rhee were cancelled. When the meal was over, the men immediately began making plans for the next day. Mango and Pic Rhee began giving a detailed description and layout of the city; each taking his turn reminding the other of some item he had neglected. From descriptions alone, Norman started a pencil sketch and Roger joined by making a projected map of the city from the information they were receiving. Constant questions, erasures and corrections were made as each bit of detail was added.

"By doing this dry run, we'll save precious time, and make fewer mistakes in the morning," Roger stated with a smile as he looked up from his map. The smile faded as his eyes met Cameron's and locked. "Don't you think so, Cameron," he finally asked.

"I most assuredly do," Cameron agreed as he tried without success to return the smile that had faded so abruptly from Roger's face. "Let Harry and I gather more chips for the fire, and build another so you'll have more light to work by."

"Yes, that would help a lot," Norman applauded, "and see if you can find me any colored pencils or paints of some kind that I could use in the morning. I'd like to make the real copy as true as I can with the material we can come up with."

"I could use a better pen, and a good straight edge," Roger added, once more looking directly at Cameron.

"We'll scrounge the entire camp," Cameron assured them, as he and Harry kindled a second fire and began gathering more chips.

Dr. Felix was in a state of extreme excitement, going back and forth from the drawing to the map; asking about each temple, bridge, street and wall as they began to take shape and form before his eyes.

When the initial work of both drawings was well underway, it was Dr. Felix's inquiries that led Mango to give them a history of the city from its founding by the ancestors of King Song-sten Cam-po in the fourth century A.D. It was this King that strongly introduced Buddhism into Tibet, and later developed into a sub-branch of the religion known as Lamaism. He told of the war between Tibet and China nearly a thousand years ago, and how the treaty between the two countries had existed shakily unto this day. He also told of how a British Colonel had fought his way to Lhasa six years before, and had obtained special privileges for English authorities, but as yet not much had come of it.

Penny was listening avidly, and did not notice when Connie left her side, but hastened to their tent immediately upon discovering her absence.

Connie was already in bed, and their quarters were pitch-dark. Undressing in the gloom, Penny slipped beneath her own robes as quietly as possible, for although she did not think Connie was asleep, she did not want to chance the fact that she might be.

The sky was cloudless, and only a slight breeze fluttered when they swung out onto a bench of the hillside about a thousand feet above Lhasa. Their view of the entire city was perfect, and they had not encountered a single person upon the trail they traveled.

When they had dismounted, Mango cautioned them all against exposing themselves to the full view of anyone that might be watching from below. "You will need an ample amount of time to complete what you have in mind; but if we are seen, and someone should realize what you are about, you may never have time to finish your drawings, much less the rest of your life." he said gravely.

"Do they have soldiers down there guarding those old walls and gates?" Harry asked innocently.

"Indeed they do," Mango replied in dead seriousness, "and they are very capable and efficient at their work, if you follow my meaning!"

"I believe I do," Harry replied with a slight shudder.

Directly below the hill on which they stood ran a small river flowing in a southeasterly direction to join the Tsang Po some thirty miles distant. The valley floor was flat and fertile, for many trees and gardens were visible both within and out of the city. The walls and gates that Harry spoke of were piles of rubble and open archways, destroyed in wars long past.

Everyone present watched as Norman and Roger set up their make-shift drawing boards, fashioned the night before from rifle containers. They had each selected the largest piece of paper they possessed, and fastened it to the boards with as many pins as they were able to borrow from the ladies. After scanning the scene for several minutes, both men set about their task in earnest.

Without even glancing at one another, both men started at the same time. Cameron thought it odd that they both began at the same spot, the large open square and the adjoining temple at the center of the city. The Forbidden City was nearly one mile square, and Cameron noted that both men had their perspective pretty well in mind; their efforts were scaled down to where they would be able to accommodate the entire city on each single sheet of paper.

Mango stood between the two of them as they worked, and he watched them closely. "The temple there by the square is called Jokhang, and is supposed to be the center of Tibet," he stated as the pictures took shape. "Pic Rhee and I will supply the names of all of the more prominent buildings and other objects as you go along."

Norman merely nodded his head, and Roger did not even look up, but went on feverishly with his work.

Cameron stepped back slightly to give them more room, then began a close scrutiny of the city on his own. His gaze went first to the immense golden roofed palace to the west, which in many respects resembled a fortress. It began at the flat floor of the valley, growing outward and upward to where it completely covered and dwarfed the hill upon which it was built. The center and lower part of the palace was bright red in color, and it was here Mango had told him the past Dali Lamas and others of great achievement were entombed. He realized that it would have taken him half the day to count the windows in the upper part of this Palace called the Potala. The sun reflecting from its golden roof hurt his eyes, and he looked down again into the city to the low mud brick houses of the poor, and the solid rock homes of the more fortunate. *It's about the same throughout the world,* he told himself. He listened as Mango pointed out the Temple of Ramoche on the north of the square, and nearby the Temple of Meru. *There's enough gold on the rooftops of this city to buy rice for the entire population of China for a year,* he mused. Then for the first time he noticed the people of the streets. Three out of every five were dressed in the gray garb of the lamas. Most everyone else wore black or another dark color. At this distance he couldn't tell the men from the women, but he was sure, with the exception of the lamas, there would be about an equal number of both. He stepped forward to see how the work was progressing, and was amazed at the speed and dexterity with which both men labored.

The drawings went on for an hour, then two, and were still not complete. The forward part of the guard had grown bored with the whole affair and without mounting, had gradually started drifting up the trail that led to the west. The guards bringing up the rear and tending the pack animals were trapped by their own position. Many of them found shady spots and went to sleep, while the others merely dozed lightly in the warmth of the morning sun.

When they had first glimpsed this fabled city they had traveled so far to see, Connie's keen interest returned, and for a while she shared the excitement of Penny with her oohs and aahs. At the end of an hour she had seen all she cared to see, and she withdrew to a cool spot beside a large boulder.

When Penny missed her sometime later, she came to her side and tried to revive her curiosity by telling her of the beautiful turquoise tiled bridge and the many flower gardens that Pic Rhee had pointed out to her. Connie listened to her patiently, but it soon became evident to Penny she wasn't doing any good.

"I wish they would hurry up and finish, so that we could move on," Connie said after a long silence. "I'm getting tired of standing here."

"So do I," Penny agreed with a small amount of heat, "but you know how men are, they want perfection."

"Let's walk up the trail a ways to break the monotony," Connie suggested without any real enthusiasm. "Surely they should be finished in a few more minutes."

"Maybe we ought to tell them first, Penny advised.

"They're so preoccupied, I doubt if they would hear if you yelled at them," Connie replied listlessly. "It will be alright, the forward guard has already moved out anyway.

"Well, if you think so." Penny ceded.

They too picked up the reins of their mounts, and began to walk slowly up the trail. Within a hundred yards or so the trail made a sharp turn to the left, forming a gentle arc as the hill dipped inward. The road was wide in most spots, though littered with stones and boulders of varying sizes. As the two women neared the point where the trail would swing on to the outward arc again, the left side of it became a vertical cliff some twenty feet high, with a jagged crest that flattened off for several hundred feet beyond what they could see.

They strolled at a leisurely pace without talking, taking notice of the different shapes of the rocks in their path, the sections of the city they could still see below now and then, and the summit of the low mountains beyond the Patola they knew they could have to cross.

Connie noticed the birds first. "Look at those stupid birds, Penny, they are flying right into that cliff ahead of us," she said with dismay. As they got closer, however, they became aware of a six-foot-wide crevice in the ledge, and it was here the birds were entering. Dozens of them, all of different species and sizes were setting up a din of loud screeches, chirps and whistles.

"I wonder what is attracting them in there?" Connie asked with reawakened awareness.

"I wouldn't have the slightest notion," Penny replied. Noting the difference in Connie's attitude she added, "we could walk in and see. It looks like a path of some sort going in there."

"Let's do it," Connie proposed with some degree of excitement in her voice. "We'll leave the horses here so the men will know we're here when they catch up."

The steep walls on both sides pulled in toward each other, and they hadn't gone thirty feet before the passage had narrowed to little more than two feet wide. It continued on this way for another ten feet, then made a sharp left turn, and instantly opened into a large chamber with dozens of large flat rocks lying on the smooth floor. The racket of the hundreds of birds within was deafening; the rocks were covered with them, the ground was teeming with them, and clusters of them clung to the sheer walls surrounding the basin. Those atop the rocks seemed to be feeding and fighting over scraps of whatever they were eating.

The eyes of both girls were fastened upon a rock near the wall where most of the birds congregated. It was at this precise moment that a double handful of unidentifiable shreds dropped from above and the scramble among the fowl developed into a minor battle.

Connie and Penny both raised their glance at the same time and saw a ledge of solid rock about six feet high, at least ten feet deep and forty foot long. Atop this shelf were four brown clad, cowl hooded, figures busily engaged in stripping the flesh from the remains of a person. They held small curved knives that moved with blinding speed, periodically glistening in the sunlight. It was an unbelievable scene; in a matter of seconds an arm, leg, head or chest was stripped of all meat, and only the bones remained. Every few seconds, one of the shrouded figures would fling a hand full of what he had cut free to the waiting birds, making sure that no section of the floor was neglected.

At first, Connie could not force herself to believe that the object they were working on was anything more than an animal of some sort. Then her eyes came to rest on the naked bodies of four or five humans laid out side-by-side within three yards of the blood covered stone being used as a table. The fresh crimson liquid slowly oozed down all three sides of the rocks she could see. She noted that the escarpment sloped naturally toward the floor where they stood; that a wide, dark-brown band came down the face of it and had discolored the sand floor for several feet around.

The entire scene was so ghoulishly unrealistic she could not believe it was really happening. She watched them neatly dismember all of the bones that remained and place them in a compact pile against the wall, with the skull at the very top. When two of them turned and deftly lifted the nearest corpse to the waiting table of rock, she knew undeniably that it was real and a terrible soul-chilling scream burst from her lungs. The frenzied sound that emitted from her throat was nearly drowned out as the mesmerized Penny faced the same stark reality and terror-stricken cries cut through Connie's.

*   *   *   *   *

The picture and the map were completed. Roger and Norman were carefully stowing them and gathering up their gear, when Cameron and Harry noticed the women were missing. Without waiting, or saying a word to anyone, they mounted their horses and headed up the trail at a brisk trot. They saw the girl's animals as soon as they came around the bend, and were dismounting when Connie's first scream pierced the air. Cameron dashed into the crevice without thinking to take a weapon. They almost knocked the girls to the ground as they burst into the basin.

The screaming had stopped by the time they arrived, and Cameron took in the entire scene instantly. The four men on the ledge stood like statues carved from stone, poised above the corpse they had begun to work on. None of them had moved a muscle since that first ear shattering sound, except to turn and stare at the two girls.

Penny had covered her mouth with both her hands, and she felt rather than saw Harry come up behind her. She whirled and stumbled blindly into his arms.

Connie's mouth was still open, but no sound came out; her eyes were vacant and immobile, and her hands were raised pressing into her breasts. Violent trembling racked her entire body, and Cameron was afraid she would collapse before he could reach her.

In one swift motion he picked her up, one arm around her shoulders, and the other behind her knees. Her body was as rigid as a piece of iron. When he came to the narrow part of the path, he had to turn sideways to get them out and he was terribly afraid he might hurt her, the confinement was so close. Once outside he wanted to lay her down, but the rigidity remained, so he lowered her to the ground in a standing position, holding her close so that she would not fall.

The severity of her trembling warned him that she was in a state near convulsions; and suddenly the thought that she might lose her mind, or die, smashed into his brain. He tilted her head back to see her face, and though her mouth had closed, the vacant stare remained. Terror raced through him as he lost control. He shouted, "Connie, Connie, for God's sake don't leave me, please, Connie, please come back. I love you, Connie, Oh, God how I love you!" He pulled her to him as tightly as he dared, pressing his lips to hers, gently at first, and as the thought of losing her grew, the pressure of his lips increased.

He had no idea of how long he had held her like this, when he felt the stiffness begin to leave her taut small frame. Then he felt her arms slowly come up and close about the back of his neck, the warmth flooding back into her lips as they parted ever so slightly and felt the wetness of her tears cruising down his cheeks.

He started to move, thinking to set her down; but she clung to him as though her life depended on it, and quite possibly it had. When the trembling had mostly stopped, she moved her mouth away from his just far enough to slide her lips across his face and down his neck, there she rested her head. He was then able to pick her up and carry her to a flat stone, where he sat down with her cradled in his lap like a small child.

It was at this moment that he thought of Harry and Penny, and he glanced about anxiously. He was greatly relieved to see them sitting side-by-side not twenty feet away, Harry caressing her, and whispering soothing words he could not hear.

He sat holding Connie for a long time until he made up his mind she was stable. "It wasn't what you thought in there a few minutes ago," he said softly, "and if you'll listen to me I'll explain it all to you, and make your fears go away."

She didn't answer him, but he knew she was listening because she snuggled even closer. "You see, dearest, these people in this land have different customs and beliefs than we do. They believe that when a person dies his spirit leaves his body to be reincarnated in another body. They think that babies are born without a soul or spirit, whatever you want to call it; and sometimes they grow up to be men or women before the right spirit finds them, and moves into their body. This is all well and good so far, but you see, there's one bad thing here, and that is that the spirit cannot tell if a body it wants to move into is asleep or dead. If the spirit were to occupy a body that was dead it would be trapped there for eternity; and that is why the flesh must be removed from the dead, and the bones dismembered, so the spirit can make no irrevocable mistake. The men you saw in the brown robes were the Raga, and it is their job to dispose of the dead in this manner. Mango told the rest of us about this when we first left Chamdo, but we didn't want to tell you or Penny for fear of upsetting you. I know it's terribly difficult to accept; but here it is a way of life, and they believe it." Now, Cameron asked softly, "does that make you feel any better?"

She did not reply immediately, and when she did her face came around to where her eyes were only inches from his. "Did you really say that you loved me, Cam?" she asked with a tremor in her voice.

"Yes, I did," he answered evenly, "I said it several times."

"Did you say it because you meant it, or were you merely trying to jar me out of my hysteria?" she asked pointedly. "I remember what you said to Roger at the camp of Cheng Wu; and I know that you really didn't mean it, and didn't want to talk to him that way, but knew you had to jolt him out of his own weakness."

"I said it, because I meant it," he replied fervently, "and because it's been burning a hole in my head ever since I first saw you back in San Francisco. I was so blind, I didn't know what it was then, but I have for a long time now. I've been eating my heart out for you for weeks now and was at the point where I didn't care if I lived or died.

"Oh, Cam, darling, I love you so very, very much," she finished as she lowered her lips back to his.

They were locked in this embrace when the balance of the company rode up with Roger in the lead. He stopped not ten feet away from them, and sat glaring down at them for a full minute before they realized they were not alone. If he thought he knew hate before, he now acknowledged he had just received an extra portion direct from hell.

Ignoring Roger completely, Cameron asked, "Do you think you are able to ride now, or would you rather rest awhile longer?"

"I can make it, I'm sure, if you'll help me up onto my horse," she replied as she kissed his cheek. "From now on I want to ride at your side at all times," she insisted.

"That's where you belong," he responded as he rose and set her on the ground. Still holding her firmly about the waist he guided her to her horse, helping her up. "Just a couple of minutes more, darling. I'd like to have a word with Mango," he stated when she was firmly in the saddle.

Cameron explained what had happened to Mango, and watched as the scowl deepened upon the Prince's face. "Don't be too harsh on your men, Prince Mango," Cameron implored, "it was not their fault. Though they knew of this place, undoubtedly they gave it no more thought than we would to an embalming parlor in my country, and none of them could have guessed that the girls would make that fatal detour on their own."

"None the less," Mango insisted, "the forward guard should never have moved out until the entire party was ready to proceed. They have been taught better than this, and stern measures will be taken!"

"I beg you, Prince Mango, to temper your judgment," Cameron appealed, "for all that came out of this experience was not bad!"

Mango had been directly behind Roger when they rode up, and he too had witnessed the end result of this horrifying ordeal.

The flashing lights of his eyes softened, and the muscles of his jaw relaxed, "Very well," he agreed reluctantly, "If that is your desire."

"Yes!" Cameron exclaimed with gratitude, "I would not want the happiness I have just found blurred by the punishment of those partially responsible for it's happening."

"I understand," Mango replied, and a full smile spread across the width of his broad features.

Cameron fairly vaulted into his saddle, and Connie moved in so close to his side that their knees touched sharply.

Mango shouted an order and they moved out swiftly.

They encountered no adversity in gaining the crest of the hill beyond the Patola, and a short time later rejoined the main caravan route. Within one mile, they passed nearby, four monasteries standing close together. "These are known as the Four Lings," Mango informed them, "and it is from one of these, that the Regent to the Dali Lama is chosen." About three miles further on, as the trail swung southward, another temple appeared. "This one is known as the Temple of Chakpori, the temple of medicine, and it is from here that many of the mysteries of this land are born."

*   *   *   *   *

Three days later, in the late afternoon, Mango called the caravan to a halt. When everyone was bunched up close enough to hear, he announced, "This is the point where we leave the caravan route." He pointed southward, "We will travel in that direction, and in two days' time should be camping on the shores of the great lake of the Yandrog Tsho." The point men and flankers already knew where they were going, for they could be seen in the distance already well away from the trail.

Cameron looked around for landmarks, and could see none. They were in the flat plateau country, and everything looked the same for miles around. There was no sign of a road or path for them to follow, and he wondered if Mango really knew the exact spot to turn off, or if he was merely guessing. He finally decided that Mango knew, and by instinct alone.

The rifle practice each evening had been discontinued for the men, as Mango had predicted, became experts in a very short time. Pic Rhee and Mango, however, were present each night when the meal was finished, and Dr. Felix went on with his explanation of the Bible. The questions of his two ardent listeners took up nearly half of the time of their instruction by the time they were into the New Testament. Dr. Felix, with a great deal of logic and a surprising amount of patience, answered each and every query.

Each night, since leaving Lhasa, Cameron and Connie would light their own small fire before his tent, and speak softly of many things long after the hour they should have been asleep. When finally they broke from each other's embrace, Connie would return to her tent and Penny, and Cameron would pull the great comforter close about himself, and drop instantly into peaceful slumber.

This night, however, when the fire was lit and they sat close together with hands entwined, Connie ask deeply serious, "Cam, tell me about your people and your boyhood."

"I guess like most other people," Cameron responded, "there really isn't a great deal to tell. For generations, my ancestors were coal miners in Cornwall, and then my grandfather decided that there must be a better way of life somewhere. He came to America to find it, and wound up digging the same coal in the pits of West Virginia. My own father, who was much like him, had the same dream, and so he came west. Though he never mined any coal, he ended up digging in the hard rock mines of Leadville, Colorado. He was a tenacious man, for within a few years he worked himself up from a common mucker to a level boss, even though he hadn't had much formal schooling."

Cameron took a deep breath, and then went on, "He had a good head on his shoulders. He knew that it was a long way from a mucker to a level boss, but he also knew that he was still in the mines his family had been trying to escape from for generations, and a level boss wasn't really that important. He decided that his only child would have a college degree, like the mine superintendent, and he would be a geologist. He worked hard and saved his money to that end, and it must have been very difficult for him after my mother died when I was fourteen. Dad lived long enough to see me finish my first year at the university, and then he died too."

He paused for a long time, thinking back, continuing, "I worked in the mines that summer to help put myself through the next year, but I didn't like any part of it. I almost didn't go back to school that year because of it, but I'm glad I did. It was shortly after my return that I met Professor Weaver, and through him I became interested in archeology. I accompanied him on my first field trip to Egypt the next summer, and though I could have made twice the amount of money in the mines, I never regretted a minute of it. I decided that if I were going to be a success in this new field that I knew very little about, I would have to study and work twice as hard as anyone else, and that's exactly what I did."

Again Cameron paused for breath, but only momentarily. "The biggest reason that I made so many finds and received so much notoriety in the years that followed was that when all the work would stop in any particular dig at the end of the day, I would stay there working for another six or seven hours. In the field I never took a day off no matter how long we were out. So you see it wasn't luck or special skill that made me somewhat of a success, but blind perseverance, and one hell of a lot of long hours. I continued to work with Professor Weaver until he got too old and finally died, then I went out on my own."

Connie had to force herself to ask her next question, and her timidity on the subject was evident. "What about your wife?" she inquired hesitantly.

"You mean my ex-wife, don't you?" Cameron rephrased her question. "Althea was a beautiful girl from a good and moderately wealthy family in Denver. She fell madly in love with me, and my work, the instant we met, and we were married six weeks later. It wasn't a one sided affair, because I believed I loved her as much as she did me. Two months after we were married she accompanied me on an expedition into Ethiopia, and within three weeks of our arrival I had to send her home. She couldn't stand the insects, the sand, the desert, the snakes; but most of all she couldn't abide the people of the land we were in, and their crude and simple way of life."

"When I returned home five months later," Cameron recalled, "she had fallen in love with a concert pianist and wanted a divorce. I gave it to her without contest. She married the pianist, and it lasted about six months or so. Then she went to Paris to start a new life, and for two years she lived with a portrait painter of some minor fame. The last I heard of her, two years ago, she was living with another artist, a sculptor I believe, somewhere in Italy, and his talent is so inadequate that she has to support him."

"For a long time," Cameron admitted, "I was deeply hurt, but as time went on my hurt changed to pity for her. I came to realize that Althea is one of those poor creatures destined to chase dreams all the days of her life; for when the dream is captured, and assumes the proportions of reality, it loses all of its radiant fascination. I truly feel sorry for her, but beyond that I have no feeling for her at all," Cameron concluded.

Connie didn't have to say anything; she pulled him close to her and kissed him several times while stroking his head and shoulders with her free hand. When her impulse came to an end, she looked at the sky and whispered. "Those stars are so close I think I could almost reach out and grab one," she laughed.

"They do seem that way, don't they?" he agreed, adding, "It's because of the rarified atmosphere at this altitude. We're able to see them much clearer here than at lower elevations."

"You and your logic," Connie giggled contentedly. "Do you have to spoil all my romantic dreams?"

No darling, I don't want to spoil any of them, and I'll remember that in the future, I promise," Cameron avowed. "Right now, young lady, I think we'd best get to bed. We've talked so long everyone else is already asleep."

They stood up, and once more Connie's arms reached out to him; then just for a split second she glanced from his face to his small tent only a few feet away, but instantly put the thought from her mind. She knew that if she were to have him even once, she would have to have him continually and that would cause a great deal of embarrassment for everyone concerned. She said goodnight, and went to her own quarters.

Just as Mango had predicted, within two days' time they arrived at the shores of the Yandrog Tsho, and made a good five miles thereafter before making camp. The lake was vast beyond belief, and from their present position they could not discern the far shore.

Roger and Norman, along with two guards, decided to miss their evening meal, and with four of the fastest mounts rode north and west beside the lake to see as much of it as they could before darkness fell. They knew they would travel in the opposite direction in the morning and they wanted to get better acquainted with the size and shape of it for their maps and log.

Pic Rhee and Mango did not wait for the meal to finish before beginning their discussion of Christianity. It was a direct violation of the rules of etiquette in this part of the world, and Dr. Felix realized instantly, and excused, their reasoning for this breach of manners. They were running out of time! He had been thinking the same thing for the past two days.

"I admire and respect the teachings of Christ, the courage, the faith and tenacity of the Apostles and those that came after," Mango began while sipping his tea. "It would be a truly magnificent thing if all the people of the world could know, believe and live these principals at the same time, but I do not see how one person or group of people can live in this manner when their neighbors and the rest of the world are barbarians, so to speak. It is a dream beyond my comprehension; and I do not believe that it can ever be completely accomplished, and unless it is full consummated, there will be erosion."

"What you say is true, to a certain degree," Dr. Felix agreed, "but as Christ explained to his Disciples, it was not going to be an easy nor short-term task. Nearly two thousand years have passed since it began, and the truth is, that his work has only recently been assured of a foothold that will last forever. Before the complete fulfillment of his teachings comes to pass it may be another two thousand or five thousand years, for that matter. In the beginning chapter of the Book we are told that God made the earth, and all that we know that exists, in six days, and on the seventh day he rested. But, who is to say how long a day is to God? He alone created the sun, and caused the earth to turn so that we have our version of night and day; but perhaps to Him a day is a thousand or a million years, for there is no other to divide his days and nights. Time, in itself, means nothing to God; and though man becomes impatient with the slowness of the fulfillment of the Prophecies, it will all come to happen just as surely as your hand will be seared if you immerse it into the flames of that fire."

"I cannot accept the concept that vengeance belongs to the Lord alone!" Pic Rhee responded after absorbing most of what the Doctor just said.

"The reason you cannot accept this, Pic Rhee," Dr. Felix replied, "is that like all men you are impatient. If a man was to do you a great injustice, and God would instantly strike him dead, would you then believe?"

"Of course I would," Pic Rhee responded without hesitation.

"What good would it do the man that He had struck dead?" Dr. Felix queried. "Would it give him the opportunity to realize the great wrong that he had done, to try in some way during the rest of his life to rectify this wrong, to repent for this sin, and thereby save his soul so that he might live in peace in the world that is yet to come? You see, that is the purpose of our lives here on this earth at this time; to test each one of us, to righteousness, mercy from cruelty, charity from greed, and give all of us the opportunity to cleanse our souls so that our ultimate destination in the infinite plan of God shall be entirely of our own doing."

"My sword shall always seek the blood of the ones that wrong me!" Pic Rhee stated with conviction.

"And mine also!" Mango concurred with heat.

"I pray that in time this may change," Dr. Felix stated with feeling. "I have come to know and love you both, and I would not like to see you do wrong unto yourselves."

For a long time both Mango and Pic Rhee sat in silence meditating on the last words of Dr. Felix. Oddly enough, it was Pic Rhee that broke the silence. "Tell us again of the Apostle called Peter and his destiny in the place called Rome."

Apparently Mango was interested also, for his eyes began to glow and he leaned closer.

Cameron had been holding Connie's hand as they listened. With a light pressure he brought her to her feet, and led her to their usual spot together near his tent.

"What are your views on religion?" Connie inquired bright-eyed after they were seated.

"To me it's an accepted fact," Cameron intoned. "My mother made sure of that. Life and the way things have been since history was recorded wouldn't make much sense if it was not."

"You sure don't talk about it like some people," said Connie.

There's no need to," Cameron smiled. "I have a working agreement with Him, and that takes care of everything."

"I don't understand," Connie said, a puzzled veil clouding her eyes.

"It's very simple," Cameron assured, "I don't expect any miracles from Him, if He doesn't expect any miraculous behavior of me."

"Isn't that blasphemous?" Connie questioned wide-eyed.

"Not really, if you stop and consider my upbringing and the way I feel about it. It's the truth and the truth in anything can be nothing else."

For a long moment Connie pondered this in quiet seriousness, smiling. "You must be right. I can't think of a single argument against it," then added, "Let's talk about something else, like us."

The intimate conversation, the short embraces and plans for the future for Cameron and Connie were cut short as Norman, Roger and the two guards rode in less than an hour later. Their voices, and the sounds of laughter, could be heard a good five minutes before they appeared in the circle of fire light. Supper had been saved for them, and the two guards joined the group for their meal also.

"It certainly is weird," Connie said when things quieted down.

"What's that," Cameron inquired idly, his head resting in her lap.

"That Roger and Norman have become such good friends," Connie stated singly.

"What's so odd about that?" Cameron asked. "They're both basically good men."

"I know that, silly," Connie said impatiently, "but their backgrounds and interests are so different. The main reason I say it is odd, though, is that Roger never really had a friend in his life before. A real friend, I mean."

"Maybe this is part of his problem," Cameron suggested.

"There are many parts to Roger's problem," Connie said absently, "I'm beginning to see that now. He's always had too much money, no responsibilities whatsoever, was overindulged by his parents and has a total lack of appreciation for what most people consider the important things in life."

"Well, it just might be that Norman could change a lot of that if they stay friends long enough," Cameron observed.

"They won't," Connie replied wistfully. "When we get back home Roger will step right back into his old self again, and immediately forget about Norman, and this entire experience."

"What makes you so sure," Cameron asked, looking up at her small face with longing.

"I've known him all his life, remember," Connie chided, "only the truth of the matter is I didn't realize what it all added up to until recently."

"You're getting much too deep for me, darling," Cameron teased as he sat up and kissed her long and hard. "For a change, let's get to sleep a little early tonight, alright?"

"Sounds like a splendid idea if you promise you won't go calling on another girl after you've sent me off to bed." Connie laughed softly.

"I promise," Cameron announced passionately, kissed her once more and they parted.

For two days they skirted the shores of the Yamdrog Tsho, first south, then due west. In the late afternoon Mango called a halt earlier than usual.

When everyone had gathered near him he pointed south away from the lake and said, "Do you see those two sharp pointed hills out there about two miles distant?" When everyone looked and nodded he continued, "When we get beyond them we will be able to see Kula Kangri. It will still be another two days ride before we reach the entrance to the valley of Kirghiz beyond that point. We could continue on for a ways yet this afternoon, but between here and the valley there is no water, and right here is the best campsite we will find. I suggest we spend the night here, and get a little extra rest. We can make up the time by starting early in the morning. Anyone have any objections?" he asked politely. When no one replied, he said,

"Then let's set up our camp, and have our dinner in the daylight for a change."

*   *   *   *   *

From the nearest of the twin hills a battered brass telescope was focused upon their actions, and the single straining eye looking through it watched intently. The eye studied each face, the equipment and all of the animals, then slammed the scope shut and dropped it into a beaten leather bag lashed to his waist. "We shall have to ride like the wind," he said to the man standing behind him, "for Tal Rashi must know of this!" They mounted their small ponies, and for the first mile proceeded southward with caution, keeping the hills between them and the people by the lake, then kicked their mounts to a fast gallop. After five miles they dismounted, and led the animals for a full mile, then remounted and resumed their course full-speed.

Twelve hours later they stood in the shabby hide tent that served as the headquarters and home of Tal Rashi. Tal Rashi lay upon a pile of dirty pelts that was his bed as he listened to their report. He asked many questions about the foreigners, the number of armed guards and the animals they had. From time to time he shook violently, and his hands trembled continuously. His hair was nearly white, and hung below his shoulders. There was so little flesh upon his frame that some of his bones were outlined through his thin clothing, and the madness glittering in his eyes had been there for a long time. "What do you believe to be their destination?" he asked in a quavering voice.

"I would have no idea, Excellency," the man with the scope replied, "but I think it possible you might. I have saved the most important news for last. The man leading this caravan is Mango Noyan!" he announced with jubilation.

The words 'Mango Noyan' brought Tal Rashi bolt upright in his bed, then instantly to his feet. In a flash he grabbed his scout by the throat violently, and shouted, "Are you sure it was he, are you positive it was Mango Noyan?" The strength remaining in this half dead man was amazing, and the scout gasp desperately for breath.

"Yes, yes, I'm certain," he managed to get out, "I have seen him many times, and could not be mistaken."

Tal Rashi released his viselike grip on the man's throat, and a vicious smile parted his lips to display his toothless gums. "Yes," he said with a cackling laugh, "I know where they are bound for. I always knew he would come back someday, and now is the time. The two of you, alert every man in camp, every man able to lift a lance, to fire a rifle or swing a sword. I want them all, do you hear? Have them armed, equipped and ready to leave at dawn. Now see to it, and be quick about it, do you hear me?" he screeched.

Without hesitation the men turned and left to do as they were bid.

Alone in his tent Tal Rashi began pacing the small confines of his floor, and talking loudly to himself. "Certainly I know where they are going; there is only one place they could be going and this time I'll be ready for them. I'll not enter that cursed valley of his this time. I'll not make that mistake again. Below the narrow inlet that guards the valley I recall where the canyon begins.

It is shallow there but the sides are strewn with large boulders and heavy brush. That will be the perfect place for the ambush. This time I have you Mango, this time you shall not escape, for you will not know what is happening until it is all over. I only hope that you are not killed outright, for I want you to know that it was I who prevailed." He slammed his bony fist down onto the low table with such force that his father's skull bounced twice, then rolled to the floor. He picked it up gently, and brought it up to within inches of his face, then stared intently into the empty sockets. "Our time has come Father; our time has come at last!"

*   *   *   *   *

The sight of Kula Kangri rising alone out of the flat plateau to its towering heights was majestic and awe-inspiring. The few places near the top where the ice and snow still remained glistened like diamonds in the early morning sun. Cameron was sure that Mango's estimate of two days before they reached it was wrong, and they would be nearly there by nightfall.

When the sun set that evening he realized how deceptive the flatness of the plateau and the actual size of the mountain had been. *It would take most of tomorrow to get there*, he admitted silently to himself.

They got an early start the next morning before daybreak, and had been on the move a full hour when the sun rose. *It will be a beautiful day*, Cameron thought, *not a cloud in the sky, and the breeze is so light you can scarcely feel it.*

Connie rode by his side, and throughout the morning occasionally she would have to reach out and touch him in some manner.

Harry and Penny riding directly behind them would glance at each other knowingly and smile. "It's truly going to be a marvelous day," Harry said, reflecting Cameron's thoughts without knowing it.

By one in the afternoon, they were close enough to clearly see the towering cliffs and the break in the rock that was the entrance to the valley of Kirghiz. Ahead of them a short distance, the first traces of a canyon leading to the valley began to form, the ground gently sloping upward from the plateau. The point men were well into the wide mouth of it, and nearing the place where it began to neck down and the sides became higher.

Without a word Mango suddenly halted.

"What is it, Prince Mango?" Pic Rhee asked in surprise.

"I don't know," Mango replied strangely. "Motion in the point men and flankers immediately," he ordered.

Pic Rhee did as he was instructed, and as the men came riding in he looked at Mango curiously.

Mango ignored him completely as his eyes scanned both sides of the canyon, every rock, bush and gully that slashed the low hillsides.

When Cameron saw all of the outriders coming in he asked Connie to stay with Penny, and he and Harry rode up to the head of the column. "Is something wrong, Mango?" Cameron asked, forgetting to use the proper form of address in his concern.

"I'm not sure," Mango replied still scrutinizing the ground ahead of them. "Suddenly I have this very strange feeling of extreme anxiety. It may be only the apprehension of returning here after so many years, and the conditions under which I left. I just can't tell," he said. "At any rate we're not going to take any chances."

He turned to Pic Rhee, "Leave four guards at the rear to take care of the pack animals, and bring all the rest up front. Instruct all of them to make sure their rifles are fully loaded, and in the ready position at all times. Tell them to check the sights, and if needed reset them to cover either side of the canyon. Cameron, I want you and the ladies to stay to the rear with the pack train. Do you have any weapons?"

"We have two pistols," Cameron replied with gravity.

"There are several of the best of the old rifles on the pack animals," Mango stated, his eyes still watching for any sign of movement on the hillsides. "If we should get into trouble, break them out, and be quick about it!"

"Yes, I will," Cameron responded.

"Now," Mango addressed Pic Rhee, "when the men are ready have them move out in a double skirmish line, well spread out and staggered. Tell them to proceed slowly and with caution, and above all be alert!" His commands were curt and to the point.

Pic Rhee nodded then turned to relay the orders to his men.

Less than a quarter of a mile up the canyon, Tal Rashi had wedged himself in beside a large piece of slanting flat rock. His searing eyes were glued to the people assembled below. "'What have they stopped for? Why don't they come on?" he whispered to himself as he slowly beat the ground with his fist.

Directly in front of Tal Rashi, and about fifteen feet below him, crouched another figure well concealed behind a thick clump of brush. The man was naked to the waist, and the scars of countless whippings completely covered his back. About his neck the heavy woven leather kang of a slave choked at his breath. In his right hand was a short spear, the only weapon he was ever allowed, and this only in times of battle. He too watched the scene below, and his apprehension was even greater than that of Tal Rashi.

"Is everything in readiness?" Mango inquired of Pic Rhee.

"Yes, Prince Mango," Pic Rhee replied, everything is done."

"Very well, then, give the order to move up!" Mango ordered tensely.

Pic Rhee nodded, spoke two words to his men, and they began inching forward.

At the end of ten minutes of slow progress, Mango was sure that he had over-reacted to his uneasy feeling and the anxiety. He knew he was going to feel very foolish when they passed through the narrows and nothing happened. He was quite sure now that it was his homecoming, after so many years had passed, that had caused him this sudden eerie sensation.

Mango and Pic Rhee both held in close behind the second line of the advancing guard, and they heard the thrashing noise at the same instant. The sound was followed by a weird gurgling screech; and they looked up to the right bank to see a man, naked to the waist, come bolting down the hillside, waving both arms wildly, and producing the unusual sounds they had heard. In one flashing instant Mango noted that the man was unarmed, but Pic Rhee had not!

In a swift liquid motion Pic Rhee's rifle rose from across his legs, and leveled on the figure darting down the slope. His finger had actually started the squeeze on the trigger, when a loud explosion shattered the stillness of the canyon.

Pic Rhee watched in complete amazement as the figure made a double somersault toward them, then rolled to the canyon floor and remained motionless. He knew that he did not fire his weapon; and for a split second he did not understand, but the answer came with his next breath.

The simultaneous firing of several dozen rifles from both sides was deafening. Figures that had been completely invisible materialized. The guards in front slid or jumped from their mounts, and began returning the fire from either a sitting or prone position.

Mango, in his preoccupation with having made a foolish mistake, the sudden appearance and sounds of the man coming down the hill, and the fact that he was not armed, had all combined to catch him off-balance. Sheer reflex brought his rifle up and leveled on the spot from where the first white puff of smoke had come, and he could now make out a head and part of one shoulder. He was never able to draw a bead on what he saw, for a shot fired from somewhere in front of him slammed into the right side of his chest, lifted him from the saddle, and crashed him to the ground. Though he never lost consciousness, it took a full two minutes for him to rise to his knees. Furiously he looked about for his weapon, but could not see it in the confusion of the free running and terrified mounts. The clouds of dust they were raising combined with rifle smoke to form a thin gauzy mist, and the thunderous din of so many shots being fired was one continuous brain-shattering roar.

He drew his sword, stood erect and looked about. His guards were firing so rapidly that he could see several ejected casings spinning in the air at the same time. He looked at their faces, and saw no fear or panic, only deep and unswerving concentration. He glanced to the rear, and saw his horse guard standing firm; he saw Cameron and Harry scrambling to open one of the packs. He saw the two girls lying flat on the ground with Dr. Felix, with Norman and Roger crouched in front of them. He saw Norman suddenly rise and roll backward, clutching the upper part of his leg.

Mango became aware that the fire was diminishing, and he looked back to the hillsides. He observed fleeting figures dashing from one bit of cover to the next in an attempt to reach the crest and safety, but he never saw one that made it! The long hours of practice his men had put in with these new weapons now proved their effectiveness.

The shooting became sporadic, then a single shot now and then, and finally silence. He heard Pic Rhee give the order for the men to split into two groups, and comb the area to make sure no one escaped.

Mango walked directly to where the first casualty of the battle lay, still grasping his sword firmly. The man was sprawled face up, with a huge gaping hole in the lower left side of his chest, and he was still alive. Mango noted the kang about his neck, and the scars covering all he could see of his body. He looked at the man's face with its crooked nose and deformed cheekbones, the long stringy brown hair, and then into his pale brown eyes that were soft and imploring. The man opened his mouth and tried to speak, and the strange gurgling noise he had heard earlier was repeated, only this time very softly. Mango saw the reason he could not speak was that his tongue had been cut out. Mango thought that the imploring look and his attempt to speak were an effort to obtain mercy. "He doesn't need mercy from me," he thought, "the poor fool will be dead in less than five minutes, if he only knew it."

Something tugged at Mango's memory, and once more he gazed into those pale brown eyes with their pleading look. He raised one hand to Mango in a beckoning gesture, then grasp each of his own forearms with the opposite hand. The customary greeting of the clan of the Blue Wolf, and suddenly Mango knew who this man was. "You're Plauyat, the younger of the two brothers who betrayed us!" Mango shouted. The man nodded twice, and rage began to boil in Mango's veins, his grip tightened on the sword in his hand.

The expression in Plauyat's eyes never changed and once more he raised his hand reaching for Mango's with a note of urgency; and it came to Mango that he knew he was dying and did not want mercy, but instead forgiveness. Mango remembered how round and smooth the boy's face had been, without blemish; and he looked again at the broken nose and cheekbones, the horrible marks covering the frail body, the kang about his neck and missing tongue. Then he thought of all of the years it had taken for this to happen, and that this was the sum of his reward for betrayal. It also came to Mango's mind that Plauyat had deliberately committed suicide in his effort to warn them of the ambush; and if he had not done so they would have been caught in close range cross fire, and most of his people would not be here now.

Mango let the sword slip from his grasp, kneeling on the ground beside Plauyat, taking his forearms firmly in the greeting of the clan. Plauyat's eyes softened and a loose smile formed upon his lips. Mango held him tightly, even at the last light faded from his eyes and his breathing ceased.

Without caution Mango made his way up the hill to the spot where he had first seen that white puff of smoke, and he found Tal Rashi lying beside the slanting slab of stone. His rifle was pinned beneath his body, and the extreme angle of his torso told Mango that his back was broken. The lower portion of Tal Rashi's jaw had been blown away, and his neck and chest were soaked with blood. Somehow, desperately, he clung to life, and wild hatred spewed from his eyes as he recognized Mango standing over him. Both of his hands formed into claws as he made a desperate attempt to lunge at Mango's throat, and was barely able to raise his arms.

The sword handle glowed like a piece of molten iron in Mango's hand, and he started the swing that would sever the head of his life-long enemy. The blade came up with all of the strength that Mango could muster, stopping in mid-air. He lowered it slowly, then laid it on the earth, and squatted beside it.

Throughout all the years he had hated this man, but now understood that his enmity was nothing compared to what Tal Rashi held for him. He looked more closely at the prone figure, and saw in entirety what his abomination of malevolence had done to him.

Tal Rashi made one last clawing gesture directed at Mango's throat, then died before his eyes. He picked up his sword, and walked slowly down the hill. He did not hear the occasional blast from a rifle, the screams of the wounded as cold steel put an end to their misery, nor hear Dr. Felix call his name as he reached the flat ground below.

Dr. Felix came to his side "Prince Mango, you've been wounded!" The Doctor said with alarm. "Come over with the rest of us, and let's see how bad it is." When Mango did not answer, the Doctor took him by the arm, and led him to where the horses had been collected and calmed. Only the horse guard was there, and the people of the expedition.

Cameron and Connie came to the doctor's aid. They sat Mango down on a rock and removed his tunic. Dr. Felix cleansed and examined the wound, then began to apply a dressing both front and behind. "You're lucky, Prince Mango, it went clear through!" he said, but the expression on his face was one of deep concern.

While he applied the bandages, Dr. Felix noticed that Mango still held his sword, and that there were no stains upon it. "Did you find Tal Rashi?" the Doctor could not refrain from asking.

"Yes, I found him," Mango replied without feeling, "and one of the men who betrayed my people."

"They were both dead then?" Dr. Felix pursued.

"No, neither of them was dead when I found them," Mango corrected.

"But your sword is clean," 'Dr. Felix stated in amazement.

"Yes, Dr. Felix, my sword is clean," Mango asserted, looking the doctor squarely in the eyes, and holding his gaze for several seconds.

"I am very thankful," Dr. Felix's reply was barely audible, and he said no more as he worked at applying the bandage to Mango's chest.

Mango looked up to see Pic Rhee standing over him, his consternation showing on his face. "How bad is it, my Prince?"

"Not too bad, I believe," Mango replied. "A few days of rest, and I shall mend."

"To my great joy," Pic Rhee said with elation.

"Did any of them escape?" Mango asked of his captain.

"Not even one of the horse tenders," was Pic Rhee's reply. "We have all of their mounts and gear, and if you so desire I will send half of our men to backtrack them, locate their camp, and destroy all that is left of the Uli Prang!" Pic Rhee stated with assurance, his sword still clutched tightly in his fist.

Mango's eyes focused on the blade that was smeared from point to hilt with drying blood. He watched with fascination as the last tiny liquid drop formed slowly at the pointed tip, then dropped and vanished in the sand. For a long moment he sat staring at the small stain that it had made, raising his eyes to look at his captain.

"No, my valiant warrior friend," Mango said resolutely, "that won't be necessary. With all of their men and mounts gone, the coming winter will dispose of all that remains of the Uli Prang; and your blade need not be stained with the blood of old women, and the few babes that you would find in their camp."

"As you wish, Prince Mango," Pic Rhee replied without emotion, but the relief he felt showed plainly in his eyes.

"How many casualties did we suffer?" Mango asked gravely.

"Three men wounded, none seriously, besides yourself and Mr. Clyde. None were killed, my Prince," Pic Rhee announced with pride.

"Good," Mango grinned. "Now take ten men, and proceed to the valley entrance. On the left side at the base of the cliff there are fortress caves that we used to guard the valley. I do not feel that you will find anyone there, but utilize great caution in your investigation. If you should run into any resistance, do not try to storm that place, but report back to me. If you find nothing there, proceed through the narrows until you are able to observe the valley above. Then come back and make your report."

"We shall be prudent," Pic Rhee assured him, then turned and left to complete his mission.

"If everything is clear," Mango spoke to Cameron, "I would like to move to the upper end of the valley where my home was before nightfall. If I should lose consciousness, see to it that this is taken care of."

"I'll take care of it, prince Mango," Cameron swore solemnly. "I think we'd best make you a couch to lie down on until Pic Rhee returns." He shot Connie a questioning glance, and without a word she went to fetch blankets.

"How serious is Norman's wound?" Mango asked compassionately.

"A very painful one, I'm afraid," Dr. Felix relied, "but aside from the danger of infection he should be as good as new in a week or two. The bullet entered high in his thigh, and emerged even higher on his backsides. He too was fortunate that it struck no bone."

"We were all very fortunate," Mango replied. "If Plauyat had not given us that warning, when he did, I doubt that any of us would be alive. As it happened, he stopped us just out of effective range for their rifles, otherwise it would have been a disaster."

Mango offered no resistance when his bed was made, and Cameron and Connie assisted him in lying down.

An hour later Pic Rhee returned to report that the narrows and the valley were clear, and they could proceed immediately.

"No one has entered or left this valley in a great number of years," Pic Rhee reported to Mango, "but there is something strange in the caves of the guard station. The skeleton of a small man is there with four loaded muskets, and four lances leaning against the wall. You told me that all of your people were accounted for with the exception of the two brothers and the two girls. Is it possible that this was one of the brothers?"

"We shall see in a few minutes," Mango responded, "Help me to my horse!"

"Wouldn't be better if we made a litter for him?" Connie directed her question to Pic Rhee.

Pic Rhee looked at her appraisingly, then said. "The only way you would ever get that man to lay still on a litter is to put a bullet between his eyes!"

Connie accepted the rebuff with a nervous smile. She then joined Cameron, and both of them went to find their mounts, as Pic Rhee and three of the guards lifted Mango into the saddle with gentle hands.

"No, this skeleton is not Jebtsun, of that I'm positive," Mango said after he had thoroughly examined the remains. "This had to be one of Tal Rashi's men; but it is very odd that he should die here, in this position, and with all those arms within his reach. I believe that there was some sort of treachery here also, but we shall never know. Help me mount again, and let us get to our camp as soon as possible, I am feeling weaker."

They made their way up the trail as rapidly as they could without jarring the wounded any more than they had to.

When they reached the upper end of the valley, Mango directed them to the great stone dais that had once been sheltered by the council yurt. "Make the camp here," he ordered, "and pitch my tent close beside that pile of stones."

When the camp was set up and the evening meal over, it was fully dark. No one ate very much, and there were a few that would eat nothing. After the sun had set it turned cold, much colder than it had been on the plateau below. Mango called Pic Rhee to his tent, and spoke to him in his native tongue.

A few minutes later Pic Rhee approached the large fire around which most of the group was gathered. He went straight to Connie. "Prince Mango would like to see you and Miss Penny in his tent, at your convenience, of course."

Connie looked at the large wrapped bundle in Pic Rhee's arms and then to Penny. Penny returned her look with a questioning lift of her shoulders. "It is convenient for us to join him at this very moment," Connie replied, even though she hated to leave the warmth of the fire. They followed Pic Rhee to Mango's tent, and then inside. A butter lamp glowed brightly at each end of his quarters; Mango lay on his couch with only his head showing above the robes.

"Well, open it," Mango tried his best to shout at Pic Rhee, but it emerged no more than a coarse whisper.

Without answering Pic Rhee complied, and held up two great coats of midnight black fur, dotted with small equally spaced spots of white. The sleeves were full length, with draw strings at the cuffs so they could be snug about the wrist, and a large hood attached to the top could be used likewise, so that only the wearer's nose might stick out if he wanted it that way. Pic Rhee extended one of the coats to each of the girls.

"These," said Mango, with a light smile upon his lips, "are gifts from Maleek. He knew you would need then when you reached the high country." The smile broadened appreciably as Mango added, "I believe you will each find them a perfect fit, for he had his servants obtain all of your measurements while they administered your bath."

"How can we ever thank him?" Connie asked, confused and embarrassed, "we'll never see him again!"

"He said to tell you," Mango stated seriously, "that the pleasure of your company for the short time you were able to stay with him was more thanks than he deserved."

Tears of joy welled in Penny's eyes, and Connie was so choked with emotion she could say nothing.

"Well, try them on and wear them," Mango whispered gruffly, "he didn't send them all this way for you to look at!"

Pic Rhee took the coat from Penny's hands, held it as she slipped into it, then repeated the process for Connie. Mango was right, they were a perfect fit, and covered the girls from the tip of their heads to their ankles.

"The two of you run along now, I must have some words with my captain and then get some rest." Mango commanded.

Both of the girls started to protest, but Mango scooted them out with a wave of his good arm he had withdrawn from the covers.

All eyes were fastened upon the girls even before they neared the fire, the rare sheen of their coats glowed, even in the darkness.

"They are gifts from the Merchant of Chamdo," Penny squealed with delight as she ran to Harry.

"Very fine and needed gifts," Harry added as he felt the fine texture of the fur.

"Could these possibly be what I think they are?" Connie asked Cameron with dismay, as she snuggled closer in his arms.

"I don't know much about this sort of thing," Cameron admitted. "How about it, Harry? This is more in your field than mine."

"It's hard to believe," Harry stated with wonderment after a thorough examination, "but unless I'm badly mistaken the entire garments are made of sable. I've never heard of such a thing before. The wealthy and those of royal blood of some countries, particularly Russia, use these furs quite intensively, but two perfectly matched coats like these! It must have taken hundreds of pelts."

"It scares me to think of what they would be worth back home." Cameron nearly choked on the thought.

"A small fortune each," Harry assured him.

"Right now I wouldn't part with mine for even a large fortune!" Connie declared. "I've never worn anything so warm, comfortable and luxurious in my entire life."

"A little while ago I was freezing to death," Penny recalled, "And now I'm nice and warm without getting close to the fire."

"It seems as though Maleek was looking out for your future," Cameron laughed.

"Yes," Connie agreed, "and what a beautiful thought it was." Her eyes were glazed and her tone filled with appreciation.

The three wounded guards were all able to resume light duty the following day, and with the aid of a makeshift crutch, Norman was able to get about the day after that.

It was a full four days, however, before Mango was strong enough to leave his couch. When the sun was warm he would spend most of his time looking out over the valley, or up toward the summit of Kula Kangri, supporting his weight by leaning against the ancient stone altar, deep in thought.

From a distance Dr. Felix and Cameron stood watching him. "He has the strength of an ox!" Dr. Felix avowed, shaking his head in wonder. "A wound such as that would have killed any lesser man almost instantly. His right lung was collapsed, though probably starting to function by now, at least partially. I can't see how the bullet passed through the chest cavity without actually damaging the lung itself. If it had he could not have survived under these conditions," the Doctor attested.

"Probably a near miss to the vital organ itself." Cameron suggested.

"Not too near I hope," the Doctor said gravely, "or he may still be in serious trouble."

Mango joined them that evening for dinner, and when the meal was finished he addressed Dr. Felix without preamble, "Doctor, I have had a lot of time to think in the last few days, and it came to my mind that you are in the wrong field of endeavor. You should have been a priest, spreading the word of your God, rather than wasting your time as a collector of religious relics."

The pale sadness that Mango had only imagined he saw before returned to alter the Doctor's countenance. For a long time he sat without moving, staring into the flames of the fire, then he finally answered softly, "I was a priest in the service of my God."

For one tiny fraction of a moment Mango wanted to ask him why he was not so now; then he erased the question from his mind as he saw how deeply, and without cause, he had opened an old wound, one that left no visible scar.

It was as though Dr. Felix had read Mango's mind, for it was he who carried the subject on after a slight hesitation. "All of my life, since I can remember, I wanted to be among those that spread the word of the Gospel. One meaning of the word Gospel is truth itself, and it can be no other way. Therefore, I must tell you the truth about myself, for I have lost too much already."

He paused briefly, then went on, "When I was many years younger I had a church of my own in a small town in Maryland.

I was zealous, confident in my work and supremely happy with the simplicity of my life. So much so, that I found it hard to understand how my congregation could have so many problems of the spirit, could become so involved in sinful activities, and find it so difficult to see the brightly lit path of righteousness. Then one day my congregation was enlarged by two, a fine young man and his wife. To spare you the details," he continued, "after a length of time I fell madly in love with this man's wife, and she in love with me. Despite everything, we ran away together to the happiness we could not deny ourselves; she away from her husband who needed her, and I away from my congregation that needed me and away from my God whom I needed."

The listeners about the fire were spellbound, and no one uttered a sound as the Doctor paused to recall his bitter memories. "We found no happiness at all! I, because of the heavy weight of the sins I had committed; being a man of God, my sins were doubled. And she, because of her great love for me, shared my horrible grief equally and there was no room for happiness, not even in each other. We could not add to the sin of adultery the legal sin of bigamy, and so we never married. Three years later she died of a broken heart, broken by her all-encompassing sadness for me. When she was gone, I wandered the country doing odd jobs to sustain my body, but nothing could be done about my soul. Purely by an unrelated accident, I became associated with the Federation, and I came to accept the fact that this was as close as I would ever come to serving my God again. So, there I have remained until we came together.

When the Doctor spoke no more, the silence became heavy and oppressive, and it was Mango's turn to speak into the flames. "Did you not tell us Doctor that everything that happens here on earth, no matter how small, somehow fits into the design and plans of your God?"

Dr. Felix merely nodded his head.

"Then why," Mango asked, "do you not believe that what has happened is not also part of His design?"

"Because I have never been able to ask for forgiveness," Dr. Felix replied without looking up.

"You told us," Mango said softly, "that though my people were here and now dead, my people are not dead because of the hundreds that left over the last six centuries. You told me that this was part of the design so that my people would blend with other people of other countries, and that someday in the far distant future we would be a brotherhood of man, as well as spirit. You told us that vengeance belonged to God alone and even though I had planned for years to destroy the Uli Prang, it was they that set the trap for us here, and by their own actions, they were destroyed. When I found Tel Rashi and Plauyat, they were both alive and I did not put my sword to either of them. You told me that your God was an all-forgiving God; and for reasons I cannot explain, even to myself, I forgave Plauyat his betrayal. I could not bring myself to forgive Tal Rashi, but before I die, that too may even come to pass with the strangeness of things that have been happening. I say I could not forgive him, but I did feel pity for him as he lay dying. The only thing that I can think of that stayed me from hacking both of them to pieces is the strength of the belief you have in your God, and what you have taught us in the past weeks. If your belief was strong enough to change me so in such a short time, why is it not strong enough for you to ask Him for forgiveness for your sins, and return to work where you belong?"

"I simply cannot." Dr. Felix replied.

"Then," said Mango with firm conviction, "even though I do not know your God, or his son Jesus, I shall pray to them both for your strength to be renewed and for your salvation." With that Mango rose.

"And I shall join him in those prayers," Pic Rhee added, as he left to walk Mango to his tent.

The Doctor raised his head and watched them go, then without a word to anyone, he too went to his quarters.

"It's getting late," Connie acknowledged when no one else seemed to have anything to say.

"Come, dear, and I'll walk with you," Cameron said.

It was not long after that Penny and Harry followed, and it was the first time since leaving Lhasa that both couples did not talk intimately and alone for a least two hours.

Within three days more most of Mango's vigor had returned, and so had his impatience. During the day his eyes were constantly going from the summit of Kula Kangri to the skies beyond the mighty mountain range to the south; and he knew their time was growing short.

He summoned a meeting of everyone, excluding his guards, at noon of this third day. He and Pic Rhee were standing directly behind the great stone dais when the rest of them arrived, and seated themselves on the ground in front.

When they all seemed comfortable, Mango addressed the group at large, "Your purpose in coming here, as I understand it, was to search for relics and artifacts of religious significance. None of you knew exactly what you were looking for, but have based this entire operation on legends that it was from this mountain that life began anew after the great waters had covered the earth. According to your version, a vast ship of some type was supposed to have landed at the top of this mountain. Your own Book tells you that this is not the mountain, that it is another in a different part of the world. Yet you say there are those that believe it was here, and that they believed it strongly enough for you to take this long journey. I spent most of my life here, at least part of each year, and I heard the legends also, but never one concerning a ship. How the people were supposed to have gotten there I do not know, but never, at any time, was I told that they arrived by a boat. I too have always believed that there was something up there of great importance, but just what it may be I could not say. We may find nothing at all of interest to you, or the people that sent you. At any rate we shall soon know, for we begin the climb tomorrow!"

"I don't believe you are strong enough for such a formidable task yet," Dr. Felix protested.

The rest of the gathering were about to express their sympathy with Dr. Felix's opinion when Mango cut them short. "Who knows better than I if I am strong enough to make this trip? Remember, I have already been more than half way there. Further," he added, "our time is running out. We do not get much snow here, a few feet at the most, and generally it will not begin until next month. But sometimes it comes early. It could begin tomorrow, and if it should, the entire mountain from here up would become a sheet of ice that would not leave until the spring thaws. It would be impossible to get out of this valley, except to go down. The temperature right here where we are standing would drop so low that nothing could live. Therefore, if we are going to attempt it at all, we must start tomorrow; we may be too late even now."

Everyone knew that they could not dispute this fact; for the whole operation had been started late from the beginning, and there had been far too many time-consuming delays.

When none offered to argue the point Mango said, "It is agreed, then? Now, as to who will go. I myself naturally, and Cameron will go. I believe Harry is strong enough in all respects to make the trip, but we should have at least one more. I was counting on Norman, but with that leg of his, that's out of the question. I cannot take Pic Rhee, for my men, as good as they are, must have a leader in the event of an emergency. Dr. Felix, you are a strong man, but I've noticed that you have difficulty breathing here, even after having a week to become acclimated to the thin air. So, you too are out of the question. How about you, Roger, are you willing to make the trip?"

Roger's reply was almost instantaneous, "I am not only willing, I have been planning on it for some time!" he announced glaring at Cameron.

"Good, it is settled then," Mango smiled. "Three would be too few, but five would be too many."

"Now, Dr. Felix, I would like to speak to you of another matter," Mango stated, changing his tone slightly. "Is your museum interested in articles relating only to the major faiths of the world, or in things associated with all types of religious beliefs?"

"The Federation is profoundly interested in any material pertaining to all spiritual beliefs known to man since the beginning of time." Dr. Felix replied instantly.

"In that case," Mango announced, "I might have some items that I think belong in that museum of yours, providing they have not been disturbed these past twenty years. I'll need your help, Pic Rhee."

The pair of them dropped out of sight behind the altar, and those sitting on the ground rose to their feet, and came to stand before the dais.

After a few moments of pondering, Mango began to manipulate four small stones that seemed to be loose in their sockets. When he was satisfied he withdrew his dagger, and instructed his captain to do the same. "Now," Mango spoke to Pic Rhee, "do you see the wide block in the center, just above the ground?"

Pic Rhee nodded his response.

"Then insert your blade in the vertical seam beside it, and pry outward when I do," Mango advised.

At first the large slab did not move, then slowly and more easily it began to inch outward. When they had it far enough projected for a good hand hold, they slid it completely free, and sat it in the clear. Mango lay on his side, and began passing articles out to Pic Rhee, who sat them on the ground beside himself. When they had finished they stood erect, and Mango began setting the sacred relics on the altar explaining the meaning of each of them.

"These," Mango announced, "are the bow, quiver, arrows, and shield of Kirghiz, the all-seeing one I told you of, Dr. Felix. This is his lance that shattered in the last battle of the conquest of China. Kirghiz was advisor and General to Genghis Khan, to his son, and later to his son Kublai Khan. He was also the spiritual leader of our faith, Tengri, and the greatest of shamans to the clan of the Blue Wolf, by which our people were known."

The next item Mango produced was the jade, gold and silver icon of the Gray Doe and the Blue Wolf. The covering had thus far remained in place, but as Mango went to remove it the many threads of silk disintegrated into puffs of white dust. The threads of gold and silver held, and the covering remained in one piece as he lifted it from the carving. The magnificent beauty of it caused a hushed murmur to flow among those watching, and they crowded closer for a better look. "This," Mango said, "was the center of our devotion, and I have already told Dr. Felix of its history and its meaning. I did not tell him that it still existed, for until this moment I was not sure myself. Dr. Felix will tell you of it when there is more time. These last two items were the ceremonial and battle headdress for the princes of the Blue Wolf clan. This one was mine, and the other my cousin-brother's. Dr. Felix will also explain the Anda and its meaning. There were also some lesser items of religious value, but they were not hidden, and were either destroyed or taken by the Uli Prang."

"Surely, Prince Mango, you can't mean that you intend to give these priceless objects to the museum?" Dr. Felix stammered.

"They mean nothing now," Mango replied slowly. "All of the people that left before have long since forgotten them, and adopted new religions. I am the only one that even knew of their existence, and I renounced them long ago. Aside from the gold, silver and jade, they are worthless to anybody except a museum. I would like to see them there so that the rest of the world might know of them, and what they once meant. As you told us in our instruction, Doctor, the world is ever changing; cities and empires are built and destroyed, nations are born and die, and even the land and the oceans change. The people of the Blue Wolf were over a thousand strong when they came here. We were a small nation of our own, and this was our Hoshun. We were born out of the conquest of China; we came here, we flourished, we died here, and no one knew about it or how we were. If you take these, Dr. Felix, and tell the story of them, I shall feel that my people live on in memory at least."

"Yes, Prince Mango, we shall take them, and tell the history behind them so that the whole world will know," Dr. Felix replied, and a tiny new light shone from his eyes.

"I am at peace then, Dr. Felix, I thank you," Mango said with sincere gratitude. "Now Pic Rhee and I shall go scout the trail up and out of this valley. Although it is not the most dangerous part of our journey, it is the most difficult physically. I want to make sure I remember it well, for we will traverse most of it in the dark." Without delaying further, Mango and Pic Rhee turned and headed for the northern wall.

The duties of the guards were few since the battle at the valley entrance and the cleanup that followed. They alternated the few hours needed in the tending, and guarding, of their now more than doubled horse herd. The luxury of idleness is a deceptive dream, for when it is finally in one's hand it soon becomes a red hot stone anxiously wanting to be rid of. And so it was that the guards, in their boredom, soon began exploring every inch of the valley that their revered leader had called his home.

When Mango and Pic Rhee returned from their reconnaissance mission late in the afternoon, two of the guards were waiting to report that they had discovered the remains of a man long dead among the rocks directly above their camp.

Thinking that it might be the remains of Jebtsun, Mango summoned Cameron and Dr. Felix, and the six of them went to investigate. In among the giant boulders, the guards led them to the skeletal remains whose severed head lay nearby. The first thing Mango noticed was that this man's weapons were also with him, and that his musket was still primed and loaded. He took special note of the size of him and his location.

When they were back at Mango's tent he thanked the two for the report, and then dismissed them. He made no comment on the discovery, and was in deep thought all the way back to his quarters. He motioned everyone to be seated.

Mango dropped to his couch, and his fatigue was evident. "It was not Jebtsun, nor any other of my people. They have all been accounted for, save him. The man we saw was in the area of the cave, which would have been directly above where he was found. It is plain to deduce that he died after the landslide that occurred when I collapsed the entrance to the cave in my escape. I have told Dr. Felix about this also, and he can relate the whole story at some later time." Weariness showed plainly in Mango's eyes, but he went on as though trying to explain something to himself, rather than to his listeners.

"I remember now," he started anew, "while I was carrying the last of my people into the cave that it started to snow lightly. Even in my state of madness there were two things I was sure of; first that Tal Rashi knew I was not among the dead, and that he had set some sort of trap for me in the narrows below. That is why I sealed the cave, even though I was not positive there was any way out." He paused for several moments, trying to recall that fateful day, and the things he had done mostly out of instinct rather than reason.

"After Tal Rashi was convinced the slaughter was complete," Mango began again, "he rationalized that the next most important thing was to protect the vast amount of wealth he had acquired. He collected the herds and flocks along with all other things of value within the camp, and had them moving away from this place even he feared. He did not know of the cave, nor that I was halfway up the mountainside. He undoubtedly left some of his men in the narrows below so that I would not escape if I was in the valley. He probably stayed with his plunder until he was sure it was safe, and then returned by himself a few days later to collect his men and hopefully my head."

"I can imagine his surprise," Mango continued, "when they returned to our camp and found only ashes, and all the bodies of the people they had slain vanished. It would have been quite a shock; especially since they were, with the exception of Tal Rashi, a very ignorant and superstitious people. The snow must have covered all traces of the new landslide. It is peculiar that I have never thought of any of this until now. Even with Tal Rashi's sense of logic he could not have explained the disappearance of all those people they had murdered, and this was probably the point at which his madness began. If the truth of what he found on his return ever got to his people he surely would have had a great deal of trouble controlling them, for they all feared this mountain long before any of this happened. My deductions are that Tal Rashi killed two of his own men, the ones he left to make certain of me, to be positive that this great mystery would never reach the ears of his tribe."

"Certainly!" Dr. Felix agreed, knowing the full story of the slaughter, and Mango's subsequent escape. "That is precisely what happened, and explains those two dead people. But, what of Jebtsun and the two girls?" the Doctor inquired. Wouldn't they have told of the cave, or the other man, what was his name?

"Plauyat," Mango answered, his eyelids drooping.

"Knowing Jebtsun, he probably demanded his woman and his share of the loot when Tal Rashi returned to his camp, and died instantly for his brashness. Undoubtedly at the same time Plauyat's tongue was cut out so that he would never be able to tell about the cave, or betray his new master as he had his own people. The poor girls never got the chance to tell anything to anyone, they were given to the men of the tribe for pleasure at their first encampment. When the men finally tired of them much later they would be given to the women as slaves, and were certain to be beaten to death in a few days. Or, they may have found a means to take their own lives in their disparity. I hope it was the latter." Mango's eyes were completely closed when he trailed off, though he still sat upright.

"I pray so too," Dr. Felix replied as he motioned to Cameron that they should quietly leave.

"A sad and pitiful thing, all of this," Cameron said once outside.

"It truly is," the Doctor concurred with feeling. "I suggest we eat early tonight and get as much rest as possible, especially Harry and Roger. The next few days are going to be trying ones for all of you."

Cameron glanced up at the summit silhouetted in the evening sky. "I have no doubt about it," he replied.

Cameron didn't know how long he had slept when he was awakened by the rustling sound at the tent flaps by his feet, he was only aware that it was pitch black and terribly cold. He felt something brush against his calf as he cautiously reached beneath the comforter for the pistol Norman had returned. His hand closed slowly on the grip when the faint scent of Connie's perfume, or whatever she used, came to his nostrils, and he released his hold on the weapon.

"What in the hell are you doing here?" he demanded in a whisper.

"I'm trying to close these tent flaps to keep the cold out," she whispered her reply.

"I meant why are you here?" he answered in bewildered exasperation. "What time is it?"

"I had to talk to you, Cam," she replied in a hushed voice, "tonight, right now. It's still early, about ten o'clock."

She brushed against him as she crawled on her hands and knees and then lay down at his side, her head close to his; the smooth richness of the hood of her fur coat swept across his cheek as she threw it back. "Now, what's all this about?" he asked. "I want to give up the plans for tomorrow," she said evenly. "I want to pack up, and get out of here fast. I no longer give a damn about what's up on top of that mountain. I'm scared, Cam, Oh, dear God I'm frightened out of my wits. I have a feeling something is going to happen up there, and I don't want you to go!"

Cameron thought over her words carefully, and his reply, before answering. "Darling," he said softly, "with all we've been through I can see how your anxiety has built up. It's been one devilish crisis after another for a long time now, and it is bound to have worn your nerves to the breaking point, but you don't seem to realize that all of the danger is behind us now. We make the trip to the top and return in a few days, accomplish what your father wanted, and safely exit through India in a matter of two or three weeks. Sweetheart, we've come halfway around the world, spent a tremendous amount of money, a good part of which is the Foundation's; we've endured all of the hardships of the journey, faced death ourselves, and witnessed death all around us. Lastly, think of all of the efforts that hundreds of people have gone through to make this whole thing possible. Now that we're actually here, with the end of it really in sight, do you honestly want me to give up and walk away?" As he spoke he felt the shivering of her body increase, even through the comforter and her coat. His bare arm felt like it was turning to ice. "Here," he said, "slide underneath the covers before you freeze to death."

She didn't answer, but he felt her roll away from him, and he raised the comforter. It was a moment before he understood what was taking her so long. He knew when he felt the weight of her coat being spread over him, but the real shock came when her cold small body came against his seeking warmth. She hadn't worn any slippers, and had nothing on under the coat!

"Oh, my God, Connie dearest, you're half frozen," he said as he put his arms about her, and pulled her against his chest. He sought her feet, and covered them with his own to transfer some of his body heat to hers., "Why in the name of Heaven didn't you at least put on some shoes?" he demanded.

He could scarcely understand her reply, her teeth were chattering so badly. "I've been so upset all evening that I didn't even think of it until I was halfway here," was the way he made it out.

He held her tightly for a long, long time until the shaking of her small exquisite form began to fade, and he could no longer hear the clicking of her teeth. "Did anyone see you coming here?" he asked with tenderness.

"No," she replied more evenly, "everyone else is asleep.

Something in the way she said it made him ask, "How about Penny, was she asleep too?"

After a slight hesitation she answered, "No, she went to be with Harry." There was another pause, and then she added, "She told me to tell you that she wasn't going to try to talk him out of going with you. That her reasons for going to him were selfishly her own, and the decision about tomorrow was yours and yours alone."

Cameron pondered Penny's message, then asked, "What about you, do you believe the decision should be mine? Remember, I'm working for you."

"I remember what it said in the will, that you would be in complete command of the expedition, and your decisions would be final." she replied softly.

"I don't want it to be my say alone, darling," he pleaded, "I want it to be ours, so that when we leave here we won't have any regrets. I know how much you loved your father, and I'm afraid that once we were on our way home you'd start reproaching yourself for not fulfilling his last wish. I already know that I would never forgive myself for not finding out what's up there, after getting so close."

He felt a warm teardrop flow across his cheek. "Oh, dearest," she sobbed, "I do so desperately want to fulfill that wish, but I love you so much, and I'm so terribly afraid something will happen to you. Darling, I've never experienced this beautiful thing that has come to me, and I can't stand the thought of losing it."

"Nothing is going to occur that we don't want to," Cameron soothed as he lightly kissed her face repeatedly. "Mango made the most arduous part of the trip this afternoon, and he said that from where he had to turn back before, he could see two separate ways that the summit could be reached quite easily by. He made the trip alone, that time, and with none of the special equipment we brought for this purpose. Now, dry your tears and stop your worrying. You know that we have to do it, and we'll do it, and nothing is going to befall us." It was becoming increasingly more difficult for him to keep his mind on what he was saying. Now that she was fully warm, her hands began to explore the contours of his face in the darkness, then his neck and shoulders.

He never got the answer to his question. Her lips found his and parted, and there was urgency in their demands. Her hands moved caressingly down across his bare chest, and the mountain was forgotten. Nothing mattered except now!

Three hours before dawn a dark blur moved swiftly among the tents. A heavy pair of men's woolen stockings left strange tracks in the light white frost that covered the ground.

* * * * *

The glacier was not nearly as wide as Mango remembered it. *But then, twenty years is a long time and many things can change,* he thought to himself as he carefully surveyed the short strip of ice remaining between the four figures roped together and the rising ledges ahead of them. *It's to our advantage too,* he mused, *we're making better time than I did alone, but then I believe we started a little earlier.*

Though Mango held them to a slow steady pace, they were making excellent progress, with rest periods every few minutes at the start. He recalled what had happened to him on the last attempt. By the time they had crossed the ice floe, they rested every other minute and he knew it wouldn't be long until he would start counting the steps.

They made the top of the ledges beyond the ice field before stopping for lunch. They ate in silence for the most part, because none of them had really caught their breath since the journey began.

When Mango thought he had recovered enough to go on he did not inquire of the others, he simply shouldered his pack, stood up, and the rest of them followed; Mango in the lead with Roger behind him about ten feet, then Harry and lastly Cameron. Mango had to lead and he wanted the strongest man at the rear, so the order of sequence was his. He never looked back unless the line grew slack, and when this would occur he would first make sure of his footing and hand holds, if any were available.

None of these people were of the mountains, and so Mango explained what they should and should not do before starting out of the valley. At first he watched them all closely when he was able to see, and found that they were all watching him, and aping his every move. As the terrain grew more treacherous, he was no longer able to keep an eye on them, but was confident none of them would do anything foolish.

By three in the afternoon, they arrived at the top of the ridge where the mountain curved back in. A short way ahead, the wide ledge would begin and the going a little easier. When Mango was finally able to speak a few words he announced, "We'll rest a little longer this time; we're a little ahead of our timing." It had been a beautiful day, not a cloud in the sky, the sun shone brightly, and though the wind was cold it was not nearly as much so as the day Mango had come alone. But then, it was much later in the year.

As they once more shouldered their packs Mango said, "A short distance ahead is the ledge shelf I spoke of earlier, the going will be smooth for a change. Except for a short span in the middle, the trail is wide, and we won't have to be anywhere near the edge. For about fifty feet it narrows down to a width not much wider than my arm is long. Even this spot won't bother us as long as you don't spend too much time looking down. It's both flat and solid."

When they arrived at the place he had spoken of, to Mango's dismay, it was neither flat nor solid. It had mostly been sheared away by an avalanche or rock slide many years past. All that remained of it was a foot or less, and this appeared badly fractured. There was no way anyone crossing could avoid looking down, for he would have to be certain of each foot hold.

Mango evaluated the situation for a good five minutes, then spoke, "We'll unfasten the long line tying us together. It should be more than enough to reach across to where it's safe again. Take three of those spikes you brought, and drive them into these cracks, right here, as high as you can reach. When we get them in, we'll pass the rope through the snap rings, and all of us put our weight on them to make sure they are solid. Then I'll tie one end of the rope about my waist, and you can feed it out to me until I reach the other side. Once I'm there I'll make the other end equally secure. In case I should fall, I want all three of you to hold that rope. When all this is accomplished, each one of you take the short line you have, tie one end about your waist so that it is tight, but not so it would become a noose if you should slip. Tie the other end to the main line in a loose knot that you can slide as you move across. Make certain this knot cannot cinch either! Do you all understand now?"

Though all three of the other men were ashen, they all three nodded in the affirmative. If Mango could carry the line across, none of them could refuse to follow!

When the pitons were firmly in place and tested, Mango very carefully tied one free end of the rope about his middle. Slowly he removed his mittens, and stuffed them inside his coat while he once more appraised the nearly sheer face of the cliff he had to breast. He looked down to see if there were any cracks, fissures or small spurs that he could use to regain the shelf if he should fall. When he was satisfied, he turned to his companions and announced, "I'll be waiting for you on the other side." There was no sign of fear in his large dark eyes, and a semblance of a smile rested on his lips.

The trio he left behind watched nervously as he inched his way out, testing each fragment of the remaining shelf before he put his weight on it. His bare fingers explored the rock blindly for any type of hand-hold from his shoulders to the limit to his reach. The distance between them lengthened as foot-by-tedious-foot he reached the center of the span.

It seemed to Cameron that it had taken him an hour to get that far, and he was wondering if he could stand the suspense of another hour of it. It actually hadn't been a full ten minutes since Mango tied the rope about himself. Cameron rubbed a mitten across his forehead, and seeing it come away damp, realized that he was sweating profusely. His heart was thudding in his chest, and several times he caught himself holding his breath; especially when Mango would be forced to move back to change the position of his footing, and this happened several times.

The three pairs of eyes that followed Mango never left him for a fraction of a second. The cold wind whispered softly, but none of them heard. They were listening too intently to the sound of the falling stones Mango dislodged periodically. They made a distinct scraping noise as they tore free, then silence for a moment followed by a loud clatter when they hit the first of the jutting projections below. The sounds would grow fainter as they fell a thousand then two-thousand feet and on to the bottom. The drop was so long that they never ran out of noise; before one hit the bottom, another had started its downward plunge.

Mango had only five feet left before he regained the solid shelf, then four and three. His motions seemed arrested to those watching, and for an interminable time they all thought he could go no further; that he had run out of places to plant his toes and finger tips, and then somehow miraculously he was standing on the far side of the trail. He did not turn to look at them, but immediately went about his work driving the pitons. He did not use the snap rings this time, instead he put a double hitch about each steel spike he had driven, pulling it snug before going to the next one.

When he finished his task he turned to face them, "Now," he said in a loud clear voice, "do the same thing as I have done, only pull the rope as tight as you can before tying it off to the first spike." The smile on Mango's face was full-blown.

The remaining men roused themselves from the spell that held them, and followed his instructions without comment.

"Alright, Roger," Mango yelled, "now it's your turn; do exactly as I told you, and you've nothing to worry about. The safety line is there to catch you, so take your time and don't be nervous!"

Roger unwound the short section of rope he carried about his body, and stepped forward to secure himself to the safety line, the rope hanging loosely in his hands. Up to this point he had followed Mango's advice and not looked down, but then in fascinated horror his gaze followed the face of the cliff all the way to the bottom; and he could not tear his eyes away from the jagged pile of rocks that littered the base of it. He stood without moving, his eyes glued to those stones so far away!

Cameron sensed the agony he was going through and stepped up beside him, thinking to help. "Why don't you let me be next, and you rest a bit longer?" Cameron suggested.

It took a while for the words to find their way through to Roger's brain, and a little while longer for his control to return in full; but when they did he whirled swiftly, ignoring his precarious position. "Like hell you will," Roger snarled, "you've been stepping in front of me for a long time now, Mr. Son-of-a-bitch, but not this time! I was assigned this second position by that man on the other side, and by God that's where I'm staying!" The pent up hate and anger that had built up in the past months flared openly in his eyes.

"I'm sorry, Roger," Cameron said evenly. "I didn't mean it that way. I don't want to take your place; I was only trying to help."

"Like all the other help you've given me on this damned trip? Like the help on the boat, the help at the General's camp and the help with Connie? Thanks, I don't need it!" Roger growled. He glared at Cameron as he lashed the rope about his waist, stepping up to the safety line. Cameron turned and walked away, visibly shaken, without a word.

"I'm terribly sorry about that," Harry tried to console as Cameron sat down beside him, "but it had to come sometime, you know. I've seen it for quite a while."

"Then why in the hell didn't you say something?" Cameron demanded.

"I was honestly hoping that it wouldn't transpire until we were done with this, and on our way home, wishfully," Harry said apologetically.

"I'm sorry, Harry," Cameron said lowering his tone. "I've been stupidly blind, and now I'm getting angry at you because of it. I knew the man didn't like me, but that's as far as I thought it went. Had I known how deep his feelings were toward me I'd never have agreed for him to make this climb!" Cameron was about to go on when Harry touched his arm, and nodded in Roger's direction.

"He's moving much too fast," Harry stated barely above a whisper, as he watched Roger, nearly a third of the way across.

"The damned stupid fool," Cameron erupted, "he's going to get himself in trouble out there!" The words had barely left Cameron's lips when it happened.

The small flat piece of stone upon which Roger had placed his entire weight broke free. He had only one hand placed in a crack above his head, and the suddenness of it stripped the skin from his fingers. As the safety line stretched, it made a strange high pitched singing noise and Roger watched in absolute terror as the free end of the rope he had fastened to it began to run through the knot he had tied. His scream started before the lines ever separated; and did not end until he slammed into the first projecting outcrop below, then there was silence, a silence so horrifying that Harry wanted to scream himself.

"Oh, my God, oh, my God," Harry finally got out as he started to rise.

Cameron put a trembling restraining arm on his shoulder. "We can't do him any good now, Harry," he said, his voice strained and quivering. "Sit still for a few minutes, and let's try to pull ourselves together."

Cameron was shaking so badly himself, he didn't know if he would be able to do anything for Harry or not. He finally managed to slip his arm about his friend's shoulder and squeezed as tightly as he could. He tried fervently to think of something to say, but his mind was filled with the imaginary echo of Roger's scream, the sight of the rope running through the knot on the safety line, and the sickening thud that had ended his cry.

It was Mango's voice, a long time later, that brought them out of it, "There is no reason for this to have happened," he stated, not fully accepting it. "Even a child should have been able to cross there now! He died through the blatancy and folly of his own imagined hate and rage. No one can hold himself responsible for what has occurred; he died by his own hand! You can't leave him down there, you know?" His voice was clear, but the ring had gone out of it.

"No," Cameron replied as he rose to his feet, "we can't leave him there; we'll have to go in from below and get him out. Can you make it back across safely?" He asked tensely, forgetting he had crossed without aid of any kind.

"Not right now," Mango replied as evenly as he could. "You and Harry will have to go back to camp for help. Get Pick Rhee and half dozen other men, stay on top of the rim of the valley when you come back up. Follow it around below the glacier and it will lead you to the point of the ridge behind you now. Continue along its base, and you will come to the rocks below. The ground is nearly flat all the way around. The only difficulty you will encounter is getting him back down the walls of the valley itself."

"What about you?" Cameron asked, still in a state of shock.

"I'm going on to the top," Mango called. "This is my last chance, and I'm not giving it up. If there's anything up there I'll find out and bring back some evidence of it; if not, I'll return empty handed within three days." A new note of imploring crept into his voice. "It's been my dream since I was a boy, and it's all I've got left. My family is gone with my people, my hate and craving for revenge are gone; and when I come down from this mountain I shall never see it again. You do understand, don't you? It's all I have left." Mango repeated.

"Yes, we understand," Cameron responded as the blood began to flow once more within him, and Harry rose to his feet. We'll get Roger out, and if you're not back by that time, we'll come up and meet you."

"Good!" Mango shouted. "You had best leave now, and find some sort of shelter before dark. If you should try to continue after night falls, they'll have to send someone out after you also!" He added sternly, knowing the state of their minds.

"Alright, Mango," Cameron agreed dumbly, "We'll do as you say."

"Then you best be moving," Mango shouted gruffly. "I'll see you in three days; he turned and moved on around the trail."

Cameron and Harry stood watching him until he was out of sight, then went back the way they came without another sound. They were still so numbed by bewilderment and grief that had there been more that one trail to follow, they would have gotten lost.

*　*　*　*　*

The oncoming tides of darkness were threatening when they reached camp the following day. It was a long and arduous descent without the expert guidance of Mango. Cameron and Harry spent the night in a deep crevasse of the ledges above the glacier, and though it afforded protection from the winds of late evening and early morning, it did little to stop the plummeting temperature. As a result they got a very scant amount of sleep and it showed in their haggard and mournful faces as they neared the early lighted fires.

The two women were the first to recognize the symptoms of disaster and came running to meet them. "What has happened?" Connie asked apprehensively, fear widening her eyes, as she took Cameron by the arm.

From the time they began their descent that morning, Cameron had been concentrating on the words he would use to tell of the tragedy that occurred, and it had kept him preoccupied throughout the day. Now that he was here, his mind would not cooperate and became a whirlpool of the events of the past two days, all of them out of context.

"Roger is dead!" Was all that he was able to utter.

"Lord God, no!" Connie and Penny shrieked almost in unison. "What happened, what went wrong?" Connie continued.

Somehow, on the downward journey, Cameron had instinctively assumed his responsibilities and gotten them off the mountain; but now delayed shock took full possession of him and he could not answer. Connie led him to the fire and sat him down in its radiating glow.

Dr. Felix, Norman, and Pic Rhee were all seated there and heard his only statement. They remained in dreadful immobility waiting for the answer to Connie's questions.

The impact of the fire's heat, the nearness of Penny and the rest of them, the sight of their camp, and the soothing sound of Penny's voice brought the nightmare to an end for Harry. He had followed Cameron blindly and speechlessly from the heights above, but he knew it was his obligation to tell them what had taken place. It was all crystal clear to him until the time he saw Mango disappear beyond the next steep ridge. He commenced to relate everything from the time they departed two days before. His voice was low, but calm and controlled.

Cameron sat listening to it all, hearing every word, and reliving every second of it.

When Harry finished, there was a long silence that no one cared to break. Each of them could see how the others felt and words seemed unnecessary. Oddly enough, Cameron was the first to speak and it was to Pic Rhee, as though no one else was present, "In the morning, when it's light enough to see, I'd like you to gather what you think is required in the way of men and equipment to bring Roger back. I'll lead you to where he is. There's no need for Harry to go; he's been through enough already."

Harry's words cut through the chill of the evening air like a knife, "I'm going back up there with you, Cameron, and help bring him down! I don't give a damn what you say to the contrary, I'm going to be there! I feel I owe him a hell of a lot more than this, but there's nothing I can do about that. Besides, I've made the trip up and down that wall once and I can be of some help next time."

In all the years Cameron had known Harry, he had never heard this positive tone of defiance and it caused him to look up at his friend in astonishment. What he saw there was a totally different person. The transition that had taken place in Harry had been so gradual that until this moment, Cameron had failed to notice any of it. He looked at his friend with surprise. The bulge around the middle, that was part of Harry, was gone; and several large pleats showed in his pants where he had gradually adjusted his belt to fit his waist. The round boyish face had grown longer by an inch, he carried his head at a different angle, his chin had a more positive thrust and a new and exciting light radiated from his eyes. His shoulders would no longer need the extra padding to give them that squarish look, and the muscles in his neck showed how he had hardened.

"If that's what you really want," Cameron relented, "I'd more than appreciate you coming along. You are the only other person here that knows how to get up and down that wall, and I know you'll be a lot of help to me and the other men." This new and aggressive Harry was a shock and the therapy was in Cameron's favor. His voice, though still quiet, was coherent and decisive.

"I think both of you had better have something to eat and then get to bed," Connie insisted calmly. "You're completely exhausted, and if you don't get some rest soon, you'll both collapse!"

When the two men had eaten what they could force down, the women led them to their respective tents and put them to bed like small children; the only difference being that there were no complaints heard.

CHAPTER 10

In the cave, high upon the mountain, Mango wakened with the rising sun, had his breakfast, and began his ascent immediately. The step like-ledges started uniformly as he had anticipated, but by mid-morning their individual height ranged from two to ten feet, and he used his short rope to hoist himself from one to the next. The effort of hauling himself up hand over hand soon began to tell on him. His right shoulder started to ache, and the cold morning air turned his lungs to fire. As he gasped for each breath his entire body was damp with sweat despite the severity of the cold.

Gradually he was forced to have his rest periods more frequently and their time longer. His legs and arms trembled continuously from overexertion, and the salt from his sweat dimmed his vision.

It was near two in the afternoon when he stood in the center of the rounded rock dome that formed the uppermost part of the mountain. He remained erect for less than a minute, taking in the once in a lifetime vista of a two-hundred mile view in all four directions, then lowered himself to the ground, and lay prone for a full half an hour.

When he rose, the perspiration had dried, and a deep chill gripped him. Forcing himself to move faster, and stir his body heat, he began to examine the entire dome that was circular in shape, slightly rounded, and barely over a quarter of a mile in diameter. There was little danger of him slipping, for though the surface looked smooth, it was actually rough as sandpaper through centuries of erosion.

At the end of two hours he had crisscrossed the area several different times, from various approaches, and found nothing. The evening winds began to rise, and on this completely exposed expanse he knew he could not survive the night. He made his way to the northeast end where he recalled the wide tableland a few hundred feet below. In the part of the mountain he had never been able to see, he found the conditions similar to those on the slope he had recently climbed, a series of steps of different heights. Once again he had to use the rope, and even though he was not climbing, he could scarcely stand the pain in his right shoulder and lung.

When he reached the flat below, he discovered it to be much larger than he had envisioned, and more than half of it covered with solid ice that never melted. He spent the rest of the evening searching for shelter for the night and finally located it near the southeast end of the ledge he had descended.

This side of the mountain was in the shade most of the afternoon and the cold was excruciatingly bitter. Mango rolled himself in his robes and nibbled at his food until he could eat no more. He drank from the leather flask of brandy and fruit juice Cameron insisted each man carry. The last rays of the setting sun turned purple overhead and night followed almost instantly. The warm glow of the liquor spread through his veins, combined with his immense fatigue, and lulled him into a delirious sleep of fitful slumber and short periods of awareness.

In the morning when he awoke, the sun had already risen and there was a small amount of warmth to it trapped in the enclosure where he had spent the night. The thought of eating made him ill. After several sips from the flask he rose, shouldered his equipment and started to explore the perimeter of the ice bed where the rock and some coarse sand were exposed. As he walked slowly it came to him that he had a fever and was somewhat dizzy. He coughed and spat upon the edge of the ice nearby and saw the red stain his spittle left. He repeated the process with the same results. *Something has broken loose inside*, he said to himself without alarm.

He was working the side belt between the ledges and the ice, when the sun's reflection came to him from something on the ground. He went to it and picked up a flat piece of bronze material about one quarter of an inch thick, three inches wide, and one-and-a-half feet long. The thickness measurement was near the center and narrowed to near nothing at all edges. The luster of it was dulled by a greenish brown stain and several small holes penetrated it at uniform locations. The perimeter of the holes had eroded to the point where he could not tell if they had once been square or round.

His scrutiny was interrupted by the sight of a similar piece three yards ahead of him, near the ice. It was an exact duplicate of the one he already had, even the holes matched. Another piece of the metal in the shape of a right angle lay nearby, and except for the sharp turn it was the same. He worked his way back and forth across the open stretch and found two shorter bars of the same type and description. The weight of all of them was growing heavy in his hands. He un-shouldered his pack and placed them all within. As he started to shoulder it once more, the dizziness he had been experiencing hit him even harder.

Dragging the pack, he made his way to the ledges where he knew the warmth would radiate from the sun. He sat carefully in the coarse sand that had accumulated near their base and lowered his head to his knees. The heat coming from the rock penetrated his clothing and calmed his shivering somewhat. When he felt recovered, he raised his head and gazed out to the hump in the middle of the ice field, a good eighth of a mile away. *That frozen mass could easily be fifty-to-one-hundred feet deep out there*, he thought to himself. *Maybe more if the ground I'm sitting on dips toward the center.*

He was about to raise himself and put both hands out to his sides to launch his weight. The fingers of his left hand touched something smooth and fine. He looked down to see a bright yellow curved band projection from the sand. His interest kindled, and with his good arm, he cleared the erosion debris away, lifting it up to have a closer look. It was a goblet of some sort, nearly five inches tall, two at the bottom and rounding out to near four at the rim. Mango dumped the sand it contained and examined it carefully. About one third of the rim was as thin as paper, and he fingered it gently so as not to break it. Not more than an inch down the material thickened to match the rest of it. It was polished smooth, and gave no indication it ever bore a marking. It had no handles, was heavy for its size, and Mango was sure it was made of solid gold. There were no stains upon it, only dullness to the yellow color. He looked at it for a long time, then pulled the pack between his legs, and placed it with the rest of his find.

It was while he was accomplishing this that he noticed the many long narrow splotches of dark brown that spattered the gray rock before him nearly every place he looked. He had walked over the top of several of them and had not paid any attention, until now. *Something has rotted out over a period of years and this is all that remains,* he mused, *several hundred logs, or slabs of wood.* He was deep in thought for several minutes and then said aloud, "I wish I had the time and the strength to climb out to that hump in the middle of the ice." But he knew he had neither, for his eyes had caught the change in the color of the skyline to the south, and he acknowledged that he must get down and away now, or he might never get another chance!

Mango took several pulls from the flask, slipped it into his pack, and with intentional slowness made his way back toward the dome, which he crossed with great effort. He had intended to commence lowering himself down the other side before stopping, but could not. His coughing started again and he left a trail of crimson spots every few feet where he traveled. He lay flattened and dead-still for nearly twenty minutes.

Painfully, Mango forced himself to his feet. He looked down at the series of gigantic steps below him, and shook his head slowly. "There's no use trying to fool myself," he said aloud, "I'd never be able to hold my own weight with this shoulder like it is. If I should pass out and fall, I'd surely break a leg, and there I'd stay." He turned to evaluate the alternate course to the west. The rock dome he was standing on sloped smoothly down to a broken ridge crest half-a-mile away. The escarpment continued on at the same angle for another two miles before he could see the beginning of the fault that doubled back to the cave below. He had no delusions that this would be an easy way down, but did not think he would be forced to use the rope.

There was no third alternative and without further consideration, he headed west.

He proceeded from the dome with deliberate patience, stopping often for rest. When he left the smoothness of the cap, he looked back and felt that he had made good time, even though it had taken him three hours.

In another three hours he looked back again and bitter disappointment grasped him by the throat. Night would fall in another three hours; he was nowhere near the halfway mark of the ridge and the distant slanting fault leading back to the cave.

He sat and leaned his torso heavily against a rock, deep in thought. *Today is the second day*, he mused, *and I told Cameron and Harry that I would be down by tomorrow night. I'll be lucky if I make it the day after that, even with their help.* Sardonically he laughed aloud, and with tremendous effort rose to his feet and went on.

As darkness fell, he studied the crest below himself, felling his way for another two hours before giving it up. It was too slow, and he was doing himself more harm than good, for he would need all the strength he could muster for the next day.

His progress the following day was even slower than it had been the day before, and it was full dark before he groped his way into the cave, rolled up in his robes and felt for the flask.

Resolutely, Mango had wanted to reach and cross the head of the precipice where the safety rope was stretched, but his condition would not permit it. It would be suicidal to attempt crossing that span in total darkness, even if he were strong enough to proceed. Obstinately, he wished there was a moon to light his way, then admitted there was no shelter between here and the cliffs above the glacier.

In the morning, when I'm rested, he thought, I can make it to the glacier and perhaps beyond. Cameron and Harry are probably on their way up now, or will be in the morning, and they can help me the rest of the way down. He refused to dwell on the problem of how he would cross that one bad spot with one useless arm. He closed his eyes and was not conscious again until the next morning.

During the night he experienced numerous spectral dreams floating out of and back into his past. He awoke to the fierce howling wail of the wind. The dimly lit walls of the cave told him the sun had not yet risen and that he must hurry. He found the flask and finished all that remained of it.

Mango sat up quickly and blackness fell over him like a shroud. He caught himself before he keeled over backward, slowed his movements, and then staggered to his feet. The pain in his chest and shoulder made him wince with each breath he took and he felt as though his lung cavity was filled with burning lava. A few minutes more, and he was able to roll his robes and place them in his pack, then slowly made his way to the entrance and the screeching wind.

He did not venture beyond the mouth of the cave. The time for the rising of the sun was long past and a titanic blizzard raged outside. The wind-blown particles were large flakes of slush that turned solid on contact with anything. It made no difference whether the surface was flat, vertical, or inverted. The entire world he could see without was a solid sheet of ice, at least eight inches thick.

He closed his eyes and tried to imagine the safety rope above the shattered stretch of ledge. All he could see was a shimmering sheet of ice, with no trace of the rope or what remained of the ledge. There was no break in the vertical wall from top to bottom. He opened his eyes and blackness sucked him into it's vortex.

*   *   *   *   *

Both Cameron and Harry were extremely grateful that Mango's predictions proved accurate. The nine-man party encountered no real problems climbing the canyon wall and the ground below the glacier and the ridges they followed was mostly dirt and broken rock. Their course was nearly level until they came into the canyon below the cliff; even here, it was nothing compared to some of the places they had been two days before.

There was little talk among them throughout any part of the journey; it was a somber mission they were on and each one of them was contemplating what they would find left of Roger.

They located his body early in the afternoon and though he was badly broken, it was not as terrifying as most of them had anticipated; he was still in one piece.

They wrapped his rigid form in two blankets, lashed it securely with rope to provide good hand holds, then rested a full hour before starting back to the valley.

Knowing they could not complete their task in one day, they made camp early in the evening in a wall-protected inlet little more than a mile from where they would drop off the valley wall. Despite the grisly burden they carried, all of them yearned for sleep. It had been a long and arduous day. Before the skies completely dimmed, all of them were in their night robes and a few already fast asleep.

Taking Roger down the nearly sheer wall of the valley was not as impossible as Harry had thought it might be. They split the party into two unequal teams, with the odd man always going to the waiting team in case something should go awry. They used the longest rope they had to relay him to the valley floor and it was a slow and tedious process; also by necessity, a merciless one. The extra man tried to guide the body clear of all obstructions as the upper men lowered it, but it proved fruitless at times.

The only sounds were the occasional groans or grunts uttered when the body would escape its guide's grasp and bang against the rocks. Even these sounds ceased by the time they reached the mid-point of the wall. It couldn't be helped and they could not hurt him anymore than he already was, a fact they accepted without saying a word to one another.

They brought him into camp at mid-afternoon and laid him in his tent for an hour while they had something to eat and rested. Four of the guards that had stayed behind carried him to a grave that had been dug that morning, a hundred yards or so above the camp toward the area of the rockslide.

Dr. Felix conducted the service. He completed it from memory, both properly and briefly, knowing the state of mind many of them were in. The two women sobbed softly as the words of the doctor were spoken and the grave refilled. None of them left until the latter was accomplished and a hurriedly carved marker placed.

The balance of the day was long for all concerned, and with this in mind, Pic Rhee put all his available men to work gathering fuel for the fires. The twenty-year-old animal droppings and the little dry brush available were getting farther and farther away from camp. Cameron and Harry both went to bed, as neither of them had fully recovered from the first part of the ordeal they had been through.

Norman hobbled to his tent, but not to rest; he wanted to be alone. Roger's death hit him exceedingly hard, for the two had become fast friends since they started sharing topographical work and records. Norman didn't make many friends, but when he did, they were friends for life; Roger was the first one he had ever lost in any manner and this was just too much for him.

Dr. Felix remained with the women, comforting them as best he could, while they tended the cook fire and he dreamed up other small chores to keep their minds and hands busy.

Pic Rhee saddled a horse, rode to the narrows, and on to the plateau country without saying a word to anyone as to his purpose or destination.

Pic Rhee returned when the evening meal was nearly over and he joined them in silence. As he finished eating, he looked at Cameron and ask, "What time do you wish to start in the morning?" His eyes flashed briefly toward the mountain top.

"Daylight will be soon enough," Cameron replied. "I'd like to have the same men we had today; they know the most difficult part of the way and seemed to have no fear. Do you suppose that would be possible?" he asked softly.

"I know it will be so," Pic Rhee said with conviction. "I'll go alert them right now, so that everything will be in readiness." Without waiting for a reply, the captain bowed slightly and left.

"I believe I'll go spend some time with Norman," Dr. Felix announced. "This has been a nightmare for all of us, but he's taking it especially hard. He's already been alone for hours and I don't think it should be much longer." He rose and went toward his tent.

"I thoroughly agree with you," Cameron called as he departed. The two remaining couples found it difficult to speak, for the words that were on their minds were meant for only two people. They let the fire die and watched the embers fade to nothing. When the warmth of it was no more, they rose and went to the tents, Penny with Harry and Connie with Cameron. They made no pretense as to who belonged where this night.

Connie lay cradled in Cameron's embrace, snuggling every few seconds, trying to get just a little bit closer. Their low whispered affections were more felt than heard. Without vocally expressing it, both of them thought that tonight it would be enough to comfort, console, and reassure each other.

Connie made a supreme effort to force the events of the past few days out of her mind, and fill it entirely with the happiness she had found in Cameron. But in so doing, she discovered she was dwelling on tomorrow and her renewed fears for him. Finally she could hold back no longer, "You're terribly worried about Mango, aren't you darling?" She asked tenderly.

"Yes, I am," he admitted softly. "He was supposed to be back tonight and I'm sure something isn't right. He said that he had, from a distance, examined both routes to the top, and neither one had any real problems that he could see. He said one way would take a day and require more exertion; the other two, with a lot less effort. The time required was from where we last saw him."

"Which route do you suppose he took?" Connie asked, trying to keep her voice down.

"That's the part that has me upset," Cameron responded. "Knowing him as I do, I'm sure he intended to take the shorter of the two, both up and down. If he did, it would have put him back here tonight."

"Maybe he took the long way up, and the short way down," Connie suggested. "That would account for an extra day."

"I believe you're right, but the other way around," Cameron reflected slowly. "I have a hunch that he came down the long way, and I'm afraid to ask myself why. After I watched him cross that gorge, I don't believe that there is anything on the mountain that could scare or hurt him. If he had been in top shape when the trip started, I wouldn't even be thinking much about him now; but we know he wasn't and we have no idea of the condition he was in when we saw him last. None of us ever got that close to him all day."

"You do think he made it to the top though?" Connie inquired, timidly postponing the question she knew she had to ask.

"It's only conjecture," Cameron shrugged, "but I think he did, and I believe He's on his way down. We'll know by tomorrow afternoon, that's for sure," Cameron said squeezing her a little tighter and thinking that the conversation was about to end.

"Yes, you will, won't you?" Connie asked, again dropping to a whisper. "You'll have to cross that same place where Roger fell to his death, won't you?"

Cameron could feel the warmth of her tears on his face and suddenly he knew the suffering she was going through. "I don't think so, he lied. We'll probably meet him somewhere this side of the glacier. He may well be so loaded down with artifacts that he had to take the long way back. Don't worry, dearest, we know the trails now and how everything should be done. There won't be any mistakes again, I promise!"

"Oh, God, darling, I hope not!" Connie breathed. "I'd give anything in the world if you didn't have to go. I'm frightened nearly out of my mind."

"We have to go," Cameron replied simply. "We can't anymore leave him up there than we could Roger. It may turn out to be nothing, and then again he may be ill or hurt and need help. We've got to go!" he finished firmly.

"Yes, I know," Connie responded gaining control of herself, but I wish with all my heart that it didn't have to be so. I love you so much, Cam, sweetheart, that I don't believe I'll be able to stand it until you get back. Hold me closer, darling, I feel like I'm drowning."

Cameron was already embracing her so tight he expected to feel a bone snap as he applied a little more pressure to her back. "Just think about me coming back and nothing else," Cameron whispered. He was about to say more, but her small mouth found his, and shut off his words. Her hands began to caress him shyly, then ardently, and within a few minutes both of them discovered love outweighed all other emotion—even grief, despair and terror.

*   *   *   *   *

The ferocious roaring of the wind woke the entire camp before dawn and only Pic Rhee was not surprised by the intensity and suddenness of the storm.

When it was light enough to see, Cameron and Connie dressed and gingerly made their way to the tent of Dr. Felix and Norman, where a thin puff of smoke could be seen now and then melting into the wind near the top of the center pole. The tent, as were all the others and the ground, was solid ice. All of the support poles of the canvas shelters could have been removed, and they would have stood by themselves, supported only by the guy ropes. The sides and roof were so stiff that even the force of a wind this strong could not riffle them.

Cameron had to grasp the flap with both hands, and heave with effort, so that he and Connie could enter. Dr. Felix and Norman both sat close to the fire and Pic Rhee stood on the other side. All three looked up as they entered. The bitterness of the cold caused the late comers to seek the fire before greetings were exchanged. "I'm afraid this is going to alter you plans." the Doctor stated as he looked Cameron squarely in the eye.

"You're probably right," Cameron admitted with a smile, trying to be cheerful. "At least temporarily," he continued. "This thing could blow over in an hour or two. Maybe by the time we eat and the sun has had a chance to work on the clouds awhile, it will all look different." He was aware that he was telling another lie, because he didn't believe a word he was saying, but he didn't want to upset them anymore than they already were.

"The men are ready and waiting," Pic Rhee interjected, "but I didn't want to bring them over here until it was decided what is to be done. There's no room for them here, and they are out of the weather in their own shelters."

"That's fine, Pic Rhee," Cameron replied still smiling, "perhaps it will let up enough for you and I to see what the valley walls look like after we have eaten." He focused his stare on the captain trying to draw his attention.

370 🌾 PERRY P. STEADMAN

Penny and Harry entered while he was speaking and edged into the fire as close as they could. The tent was small and was getting crowded. "Would you like me to accompany you?" Harry stammered through clicking teeth.

"Not much point in it, Harry," Cameron shrugged. "The two of us can see all we need to." He saw Connie watching him intently, adding, "We don't plan to do any climbing, only see how bad the ice has coated the cliffs." He watched the tight expression disappear from around her mouth and the outline of a tentative smile replace it.

Pic Rhee caught the cue and waited his turn to speak. "Whether it lets up or not, I think it might be a good idea to walk over and have a look. Then we'll know our situation better."

"Good," Cameron nodded; this time the smile was genuine. "When we all get unthawed, we'll have to fix our own breakfast. I don't want any of the men to be out on a morning like this, unless it's necessary."

"Connie and I can take care of that," Penny stated eagerly, "can't we?" she asked turning to Connie.

"We sure can," Connie grinned, "All they have to do is give us a little more room next to the fire. We'll get warm while they freeze, but at least they'll have a full belly."

"I knew the two of you had some ulterior motive for volunteering," Harry laughed as Penny pulled away from him.

Cameron and Pick Rhee stood peering at what they could see of the cliffs about one-hundred feet away. This was as close as they could get. Where the walls met the valley floor, an accumulation of dirt and rubble formed a small shoulder-like hill the full length of the valley and on both sides. The ice was so treacherous they were unable even to gain the cliff base.

Finally Cameron looked at the captain and spoke dejectedly, "There's no point in fooling ourselves any longer. With the equipment we have, there is no way we can get up there. We just didn't come prepared for full winter climbing conditions."

"You're still not acknowledging the obvious," Pic Rhee shouted above the wind, as he wiped the sleet from his face. "You knew all this before we came out here. You know full well that if we should attempt it, one or more of us might be killed. You knew that our fuel supply won't last through the coming night, nor will the horses. You also know that if the storm should let up, it will get twice as cold as it is now, and nothing in the upper end of this valley will survive."

"Yes," Cameron shouted back, "it's just that I wanted to hear it from someone else. I want know what you think we should do."

"I've already been told what to do," was Pic Rhee's answer, "and the first thing is to get back to our camp." He took Cameron by the arm, heading him in the right direction, walking close by his side so he could be heard. "The next thing we've got to do is get all of the horses we're not going to need started down to the plateau. I've already picked out a spot down there where there's enough feed for the animals and fuel for our fires. I'll have some of the men take them and the ladies down as soon as they are ready. The rest of us will stay here and build fires in every tent until they get warm enough to knock the ice loose and fold up. We'd best have everything we need packed before then. If we didn't need them so badly, I'd suggest leaving the tents and go now. The night before you left, Mango told me that if anything like this happened, I was to get everyone left in the valley down out of here. When we get out, we'll set up camp, wait a few days, and see what happens."

"As much as I dislike the whole idea, I know it's the only way," Cameron shouted, as he carefully quickened his pace. "Let's get them started!"

The evacuation went more rapidly than any of them thought possible, but neither of the women would leave until their men rode by their side.

They dropped below the storm a mile above the narrows, but the wind continued to howl and increased in velocity where it necked down while entering the valley. It was uncanny how the wind began to lower, and the temperature rise, once they were past the place of Tal Rashi's ambush. There was neither ice nor sleet, even though the clouds hung little more than two thousand feet above them.

Penny's eyes grew wide and a trembling sensation cruised her spine, as she involuntarily scanned the slopes of the canyon. Though she could see none of them with her eyes, she knew the remains of the Uli Prang littered the hillsides. She kneed her mount closer to Harry and forced her gaze to his reassuring features.

*   *   *   *   *

Mango had no inkling of how long he had been lying there. The early winter storm still raged with even more vigor, his hands and feet were numb with cold, and one side of his face was stinging where small frozen particles clung. He raised himself to all fours and laboriously crawled back into the cave. He went deeper into the gloom this time, for the force of the wind was so strong it was siphoning off the warmth his shelter had held through the night.

He stopped and lay against the far wall, ten or twelve feet from the fire pit. He was totally spent, though vibrantly aware. As he lay there, he thought of the people in the valley below. *They could be trapped just as I am. It's hard to tell about these freak storms; it could be worse down there than it is here. They have come so far and suffered so much, only to prove or disprove a theory someone else had. If they could only know that there is something up here! If they could examine what I have with me, and what I have seen, perhaps they could decipher what it means. The shape and style of the goblet or the bronze bars might signify something to them. But, they will never see them now,* he speculated sadly.

Mango lay still, thinking of the tragedies of the entire expedition for a long time. Then his mental process took a different turn. *It just might be that if they felt this strongly, there will be other people in the future that will feel the same way, and someone else will come to this mountain. They will have to come this way. When they see the steel spikes driven into the walls where the safety rope is they will know that others have been here, and will find some way to get across. The rope, and all traces of it will be gone in a few years, but the spikes will last several centuries, even in their location. When they arrive here, they must see what I have found; then they will have to go on to the summit, and find out what it all means. Maybe by then the ice sheet will have melted some, and they will be able to see even more than I did.*

Mango rolled from side to side, and managed to shift himself out of his pack. He worked the robes loose with his un-responding fingers and his teeth. He hooked the pack with his left arm, and crawled to the fire pit. *If I put them up there on the flat stones they will not become buried in the dust and will be easily seen,* he rationally deduced. He got to his knees again, and using his arms as clubs, he drew the goblet from his pack and placed it on the center stone slab. It was a long and painful operation and although he did not cough much, a tiny trickle of blood threaded its way down his chin from each corner of his mouth. He finally retrieved the last small bar of bronze and laid it gently at the end of the arc his display formed. "No one could possibly miss that now! he stated aloud, "no matter how long it takes them to get here," he added positively.

He inched his way back to the wall on his knees and sat facing the entrance. The expended effort caused him to start coughing again and it was a full five minutes before he could control the spasm. He unrolled his robes and spread them across his feet and legs, then worked them in and around his hips and waist, and placed his mittened hands beneath the furs. He leaned back against the cold stone for support; his energy completely gone, and sat staring into the swirling mass outside.

I wish that the skies were clear so that I might gaze out into the blueness of it, and imagine the beauty and peace of the valley below,

Mango thought. Although his spirit and subconscious knew that this was the end and had accepted it, it never really entered his searching consciousness.

"Oh, Gariu," he said aloud, "if you could only know that I sit directly above you looking out on the world just as yourself." The words were like lightening flashing within his skull, and for a while their impact staggered his mental capacity. He groped blindly for the exact phrases Dilow Kampi had used to quote the final passage from the Yassa of Kirghiz. At last it framed itself, and he said the words aloud in disbelief, "And the Princes of the Blue Wolf shall abide in this valley forever, looking out upon the world from both on high and from within!"

"He knew it! He knew it all the time. Kirghiz knew exactly what would happen to you and me, Gariu," Mango said, talking to his cousin far beneath him. "Even knowing what would happen in the end, he led our people here and established our Hoshun." Mango digested these facts slowly, then spoke anew. "Kirghiz was right in all of it Gariu. He was aware of our end as a clan, but he also knew that hundreds upon hundreds would leave over the years and blend with others of the world to form a new and better people. He knew we would have over six hundred years of peace and happiness and the ones that stayed in China would have less than one third of that. He knew the Uli Prang would not hound us forever and that before the end we would triumph. He understood the impelling force that drew me to the top of Kula Kangri and all it would bring about. There is more to come my brother that you and I shall not know of, but it does not matter. We have done our part and we can both now be at peace again. In all things I am content."

As he finished speaking, the constant pain in his groins, armpits, chest and shoulder fluttered, eased and left. His vision cleared, and although he could see nothing but the whiteness of the clouds, he was sure that they were not moving and the wind was gone. A weird vacuum of silence filled the air. He felt, before he saw, the golden pinkish glow of the cavern walls and a warm tingling sensation started in the soles of his feet and flowed through his body.

He transferred his line-of-sight from the walls to the fire pit and his nerves jangled instinctively. The artifacts he had placed there a short time ago glowed with the radiance of liquid gold. The light coming through the opening in the ceiling nearly blinded him as he looked up. He returned his stare to the goblet and the bars, the reflections of which seemed to be alive and moving. As he watched, an image began to shape in the center of the fire pit, faintly at first, then the form of a man was standing there smiling down at him. His soft brown hair fell below his shoulders and he had whiskers on his face. Mango could not tell the color of his eyes, for they changed as did the aura of light and warmth emanating from him. A long white robe enveloped him and his feet were bare. "It has to be Him," Mango said aloud, "the One Dr. Felix spoke of so many times. It is Him!" Mango forced his entire attention on the figure. He smiled gently, as one bare arm reached out to Mango, beckoning. When Mango did not move, the figure stretched out both arms, and the eyes implored softly.

"He is the one that has taken away my pain and put life back within me," Mango spoke as if still talking to Gariu. "He gave me the warmth I needed so vitally. I am going with Him!" Mango rose to his feet and walked without hesitation to the outstretched arms. "You see, Gariu, He greets me as you do, grasping my forearms."

Slowly the radiance within the cave faded and the gray gloom of it returned; the wind murmured timidly, then roared with impatience, and the blizzard without came back with renewed intensity.

CHAPTER 11

———◆•◆•◆———

Pic Rhee came to the place where the low canyon sides dumped into the flatness of the plateau, and raised his hand high to call a halt. Half-a-mile further ahead he could see the horse herd and the fires of their tenders resting snugly in the shallow depression he had selected the night before. The mount he rode, and the ones behind him, looked like phantom steeds, fully crusted with a layer of thick foamy ice. As they stood, the casing began to break away in pieces and fall to the ground. They reminded Pic Rhee of snakes he had seen shedding their skins late in the month of August. He dismounted and scraped the rest of it from his pony's back, neck, and shoulders. When his horse was perfectly clear of ice, he turned his attention to himself. Dr. Felix and Norman were immediately behind him and followed his example.

Within a few minutes, the entire party was bunched up, cleaning horses, themselves, and each other. With the relief of being out of the valley, the storm, and being warm, they began to laugh and shout. Even the guards to the rear of the pack animals caught the spirit.

It was Pic Rhee that noticed it first, the unearthly stillness; there was not even a trace of a breeze. He walked out away from the others ten or twelve paces, and listened keenly, but could neither hear nor feel anything. Then he looked up at the mountains, and his eyes grew wide, and the twin points of his beard began to tremble. The cloud bank was rolling back up the mountain, pushed by a wind of hurricane force, and yet there was no sound.

Dr. Felix and Norman noticed his odd behavior and came out to see if something was wrong with him. They didn't speak. By the time they reached his side, they too were watching this weird phenomenon. They were soon joined by Cameron and Connie, then Harry and Penny; the rear guards formed a group of their own three hundred feet closer to the narrows. By the time Harry and Penny came up, all movement on the mountain had stopped and only the dome remained hidden from view. The magnificent grandeur of it was hard to encompass, standing there in its solid sheeting of sparkling ice. It looked more like a painting than a reality.

Connie sucked in her breath with a loud gasping noise, as a thin brilliant ray of sunlight split the clouds and stabbed into the mountain slightly southwest of the huge gorge that was in the center of their view.

That's about the same place where we last saw Mango," Cameron whispered to Harry, never taking his eyes from the beam of light.

"Or the cave he spoke of," Harry replied as low as he could.

The radiant beam gave the impression of being anchored to the stationary clouds and imbedded into the mountain, for nothing moved or wavered. A full minute went by, then two and three. There were several loud gasping noises as the people that had been holding their breath gulped for air. The light still held.

Then, at the very base of the shaft there was a disturbance, and a chromatic dispersion boiled in confusion. From this, a solid band of colors arched upward like a rocket, bounced off the bottom of the clouds, and slammed back into the mountain east of the glacier, forming a perfect arch. The aura of it was so bright, it made their eyes water to look at it very long.

It all happened so fast that Cameron thought he might be seeing things, especially after the hellish morning all of them had spent. He looked down at the ground and back again. It was still there! After two more minutes Cameron saw the arch begin to fade, then melt away to nothing, and next the sunbeam did the same thing. There was nothing swift in the departure of either. Cameron watched with unbelieving eyes as the clouds rolled slowly down the mountain to where they had been before.

"Noyan is gone!" Pic Rhee stated in a strained voice, as he turned to Dr. Felix at his side.

"I know," the Doctor replied softly, never taking his eyes from the mountain. Slowly and deliberately he dropped to his knees, clasped his hands and raised them in prayer. His words were low and in Latin and no one except Norman could understand what he was saying. Although the mountain was hidden from his view, his eyes remained fastened on the spot where the light had touched.

When the doctor rose to his feet, Norman took his place, grimacing from the pain in his leg. He uttered his prayer in English and it was not as long as Dr. Felix's. But then, he hadn't been acquainted with Roger or Mango long enough to really know much about them, so the prayer was brief.

"What does it mean, Dr. Felix?" Cameron finally asked when it was apparent that no one else would for the moment.

For one thing it means that Prince Mango is gone," the Doctor replied, with a strange new quality to his voice. "Don't ask me how I know, for I can't explain it. Pic Rhee knows it also." The captain nodded his head several times. "I also know that he is at peace and contented, and that his life and the lives of his people were not in vain. Another thing I am sure of is that there is something sacred about this mountain. The rainbow you saw is the symbol of the everlasting covenant that God made with man after the deluge. Beyond that I can only guess, as you can."

But, but . . ." Cameron stammered, "Everything we witnessed here are physical impossibilities. Clouds cannot remain absolutely stationary, sunbeams cannot hold without drifting, winds of that force are not noiseless, and rainbows are not formed out of snow storms!"

"They are impossible for the minds of man!" Dr. Felix replied in the same tone of voice.

"How are we going to explain this when we get home?" Harry interrupted.

"I wouldn't even try if I were you," Dr. Felix smiled. "No one will believe you no matter how you explain it. Just be thankful you were here to witness it. It doesn't happen to many people on this earth." The doctor looked to Norman, who returned his smile knowingly. It was the first time he had smiled since the news of Roger's death.

Pic Rhee looked out toward the horse herd, then at Cameron. "There is no reason for us to remain here if you wish to take advantage of what daylight is left us. We could gain almost half-a-day's-march."

"That's true," Cameron agreed, when he realized there was no point in making camp here. "What do the rest of you feel about going on for the balance of the day?" He swung his head around to take them all in.

The doctor and Norman merely nodded their approval. Connie squealed her delight, and Harry replied, "This is the part of the trip we've been looking forward to the most." He slipped his arms around Penny's waist and hugged her tightly.

"That's the answer, Captain," Cameron grinned brightly.

"In that case," Pic Rhee responded, glowing himself "I'll start the horse herd back for Chamdo now. They've had plenty of time to unfreeze and eat. The six men we have with us will be enough to guard and take care of the other essentials. I'll have them prepare something to eat now. In less than a week's time, we'll be at the British outpost in the Chumbi Valley. You're going to be amazed at how fast they shuttle you on down to Calcutta and out of the country. You're considered a burdensome annoyance in that country right now, and the quicker they get you on your way home, the better they'll like it." Pic Rhee grinned once more, and there was even a twinkle in his eye.

"It can't be any too soon for us," Connie laughed, and put her arm about Cameron as the captain bowed, then mounted and rode first to the men at the rear, and the out onto the plateau.

"It's really odd, isn't it, how this trip brought the two of them together?" Penny whispered to Harry as she looked at Connie and Cameron across the fire.

"Not any stranger than what has happened to you and me," Harry avowed. "Remember, I was forced into this in the beginning. Now I have nightmares that I didn't go and that I never met you at all. It's terrible to even to think of. Do you know that?"

"Yes, darling, I know," Penny replied sincerely. "I have bad dreams like that too, only different. In mine, we make the entire trip together and you never pay any attention to me at all. For a long time I thought that was the way it was going to be," she confessed.

If we had only understood each other's feelings sooner, wouldn't that have been wonderful?" Harry blushed.

"The not knowing made it all the more beautiful right now, dearest," Penny sighed. "We've got the rest of our lives to spend together. Let's not waste any worrying about the little we've lost."

"You're absolutely right, dear girl," Harry laughed "It's up to you to keep me straight on things like that, you know!"

As Connie finished drinking her last cup of tea, she sat regarding the remarkable change in Dr. Felix; the new glow in his eyes, how the deep lines in his forehead and around his mouth had smoothed, and the sadness that was always near him had vanished. "What are your plans when we arrive home, Doctor?" she inquired finally.

"Just as soon as this trek is finalized by disposition of the artifacts, completion of the log, maps, drawings and other business matters settled, I'm returning to my life in the church, where I belong!" Dr. Felix announced with pride. "I don't care how menial my position there might be; I'll be happy with it and spend the rest of my life doing what I know I was meant to do."

"That's marvelous, Doctor!" Connie exclaimed. "We're all so very happy for you; the change is already showing through."

"Yes, Doctor," Cameron interjected, "we are all grateful that this trip has had some special meaning for you!"

"I'm humbly grateful myself," Dr. Felix assured them, looking at each one of them individually.

"What about you, Norman?" Connie continued curiously.

Dr. Felix didn't give him time to answer, "Norman is going to take my place at the museum, that's some of the business I mentioned. The Foundation will automatically appoint him on his own merits, but with my recommendation, there's no doubt about it."

"I, I don't know what to say, Doctor," Norman stammered in confusion. "This comes as a complete surprise." He lowered his head shyly for a moment.

"No need to say anything, Norman," Dr. Felix soothed, "You've earned it twice over." He looked at Norman benevolently for several seconds and then turned to Connie. I don't believe I need to ask the plans of the four of you," he added with a smile. "They've been evident for quite sometime now."

Pic Rhee glanced at the sullen skies, and anxious to be on his way interrupted, "There is one thing yet to be done before we can leave, but first I would like to show you something." The captain raised his hand high from his sitting position, and two guards ran up, each carrying a long object wrapped and bound with horse hide. On his nod the guards quickly undid the coverings, standing at attention proudly. In the right hand of each man, an eight-foot war lance bearing the banner of the Blue Wolf was held straight and tall, the butt end of each iron wood shaft firmly on the ground.

"The men and I them made over ten years ago," Pic Rhee stated with slight self-indulgence. "Mango Noyan would never let us display them. He said that they could be unfurled only on the Hoshun of the Blue Wolf, and now they are where they belong, and here they will stay!"

Cameron scrutinized them closely. The hard solid shafts were over an inch thick and the blades of tempered and burnished steel a foot long. The pennants were of a material Cameron could not identify, heavy and closely woven, about five-feet-long and two at the base. The large head of a snarling wolf was meticulously worked into the center, with dark, blue thread against a background of gold. "They are breathtaking!" Cameron said with awe.

Each member of the party came forward to admire and touch them lovingly. There were more than a few eyes clouded by tears. Dr. Felix waited until last, then he too caressed both briefly, then got to his knees and uttered a short prayer. When the doctor rose, Pic Rhee spoke to the standard bearers in their own tongue. They snappily shouldered the lances and wheeled about, one in one direction and the other in the opposite.

As he two men marched to the low hills that marked the beginning of the canyon, they were each joined by a second. When they reached the top, the late coming guards drew their swords and gouged a hole into the earth. The butt of each shaft was inserted, the loose earth replaced, tamped down, and conical piles of rocks placed high on top of each one. When it was done, the four men stood at attention a full minute, then returned to their places. The light breeze was not strong enough to lift the banners and they dangled with a slight shipping motion.

Except for the sounds created by the men doing the honors, the ceremony was quiet. Pic Rhee's impatience returned and he gathered up the little gear he carried. Once more, he looked toward the northeast where the horse herd had disappeared, then strode to his mount. "Now we had best move!" he said quietly as he swung up into the saddle and pointed his horse southwest.

The doctor and Norman fell in behind him. Harry helped Penny up hesitantly, took a long last look as if he was trying to stamp it all indelibly into his mind, then with practiced skill, mounted his own animal. He gave Cameron and Connie the benefit of a shrug and a lopsided grin as he rode by. Cameron made no attempt to move and Connie didn't ask him why, but stood close holding his hand. He wanted to solidify his own impressions and he wanted the two of them to be alone for it.

The guards apparently understood their needs, for they rode by rapidly; some with their eyes averted, others with a friendly smile and a finger touched to the forehead.

"I wondered many times if either of us would live to see this day," Cameron said after many minutes of silence, and after he felt that his surroundings had permeated his mind and soul.

"I didn't!" Connie replied emphatically, "not after I recognized all of the meanings of my father insisting you be the one to guide and protect us," she looked up at him longingly.

A faint flush colored the exposed part of Cameron's neck. "I think we'd better go," he replied tenderly, "or we'll have a hard time catching up!" He pulled her to him and kissed her several times.

As they walked to their horses, an impish grin formed on Connie's lips. "How soon will we be going on our next expedition?" she asked soberly.

"If you so much as mention that word for the next year, I'm going to turn you over my knee, and that's a promise!" Cameron snapped playfully, as he legged her up into the saddle.

"If you should turn me over you knee, you might be letting yourself in for a big surprise," Connie answered in a similar playful tone.

He looked up at her on her high perch, and saw the beautiful curve of her mouth and the blue-green fire dancing in her eyes. His heart winced at the enormity of his love for her. "I wouldn't doubt that in the least," he answered, and was barely able to tear his glance away from her and proceed to his own mount.

He was about to swing up, when a strong gust of wind clutched the lance banners and gave them life. He watched the slashing jaws and the flashing eyes with hypnotic fascination. *The banners will be gone in a few years,* he thought, *but the lances will stand for a hundred years, maybe two. By then, the stories of what happened here will have spread across the continent and the Hoshun of the Blue Wolf will be established for a time in the minds of man. The legend of it may even last as long as the one of Kula Kangri and no one passing by will ask to whom this mountain belongs.* He closed his eyes in a silent prayer of his own, then mounted, and rode up beside Connie to take her outstretched hand.

Ten minutes later he turned to look back again, smiling broadly.

"What are you thinking, Cam?" Connie inquired with aroused curiosity.

"I'm thinking how lucky you and I are going to be in our old age," Cameron replied still smiling.

"How so?" Connie laughed.

"Because," he intoned serenely, "we'll have each other to assure ourselves that all of this was not a dream, but a living truth!"

THE END